*Critical Essays on*
# HENRY FIELDING

# CRITICAL ESSAYS
## ON
# BRITISH LITERATURE

Zack Bowen, General Editor

*University of Miami*

*Critical Essays on*
# HENRY FIELDING

*edited by*
ALBERT J. RIVERO

*G. K. Hall & Co.*

*New York*

G. K. Hall & Co.

1633 Broadway
New York, NY 10019

Library of Congress Cataloging-in-Publication Data

Critical essays on Henry Fielding / edited by Albert J. Rivero.
        p. cm. — (Critical essays on British literature)
    Includes index.
    ISBN 0–7838–0059–2
    1. Fielding, Henry, 1707–1754—Criticism and interpretation.
I. Rivero, Albert J., 1953–   . II. Series.
PR3457.C69  1998
823'.5—dc21                                          97-34644
                                                        CIP

The paper meets the requirements of ANSI/NISO Z3948-1992 Permanence of Paper.

10 9 8 7 6 5 4 3 2

Printed in the United States of America

*For My Students*

# Contents

# General Editor's Note

◆

The Critical Essays on British Literature series provides a variety of approaches to both classical and contemporary writers of Britain and Ireland. The formats of the volumes in the series vary with the thematic designs of individual editors and with the amount and nature of existing reviews and criticism, augmented, where appropriate, by original essays by recognized authorities. It is hoped that each volume will be unique in developing a new overall perspective on its particular subject.

Albert J. Rivero's introduction begins by outlining the long-standing debate regarding Fielding's morality versus his reputation as a realistic novelist, and his evolution through "Christian Humanism" to the more ambiguous moral intent of later works like *Amelia,* which retreated from the Christian paradigm. Along the way Rivero explores how Fielding's directions inside the texts themselves shaped readerly responses in ways that his rival Richardson was not allowed in his own unobtrusive presentations of material that inspired what Richardson regarded as misreadings of authorial intent.

Rivero also points out that Fielding was a dominant figure on the British stage in the 1730s and has only recently received major critical attention as a dramatist. Rivero also recounts how early feminist concentration on Fielding's misogyny has evolved into a healthy revaluation of the contributions of newly rediscovered women's narratives to the shape and substance of the novel—Fielding's as well as the entire genre.

Rivero's selection of essays includes one on Fielding's drama; multiple treatments of *Jonathan Wild, Joseph Andrews, Tom Jones,* and *Amelia;* as well as some on diverse topics involving several works.

ZACK BOWEN
*University of Miami*

# *Publisher's Note*

◆

Producing a volume that contains both newly commissioned and reprinted material presents the publisher with the challenge of balancing the desire to achieve stylistic consistency with the need to preserve the integrity of works first published elsewhere. In the Critical Essays series, essays commissioned especially for a particular volume are edited to be consistent with G. K. Hall's house style; reprinted essays appear in the style in which they were first published, with only typographical errors corrected. Consequently, shifts in style from one essay to another are the result of our efforts to be faithful to each text as it was originally published.

# Introduction

ALBERT J. RIVERO

This volume contains 14 essays on Henry Fielding published during the 1980s and 1990s. I have chosen to reprint this recent material primarily because several readily available anthologies of earlier criticism already exist. Three of these deserve special attention. *Henry Fielding: The Critical Heritage* (1969), edited by Ronald Paulson and Thomas Lockwood, documents the responses of Fielding's contemporaries and near-contemporaries to both the man and the works.[1] In these responses, we can discern the emergence of the long-standing debate between those who regard Fielding's morality as beyond dispute and those who see it as always suspect. When Samuel Johnson weighed in on the side of Samuel Richardson's fictions of virtue rather than Fielding's representations of vice, he ensured that future champions of Fielding the moralist would have to conduct their critical battles on Johnsonian ground. Johnson's assertion that Richardson "knew how a watch was made" while Fielding could only "tell the hour by looking on the dial-plate" has also shaped subsequent criticism.[2] Thus Ian Watt, in his influential *The Rise of the Novel* (1957), has distinguished between the depths found in what he calls Richardson's "formal realism" and the more superficial treatment of life evident in what he terms Fielding's "realism of assessment." In attributing a moral purpose to Fielding while denying him "realism of presentation," Watt strikes a compromise between Johnson's two seemingly contradictory positions that Fielding is either too realistic and therefore morally dangerous, or not realistic enough and therefore artistically deficient. That Watt, in his defense of Fielding the moralist, still gives the nod to Richardson the realistic novelist reminds us of the peculiar fact that defenders of Fielding's morality have often done so at the expense of his "realism"; that, in choosing to focus their attention on Fielding's moral precepts, they have often downplayed his fictional examples.[3]

This curious aspect of Fielding criticism is captured in Paulson's *Fielding: A Collection of Critical Essays* (1962), which offers an excellent sampling of criticism from the 1920s to the early 1960s. In his introduction, Paulson suggests that "the effect of twentieth century Fielding criticism has been to prove him moral." Although Paulson sees this as "an important corrective" to the nineteenth-century view of Fielding as "interesting but immoral," the "Christianizing of Fielding stresses an aspect of his work that is neither the most characteristic nor (I am sure readers of Fielding will agree) the most interesting one."[4] What Paulson is referring to here is the reassessment of Fielding's life and works begun by Wilbur L. Cross's *The History of Henry Fielding* (1918);[5] continued by James Work's "Henry Fielding, Christian Censor" (1949);[6] and wrought to critical perfection by Martin C. Battestin, who, by the time of publication of Paulson's anthology, had already published his influential *The Moral Basis of Fielding's Art: A Study of "Joseph Andrews"* (1959).[7] Even though Paulson lists Battestin's book in his bibliography, calls it "an important study," and does not identify it explicitly in his introduction as one of the recent critical works contributing to the "dulling" of Fielding, he does not reprint any excerpts from it in his collection. Paulson's main argument against those who wish to moralize Fielding is that they do not really read his works. To abstract religious maxims from Fielding's textual particulars requires the suppression of those particulars. This is why Paulson reprints essays that, as he puts it, are "concerned primarily with Fielding's literary works, not with the man, his life or ideas in isolation."[8]

By the time of Harold Bloom's *Modern Critical Views: Henry Fielding* (1987), published 25 years after Paulson's collection, several changes had occurred in Fielding criticism. In spite of Paulson's vehement warnings and such loud dissenting voices as Claude J. Rawson's, the "Christianizing of Fielding" continued to thrive during the 1960s and early 1970s. For these two decades Fielding, triumphing over the momentarily devalued Richardson, became the canonical eighteenth-century British novelist, whose works, unlike those of his rival, began to appear in a "definitive" critical edition. The ascendancy of the Christian Fielding came about primarily because of the enormous influence of Martin C. Battestin's editions of the novels. In his introduction to the widely disseminated Riverside edition of *Joseph Andrews* and *Shamela* (1961), and in his introductions and annotations to *Joseph Andrews* (1967) and *Tom Jones* (1974) for the *Wesleyan Edition of the Works of Henry Fielding,* Battestin puts forth the argument, advanced in his book on *Joseph Andrews* cited above and repeated in several articles published between 1960 and 1974, that Latitudinarian sermons provide the best context in which to understand Fielding's works. There is, to be sure, a lot more in Battestin's rich annotations to the novels than footnotes to Latitudinarian sermons, but his main thrust throughout, especially in his introductions, is that Fielding's works in general and his novels in particular can be properly understood only if viewed as embodiments of their author's Christian Humanism. The image of Henry Fielding, Christian Censor, thus conveyed to many readers in the authoritative Wesleyan edition of the novels, offered a powerful corrective to Johnson's version of Fielding, the corruptor of "the young, the ignorant, and the idle."[9]

The image of Fielding as mellow moralist, sitting in his magistrate's chair passing judgment on human follies, is persuasive because it squares very nicely with the image of himself that Fielding fashions in his own prefaces and introductions. That is, adherents of the moral Fielding take seriously Fielding's representations of his moral purpose, whereas critics imbued with the skeptical Johnsonian ether regard those representations with suspicion. But one does not have to agree fully with Johnson's view of Fielding as moral blockhead to see that, in Fielding's novels, discrepancies exist at times between what he says he is doing and what he actually does. The "Christian-izing of Fielding" tends to paper over those discrepancies and to present a Fielding who is much more consistent in his views than his texts would seem to allow. That inconsistent, unruly Fielding is the Fielding Harold Bloom values in his introduction to *Modern Critical Views: Henry Fielding*. In Bloom's view, Fielding's "most surprising strength" is his representation of "the violent, daemonic, mindless energy of Squire Western."[10] Although Bloom reprints a section on *Tom Jones* from Battestin's *The Providence of Wit: Aspects of Form in Augustan Literature and the Arts* (1974)[11] and a chapter on *Tom Jones* and providential fiction from Leopold Damrosch's *God's Plot and Man's Stories: Studies in the Fictional Imagination from Milton to Fielding* (1985),[12] the majority of the essays in his collection, two of which also appear in Paulson's 1962 anthology, present a morally problematic and textually divided Fielding. The supreme exponent of a well-ordered neoclassical world view appears side by side with the tentative existentialist hero of Claude J. Rawson's *Henry Fielding and the Augustan Ideal under Stress* (1972)[13] and the troubled prisoner of history of J. Paul Hunter's *Occasional Form: Henry Fielding and the Chains of Circumstance* (1975).[14]

As textual discontinuities and fissures began to be privileged in critical discourse in the 1970s, Fielding's fictions, thanks in large part to the influential work of Wolfgang Iser, were viewed less and less as placid repositories of moral maxims and more and more as contested sites on which Fielding and his readers struggle for mastery of the text.[15] It could be argued, of course, that very few critics have ever viewed Fielding's fictions as placid repositories of anything, that the accusation of underreading brought against those who have read Fielding's fictions as allegories of Christian Humanism is nothing more than the exaggerated rhetoric of critics struggling to carve out a space for their own critical positions. But there can be little doubt that, while proponents of the Christian Fielding privilege his role as author, as the god of his literary creations, the emphasis during the 1970s began to be placed on the role of the reader. It could be argued, again, that this "new" emphasis on the reader merely replicates a critical procedure Fielding himself has encoded in his fiction, that critical theory, in this instance, has finally caught up with authorial practice. Like Richardson, Fielding knows that he is at the mercy of his readers, though Richardson usually seems shocked when he descries a misreading whereas Fielding seems to understand that that is what readers have always done to authors. Readers will often read against the prescriptions of authors and write their own texts—turning, for instance, a Pamela into a Shamela, or sympathizing with the diabolical Lovelace. This is why, throughout *Tom Jones,* Fielding cajoles, flatters, and bullies his readers into "correct" readings. Fielding anticipates the "misreadings" of his readers and attempts to correct them, in explicit statements sprinkled throughout his texts. Richardson, on the other hand, can correct misreadings only after they have occurred—in future editions, prefaces, letters, and other after-the-fiction authorial interventions. This is the disadvantage of writing to the moment, without an intrusive author on hand to guide the reader's responses. Richardson's disadvantage, however, has turned out to be a boon to his modern critics. Although Fielding criticism benefited initially from the turn to the reader, Richardson criticism has benefited even more. To borrow the still-useful distinction made by Roland Barthes, Richardson's writerly fictions were more amenable than Fielding's readerly narratives to the practitioners of deconstruction, reader-response criticism, and reception theory.

But another version of Fielding was also beginning to emerge in the 1970s and 1980s. If Martin C. Battestin had been largely responsible for the canonization of the Christian Fielding in the 1960s and early 1970s, in the late 1970s and 1980s he began to reveal, as a result of his research for a new biography, a more complex *historical* Fielding. The Christian Fielding, though fashioned out of such historical materials as sermons and religious pamphlets, was in many ways a historical abstraction, an idealized Fielding operating in a doctrinal realm divorced from the strife of day-to-day living. This disembodied Fielding, inhabiting a golden, providentially ordered fictional world, now gives way to a Fielding struggling to make ends meet, embroiled in political controversies; an angry, bitter Fielding, whose Christianity is tested by the evils of humanity parading daily before his magistrate's bench; a Fielding who, dying by degrees, reminds us more of King Lear than Squire Allworthy. This all-too-human Fielding, fully fleshed out in Martin and Ruthe Battestin's *Henry Fielding: A Life* (1989),[16] is glimpsed first in Martin Battestin's introduction to the Wesleyan *Amelia* (1983). As Battestin briefly demonstrates, *Amelia,* "to a greater degree than any other of Fielding's novels," is deeply "rooted in the history of its time and in its author's personal experience."[17] Its chaotic action significantly opening on April Fools' Day in Newgate prison, *Amelia* presents a gritty Hobbesian world in which "every Man is taught to consider himself as the Centre of Gravity," in which private and public vices trump virtue nearly every time.[18] Unlike the triumphantly celebratory conclusions of *Joseph Andrews* and *Tom Jones,* the "happy" ending of *Amelia* fails either to uplift or to convince. That the good Dr. Harrison purports to read the glad tidings of the restitution of Amelia's fortune from a newspaper advertisement suggests that providential endings are now matters of local interest, not cosmic significance, of no more importance, perhaps, than the latest dentifrice or cure for venereal disease. *Amelia,* in short, is Fielding's most "realistic" novel. Bursting with the troubling details of a decaying metropolis, it resists interpretation as yet another comforting Christian parable of good triumphing over evil.

Because of its messiness, *Amelia* has always been the test case for the validity of the hypothesis of an aesthetically and doctrinally pleasing Fielding. Although one could argue that the assured, well-wrought literary form of *Tom Jones* reflects its author's belief in a providentially ordered universe, it would be hard to make a similar case based on the tentative, chaotic contours of *Amelia. Amelia* is a morally complex work precisely because it does not deliver its morality in a neatly wrapped formal package. This is why the novel has often been regarded as Richardsonian and why Johnson is reputed to have liked it. By and large, critics sympathetic to the Christian Fielding position have found the work problematic and have often attempted to explain its difficulties by suggesting that it is not up to its author's previous standards, either because Fielding's increasing bitterness toward the world had vitiated his artistic vision or because his decision to imitate Richardson by focusing his story on a woman was ill-advised for such a manly author as Fielding.[19] But for other critics *Amelia* has proved the most compelling of Fielding's novels. Rawson, for example, reads the novel as "a (partly deliberate) rendering of a larger struggle between Fielding's rage for order and the senseless brutality of fact."[20] This self-divided Fielding is very similar to the Fielding Battestin portrays in his introduction to the Wesleyan *Amelia.* For Battestin, however, Fielding still remains a fully Christian and fully "deliberate" artist. This curious affinity between such methodologically different critics suggests that the usefulness of the Christian Fielding paradigm diminishes as we move from the early Fielding (up to *Tom Jones*) to the later Fielding of *Amelia;* the social pamphlets, especially the *Enquiry into the Causes of the late Increase of Robbers* (1751), which both Battestin and Rawson connect to *Amelia;* and the profoundly pessimistic (and posthumously published) *Journal of a Voyage to Lisbon* (1755).

So far the story of Fielding criticism I have been telling has focused almost exclusively on the three major novels, primarily because critics, though they have occasionally dealt with Fielding's other works, have concentrated their attention on what many of them regard as his major artistic accomplishments. Thus it was not until the late 1980s that Fielding's plays began to receive extended critical attention, in books devoted exclusively to them. To be sure, important work on the plays had appeared earlier, especially during the 1960s and 1970s when such eminent Fielding scholars as Hunter, Paulson, and Rawson offered incisive readings of various aspects of Fielding's dramatic career.[21] But the consensus seemed to be that the plays were worthy of critical attention only as prologues to the novels. This attitude is captured in the title of the only book on the plays published before 1988, Jean Ducrocq's *Le théatre de Fielding, 1728–1737, et ses prolongements dans l'oeuvre romanesque* (1975).[22] Given that from 1730 until 1737 Fielding was the most successful and prolific English playwright, the relative critical neglect of his dramatic works until quite recently is puzzling.

The reasons for that neglect might derive not so much from the plays themselves as from the methodological constraints of some of their earlier twentieth-century critics. To begin, New Critics trained to savor the ironies and structural intricacies of well-wrought urns would not look favorably on works that appear shapeless and hastily put together. Fielding's best plays are irregular, works in process shaped by the vibrant political and theatrical realities of London in the 1730s. Their overt materiality and identification with "low" culture would also run counter to the New Critics' predilection for "high" art, for lofty rhymes wafting safely above the embarrassing ferment of history. As such critics as Erich Auerbach and M. M. Bakhtin have reminded us, the novel is also a "low," historically oriented genre. This, of course, would not have been news to some of Fielding's contemporaries who, spearheaded by Johnson, regarded his novels as "low" representations of "low" life. Helped along by the strenuous assertions of high moral and artistic purpose made by Fielding and Richardson—and by the grandiose claims of later novelists like Flaubert, James, and Joyce—the elevation of this "low" species of writing had been so successful by the middle of the twentieth century that it allowed New Critics to suppress the novel's less than patrician origins and to regard certain novels—those well-plotted eternal monuments, usually written by men—as worthy of the same critical scrutiny as the most complex poetical artifact. Since the fashioning of the Christian Fielding reached its zenith when its doctrinal generalizations could finally be supported with the analysis of textual evidence made possible by the practitioners of New Criticism—so that, for example, *Joseph Andrews* stops being episodic and becomes a coherent work of art evincing its author's belief in Providence—the morally indifferent and aesthetically flawed plays did not quite live up to their author's future stature as moral and artistic paragon. This is why they merited critical attention only as they looked forward to the author's novelistic triumphs, especially *Tom Jones,* the quintessential Fielding novel.

In 1988, however, Robert D. Hume published *Henry Fielding and the London Theatre 1728–1737*.[23] Written from the perspective of a theater historian, Hume's book offers a rich historical survey of Fielding's plays in the context of contemporary dramatic and theatrical events. When in 1989 the Battestins published what is in effect a small book on Fielding's theatrical career in the second part of their biography, the plays had finally achieved eminence in their own right, though both Hume and the Battestins, writing as historians, do not offer critical analyses of individual plays. My own *The Plays of Henry Fielding: A Critical Study of His Dramatic Career,* also published in 1989, supplements these two historical accounts by offering critical analyses of 10 representative plays.[24] More recently, Jill Campbell has approached the plays from a feminist perspective in *Natural Masques: Gender and Identity in Field-*

*ing's Plays and Novels* (1995), though, as her title suggests, her concern with Fielding's drama is part of a larger interrogation of sexual ambiguity and political instability evident, she argues, both in Fielding's works and in eighteenth-century British culture.[25] We still need a book that examines *all* the plays critically in their complex historical context, a task now made easier by the thoroughness of Hume's and the Battestins' historical accounts and undoubtedly to be expedited greatly in the future when the plays appear with full annotations and introductions in the Wesleyan edition currently being prepared by Thomas Lockwood.

The year 1989 was also memorable because of the appearance of the first book on Fielding written from a feminist critical perspective: Angela J. Smallwood's *Fielding and the Woman Question: The Novels of Henry Fielding and the Feminist Debate 1700–1750*.[26] Unlike other feminist critics, Smallwood does not summarily dismiss Fielding as a misogynist. She presents a Fielding whose views on women are at least as enlightened as those of Richardson. Although some subsequent feminist critics have disagreed with Smallwood's version of Fielding, thanks to her efforts we now have a more nuanced and accurate picture of Fielding, neither the supremely masculine artist relished by some male critics nor the misogynist monster of earlier feminist lore. Indeed, one could argue that the rise of Richardson to the role of preeminent eighteenth-century British novelist in the 1980s and 1990s, while originally assisted by the turn to the reader in critical theory and practice in the 1970s, was given final and definitive impetus by the ascendancy of feminist criticism. Simply put, the sentimental travails of Richardson's heroines appealed more to feminist critical sensibilities than did the sexual escapades of Tom Jones.

But this feminist turn toward Richardson, though not salutary to Fielding's critical fortunes, especially when panegyrics on Richardson's protofeminism have been accompanied by castigations of Fielding's unenlightened views, has led to a welcome revival in interest in those novelists, mostly female, whose works, though dismissed by both Richardson and Fielding, nonetheless influenced and shaped their novelistic careers. Thus we are now in a position to view the emergence of the British novel not as the product of the agon in the 1740s and 1750s between two highly gifted male authors, but as the result of the pioneering efforts of such popular female authors as Aphra Behn, Delarivier Manley, and Eliza Haywood. In this new history, Richardson and Fielding are not so much the undisputed fathers of the British novel as the reluctant sons of mothers they would rather not acknowledge, with Richardson pretending that his loudly proclaimed moral purpose severs his ties to earlier female fiction, while Fielding, rightly identifying Richardson with earlier female fiction, argues instead that he is following such male models as Homer and Cervantes. This more accurate, feminocentric history of the British novel should yield yet another version of Fielding to supplement those we have noted in this brief introduction, a Fielding whose quarrels with Richardson and proclamations of classical antecedents have occluded his far more intriguing indebtedness to women authors. In short, much work remains to be done by Fielding's future critics. I hope that they will find the essays in this collection useful places to begin their inquiries.[27]

## Notes

1. Ronald Paulson and Thomas Lockwood, *Henry Fielding: The Critical Heritage* (London: Routledge and Kegan Paul, 1969).

2. James Boswell, *Life of Johnson,* ed. R. W. Chapman, rev. J. D. Fleeman (Oxford: Oxford Univ. Press, 1980), 389. I wish to thank Michael Patrick Gillespie, George Justice, and Alexander Pettit for their generous assistance in the preparation of this introduction.

3. Ian Watt, *The Rise of the Novel: Studies in Defoe, Richardson and Fielding* (Berkeley: Univ. of California Press, 1957), 30–34, 256–57, 288–89, passim.

4. Ronald Paulson, ed., *Fielding: A Collection of Critical Essays* (Englewood Cliffs, N.J.: Prentice-Hall, 1962), 1.

5. Wilbur L. Cross, *The History of Henry Fielding,* 3 vols. (New Haven: Yale Univ. Press, 1918).

6. James A. Work, "Henry Fielding, Christian Censor," in *The Age of Johnson: Essays Presented to Chauncey Brewster Tinker,* ed. Frederick W. Hilles (New Haven: Yale Univ. Press, 1949), 139–48.

7. Martin C. Battestin, *The Moral Basis of Fielding's Art: A Study of "Joseph Andrews"* (Middletown, Conn.: Wesleyan Univ. Press, 1959).

8. Paulson, 10.

9. Samuel Johnson, *The Rambler,* no. 4, in *Selected Essays from the Rambler, Adventurer, and Idler,* ed. W. J. Bate (New Haven: Yale Univ. Press, 1968), 11. Although Johnson does not name Henry Fielding, scholars have traditionally assumed that his attack here is aimed at Fielding's *Tom Jones* (1749) and perhaps Tobias Smollett's *Roderick Random* (1748).

10. Harold Bloom, ed., *Modern Critical Views: Henry Fielding* (New York: Chelsea House, 1987), 2, 5.

11. Martin C. Battestin, *The Providence of Wit: Aspects of Form in Augustan Literature and the Arts* (Oxford: Clarendon Press, 1974).

12. Leopold Damrosch, *God's Plot and Man's Stories: Studies in the Fictional Imagination from Milton to Fielding* (Chicago: Univ. of Chicago Press, 1985).

13. C. J. Rawson, *Henry Fielding and the Augustan Ideal under Stress: "Nature's Dance of Death" and Other Studies* (London: Routledge & Kegan Paul, 1972), 68.

14. J. Paul Hunter, *Occasional Form: Henry Fielding and the Chains of Circumstance* (Baltimore: Johns Hopkins Univ. Press, 1975).

15. See, for example, Wolfgang Iser, "The Role of the Reader in Fielding's *Joseph Andrews* and *Tom Jones,"* in Iser, *The Implied Reader: Patterns of Communication in Prose Fiction from Bunyan to Beckett* (Baltimore: Johns Hopkins Univ. Press, 1974), 29–56. For an important pre-Iser work on this topic, see John Preston, *The Created Self: The Reader's Role in Eighteenth-Century Fiction* (New York: Barnes & Noble, 1970); for Preston's two chapters on *Tom Jones,* see 94–132.

16. Martin C. Battestin, with Ruthe R. Battestin, *Henry Fielding: A Life* (London: Routledge, 1989).

17. Henry Fielding, *Amelia,* ed. Martin C. Battestin (Middletown, Conn.: Wesleyan Univ. Press, 1983), xxxix.

18. Ibid., 21.

19. See, for instance, Eustace Palmer, *"Amelia*—The Decline of Fielding's Art," *Essays in Criticism* 21 (1971): 135–51.

20. An important exception to this critical view is offered in Martin C. Battestin, "The Problem of *Amelia:* Hume, Barrow, and the Conversion of Captain Booth," ELH 41 (1974): 613–48.

21. J. Paul Hunter, *Occasional Form,* 23–74; Ronald Paulson, *Satire and the Novel in Eighteenth-Century England* (New Haven: Yale Univ. Press, 1967), 85–95; Claude J. Rawson, "Some Considerations on Authorial Intrusion in Fielding's Novels and Plays," *Durham University Journal* 33 (1971): 32–44.

22. Jean Ducrocq, *Le théatre de Fielding, 1728–1737, et ses prolongements dans l'oeuvre romanesque* (Paris: Didier, 1975).

23. Robert D. Hume, *Henry Fielding and the London Theatre 1728–1737* (Oxford: Clarendon Press, 1988).

24. Albert J. Rivero, *The Plays of Henry Fielding: A Critical Study of His Dramatic Career* (Charlottesville: Univ. Press of Virginia, 1989).

25. Jill Campbell, *Natural Masques: Gender and Identity in Fielding's Plays and Novels* (Stanford: Stanford Univ. Press, 1995).

26. Angela J. Smallwood, *Fielding and the Woman Question: The Novels of Henry Fielding and the Feminist Debate 1700–1750* (New York: St. Martin's Press, 1989).

27. Although Fielding criticism in the twentieth century has been dominated by the emergence of the moral, Christian Fielding, I do not wish to leave the impression that this is the only approach to Fielding's works worth emphasizing. For the sake of brevity and coherence, I have had to sketch out a complex history with a few broad strokes and thus reduced the multiple plots of Fielding criticism to fit a single story line. As I hope I have suggested throughout, there have been other critical voices in what has been a long and diverse conversation. Building on the rich legacy of earlier Fielding criticism and on the expansion of critical approaches during the last two decades, the essays that follow reflect many critical perspectives.

# The Politics of the Playhouse:
## *Pasquin* and *The Historical Register for the Year 1736*

ALBERT J. RIVERO

Fielding's last five plays before the Licensing Act—*Pasquin, Tumble-Down Dick, Eurydice, The Historical Register for the Year 1736,* and *Eurydice Hiss'd*—were written on the model of *The Author's Farce.* All five plays rely on the rehearsal structure and techniques of his first irregular piece; all five continue his satire on the pleasures of the town; all five, unlike their prototype, deal specifically with politics. Politics had never been totally absent from Fielding's drama; no dramatist of the 1730s, if he wished to be truthful to nature, could have avoided the most prominent concern of the age. But in the 1730 version of *The Author's Farce,* for instance, or in the *Tom Thumb* plays, politics are referred to only by isolated allusions. One of these allusions, however, deserves notice. In *The Author's Farce* Witmore attributes the contemporary decline in taste to "party and prejudice" (p. 16). Although Witmore's observation is a commonplace—the type of blanket indictment of modernity ridiculed in *The Historical Register* in the first player's notion of drama as a "humming deal of satire"[1]—it nonetheless marks the first explicit connection in Fielding's plays between theatrical and political spheres. Fielding would elaborate on this connection in *The Welsh Opera,* where the seemingly innocuous transactions of the Apshinkens and their servants point clearly in the direction of the royal family and the ministry. Dramatic actions thus become analogies for political actions, as actors on one stage remind the audience of actors on another stage.

In his last plays—particularly in *The Historical Register* and *Eurydice Hiss'd*—Fielding would carry this process of dramatic analogy to its logical conclusion and represent political events, not in terms of the humorous mishaps of a Welsh family, but in terms of the theater itself. Medley, the author of a play titled *The Historical Register,* enlightens the critic Sourwit

Reprinted from Albert J. Rivero, *The Plays of Henry Fielding: A Critical Study of His Dramatic Career* (1989), by permission of the University Press of Virginia.

about "how [his] political is connected with [his] theatrical": "When my politics come to a farce, they very naturally lead to the playhouse where, let me tell you, there are some politicians too, where there is lying, flattering, dissembling, promising, deceiving, and undermining, as well as in any court in Christendom."[2] This natural connection between the politics of the playhouse and the politics of Walpole's England, between affairs of stage and affairs of state, caused Fielding to return to the scriblerian strategies of his first irregular play with renewed interest and with the conviction that he could discover new dramatic possibilities in the rehearsal of the pleasures of the town.

One of the lessons Fielding had learned while rehearsing the pleasures of the town in *The Author's Farce* had been that contemporary amusements are virtually interchangeable, that Don Tragedio's professions of linguistic excellence, to select a familiar example, "very naturally lead" to the equally extravagant claims of Sir Farcical, and these, in turn, lead to those of Dr. Orator, and so on. The protean nature of modern diversions is, therefore, reflected in the play's dizzying movement from comedy to farce to puppet show, in its fluid pageant of personified literary genres, now no longer what they once were, in its climactic confusion of characters and puppets. These strange metamorphoses continue into the epilogue, as the play ends by projecting itself into a chaotic future where no end exists, where flux reigns supreme. When Fielding in *Tom Thumb* wrestles with this modern Proteus and tries to hold him down to one single shape, he finds that the creature keeps changing, that the satiric object refuses to be objectified, that one pleasure of the town cannot be invoked without conjuring up all others. This apparent catastrophe is actually a gain: the satirist's task is simplified once he recognizes that one modern aberration inevitably calls to mind the whole context of modernity. Thus, in *The Modern Husband* Fielding can represent the Moderns' sordid practices metaphorically, with the play's ludic structure mirroring the moral frivolity of fashionable London, where human actions, from courtship to marriage to playgoing, are reduced to, and interpreted as, games. *The Modern Husband,* in short, discovers the quintessence of modernity, its deep ludic structure, and embodies it in a complex dramatic metaphor. The dramatic metaphor of Fielding's last plays draws its power from the quintessential connections between the political and the theatrical.

The word *quintessence* belongs to Medley. The prologue to his new play is an "Ode to the New Year," a hodgepodge of clichés and imbecilities ("the sun shall rise," "the moon shall be bright," etc.) extracted from the sublime effusions lovingly crafted by the poet laureate to commemorate the king's birthday and New Year's Day.[3] When the singers have finished singing his ode, Medley exclaims that "that's the very quintessence and cream of all the odes I have seen for several years" (p. 17). That is, Medley has studied contemporary odes long and hard, as Fielding had studied regular comedy before writing *Love in Several Masques,* and discovered their deep structure. Hence he can compose an ode that is the "quintessence"—the Platonic Idea, as it were—

of all odes written within recent memory, an ode which not only refers to all Cibberian odes but also an ode to which, by virtue of the modern principle of *hysteron proteron* so learnedly enunciated in Scriblerus's preface to *The Tragedy of Tragedies* (pp. 42–43), all Cibberian odes can now refer. The concept of quintessence is the cornerstone of Medley's dramatic method in *The Historical Register,* and of Fielding's model both in *Pasquin,* where Sneerwell calls it "Emblematical,"[4] and in *The Historical Register for the Year 1736,* which "is writ," in Medley's words, "in allegory" (p. 27).

*Pasquin* opened on 5 March 1736 and ran, with few interruptions, for fifty-nine nights; its popularity carried over into the following season, when another production by the Great Mogul's Company of Comedians, *The Historical Register for the Year 1736,* became the town's favorite entertainment.[5] Praise for Fielding's "Dramatick SATIRE *on the* TIMES" was nearly unanimous,[6] though there were some dissenting voices, most notably that of Marforio in the *Grub-Street Journal.*[7] The object of all this attention was a five-act "REHEARSAL of Two PLAYS, *viz.* A COMEDY call'd, THE ELECTION; And a TRAGEDY call'd, The LIFE and DEATH of COMMON-SENSE" (title page), the joke presumably being that, in order to fill up a regular five-act structure, one needed to act both a modern comedy and a modern tragedy. Each play-within is rehearsed in its entirety, with each rehearsal taking up approximately two and a half acts of *Pasquin.* The comedy is regular; the tragedy, on the other hand, is irregular, consisting of only three acts. As Fustian explains to Sneerwell, his piece may be "immethodical," but he has an excellent reason for contravening the most revered Aristotelian rule of them all: "I spun it [his tragedy] out as long as I could keep *Common-Sense* alive; ay, or even her Ghost" (4 [38]). Unlike the surprisingly commonsensical Fustian, most modern tragedians follow the advice of critics like Sneerwell and thereby reduce all dramatic art to Aristotelian or Horatian clichés; such blind devotion to convention for the sake of convention inevitably gives rise to five-act plays on topics that merit, at best, only three—or, what is often closer to the truth, none whatsoever. In this respect, Fustian's name, like Trapwit's, actually belies his understanding of the craft he practices. Unlike the wholly inept dramatic hacks ridiculed in rehearsal plays from Buckingham onward, both Fustian and Trapwit, in spite of some regrettable lapses, know what they are doing most of the time. Neither Fustian's tragedy nor Trapwit's comedy can be said to resemble the typically bad play-within of the traditional rehearsal; neither play is the primary object of Fielding's satire in *Pasquin.* Instead, each one of these miniature sketches presents, within its reduced frame, a "Dramatick SATIRE *on the* TIMES," as Fielding discovers in Fustian and Trapwit two unlikely allies in his war against the pleasures of the town.

The pleasures of the town ridiculed in Trapwit's play are explicitly political, centering around a disputed election in a country borough. In fact, Trapwit's comedy is, in many ways, a rewriting of Fielding's own *Don Quixote in England.* As in the earlier play, the political satire is general and even-handed: Trapwit demonstrates that all politicians, whether "Whig and Tory; Or Court and Country Party" (1 [5]), are equally corrupt. The quintessential truth about modern elections, Trapwit and Fielding suggest, is that both parties will "Bribe away with Right and Left" (p. 7), though some candidates, like Sir Harry, do their bribing indirectly, as Trapwit explains, while others, like Lord Place, do so more directly, but because of the forgetfulness of the prop man, do so without money (p. 8). The stage, in short, is such a faithful mirror of "nature" (Trapwit's word) that even when it appears to fail in its representation of political corruption, it actually manages to be more accurate than the beleaguered playwright suspects. As Fustian puts it, "The Actor has out-done the Author; this Bribing with an empty Hand is quite in the Character of a Courtier" (ibid.). Fustian is wrong to exult in his colleague's apparent failure: Trapwit has written a scene in which either outcome would be true to nature; the prop man, by his carelessness, has unwittingly turned a good scene into an even better one. Trapwit, after all, knows that "the Art of a Writer . . . is, to diversifie his Matter, and do the same thing several ways" (ibid.). That "same thing," variously represented, is the quintessential corruption of modern political life; and that political quintessence cannot be better captured than in a playhouse that is quintessentially in disarray and in political turmoil. Men like Rich and the Cibbers, through their greed and political machinations, have turned the theater into a perfect mirror of the times; a satirist need be only passingly competent to score points off such easy targets.

If Trapwit's comedy, whatever its demerits, faithfully captures the quintessence of modern politics by satirizing that most quintessential of political transactions, the election, Fustian's tragedy carries the process of quintessential representation one step farther by dramatizing the underlying pattern that serves as the metaphorical link between stage and state actions. That link, for Fustian and Fielding, can be found in the modern disregard for traditional moral and intellectual imperatives, or, in Fustian's "Emblematical" terms, in the modern worship of Queen Ignorance and disdain for Queen Common-Sense. But even while staging his dramatic emblem for the decline of civilization as he knew it, Fielding introduces some additional complications. His original audiences at the Haymarket would have noted that the actress playing Queen Common-Sense had acted the part of Mrs. Mayoress in Trapwit's comedy. This doubling of parts would have planted a seed of suspicion in the audiences's collective mind: how can we trust a deity one has just seen in the role of a very earthly, very foolish old woman? Queen Common-Sense seems admirable enough, but the *visual* evidence appears to undermine her admirable character. This is, of course, the problem with the modern world: one can never be sure whether the appearance corresponds to reality, whether one is being deluded by a performance, whether Queen Common-Sense, as in the dedication the poet vows to write (5 [49]), is Queen Ignorance in disguise. Folly reveals and conceals itself under several masks.

What *Pasquin* does, in short, by offering us these fleeting moments of uneasy recognition, by constantly exposing the underlying mechanism of the theatrical illusion, is to emphasize the importance and wisdom of observing life as though it were a theatrical performance—a quintessential point Fielding raises over and over in his dramatic career, beginning with the opening scene of *Love in Several Masques* and the play's subsequent concern with the reading of acting. We may note in the playhouse that one actor or actress is playing several parts, that life on stage is performance, but in life, because we are so caught up in our own performances, we seldom recognize the histrionic basis of all human behavior. This is why we are easily deceived by the actions of others, even though, as Fielding would later remark, we tend to speak of human activities in the language of the stage.[8] But this stage language, like most metaphorical language—as illustrated by the characters in *Tom Thumb* and *The Tragedy of Tragedies*—is often used without awareness of the underlying metaphor, without a thought about its implications and consequences. We all know that the world is a stage, but through mindless repetition we no longer understand what the analogy between world and stage involves, what it can teach us about our behavior and the behavior of others. In *Pasquin* Fielding revitalizes this theatrical commonplace by dramatizing, in "Emblematical" detail, the connections between life as acted on stage and life as acted in the world. And the world, for Fielding and his contemporaries, pullulated with political meaning. *Pasquin* may not have been as "bitterly satiric [as] other political satires of the time,"[9] but the lessons it taught its audience, because taught with such subtlety and such apparent good nature, must have deeply disturbed those in power. Any play that seeks to heighten the perceptions of its audience, that challenges its viewers to read the world with histrionic detachment, makes an emphatic political statement. *The Historical Register for the Year 1736* would differ from *Pasquin* in directing that political statement, explicitly and unequivocally, at Walpole and his ministers, in inviting its spectators and readers to find specific partisan applications in its transparent political allegory.

The unmistakable anti-Walpole applications of the dramatic allegory of *The Historical Register* have often been cited—at least since Colley Cibber's celebrated pronouncement on the subject in his irrepressible *Apology for His Life* (1740)—as one of the main factors contributing to the passage of the Licensing Act. While it would be difficult to establish that *The Historical Register* was one of the principal protagonists in this dramatic tragedy—the law, after all, was already on the books and efforts to enforce it had begun as early as 1735—it is almost as difficult to deny it its prominent role.[10] The play, as any reader can plainly see, was intended to offend: "He who maketh any wrong application thereof," as Fielding himself devilishly suggests in his dedication to the public, "might as well mistake the name of Thomas for John, or Old Nick for Old Bob" (p. 8). Indeed, even though Fielding does not develop the diabolical connections of Walpole and his minions with the thoroughness that the dedication might lead us to expect, there is a scene (pp. 36–37) in which these connections are perhaps suggested through Miltonic and biblical allusions. Pistol, Theophilus Cibber's dramatic alter ego, storms the stage and speaks to the mob of his part in the "glorious enterprise," a reference to the well-known spat between his wife Susanna and Kitty Clive over the role of Polly; Satan speaks to his cohorts of their "Glorious Enterprise" in his first speech in *Paradise Lost* (1.89). The citizens then express their sentiments on Cibber's "successless" mission with a theatrical hiss. "That hiss," Pistol tells his audience,

> speaks their assent.
> Such was the hiss that spoke the great applause
> Our mighty father met with when he brought
> His *Riddle* on the stage.

When Satan returns to Hell, "successful beyond hope" (463), after carrying out his temptation of Eve, his companions hiss their approval:

> So having said, a while he stood, expecting
> Their universal shout and high applause
> To fill his ear, when contrary he hears
> On all sides, from innumerable tongues
> A dismal universal hiss, the sound
> Of public scorn.
>
> (10.504–9)

Finally, after Cibber/Pistol finishes his oration, Medley dismisses him with "Get thee gone," a possible echo of Christ's words to Satan in the wilderness, "Get thee hence" (Matthew 4:10) and "Get thee behind me" (Luke 4:8).[11] These hits at the Cibbers, together with Fielding's usual roasting of beaux, auctions, and other inhabitants and pleasures of Old England, constitute the brilliant dramatic fabric of the Great Mogul's most exuberant acting play.[12]

As a critical term, *exuberance* does not seem promising, yet it would be hard to come up with a word that better describes Fielding's dramatic art. *Love in Several Masques* and *The Temple Beau* offer a compendium of clichés borrowed from Restoration and early eighteenth-century comedy, but, as I have suggested at the beginning of this study, Fielding's precocious confidence in his dramatic powers breathes new life into the old conventions. In *The Author's Farce* Fielding's energy and exuberance are omnipresent: the play refuses to hold still; it holds a mirror up to its maker's hyperactive imagination. *The Author's Farce* is thus always threatening to run out of control, to become one with the chaos it must hold at bay to make its satiric statement. There is, in other words, more than a hint of immaturity lurking in the play's brilliant execution. The modern world may be an amorphous heap, but art, if it is to perform its didactic function, must erect boundaries to stave off dissolution. Art must make a statement: it must not merely record; it must also interpret and organize. In *The Author's Farce* Fielding senses that he is letting his exuberance control his art, and, as a result, he feels that he must apologize for what he is doing.

In *The Historical Register* there are no apologies, no intimations of uneasiness, because Fielding has discovered a new way of representing the pleasures of the town. In *The Author's Farce* Fielding is constantly insinuating that he is not the real author of Luckless's puppet show; indeed, even Luckless himself tries to disown his own work. As we sit in the theater, we are asked to believe that this particular puppet show is a parody, that there is a satiric purpose to all this nonsense. The play, therefore, breaks up into a foreground of commentary and a background of modern diversions, into the frame provided by the "reading" romantic comedy and the "acting" puppet show that refuses to be contained within that conventional frame. Like the *Tom Thumb* plays, *The Author's Farce* aims to convey its satiric intent to its viewers by making them aware of the discontinuities in its representation. *The Historical Register* and *Pasquin,* on the other hand, present virtually seamless fabrics. To be sure, these plays still offer internal sketches with external commentary, but here commentary and play-within are leading toward the same goal; as we have noted, the works of Trapwit and Fustian, like Medley's brief skits, are not so much the objects of satire as the agents of it. And the audience cannot mistake the satiric intent of these internal objects because they, unlike those found in *The Author's Farce,* have unmistakable political applications. That is to say, in *Pasquin* and *The Historical Register*—to recall the critical terminology of my earlier analysis—politics is the distancing device that prevents misinterpretation. The plays' exuberance derives from Fielding's knowledge that he is fully in control, that his motives cannot possibly be misinterpreted, because he has discovered a dramatic metaphor that yokes together all the potentially fissiparous elements of modernity, the quintessential link connecting all the pleasures of the town to their political source.

The political state of Walpole's England, then, is the tenor of Fielding's dramatic metaphor in his last plays; the theatrical representation of the pleasures of the town, with all the difficulties involved in that representation, is the vehicle. *The Historical Register* and *Eurydice Hiss'd* give special bite to the dramatic metaphor by particularizing the satire, by choosing sides. In *The Historical Register* Fielding mocks those who, like the first player and perhaps like the author of *Pasquin,* believe that satire is simply the repetition of general and hackneyed condemnations. In the first player's words, "I would repeat in every page that courtiers are cheats and don't pay their debts, that lawyers are rogues, physicians blockheads, soldiers cowards, and ministers" (1 [13]). Just at the moment when he appears to hit a specific target, the first player draws back: "I'll only name 'em, that's enough to set the audience a-hooting" (ibid.). Like the writers of "simple" farces, a term Honestus uses in

*Eurydice Hiss'd* (Appleton, ed., p. 68) to classify *Eurydice,* the first player is satisfied with an automatic response. A response of any kind, as Fielding well understood, is better than no response: it is preferable "to set the audience a-hooting" than a-sleeping. The playwright's first goal is to entertain his audience. As Medley observes with tongue in cheek, the "main design" of his "several plots"—"some pretty deep and some but shallow"—is "to divert the town and bring full houses" (1 [15]). But drama must also teach, must have a moral (ibid.). It is not enough to "extract" satirical tags from "above a dozen plays" (p. 13), as the first player admits; one must aim for specificity, one must select what is really important, what is historically meaningful. One must, in short, write a quintessential play like *The Historical Register,* though Medley is less than candid when he says, like Tacitus at the beginning of his *Annals,* that his "design is to ridicule the vicious and foolish customs of the age, and that in a fair manner, without fear, favor, or ill-nature" (p. 15). What distinguishes Medley's quintessential "design" from the first player's "humming deal of satire"—and from Fielding's previous plays—is its "favor," its ill-natured barbs at the ministry, its specific partisan applications. In Walpole's England, a "humming deal of satire" is not enough; the socially conscious dramatist can no longer play along with the general farce and "screen" the culprit;[13] he no longer has the easy alternative, the cowardly luxury, of writing *sine ira et studio.*

This irruption of political reality into the playhouse is reflected in the odd title of Medley's new play, *The Historical Register,* a title made even more specific in Fielding's *Historical Register for the Year 1736.* Sourwit, as he tells Medley, is "a little staggered at the name of your piece. Doubtless, sir, you know the rules of writing, and I can't guess how you can bring the actions of a whole year into the circumference of four-and-twenty-hours" (p. 14). Like all carping critics in rehearsal plays, Sourwit is a devout Aristotelian and cannot imagine how a "whole year" can be compressed into that all-important dramatic "day"; of course, he fails to take into account that he has never seen a twenty-four-hour play, that the quintessence of the dramatist's art is selection. Medley now reminds him of this curious property of the dramatist's mirror. His new play, he points out, is not like "vulgar" newspapers, often "filled . . . with trash for lack of news" (p. 15). Its journalistic title, in this respect, has misled the literal-minded critic. Instead, his "piece," as Sourwit calls it, selects or "extracts," from the larger register of historical events, what is truly significant; hence, it can depict, "in half an hour," every single action that captures the quintessence of the year. In fact, Medley's model is so successful that, with only a few strokes of his satiric brush, in his scene on taxation he can portray ("comprise" is Medley's word) "the full account of the whole history of Europe" (p. 21). But Medley's dramatic allegory, its artistic transformations notwithstanding, is firmly grounded in history. The allegorical scenes of *The Historical Register* may have wider applications to—in Hume's oft-quoted phrase—the constant and universal principles of human nature. But their most important connection is to specific events in a specific place (England) during a specific year (1736).

One of the most newsworthy events of the year, as the town well knew, had occurred not in the turbulent world of politics, where all eyes (and ears) had been riveted in fascination and evermounting anxiety, but in the lesser, though equally volatile, world of the theater. On the night of 19 February 1737, *Eurydice,* Fielding's one-act afterpiece to Addison's *Cato,* had been damned at Drury Lane, drowned in a deafening din of hisses, whistles, and catcalls, by a mob of unruly footmen. This disastrous event had apparently occurred too late in the calendar year—then reckoned to run until March—to be included in the dramatic allegory of *The Historical Register for the Year 1736* when the play opened on 21 March 1737.[14] On 13 April, however, Fielding corrected this omission and added to his already popular play what was in effect a new act, *Eurydice Hiss'd or A Word to the Wise.* In this brief sketch Fielding extended his dramatic allegory to its boldest application yet, as the playwright-within of Spatter's "tragedy," the "very Great Man" Pillage (p. 56), becomes not only the symbol of the corrupt man of the theater who will balk at nothing to make a profit—Fielding's most honest self-portrait—but also the dramatic counterpart of the Great Man of English politics, Sir Robert Walpole, who had recently failed in what was widely regarded as one of his crudest attempts on the liberties of the king's long-suffering subjects. Just as Fielding and his ill-fated *Eurydice* had been hooted off the stage at Drury Lane, so had Walpole and his ministers been soundly humiliated, both in the press and in Parliament, for trying to act out their little public farce known as the Excise Bill. As the earl of Egmont noted in his diary, the parallels between stage and state could not be mistaken: "To the Haymarket playhouse where a farce was acted called *Eurydice First* [*sic*] an allegory on the loss of the Excise Bill. The whole was a satire on Sir Robert Walpole, and I observed that when any strong passages fell, the Prince [Frederick] who was there, clapped, especially when in favor of liberty."[15]

But, as he would continue to do until 1742, Sir Robert had the last laugh. On 21 June 1737 the Licensing Act received the royal assent, and three days later, on 24 June, the Little Theatre in the Haymarket closed its doors. Like the "actor standing in the wings laugh[ing] loudly" in *The Historical Register,* Sir Robert, his nose tweaked once too often by the Opposition wits, had been plotting "behind the scenes" (p. 46). As the curtain fell for the last time on that gloomy summer's evening at Mr. Fielding's "scandal-shop," the Great Man stepped forward to speak his triumphant epilogue, while the Great Mogul, no match for his allegorical double, fled backstage, followed by his "Company of Comedians," to pick up the pieces of his shattered satiric mirror. That satiric mirror, wondrously reconstituted, would, like the ghost of Queen Common-Sense, continue to haunt the prime minister—in the *Cham-*

*pion,* in *Jonathan Wild*—but it would never again recapture its original efful-
gence, the bright, living images of flesh and blood it projected onto the London stage during the glorious final days of Fielding's dramatic career.[16]

## Notes

1. William W. Appleton, ed., *The Historical Register for the Year 1736 and Eurydice Hiss'd*
(Lincoln: Univ. of Nebraska Press, 1967), p. 13.

2. Ibid., p. 16. On the meaning of "farce" and the correspondences between stage and
state in Fielding's plays, see Ronald Paulson, *Satire and the Novel in Eighteenth-Century England*
(New Haven: Yale Univ. Press, 1967), pp. 85–95. For an excellent discussion of Fielding's
strategies in his last "reflexive plays," see Hunter, *Occasional Form,* pp. 49–74.

3. In *The Egoist: or, Colley upon Cibber* (London, 1743) Cibber, while pointedly refusing
to name his antagonist, records his "good-natured" reaction to Fielding's attack: "Don't you
remember, at the little Theatre in the *Hay-Market,* upon the first Day of acting some new Piece
there? when a personal Jest upon me flew souce in my Face, while I sat in the Eye of a full
Audience, was not I as suddenly loud in my Laugh and Applause, as any common Spectator?
Now as I could have no Warning of the Shot, was not my manner of receiving it a plain Proof
that I was more pleased with the Conceit, than hurt with the Intention of it?" (pp. 27–28).
This little pamphlet is also remarkable in revealing that Cibber, after having "been so used to
play[ing] the Fool in Comedy," had begun "to be quite as easy, in the same Character, in real
Life" (p. 35): "Why, how do you think I could have given you so finish'd a Coxcomb [Lord Fop-
pington] if I had not found a good deal of the same Stuff in myself to make him with?" (p. 38).

4. O. M. Brack, Jr., William Kupersmith, and Curt A. Zimansky, eds., *Pasquin* (Iowa
City: Univ. of Iowa Press, 1973), p. 37.

5. For the stage history of *Pasquin,* see the Introduction by Brack et al., pp. vii–xviii;
and Hume, *Fielding and the London Theatre,* pp. 209–20.

6. Cited from facsimile of original title page, in *Pasquin,* p. 1.

7. See the *Grub-Street Journal,* no. 330 (22 April 1736) and no. 332 (6 May 1736).
Marforio here offers an uninspired rebuttal to what was perhaps the most interesting contemporary analysis (in terms of painting) of the play's dramatic method, Aaron Hill's commenda-
tory essay in *The Prompter* (2 April 1736). These three pieces, together with other contemporary documents dealing with *Pasquin* and *The Historical Register,* are reprinted in *Henry Fielding:
The Critical Heritage,* pp. 77–110.

8. See the *Champion* (19 August 1740). Cf. *Tom Jones,* 7.1 "A Comparison between the
World and the Stage."

9. Goldgar, *Walpole and the Wits,* p. 151. Goldgar is here speaking of all Fielding's
plays from *Don Quixote in England* to *Eurydice Hiss'd:* "Nor are the plays . . . heavily or bitterly satiric, not at least when compared to other political satires of the time. Fielding's persistent themes, aside from the perennial topic of corruption, are political motifs which have
the maximum *literary* significance: that is, he is acutely sensitive to the triumph of the 'sons
of dullness' over men of wit and merit and to efforts to limit the freedom of the stage." I
agree with Goldgar, but would add that few of Fielding's patrons at the Haymarket would
have failed to notice that the vast majority of the "sons of dullness" seemed to belong to
Walpole's camp; moreover, *The Historical Register,* though it may not have been "heavily or
bitterly satiric" in performance, becomes downright offensive when read after Fielding's
Dedication to the Public.

10. In 1729, for example, Walpole had revived the old statute and suppressed Gay's
*Polly.* Although the Licensing Act provides the catastrophe for Fielding's dramatic career, its
story does not really belong in a critical study of his plays. For the definitive study of the

subject, see Vincent J. Liesenfeld, *The Licensing Act of 1737* (Madison: Univ. of Wisconsin Press, 1984). On Fielding and the Licensing Act, see Hume, *Fielding and the London Theatre,* pp. 248–53.

11. Biblical quotations are from the King James Version; those of *Paradise Lost* from Merritt Y. Hughes, ed., *John Milton: Complete Poems and Major Prose* (New York: Odyssey, 1957).

12. See Charles W. Nichols, "Social Satire in *Pasquin* and *The Historical Register,*" *Philological Quarterly* 3 (1924): 309–17. On Fielding's fun at the Cibbers' expense, see, in addition to the sources already cited, Charles W. Nichols, "Fielding and the Cibbers," *Philological Quarterly* 1 (1922): 278–89; and Houghton W. Taylor, "Fielding upon Cibber," *Modern Philology* 29 (1931): 73–90.

13. The *Craftsman,* no. 403 (23 March 1734) offers a discussion of the popular stage-state term *screen:* "A *Screen* in the metaphorical Sense, means any Device, or Contrivance, to protect Men from the Fury of their Enemies, or the Pursuit of Justice. . . . Hence it appears, *Screening* is absolutely necessary, when *publick Corruption grows prevalent;* and in whom can this great Privilege be so properly reposed, as in a *Prime Minister,* who conducts the whole Machine of Government, and is therefore the best Judge who are the proper Objects of Favour." This piece is attributed to Fielding in Martin C. Battestin's forthcoming *New Essays by Henry Fielding* (University Press of Virginia).

14. For the stage history of *The Historical Register* and *Eurydice Hiss'd,* see Appleton's introduction, pp. xii–xviii.

15. Ibid., p. xiii. Appleton cites other relevant entries from Egmont's diary on p. xii.

16. On the last days of the Great Mogul's Company—including Fielding's scheme for building a new theatre as well as the tantalizing probability that, at the end, Fielding was bought off by Walpole—see Hume, *Fielding and the London Theatre,* pp. 239–53.

# What the Drama Does
# in Fielding's *Jonathan Wild*

ALEXANDER PETTIT

Fielding's *The Life of Mr. Jonathan Wild the Great* was first published in his generically chequered *Miscellanies* (1743), but was probably drafted and possibly written before *Joseph Andrews* (1742); it belongs equally to his career as dramatist and as novelist. Many readers have remarked that the anti-Walpole strain recalls Fielding's later drama at the Little Haymarket theatre. *Jonathan Wild* can tell us more about the shape of Fielding's career, however, if we read it as a study of genre in transition, a working-out of the question of what counts—or what works—in a genre new to Fielding and still uncertain of its own formal parameters. Fielding calls attention to the absurdity of his protagonist by presenting him as an actor unaware that his overblown theatricality denies or contradicts the generic requirements of the novel. Wild "acts," habitually and very much as an actor acts, but without realizing that his acting is a behaviour both granted by and mocked by a narrator who abdicates his role as the controller of the narrative whenever he is especially eager that his protagonist discredit himself.[1]

I shall first suggest that *Jonathan Wild* is structurally and thematically allied to the drama of the Restoration and the early eighteenth century; secondly, I shall examine the parodic and evaluative functions of the drama in *Jonathan Wild*—the manner in which the drama is used to indicate its own limitations. I hope to demonstrate that *Jonathan Wild* offers a self-conscious evaluation of, and a judgment against, the appropriateness to the novel of the conventions of the drama.

Robert Hume designates the period 1728 to 1737 the "New Wave" of English eighteenth-century drama, introduced by the great commercial successes of *The Beggar's Opera* and Vanbrugh and Cibber's *The Provok'd Husband,* and brought to an abrupt close by Walpole's Licensing Act; he notes

Reprinted from *Eighteenth-Century Fiction* 6 (1994): 153–68, by permission of the publisher.

that the period is characterized by "writers [who] experiment vigorously in new play types."[2] The conservative resonance of his occasional pseudonym "H. Scriblerus Secundus" aside, Fielding was throughout the 1730s experimenting as broadly as any of his contemporaries. The vigour in Fielding's plays manifests itself as an intolerance for rules and conventions, a youthful, joyous, and relaxed irreverence that defines the central difference between the *Peri Bathous* of "Martinus Scriblerus" (1727) and a piece in many ways indebted to it, *The Tragedy of Tragedies* of "Scriblerus Secundus" (1731). *Jonathan Wild* transposes the great creative energy of 1730s drama into the novel, punching through generic boundaries as surely as *The Tragedy of Tragedies* and *The Historical Register for the Year 1736* (1737) did.

A bantering and propulsive, if finally novel-centric, relationship between genres is evident throughout *Jonathan Wild:* the distance that separates the literalistic and prose-bound Partridge from the actor Garrick in *Tom Jones* is never taken for granted in the earlier novel. Dramatic convention, which embellishes theme, character, and narrative in *Tom Jones* (1749), is integral to theme in *Jonathan Wild,* in which Fielding presents one chapter as a "soliloquy" and three as "dialogues." Wild's dialogues with Laetitia Snap and the ordinary of Newgate obviously derive more from dramatic farce than from prose fiction; Fielding, in fact, later rewrote what looks like a stage direction in Wild and Laetitia's "dialogue matrimonial" as if he had recognized and rejected the "prompt-book" style of the earlier version. Many characters have an unmistakable affiliation with the dramatic tradition. Allusions to plays and playwrights are numerous, as are plainly allusive references to or puns on "the hero," "performance," "character," "catastrophe," "conservation of character," and so forth; the pattern is supported by periodic uses of the durable world/stage metaphor.[3]

The disguise or masquerade motif that had migrated from the drama to prose fiction appears in *Jonathan Wild* in theatrical rather than novelistic form. The day after Wild has enjoyed the "endearments and caresses" of Molly Straddle (p. 92), she fails at first to recognize him when, with no apparent alteration other than a softening of his voice, Wild "personate[s]" the jeweller Heartfree in Heartfree's shop (pp. 99–100). The simplicity and the effectiveness of Wild's posing recall the Elizabethan or Restoration drama—or, closer to home, the transparent disguise of Old Laroon in Fielding's *The Old Debauchees* (1732)—and anticipate the sartorial gamesmanship of *She Stoops to Conquer* (1773) and *The Rivals* (1775). As readers of Terry Castle's work on the masquerade in eighteenth-century fiction will recognize, Fielding's use of the disguise motif in *Jonathan Wild* is not typical of the eighteenth-century novel.[4] In Haywood's masquerade novels, Defoe's *Roxana* (1724), and Fielding's own later *Amelia* (1751), disguise is a more elaborate affair, tied to deeper deceptions and more fundamental questions of self-identity, and susceptible to the sustained scrutiny of the reader rather than to the fleeting and habituated aural and ocular observation of the viewer.

There is a thematic similarity between *Jonathan Wild* and Fielding's drama that suggests a correspondence between phases of Fielding's career and between *Jonathan Wild* and the recent drama. *Joseph Andrews* and *Tom Jones* are journeys towards romantic marriage; Booth and Amelia are married when *Amelia* opens, but closure is defined by their belated realization of a sentimental mutuality. In *Wild* the marriage interest is subverted. The romantic and generative marriage of Mr and Mrs Heartfree pre-dates the opening of the narrative and remains emotionally static throughout it; it functions as a normative commentary on the corrupt, mutable, and more carefully developed courtship and marriage of Wild and Laetitia.

As Fielding is about to marry "the great man" Wild off to "the chaste Laetitia," he comments on genre, marriage, and teleology. The passage accents Wild's odd generic status and its affinity with Fielding's drama.

> Most private histories, as well as comedies, end at this period; the historian and the poet both concluding they have done enough for their hero when they have married him; or intimating rather that the rest of his life must be a dull calm of happiness, very delightful indeed to pass through, but somewhat insipid to relate. (p. 142)

The categorical syllogism that Fielding initiates, and what it implies about Wild, is clear enough: heroes get married at the ends of histories and comedies, and Wild marries in mid-text. But if we read the passage as initiating a hypothetical syllogism, its meaning is different. Consider the following hypothetical syllogism, based on the rejection by the minor premise of the consequent, or the "then" clause: if *Jonathan Wild* is a history or a comedy, then its hero will marry at the end of the narrative; Wild does not marry at the end of the narrative; therefore, *Jonathan Wild* is neither a history nor a comedy. The syllogism calls attention to the generic ambiguity of Fielding's narrative.

The text supports the conclusion of the hypothetical syllogism, as does a third, if less precisely classical, syllogism. We could consider that in this passage Fielding tacitly reaffirms his major satirical premise that Wild is a worthy "hero" and adds the minor premise that heroes in prose fiction and comedy tend towards such-and-such an end. The major premise is transparent, designedly false, given the satiric and allegorical strains in the narrative; but the truth-value of the minor premise is beyond dispute. While Fielding leaves the categorical and hypothetical syllogisms to complete themselves, he encourages his reader to consider the collapse of the substitute syllogism, weakened by the fallacy of its major premise:

> but, whether it was that nature and fortune had great designs for him to execute, and would not suffer his vast abilities to be lost and sunk in the arms of a wife, or whether neither nature nor fortune had any hand in the matter, is a point I will not determine. Certain it is that this match did not produce that

serene state we have mentioned above, but resembled the most turbulent and ruffled, rather than the most calm sea. (p. 143)

In the revised syllogism we have a major premise that Fielding has asked us to believe and a minor premise that we cannot deny; but we are obviously disallowed the conclusion—the dull and happy marriage of Wild—towards which they tend. Satire, however, has its own logic; and if we cede too easily the point that Wild is not "great," then Fielding's satire loses its sustaining oscillation between intended and pretended meanings, and runs the risk of becoming polemic or mere sarcasm. The momentum of the satire tempts us to accept the major premise's inversion of hero and crook, and to recognize the indeterminacy of the narrative as a surrogate conclusion. The violation of the marriage closure finally identifies a self-consciously unorthodox approach to genre and teleology.

Another look at these passages underscores *Jonathan Wild*'s awkward relationship to the novel as a genre and its proximity to the drama. The attempt to distinguish one's work from "most private histories" is of course a stock affectation in earlier prose fiction: Defoe's preface to *Roxana* provides a striking but not extraordinary example. At least by the time he wrote *Joseph Andrews* and its preface, the classically mannered Fielding was taking this claim a good deal more seriously than his predecessors had. *Jonathan Wild,* like *Joseph Andrews,* is no "private history": the generalized and broadly public satire that Fielding intended in both novels ensures this.[5] His attempt to distinguish *Jonathan Wild* from "comedies" (dramatic or otherwise) would be out of place in his later work and would contradict the generic foundation of the "comic epic in prose" (*Joseph Andrews*) as well as the teleological impetus of *Joseph Andrews* and *Tom Jones.* And Fielding's dissociation is misleading unless we remark that the plays that he himself designated comedies—for instance, *The Modern Husband* (1732), *The Old Debauchees* (1732), and *The Miser* (1733)—are more concerned with the satire generated by their plots—in these cases, satires of bad marriage, bad religion, and venality—than with the comic marriage motif that concludes the plots. So Fielding does not, in *Jonathan Wild,* distinguish his prose narrative from his own comic dramas. The union of Charlotte Gaywit and Captain Bellamant in *The Modern Husband* is not designed to purge our memories of the ill spirits that have dominated the play, and we are left unconvinced of the charm or even the utility of the new order. As a summary of narrative intention, the marriage of Gaywit and Bellamant is of considerably less moment than the marriages of Joseph Andrews and Fanny, and Tom Jones and Sophia Western. By focusing on the denunciation of corrupt marriage rather than on the glorification of romantic marriage, Fielding sounds more like the satirical dramatist who wrote *The Modern Husband* and *The Virgin Unmask'd* (1735) than the novelist who wrote *Joseph Andrews, Tom Jones,* and *Amelia,* or, to bring in two of Fielding's occasional adversaries, more like Cibber in *The Careless Husband* (1705) than Richardson in *Pamela* (1741).

In his treatment of his protagonist's marriage, Fielding could draw on the tradition of what Hume calls the "marital discord comedy" of the late seventeenth and early eighteenth centuries—a tradition, although Hume does not note this, at odds with the eighteenth-century novel, and one that poses an alternative to the wedding-bells closure that the novel was importing from the drama. Hume's parameters for this subgenre are Dryden's *Marriage A-la-Mode* (1671) and Fielding's *The Modern Husband* (1732). He proposes the additional category of the "problem plays" of Otway (*The Atheist,* 1683), Southerne (*The Wives Excuse,* 1691), and Vanbrugh (*The Provok'd Wife,* 1697), which, unlike the "happy-ending plays" of Steele, Cibber, Charles Johnson, and others, "[spring] from a recognition of the intractability of the [marital] problem, and [move] only to impasse."[6]

While the eighteenth-century novel on the whole embraced neither strain of the marital discord comedy, I suggest that *Jonathan Wild* behaves very much like Hume's "problem play": the central marriage is rotten in the manner of Otway's and Southerne's marriages (although it provides us a good deal more laughter); and the compensatory vision of the Heartfrees' marriage obliquely recalls the pairing of Belinda and (again) Heartfree in Vanbrugh's play.[7] The "impasse" that Hume identifies is escaped only because Wild is hanged. The last we see of a marriage that has been defined by ignorance and delusion on one side (Wild's) and unabashed calculation on the other (Laetitia's) is a scene in which Wild, awaiting the cart that will take him from Newgate to Tyburn, declares Laetitia "the vilest of b—s," a sentiment to which Laetitia responds with "a recapitulation of his faults in an exacter order, and with more perfect memory, than one would have imagined her capable." Wild ends the conference by "[catching] her by the hair and [kicking] her, as heartily as his chains would suffer him, out of the room" (p. 212).[8] Violent marital incompatibility is not a big issue in the novel before the Gothic and historical novels of the later eighteenth century—can anyone imagine *The History of Mr. and Mrs. Tow-wouse,* or *Mrs. Mirvan Gets Mad?*—and is in fact one of the elements of the romance to which the novel proved least hospitable. But the problem had been taken up in the genre in which Fielding had made his mark, and here again Fielding seems to have borrowed from the drama.

The drama does more in *Jonathan Wild* than provide a sense of historical and generic association: it allows Fielding to build a case for the inadequacy of his protagonist and becomes a vehicle for his commentary on phony "greatness," another means of emphasizing the disjunction between what Wild is and what he thinks he is. Mikhail Bakhtin's theory of "novelization" is useful here. Bakhtin argues that "the novel parodies other genres (precisely in their role as genres); it exposes the conventionality of their forms and their language; it squeezes out some genres and incorporates others into its own peculiar structure, reformulating and reaccentuating them."[9] *Jonathan Wild* certainly "incorporates" the drama into its own narrative; furthermore, in doing so it comments parodically on the sometimes restrictive "conventionality" of the genre it has appropriated by making Wild a travesty of an actor and *Jonathan Wild* a travesty of the drama.

Fielding likens Wild to an actor—a "clown," as Claude Rawson would have it, whose "comic diminutions" recall "the deadpan expression of a stage-comic."[10] Wild's mother was an orange-seller at a theatre. Speaking of Wild's birth, Fielding observes that Wild "made his first appearance on this great theatre the very day when the plague first broke out in 1665" (p. 45). If we conflate "Wild" and "plague," as Fielding invites us to, emphasizing the point by implying prostitution in Wild's family and incest in his marriage, then we see Wild as a sort of actor-virus whose theatricalism is not restricted to the stage, but enters indiscriminately into other and less appropriate spheres of life. Instead of simply "saying," Wild "repeat[s] a speech" to Laetitia (p. 94). Stressing Wild's disjunctive personality, Fielding notes that Wild demonstrates "that perfect mastery of his temper, or rather of his muscles, which is as necessary to the forming a great character as to the personating it on the stage" (p. 93). Wild's inability to distinguish between literal and figurative meanings of "stage," suggested syntactically by the ambiguous "character," identifies the trespass that makes Wild the subject of parody (he offends generic context) as well as satire (he offends moral decency).

The narrative structure of *Jonathan Wild* negotiates between the drama, in which the author usually does not appear *in propria persona* and must therefore exert control discreetly, and the third-person novel, in which the narrator is a more or less overt and authoritarian presence. In this *Jonathan Wild* again participates in both periods of Fielding's career, reflecting the playwright's occasional dissatisfaction with the exclusion of the dramatist from the drama and anticipating the novelist's interest in ways of including himself in his narratives.[11]

Fielding goes a step further than he had done in the plays or would do in the novels, and constructs a dialogue between dramatic and novelistic modes of control. "Authority" and "persona" are ultimately retained by the novelist Fielding, but these values are sometimes loaned by him to the actor Wild. Fielding grants Wild the illusion of narrative control, minimizing his own presence in the narrative or retreating from it at those moments when Wild speaks in soliloquy, in dialogue, or oratorically. In this way Fielding presents Wild as a windbag and a buffoon: a soliloquist in a narrative environment that prefers a more professed heteroglossia, a dialogist unable to master the rules of the dialogue, and an orator increasingly ineffective with his audiences. The novel, which ends not with Wild's death but with Fielding's mordant commentary on the characters that he has created, finally insists on an authorial control against which Wild has been allowed to struggle, and so declares against the drama that has accommodated the struggle.[12]

From a narratological point of view, Wild's theatricality is usually unnecessary: the outbursts of theatrical discourse achieve no narrative end that thinking, chatting, or (more to the point in Fielding) being quoted indirectly could not accomplish with equal expediency and less ponderousness. But ponderousness—or the ponderous self-consciousness of misplaced characters—is precisely what Fielding is up to. Wild is always aware of what he regards as his own rhetorical savvy, but always ignorant of the inappropriateness of his verbal method to its matter. Consider some of the subjects of Wild's soliloquies or orations: "priggism," pretended "greatness," Laetitia's extravagant infidelity, his innocent "friend" Heartfree whom he has consigned to the hangman, and the ingratitude of his cut-throat companion Fireblood. Consider as well the heightened diction of these passages, and the impression created by them of a fine mind working through momentous metaphysical problems. "Thee's" and "thou's" are everywhere; and traces of formal rhetoric often adorn Wild's language, for instance in the soliloquy on the condemned Heartfree, in which Wild employs, unconvincingly, the figure of *ratiocinatio*, posing and answering a series of questions until he arrives at the exoneration that he desires (pp. 177–78). The figure here is not a self-contained dialectical approach to truth, but rather the means to an apology for self-interest, and as such, to Fielding, an instrument of parody and satire, a subtly distanced commentary on the rhetorical and moral failings of his protagonist.

Fielding treats Wild's penchant for fustian as an exercise in bathos, as when the penniless Wild strolls into a tavern, orders "a sneaker of punch," and begins to speak in "soliloquy":

> "How vain is human GREATNESS! What avail superior abilities, and a noble defiance of those narrow rules and bounds which confine the vulgar, when our best-concerted schemes are liable to be defeated! How unhappy is that state of PRIGGISM!" (p. 96)

Here again Fielding gives Wild enough rope to hang himself: the metaphor is useful as well as irresistible. The bathetic tumble from "GREATNESS" to "PRIGGISM," exquisite in any case, is all the more so for passing through the lament about vulgarity. We learn shortly that Wild's "soliloquy and his punch concluded together; for he had at every pause comforted himself with a sip" (p. 97). The aural and visual punctuation suggested here is highly theatrical, and the one-time playwright wishes us to imagine it as literally as possible: "Why then should any man wish to be a *prig,* or where is his greatness?"— pause, sip—"I answer, in his mind"—another sip, maybe longer this time, as the orator prepares himself for the strenuous balderdash that will follow— " 'tis the inward glory, the secret consciousness of doing great and wonderful actions, which can alone support the truly GREAT man, whether he be a

CONQUEROR, a TYRANT, a STATESMAN or a PRIG"—pause, sip, burp—and so forth (p. 96). Similarly, after lecturing the count on statecraft and priggery and having bored him sufficiently that he falls "fast asleep" during his speech, Wild relieves his friend of three shillings and repairs to a night-cellar (p. 55). A dialogue thus becomes a soliloquy and finally a means to more punch. In both cases, as elsewhere in *Wild,* dramatic amplitude exists in the service of bathos and inescapably points to the shabbiness of the hero.

Fielding's use of formal dialogue allows him to achieve the illusion of unmediated characterization in a way uncharacteristic of the novel as a genre.[13] The parodic impulse is again localized in the verbal habits of the characters themselves, assigned to them by an author exercising the playwright's prerogative of indirection. In *Jonathan Wild,* as in *The Modern Husband* but with considerably more good humour, Fielding advances his argument, jarringly, by allowing his characters to speak overtly the truths that he means to suggest obliquely and ironically.

Introducing the "dialogue matrimonial" between Wild and Laetitia, Fielding claims that he has "taken [it] down verbatim" (p. 143); later, speaking of the "dialogue" between Wild and the ordinary of Newgate, Fielding says that he will "transcribe it . . . exactly in the same form and words we received it" (p. 205). Fielding thus abdicates responsibility for his text much as, among others, Behn and Defoe had done, much as Richardson, to Fielding's displeasure, was doing, and much as dramatists—historical dramatists in particular—had done for a very long time. In the "dialogue matrimonial," Laetitia, suddenly, is no longer the "chaste Laetitia" on whom Fielding has insisted and in whom Wild has believed. Rather, she is Wild's nemesis, a conniving virago like Mrs Modern or Shamela, the force that gives the lie to Wild's improbably conventional notions of romantic courtship and marriage. Proclaiming her intention to continue her adventures with Jack Strongbow, Laetitia says, "I suppose you took me for a raw senseless girl, who knew nothing what other married women do!" (p. 144). In response to Wild's query about why she married him, Laetitia replies, "Because it was convenient, and my parents forced me" (p. 145). Later, "You agree I shall converse with whomsoever I please?" (p. 147). Wild proposes a truce, suggests a treaty of mutual infidelity that Laetitia willingly accepts, and ratifies it with a kiss, unaware that the primary accomplishment of the dialogue has been the exposition of his own sexual inadequacy.

This raw comedy is the antithesis of irony; the voices invade an authorial vacuum that we do not find in Fielding's later work. For the moment at least, Wild and Laetitia are not the property of the agile satirist; but Laetitia's forthrightness here conspires with Fielding's irony elsewhere to ridicule Wild, effortlessly outclassed when he is tempted from soliloquy to dialogue. The drama perhaps never produced a more confident cuckold, although the type is familiar enough.

Prose fiction, like much satirical poetry, generally reserves such truthtelling as Laetitia's for the narrator in his or her own voice. Fielding's familiar attacks on venality and hypocrisy and Pope's anaphoric outrages operate differently from analogous moments in the drama, in which the characters are forced to a collaborative sort of revelation by the absence of a controlling authorial voice. Gay's satire in *The Beggar's Opera* works through the accretion of similar or analogous voices saying similar or analogous things in slightly different ways; *The Modern Husband* and the dialogue portions of *Jonathan Wild* work this way as well. We know that Mr and Mrs Tow-wouse in *Joseph Andrews* have an unpleasant marriage because Fielding shows it to us and discusses it with us; we know that Wild and Laetitia have one because they act out their problems before us, often without much embellishment from Fielding.

Wild is given to oratory throughout the book: the tendency allows Fielding to accent Wild's addiction to theatrical language and behaviour and to suggest a decrease in Wild's effectiveness as his language, itself unchanging, more and more falls short of its mark. Fielding designates as "speeches" Wild's lectures to Marybone (pp. 130–31), Fireblood (pp. 197–98), and various assemblages of thieves (pp. 103–4, 172–73). Wild's "dialogue" with the Count la Ruse (pp. 51–55) and his lectures to Bagshot (pp. 60–62), the count (pp. 70–71), and a group of incarcerated gamblers (pp. 74–75) are rhetorically similar occasions, replicating, as Fielding indicates, the relationship between actor and audience. As he does in the "dialogue matrimonial," the usually nimble narrator typically retreats during Wild's euphuistic speeches: the Fielding recognizable in, for instance, the passage on Wild's "turbulent" marriage—the Fielding we come to know so well in *Tom Jones*—limits his commentary during Wild's orations to dull, minimalist insertions such as "Mr Wild answered" (p. 51), "the count replied as follows" (p. 52), "the count answered" (p. 71), "answered Fireblood" (p. 198), and "says Wild" (p. 198).[14] Like Wild's other listeners, Fielding fades into the background at these times, and leaves the reader to recognize Wild's pomposity for what it is.

Early on, Wild is a persuasive orator. In book 1, he triumphs in his "dialogue" with the Count la Ruse, in his logic-busting lecture to Bagshot in a public tavern, and in Mr Snap's lock-up before the assembled gamblers. Wild's boorish persistence pays off when he picks the count's pocket and again when he quells a disturbance at Snap's. On both occasions, Wild calculates the rhetorical task required of him, and speaks in a stylized and anti-conversational manner until he achieves his end, descending only to that staple of the Restoration stage—drawing one's sword—when the uncouth Bagshot proves incapable of understanding his tortuous rhetoric.

Imprisoned at the lock-up, Wild weighs Bagshot's accusation that he, Bagshot, has had his pocket picked at cards. The passage introduces a pattern of deictic phrases, each signalled by a form of "follow" and each distinguishing

Fielding's prose from Wild's and stressing Wild's awareness of his position as a speaker before an audience:

> At last Mr Wild, our hero, rising slowly from his seat, and having fixed the attention of all present, began as follows: "I have heard with infinite pleasure everything which the two gentlemen who spoke last have said with relation to honour, nor can any man possibly entertain a higher and nobler sense of that word, nor a greater esteem of its inestimable value, than myself. . . ." (p. 74)

Wild runs on at some length in this manner, scattering allusions to Iago on "honour," and gradually making the speech an apology for honour as appearance.

We know of course that this is only bombast. But the effectiveness of bombast depends on an actor's ability to perform; and at this point in the narrative at least, Wild is performing fairly well. When Bagshot persists in his accusations, however, Fielding asserts his own presence and parodies Wild's theatricalism by constructing an alternate rhetorical version of Wild, saying much the same thing as Wild did, but in a different way and to a different end: "Wild, rapping out a hearty oath, swore [the accused] had not taken a single farthing, adding that whoever asserted the contrary gave him the lie, and he would resent it" (p. 75). The coarseness of Wild's indirectly represented speech contradicts the characterization implied by the loftier tone of the speech directly quoted. The cursing, the easy slang, and the emphasized money-term—all comment on Wild's character by ascribing to Wild a linguistic lowness that Wild scrupulously keeps from his own talk. In contrast, Fielding represents Bagshot's coarseness and simplicity in direct quotation: "I thought I had been among gentlemen and men of honour, but d—n me, I find we have a pickpocket in company" (p. 73); and, to Wild, "Let him give me my money again first . . . and then I will call him a man of honour with all my heart" (p. 75). Fielding's addendum to Wild's speech calls attention to the distance between Wild as eloquent orator (or Wild on Wild) and Wild as travesty of eloquence (or Fielding on Wild). Bagshot's comedy is simpler and less disjunctive and becomes comedy, in fact, only as part of a larger commentary on Wild's attempts to act.

Wild's success before audiences is again evident in his justification of his betrayal of the thief Fierce. His sense of occasion is clear, as is the distinction between performer and audience: "Wild . . . having assembled them all at an alehouse on the night after Fierce's execution, and perceiving evident marks of their misunderstanding . . . addressed them in the following gentle, but forcible manner" (p. 103). Like Mark Antony, Wild seduces his audience by repeating key words and ideas in order to suggest a correspondence among them and to obscure the purpose of his speech: the maintenance of power. "Hats," "prig," and "prigs," and various words connoting gentility combine to produce the effect that Wild desires: "He thus ended his speech, which was followed by a murmuring applause, and immediately all present tossed their hats together as he had commanded them" (p. 104). Fielding inserts a footnote on Aristotle's lost chapter on, as he would have it, hats; not only is he poking fun at his own pet scholarly preoccupation with the lost Aristotle, but he is observing the distance between the high dramatic tradition and a low-life parody of that tradition—a useful analogue to the ironic distance between tone and subject in Wild's rhetoric.[15] Leo Braudy remarks that Wild is "ultimately trapped" by "his emphasis on rhetorical form."[16] Certainly the theatrical rhetoric that serves Wild well for roughly the first half of the novel becomes less useful to him as the novel progresses, and increasingly signals his absurdity rather than his success or even his cleverness. A significant moment occurs when Wild, tossed overboard after having attempted to ravish Mrs Heartfree, finds himself alone and self-pitying in a small boat. Wild revives himself by reverting, as he often does, to a self-conscious and stylized soliloquy: "At length, finding himself descending too much into the language of meanness and complaint, he stopped short, and soon after broke forth as follows" (p. 116). Alan McKenzie calls this a "wonderfully theatrical passage" and observes that Wild's rhetorical failure here "depends on the absence of an audience"—the realization of which comes slowly to the self-absorbed and finally befuddled Wild.[17] The scene marks the beginning of a series of failures that continues for the rest of the novel.

Wild's next "speech" is a failed attempt to make a murderer of the thief Marybone (p. 131); Wild fares poorly as well with the inmates after his incarceration at Newgate. In an endeavour to overthrow Newgate's "great man" Roger Johnson, Wild, once more preposterously echoing Shakespearean tragedy, "assembled [the inmates] together, and spoke to them in the following florid manner: 'Friends and fellow-citizens. . . .' " (p. 172). The performance does not sway its audience, and Fielding interrupts Wild midsentence, claiming that "the only copy which we could procure of this speech breaks off abruptly" (p. 173). The inmates apparently share Fielding's impatience, and they remain sceptical about the superiority of Wild to Johnson, rebelling against Wild as soon as he topples Johnson. The transition is charted structurally and rhetorically: Wild holds on to power for one paragraph of middling length before being toppled by the rote recitation of a nameless "grave man" (p. 174) before an audience designated only as *prigs* (p. 173). This "speech," Fielding notes, "was received with much applause" (p. 175). A failed but engaging drama of exaggerated personality has given way to an unambitious drama that disregards the identities of actor and audience. We are left with the form of the drama, but we have lost the idea of *acting*. Not only does the "grave man" not create alternate identities, he has no identity in the first place; he is a cipher who serves the plot, not, like Wild, a character who motivates it.

Wild has become an easy target for anyone able to master the forms of discourse at which he himself once excelled. One of Fielding's final movements in *Jonathan Wild* is the conflation, both rhetorical (the thieves all start to sound alike) and teleological (they are all hanged), of the grasping participants in "those farces . . . acted almost daily in every village in the kingdom," directed by puppet-masters, and accepted by audiences willing to be duped (pp. 154–55)—the metaphor illustrates the transparency and finally the commonness of a theatrical rhetoric that has escaped the theatre. In its incendiary repetitions and in its alternation of facile interrogatives and pat declaratives, the grave man's speech is modelled upon Wild's earlier ratiocination. And Wild stumbles before the parody of his own showmanship: the speech succeeds in undermining his authority among the inmates. The notion of individual "greatness" is threatened by the rhetorical similarities between Johnson and Wild and by the displacement of Johnson by Wild and Wild by the nameless orator. A meaningless generational shift is almost palpable, and Wild loses the uniqueness that defined his charm earlier in the narrative. Hereafter, his life is that of a pensioned actor:

> Wild continued as before to levy contributions among the prisoners, to apply the garnish to his own use, and to strut openly in the ornaments which he had stripped from Johnson. To speak sincerely, there was more bravado than real use or advantage in these trappings. As for the nightgown, its outside indeed made a glittering tinsel appearance, but it kept him not warm, nor could the finery of it do him much honour, since every one knew it did not properly belong to him; as to the waistcoat, it fitted him very ill, being infinitely too big for him; and the cap was so heavy that it made his head ache. . . . These clothes . . . afforded very little use or honour to the wearer; nay, could scarce serve to amuse his own vanity when this was cool enough to reflect with the least seriousness. (pp. 175–76)

This is the first occasion on which Fielding has "spoken sincerely" about Wild's elaborate theatricalism; and he condemns Wild by describing his costume as tawdry and, moreover, useless, now, even as a means of self-delusion.

Wild's subsequent speech to Fireblood about Laetitia's infidelity seems to express a confident grasp of the particulars of the case and certainly conveys Wild's continuing belief in his own rhetorical power. But Fireblood easily deflates the speech, rising from the simple exclamatory "My [arse] in a bandbox!" to a shrill but irresistible attack on Wild's suasion, couched in Wild's own familiar vocabulary of "blood" and "honour" (p. 198). For the first time, Wild descends to fisticuffs, a burlesque of heroic combat in which the enchained participants are reduced to whispering impossible promises of vengeance as the audience parts them without any great show of effort or interest. The "great man" will soon botch a suicide attempt—tragedy becomes bathos—and will subsequently close what Fielding calls Wild's "fifth act" (p. 211) by swinging from this world to the next to the "universal applause" (p. 214) of his audience. The language of the catastrophe recalls the criminal biography and the playhouse, as indeed throughout *Jonathan Wild*

Fielding blurs generic boundaries in what looks like an enthusiastic overture to prose fiction, and a measured, affectionate, and decisive farewell to the drama.

## Notes

1. For the dating of *Jonathan Wild*, see Martin Battestin, *Henry Fielding: A Life* (London: Routledge, 1989), pp. 281–82, 655n37. While many critics note in passing the dramatic trimmings of *Jonathan Wild*, Simon Varey's survey is the most useful. See Varey, *Henry Fielding* (Cambridge: Cambridge University Press, 1986), pp. 39–41. Only Claude Rawson analyses the presence of the drama in *Jonathan Wild;* see Rawson, *Henry Fielding and the Augustan Ideal under Stress* (London: Routledge, 1972; Atlantic Highlands, NJ: Humanities Press International, 1991), pp. 101–259; and *Order from Confusion Sprung: Studies in Eighteenth-Century Literature from Swift to Cowper* (London: Allen and Unwin, 1985; Atlantic Highlands, NJ: Humanities Press International, 1992), pp. 261–310. In *The Drama and Fielding's Novels* (New York: Garland, 1988), Charles Trainor claims that Fielding "borrows" several characters from the drama (pp. 7–8), and notes the dramatic structure of the Heartfree plot (p. 41) and the sentimental strain in the novel (pp. 100–101). Trainor believes that *"Jonathan Wild* portrays a lower-class world far removed from the privileged circles of Restoration comedy, and for the most part the novel shows little influence from the genre" (p. 59); the present essay rejects this position.

2. Robert D. Hume, *The Rakish Stage: Studies in English Drama, 1660–1800* (Carbondale: Southern Illinois University Press, 1983), p. 216.

3. Fielding designates book 1, chap. 5; book 3, chap. 8; and book 4, chap. 13 as "dialogue[s]"; book 3, chap. 2 is Heartfree's "soliloquy." Wild speaks explicitly in "soliloquy" in book 2, chap. 4, and recognizably so elsewhere. Unless otherwise noted, references are to *Jonathan Wild*, ed. David Nokes (Harmondsworth: Penguin, 1982). In the 1743 edition the "dialogue matrimonial" includes the parenthetical remark, *"These Words to be spoken with a very great Air, and Toss of the Head," Miscellanies* (3 vols), 3:238; cf. Fielding's revised edition of 1754, the copytext for modern editions, *"These Words were spoken with a very great Air, and Toss of the Head"* (p. 151). The change from the infinitive to the past tense suggests a shift from directing to recounting, from the drama to the novel. For the world/stage metaphor in opposition literature when *Jonathan Wild* was written, see Morris Golden, "Public Context and Imagining Self in *Joseph Andrews* and *Jonathan Wild," JEPG: Journal of English and Germanic Philology* 88 (1989), 505–6.

4. Terry Castle, *Masquerade and Civilization: The Carnivalesque in Eighteenth-Century Culture and Fiction* (Stanford: Stanford University Press, 1986), especially pp. 116–25. Castle does not mention *Jonathan Wild.*

5. Fielding's Preface to the 1743 edition stresses *Jonathan Wild's* general satire and its theatricality: "My narrative is rather of such actions which [Wild] might have performed, or would, or should have performed, than what he really did; and may, in reality, as well suit any other such great man, as the person himself whose name it bears" (*Miscellanies,* 3:29).

6. Hume, p. 204. See also pp. 176–213 for "marital discord comedy," and pp. 187–206 for the "problem plays." See *Jonathan Wild*, p. 47, for Wild's fondness for Otway.

7. Hume does not mention *Jonathan Wild*, but finds in *The Modern Husband* a thematic anticipation of *Amelia* (pp. 211–12). *The Modern Husband* and *Jonathan Wild*, however, seem related to Vanbrugh's sort of problem play, and *Amelia* to the "happy-ending" plays, in which marital problems finally have solutions.

8. Hume calls act 5, scene 4 of *The Beaux Stratagem* (1707) "an amusing inversion of a proviso scene" in which "the Sullens agree only that they have no use for each other" (p. 202).

Wild and Laetitia's parting recalls Farquhar; and as Mrs Sullen may wed the urbane Archer, Laetitia will presumably sport further with the sexually adept Fireblood.

9. *The Dialogic Imagination: Four Essays by M.M. Bakhtin,* trans. Caryl Emerson and Michael Holquist (Austin: University of Texas Press, 1981), p. 5.

10. *Fielding and the Augustan Ideal,* p. 107. Bakhtin claims that the clown and fool, transplants from folklore, demonstrate "a naïveté expressed as the inability to understand stupid conventions" (p. 163); the claim is applicable if we consider that Wild misunderstands those positive moral and legal "conventions" that the satirist Fielding presents, transparently, as "stupid."

11. Rawson notes that "plays do not normally accommodate the open presence of a narrator or author. [Fielding's] *Rehearsal*-plays (*The Author's Farce* [1730], *Pasquin* [1736], *The Historical Register, Eurydice* [1737], etc.) are partly an exception, since they contain authors-within-the-play who stand outside their own play" (*Order from Confusion Sprung,* p. 271). The Scriblerian apparatus of *The Tragedy of Tragedies* and the presence of the playwright Scriblerus in the introduction to *The Grub-Street Opera* (1731) suggest that Fielding was interested in authorial presence elsewhere in his career as a playwright.

12. John Bender, writing about *Jonathan Wild,* argues that "Fielding's overriding concern—in his novels, his judicial practice, and his reformist writings—[is] with the deployment of narrative as an authoritative resource." *Imagining the Penitentiary: Fiction and the Architecture of Mind in Eighteenth-Century England* (Chicago: University of Chicago Press, 1987), p. 139. But Fielding surrenders this "authority" in *Jonathan Wild*'s more theatrical moments.

13. Fielding uses dialogue form in non-dramatic and non-novelistic writing; see, for instance, "A Dialogue between Alexander the Great and Diogenes the Cynic" (c. 1743), *A Dialogue between the Devil, the Pope, and the Pretender* (1745), and *Covent-Garden Journal* 54 (11 July 1752). Rawson notes the practice in Defoe, and observes that it "is not unknown in Fielding, but it is rare and . . . never neutral" (*Order from Confusion Sprung,* p. 265). Rawson rightly considers Fielding's chapter heading to the "dialogue matrimonial" "a strongly marked authorial statement"; but his claim that " 'immediacy' is not what Fielding is after, in any of his fiction" (*Order,* p. 266) should be qualified. The alternation between "strong" authorial statements and *apparent* "immediacy" perhaps better describes Fielding's intention in *Jonathan Wild.*

14. The "medial inquits" that Rawson (after Helmut Bonheim) finds throughout *Tom Jones* have a less marked dramatic effect than the sections I cite from *Jonathan Wild,* which are set off from the spoken words in three of my examples by a colon and thus suggest authorial distance and perhaps the dramatic script; see Rawson, *Order from Confusion Sprung,* pp. 268–69.

15. For Wild as problematically mock-heroic, see Rawson, *Fielding and the Augustan Ideal,* pp. 157–65, *Order from Confusion Sprung,* pp. 207–12; and Michael McKeon, *The Origins of the English Novel, 1600–1740* (Baltimore: Johns Hopkins University Press, 1987), pp. 383–84.

16. Leo Braudy, *Narrative Form in History and Fiction* (Princeton: Princeton University Press, 1970), p. 123.

17. "The Physiology of Deceit in Fielding's Works," *Dalhousie Review* 62 (1982), 143.

# Jonathan Wild

## BERTRAND A. GOLDGAR

In the Preface to the *Miscellanies* Fielding makes eminently plain that he will not be attempting in Volume Three a "faithful Portrait" of the historical Jonathan Wild, the thief, gang leader, receiver of stolen goods, and self-styled *"Thief-Catcher-General of Great Britain,"*[1] who despite his pleas of public service was tried at the Old Bailey and hanged at Tyburn on 25 May 1725. Fielding has no wish, he says, to compete with "historians" like Defoe or others who have given the public such a variety of biographical accounts of Wild for the past eighteen years. In short, he warns his readers not to expect a criminal biography; he has little knowledge and only limited interest in Wild himself. Instead, he asserts, "my Narrative is rather of such Actions which he might have performed, than what he really did; and may, in Reality, as well suit any other such great Man, as the Person himself whose Name it bears."[2] And indeed the definitive modern work on the historical Wild agrees that Fielding in *Jonathan Wild* is concerned with his hero mainly as a symbol of all villainy; "of the real Wild," says Gerald Howson, "or the real criminal underworld, his book tells us hardly anything, whatever its virtues may be as a satire on 'Great Men.' "[3]

To be sure, Fielding shows some familiarity with the Wild "tradition" and even makes some use of the details of the man's case, especially near the end of the novel; thus several "true" incidents, like "Blueksin's" assault on Wild in Newgate and the hero's attempt to cheat the gallows by overdosing himself with laudanum, find a place in the book.[4] Actual biographical facts are, however, very few, as Fielding has warned us will be the case. It is more important to note that some of the accounts in the Wild tradition, accounts Fielding may have seen, take the same mocking and even mock-heroic tone about criminals that Fielding uses in his novel. His library contained one work with a substantial account of the Wild story: *Select Trials at the Old-Bailey* (1742), an account which claimed to avoid "the fictitious, extravagant, and improbable Stories which all other Accounts of him hitherto publish'd are

Reprinted from General Introduction to *Miscellanies by Henry Fielding, Esq.,* vol. 3 (1997), ed. Bertrand A. Goldgar and Hugh Amory, by permission of Oxford University Press and University Press of New England/Wesleyan University Press. ©Bertrand A. Goldgar and Hugh Amory.

stuft with."[5] Here one finds some of the features later made familiar by Fielding: details of the trial; the use of the word "Prig"; speeches made by Wild,
including one given "after convening some of his chief *Prigs*"; extracts of documents by Wild and others, including a list of "Flash Words," some of which
were used by Fielding; and the conventional account of the criminal by the
Ordinary of Newgate. One other item included in the *Select Trials* version
strikes the note Fielding seems to have sought, an "Elegy" dating back to
1725 called "The Complaint of Jonathan Wild," in which the arch-criminal
adopts an absurdly heroic tone in making his usual claim of having performed
a service to the public:

> Ingrateful Country! Zealous for thy Good,
> How often have I hazarded my Blood?
> Nor have I Arms alone, but Arts employ'd,
> Swords, Pistols, and Damnation have defy'd.
> Warm in thy Cause, of Dangers not afraid,
> How great a Slaughter has by me been made?[6]

Something about Wild's assumed "greatness" seems to have aroused a
similar tone in some of the other contemporary accounts of his activities and
those of his fellows. *Select Trials,* in reporting on the trial of Jack Sheppard (in
which Wild also figured), reprinted a Lucianic dialogue from the *British Journal* between Caesar and Sheppard, who are referred to as *"an ancient and a
modern Hero."* Even *The Regulator* (1718), a barely literate attack on Wild by
Charles Hitchin, a corrupt Under City-Marshall, indulges in epithets for him
like "King of the *Gipsies,*" "Captain-general of the Army of Plunderers, . . .
Ambassador Extraordinary from the Prince of the Air," and "his *Skittish* and
*Baboonish* Majesty."[7] In the same way the Introduction to *Lives of the Highwaymen* (1734) by "Capt. Charles Johnson" adopts a tone close to that Fielding
was to give his narrator; all great men, says this author, are robbers and plunderers, and he cites as instances Nimrod, Alexander, and Caesar. Of the last
he writes, "What better can we call any of his Successors who have sacrific'd
the Lives and Liberties of Thousands of their Fellow-Creatures to an extravagant Passion? Whether we name it Tyranny or only Greatness of Soul, 'tis
much the same, while the Effects of it are so very terrible."[8] And an early but
fine example of the way such mock-heroic attitudes and language seemed to
cling to Wild comes in *The Life of Jonathan Wild, from his Birth to his Death*
(1725) by "H. D." (sometimes attributed to Defoe), as part of a description of
Wild's assault on a cheesemonger: "So have I seen, and with as little Mercy, a
gallant Ox fell'd to the Ground by some Fierce Butcher; and so, like *Jonathan,*
have I seen him bestride the mighty Beast, and strip him of his Skin."[9]
"H.D."'s pamphlet contains much of this sort of tongue-in-cheek language,
crediting Wild with a wisdom superior to that of a governor of a common-
wealth and with inventing "a System of Politicks unknown to *Machiavel*";

there were stratagems invented by this "Fellow without Learning" which were deeper "than are to be met with in the Conduct of the greatest States-men, who have been at the Heads of Governments."[10]

Whatever his lack of interest in the historical Wild, then, Fielding may have inherited from the mass of writing about him not only minor details of plot but some of the ironic tone and mocking manner of treatment of this form of "greatness." Yet if the ironic treatment of false greatness which is at the heart of Fielding's novel was to some extent a feature of criminal biographies and of the Wild tradition in particular, the primary genre which Fielding chooses for his account was not narratives of criminal lives but serious history and biography. The work opens with paragraphs praising the lives of great men as "the Quintessence of History" which enables readers to survey "the true Beauty of Virtue, and Deformity of Vice" and detailing the lessons that may be learned from Plutarch, Nepos, Suetonius and other biographers, especially the lesson that good and evil may be so mixed in the same character that "it may require a very accurate Judgment and elaborate Inquiry to deter-mine which side the Ballance turns." Though some have seen these para-graphs as satirizing by parody the genres of serious history and biography, that was surely not Fielding's intention. His point, as William J. Farrell has shown, is to take the language and the *topoi* of classical biography and history, those forms associated with traditional accounts of the great, and make them applicable to an ordinary criminal. The result is irony at the expense of popu-lar notions of greatness. As Farrell puts it, "when a literary genre associated with the heroes of all times presents the life of a common thief that form becomes an ironic commentary on the traditional notion of a hero."[11] These passages, Farrell shows, are close in tone and manner to the opening sections of Conyers Middleton's *Life of Cicero,* which provide the air of "high biogra-phy" necessary for a mock-heroic, and he demonstrates that there are clear parallels between Fielding's life of Jonathan Wild and Plutarch's life of Alexander the Great.[12]

Fielding's playful use of serious history and biography as the vehicle for his satirical indictment of false or bombastic greatness should thus not be misunderstood as attack on those genres themselves, which he well under-stood to be appropriate for the study of the truly great. He both admired and made serious use of Middleton's work, for example, despite his ridicule in *Shamela* of the dedication to Lord Hervey;[13] the irony of these passages is not at the expense of history but at the expense of the false greatness of an Alexander or Charles XII as glorified by some writers.[14] Indeed in *Jonathan Wild* Fielding's tone is consistently mock-historical (rather than mock-heroic), and his irony no more impugns the value of genuine biographies or histories than the *Rape of the Lock* ridicules Homer or Milton. Thus when the narrator says in praise of the aptness of Jonathan's death, "we could almost wish, that whenever Fortune seems wantonly to deviate from her Purpose and leave her work imperfect in this Particular [by a less satisfying death], the Historian would indulge himself in the Licence of Poetry and Romance and even do a Violence to Truth to oblige his Reader" (IV. xv), the irony rests on firm distinctions between the "Truth of History" and "the Latitude of Fiction," terms used a few pages later. The narrator has much of this sort to say about history, but he is not literally voicing Fielding's own thoughts on historiography—the distinction between them shows itself even in small ways, such as the narrator's reference to "one Herodotus" (III. i. 93), a touch of pretended ignorance Fielding sometimes uses for his personae in his efforts at irony.[15]

It has, however, long been alleged that Fielding's mock-heroic satire in *Jonathan Wild* has a more specific target than the general moral vice of false greatness. Ever since an essay by Thomas Keightley in 1858,[16] critics have tended to assume the fiction is intended, primarily or secondarily—the degree depends on the writer—as the vehicle for satire on Sir Robert Walpole. Fielding wrote this book "with his eye steadily on the Great Man of the Age," wrote J. E. Wells in 1913.[17] Since Walpole fell from power in February 1742, more than a year before *Wild* saw its first publication, the presence or absence of satire on Walpole may have crucial implications about the time and method of the work's composition. Before turning to the issue of the stages or period of composition, however, we need to look more closely at the entire question of its supposedly specific political satire.

The equation of political and criminal greatness, which of course received its most popular expression in Gay's *Beggar's Opera* (1728), was applied in the political press to Wild almost immediately after his execution in May 1725. It seemed a natural enough analogy, since Wild was charged with forming "a Kind of Corporation of Thieves, of which he was the Head or Director" and was claimed to have "divided the Town and Country into so many Districts, and appointed distinct Gangs for each."[18] Shortly after this criminal/governor was hanged, Nathaniel Mist's crypto-Jacobite *Weekly Journal* for 12 and 19 June 1725 ran an account of "that celebrated Statesman and Politician" Jonathan Wild. Praising his "System of Government," Mist argues that a man may be a rogue "and yet be a great Man." Wild is given credit for the South Sea scheme (as was Walpole), is linked to the philosophy of Mandeville, and is called a "right Modern Whig," who lives up to the modern Whig motto, *"Keep what you get, and get what you can."* The politicizing of the rogue-hero is obvious enough, but in this instance Mist's satire is very mild, directed at no one great man with any specificity. In the years that followed, the Wild legend was applied more pointedly to Walpole in political journalism, though it was not really a common device. A writer for *Common Sense* on 23 December 1738, for example, pretends, like Mist, that he will lay politics aside for a day so as to present the memoirs of a *"certain great Man, deceased"*; the account that follows (drawn heavily from the *Select Trials*) intermixes the facts of the Wild case with conventional images associated with Walpole: Wild "seem'd rather born to a Ribband about his Shoulders, than a

Rope about his Neck"; he holds a "Levee"; and he has been "the *Screen* and *Bulwark* of his Party."[19]

Although such clear use of the Wild/Walpole equation in the Opposition press was much less frequent than is sometimes claimed—the "Wild" parallel could hardly compete with the "Cardinal Wolsey" analogue, for example, or with such conventional epithets as "Robin Brass," "Dr. Robert King," and the like—the satiric connection of the two figures was a recognized device, one Fielding would not have been likely to miss in his years as a journalist and playwright. And some of the journalistic ploys seem familiar to later readers of his novel. Thus *Common Sense* for 3 March 1739 gives the speech of "Bob Booty" to his gang, a speech including such reflections as "you know I always told you, that Right and Wrong consists in nothing but Power, and the Strength of Numbers" and promising that some day "instead of Halters about our Necks, we may have Ribbons about our Shoulders."[20] Wild's speeches to his gang, as Fielding represents them, seem anticipated here. Again, in the *Champion* for 16 September 1740 a fairly vicious poem in imitation of a Horatian ode makes the Wild/Walpole comparison, while promising that the Muses and poets will provide Sir Robert with the punishment he deserves:

> Not *Shepherd,* who could shift the Scene,
> From Jail to Jail, like Harlequin,
> Nor *Wild,* great Man! who had his Day,
> Can live in *Newgate's* Rolls so long
> As thou, thou greater R———! in Song.

Despite its appearance in the *Champion* there is no reason to believe Fielding wrote this poem, but there is every reason to believe that by 1740 its criminal/political rhetorical strategy was a commonplace for him and his readers.[21] Pope in 1738, in his sarcastic farewell to the power of satire, could say "Arraign no mightier Thief than wretched *Wild,*"[22] but satire on at least a few occasions still employed the wretched Wild to arraign a mightier thief.

Given this background, it is not surprising that Fielding felt called upon to deny any personal application of the satire. In the Preface to the *Miscellanies* he asserts that just as the work "is not a very faithful Portrait of *Jonathan Wild* himself, so neither is it intended to represent the Features of any other Person. Roguery, and not a Rogue, is my Subject; and as I have been so far from endeavouring to particularize any Individual, that I have with my utmost Art avoided it; so will any such Application be unfair in my Reader."[23] Any reader who makes such a personal application, he adds, will not only be acting unfairly, but betraying his ignorance of "the Great World," where he would be acquainted "with more than one on whom he can fix the Resemblance."[24] In the "Advertisement from the Publisher" in the revised edition of 1754, Fielding (one assumes he is the author of the notice), despite the fact that as far as we know there had been no specific charge that his novel reflected on Walpole, again warned against such individualized application of the satire, linking it to one of his favourite topics, the fathering on him of the scurrility of others: "That any personal Application could have ever been possibly drawn from them, will surprise all who are not deeply versed in the black Art . . . of deciphering Mens Meaning when couched in obscure ambiguous or allegorical Expressions: This Art hath been exercised more than once on the Author of our little Book, who hath contracted a considerable Degree of Odium from having had the Scurrillity of others imputed to him." The Advertisement concludes with the suggestion that "as a very corrupt State of Morals is here represented," the Newgate scene is highly appropriate, without "introducing any Allegory at all," though readers will agree that some outside Newgate may be "of worse Morals than those within" and have "a Right to change Places with its present Inhabitants." Fielding concludes by recommending to such corrupt figures the speech of the "grave Man" (IV. iii), a speech which denounces all "party" allegiances and stresses instead that we all are "Members of one Community, to the public Good of which we are to sacrifice our private Views." Despite his final concession to the possibility of a figurative reading, Fielding's denial of personal satire seems unambiguous.

Should it be taken at face value? Until very recently commentators have seen Fielding's pleas as disingenuous, at odds with what seemed to them the "clear" and "extensive" satire on Walpole in the work.[25] At least one recent scholar, however, has taken a strong stand against such a reading, and indeed there is good reason to take a fresh look at the question.[26] The most fruitful approach will be to lay aside, at least for the moment, speculation about supposed "stages" of composition and confine the discussion to the text itself, as it was delivered to readers in 1743.

With that stipulation, it can be argued that for the most part the entire text can and should be read merely as a satire on False Greatness, although such a theme is obviously one which includes "great" politicians. Once this argument is made, certain corollaries naturally follow. First, particular images or details *may* have been conceived earlier or even written earlier with Walpole in mind, but there is no way to demonstrate this, nor is speculation about it helpful in explaining anything in the text. Second, it is doubtless the case that some readers in 1743 would be likely to think of Walpole in many places and make that specific application of Fielding's general themes and observations, especially given the fact that, as described above, there was a tradition, however attenuated, of identifying Walpole with Wild in political satire of the 1730s.

Moreover, it is undoubtedly true that readers might still have Walpole in mind even though he was no longer in office. Some critics, assuming the novel is mainly an attack on Walpole, have accused Fielding of "flogging a dead horse." But the fact is that not only did satires on Walpole continue all through 1742 and 1743, but as committees met to inquire into his alleged crimes and his former opponents clamoured for his punishment, the parallels with Wild and other criminals seemed to be drawn with increasing frequency in the press. In July 1742 the old Opposition papers were calling him a "Felon," a "Robber and Oppressor," a "Criminal" in need of legal punishment. *Common Sense* for 16 October 1742 described Walpole (now Earl of Orford) as "the late Corrupter General," happy with his "Plunder" and generous only in the manner of "the Gentlemen of the Road, who collect in Gangs."[27] The following month the *Craftsman* for 20 November compared his hypocrisy to that of "a *Wild*, a *Charteris*" and a Cromwell.[28] And as late as March 1743, just weeks before the *Miscellanies* appeared, *Common Sense* was still inveighing against the former minister and complaining that he seems to triumph in his guilt, though of course "Axes, Gibbets, and Halters may . . . frighten and reclaim less[er] Criminals."[29]

With journalists, politicians, and print-makers demanding prosecution, Walpole was thus still inescapably in the public eye. Since attacks upon him did not cease with his fall from power, the fact that he was out of office when Fielding's book appeared is no argument either for or against any particular theory of composition or any particular assessment of the level of specific political satire.

But although the general themes can be read and doubtless were read by some with a particular application to Walpole, that is not to say that the work was conceived or intended with that application primarily or largely in Fielding's mind. In short, on the evidence of the 1743 text itself we have no reason not to take the book as the Preface to the *Miscellanies* describes it, especially if the work is compared to some clear and pointed anti-Walpole satire from the heyday of the Opposition—say, Pope's *Dialogues* or Fielding's own *Vernoniad*. Indeed, it can be argued that there are only a few details or passages in the book worth considering as obvious hits at Walpole, or which could be taken as such in 1743, and none of them are as clearly personal or as specifically directed as would be the case in a typical Opposition satire before 1742 or in one of the pieces of post-lapsarian anti-Walpole journalism cited above.

The first of these details, and one frequently cited as a feature directly pointed at Walpole, is Fielding's use of the terms "Great Man" and "Prime Minister," the latter broadened in Fielding's revision of 1754 to "Statesman." Such terms were indeed used to designate Walpole during his years of power, but they were generic, not specific. As Hollis Rinehart has pointed out, "great Man" was a term commonly used to indicate a member of the ruling classes, a matter of birth or social station; Sir Robert's enemies in their constant use of the term thus suggest ironically that he is only a pretender to the style of life of his social superiors.[30] And Rinehart might have added that its use varied from a common term for all in political power (for example, "the *great* Men in Power" in one satire of 1742 describing the politicians who *followed* Walpole)[31] to a designation of those who (like Wild) succeed in criminal leadership at the other extreme of society: an early anecdote about Wild has him praising a thieving young boy to his mother, "*My Life on't, he'll prove a great Man*—."[32] In this context, such use of the phrase "great Man" in praise of criminal expertise has no political connotations at all. As for "prime minister," Mr Rinehart argues that this was also a term of abuse, suggesting one who has usurped powers rightfully belonging to the monarch.[33] Thus Fielding himself defined a prime minister as "a Magistrate, who tho' not consistent with our Constitution, nor countenanc'd by our Laws, hath often found Means to insinuate himself into the political Machine, and sometimes hath made a Handle of the Prerogative."[34] Wolsey is Fielding's example, and though the essay is clearly anti-Walpole the complaint is put in general terms. The same, Rinehart argues, could be said about the term "prime minister" in *Jonathan Wild.* Mr Rinehart tends to ignore the degree to which Walpole in particular was blamed for virtually creating this unconstitutional office and was thus personally associated with the phrase, but his main point about *Jonathan Wild* remains crucial: although many readers would be very likely to think of the recently defeated minister when prompted by the phrase "prime minister," it fits other "great Men" as well, as do allusions to non-specified palaces, pictures, ribbons, and honours; Fielding's quarry here is all such "bombast Greatness." As Rinehart puts it, "It must be recalled that Fielding did not claim that there was nothing in *Jonathan Wild* which would fit Walpole. He merely claimed that to the best of his ability he has avoided particularizing any individual—that is, that there was nothing . . . which would fit *only* Walpole."[35]

The same distinction applies to the other images or allusions that seem to have identifiable referents, such as the narrator's obvious sarcasm about the Licensing Act (III. v. 105). A few of these passages have a world-weary air of describing events long past, such as the reference to two great men in former times who hacked and hewed each other (III. xi), possibly, if specific, an allusion to Pulteney and Walpole. The Johnson–Wild battle in Newgate (IV. iii) provides Wild (not Johnson) with some highly recognizable anti-Walpole rhetoric, and many have very reasonably seen in the chapter another expression of Fielding's disillusionment with the Patriot opposition.[36] But it is a spirit of general disgust with the political process that is the hallmark of that chapter, and perhaps of the whole book. The speech of the "grave Man" in that section urges the debtors in Newgate to remember that both factions are "*Prigs*" and that the only hope is in a turn to public rather than private interest; interestingly, it is that speech which Fielding in 1754 urges his readers to remember rather than seeking to discover particular politicians allegorized in the narrative. Such dark political realism, which also dominates the "Hats" chapter (II. vi), sits very uneasily with any notion of partisan Opposition satire.

In its general commentary on political life *Jonathan Wild* is a work which harbours no political illusions. And it is as a general satire that Fielding urges us to read it. Though he may, as even Rinehart suggests, protest a bit too much, the text as we have it encourages us to take him seriously when he disclaims personal or particularized satire. In my own view, the details or images that are sometimes cited as pointing directly to Robert Walpole, and which the notes will identify, are far from compelling (Wild's genealogy, Tishy's red ribbons, and the like). In fact, given the general themes, even if we take all such items as reminders of Opposition satiric motifs, the proportion of such passages is very low, especially when compared to those in any typical anti-Walpole satire from the 1730s. Moreover, unlike *A Journey from This World to the Next,* there is in this work very little that seems to constitute "remnants" or a mixture of different types of specific, partisan political satire.[37] If *Jonathan Wild* is anti-Walpole, it is so by virtue of its general fable satirizing false greatness rather than by a series of inserted "giveaway" details.

Obviously this judgement bears directly on the question of when the novel was composed, an issue which has sharply divided critical and scholarly opinion. As demonstrated above, Walpole continued to be an object of satiric attack after his fall from office, especially as a "criminal" deserving prosecution. Nevertheless, most commentators who assume Walpole at some stage to have been the prime target of Fielding's irony have felt that a theory of composition seems to follow which places the conception and perhaps the earliest version before the fall of the minister in February 1742, before the publication of *Joseph Andrews* in that same month, and also, presumably, before Fielding's disillusionment with the Opposition and apparent change of heart about Walpole himself (that is, perhaps before the spring of 1741 and certainly before December 1741, when his satire *The Opposition* appeared). Until recently, in fact, some version of such a theory has been more or less the received opinion. On the other hand, one of the benefits of recognizing that the anti-Walpole satire is minimal in the version we have, and that it need never have been any more dominant, is that we need not then be driven by thoughts of Walpole to any hypothesis about an "Ur-*Wild*," as Hugh Amory has phrased it. Although the main biographical and interpretive arguments about time of composition will be summarized here, the notion of an "Ur-*Wild*," as a distinct textual issue, receives more detailed and fuller argument in Mr Amory's Textual Introduction to the Wesleyan Edition.

Before reviewing the commonly accepted theory and its rivals, however, we will do well to note the few allusions and references in the 1743 text that might point to a time of composition. For it cannot be emphasized too strongly that no hard evidence whatsoever exists outside the text that can provide anything like "probability," much less proof, of a date of composition or of earlier versions or stages of the work. All such hypotheses are efforts, many of them highly ingenious, to fit the work into Fielding's bewildering shifts in political attitudes or to account, by guesses about stages of composition, for what to the critics appear to be artistically weaker portions of the book. And all such hypotheses are necessarily dependent solely on conjecture and speculation.

What, then, can be said with certainty about the date of *Jonathan Wild?* Only that Fielding was writing or revising it in the spring and summer of 1742, as several references in the text make unmistakable. First, and this is by far the most concrete evidence for showing that he was still working on the book in 1742, the chapter "Of Proverbs" (II. xii, and omitted in the revised edition) is mostly taken verbatim from the fifth edition of *Joe Miller's Jests: or, the Wit's Vade-Mecum*, published on 5 July 1742.[38] These proverbs, none of which are in earlier editions of *Joe Miller*, include, incidentally, a line about "debauching a Member of the House of Commons from his Principles, and creating him a Peer" that used to be thought of erroneously as Fielding's own comment on Pulteney's accepting a peerage in the summer of 1742. Second, Fielding quotes (III. ii) from Edward Young's *The Complaint: or, Night-Thoughts* ("Night the First"), first published on 31 May 1742. Again, the narrator's comment on the "many Occurrences of the Phænomenous Kind which have lately appeared in this our Hemisphere" (II. xiii. 87), Wilbur Cross suggested, perhaps refers to the much-discussed comet of 1742, which appeared on 20 February and was visible throughout March; but Fielding uses similar language elsewhere figuratively rather than literally, so that this allusion is less precise an indication of date than Cross believed.[39] One other allusion that has sometimes figured in efforts to date the book can be discounted: Fielding, after one of his similes (I. xiv. 45), refers to "the Hills near *Bath,* where the simile was indeed made," but even if taken literally this is of little help in fixing a date, for he visited Bath in the summers of both 1741 and 1742.[40]

As a sub-topic of the debate some critics have also argued about whether *Jonathan Wild,* in substance, was composed before or after *Joseph Andrews,* which appeared in February 1742. Again, almost all such arguments are conjectural, deriving usually from the particular writer's sense of what would or would not have been Fielding's style or tone at a given time or the expected course of his artistic development. In fact, what little evidence there is on this point, like the datable allusions mentioned above, suggests that *Wild* is the later book. The most reliable detail is the appearance (perhaps the reappearance) of Peter Pounce, who refuses to pay a debt to Heartfree (II. vii. 72). Somewhat less reliable, but none the less striking, are what appear to be a number of verbal stylistic echoes of *Joseph Andrews* in *Jonathan Wild;* as Cross warned many years ago, such parallels alone cannot be relied upon for dating Fielding's works, considering his habit of revamping old ideas and materials.[41] Nevertheless, given the appearance of Peter Pounce in the 1743 novel, a few of these resemblances are highly suggestive. As an example, one may compare *Jonathan Wild* (I. xiv. 45), where the narrator says (in the same style and tone as in *Joseph Andrews*), "And now, Reader, if thou pleasest, as we are in no great Haste, we will stop and make a Simile" and there follows a long simile about a huntsman gathering hunting dogs to their kennel, with the hunting adventure in *Joseph Andrews* (III. vi), where the narrator says "Reader, we would make a Simile on this Occasion, but for two Reasons. . . ." Another long mock-epic simile in the style of *Joseph Andrews,* about a bull and cows, occurs in *Wild* (IV. xi. 170). And one is struck also by the comparison of this passage in *Wild:* "When the Boy *Hymen* had with his lighted Torch driven the Boy *Cupid* out of Doors; that is to say, in common Phrase, when the Violence of Mr. *Wild*'s Passion (or rather Appetite) for the chaste *Laetitia* began to abate . . ." (III. ix) with such formulae in *Joseph Andrews* as "Now the Rake *Hesperus* had called for his Breeches, . . . In vulgar Language, it was in the Evening when *Joseph* attended his Lady's Orders" (I. viii). Finally, Heartfree's "wicked Sentiment" "*That he believed a sincere* Turk *would be saved*" is close to the comment Parson Adams makes to Parson Barnabas, "that a virtuous and good *Turk,* or Heathen, are more acceptable in the sight of their Creator, than a vicious and wicked Christian" (I. xvii).[42] Such apparent echoes may actually, of course, be "anticipations," but taken together with the other datable allusions they make the case for pre-1742 composition at least slightly more problematical.

Nevertheless, it is that case which most scholars have sought to make in one form or another, although all realize that fixing a date in the absence of external evidence is a speculative enterprise. Acting on the assumptions that *Jonathan Wild* is a work "whose satire is aimed chiefly at Walpole"[43] and that such satire would be irrelevant after the minister's fall in February 1742—both assumptions which, as indicated above, are highly questionable—most commentators have speculated that the earliest version of the book was an anti-Walpole satire composed during Fielding's most active years in the Opposition, perhaps during 1739–40, when he was contributing heavily to the *Champion.* The leading Fielding scholar Martin Battestin, for example, in his authoritative biography, concludes that it "seems likely" Fielding, encouraged by that exemplar of "true Greatness" Bubb Dodington, undertook such a satire with Wild as the vehicle:[44] With small variations and sometimes differing political interpretations of specific scenes or characters in the novel, Keightley, Austin Dobson, Aurélien Digeon, and Thomas Cleary have advanced the same notion.[45] Cleary, to cite one example, guesses that the "boring and pointless" chapters of Mrs Heartfree's travels were written second and then tacked on to the original satire to fill out a volume after Walpole's resignation had made the satire "dated"; yet at the same time, with only slight signs of a scuffle, he finds that some portions refer to later political events, especially the displacement in Newgate of Johnson by Wild (IV. ii), which he sees as an allegorical attack on those betrayers of the Opposition, Pulteney and Carteret. Both his speculations and those of the other proponents of an "Ur-*Wild*" receive detailed and cogent analysis in Mr Amory's Textual Introduction to the Wesleyan Edition.

Those who argue for an early date of composition must also provide some explanation of why Fielding failed to publish before the end of the Walpole administration what was (in their hypothesis) a more pointed attack on

Walpole than the text in the 1743 *Miscellanies.* Martin Battestin's explanation is straightforward enough: Fielding withheld publication because he was paid to do so. After rumours and innuendoes in the ministerial press in the autumn and winter of 1740/41 about his "defection" from the Opposition cause, early in 1741 he finally ceased writing for the *Champion* and, indeed, brought a complete end to all his work for the Opposition, with the final break signalled by his flattery of Walpole and his slashing attack on Opposition leaders in *The Opposition: A Vision* (December 1741). Moreover, in the view of Professor Battestin and of many other scholars as well, he was very likely rewarded for this shift of political loyalties.[46] The incident during this season of tergiversation which may bear directly on *Jonathan Wild* was the appearance in the *Champion* for 4 October 1740 of a leader by Fielding which if taken at face value admits that he has already accepted one bribe to silence his pen. In the essay the speaker claims to have been offered "Pills" from the quack doctor Roberto, some for remaining silent and more in return for his praise. Fielding (or his persona) rejects the offer and adds: "If I mistake not the Hand, it is one whose Pills I formerly refused on the like Conditions now offer'd, tho' I own, being in an ill State of Health, I accepted a few to stop the Publication of a Book, which I had written against his Practice, and which he threaten'd to take the Law of me, if I publish'd." Professor Battestin suggests that the only "Book" which seems to fit the case and which Fielding might have taken money from Walpole to suppress is *Jonathan Wild.*[47] Yet, as Mr Amory points out, there are not only a number of other reasonable candidates for this "Book" but also several grave difficulties with identifying it as a version of *Jonathan Wild.*[48] Although if taken literally the passage in the *Champion* tells us much about Fielding's relations with Walpole, it does not constitute hard evidence for the early composition of *Jonathan Wild.*

Perhaps, Professor Battestin suggests further, it was as part of his "pills" or reward for withdrawing his journalistic support from the Opposition that Fielding obtained an unusually handsome subscription to the *Miscellanies* from Walpole himself, who paid 20 guineas for ten sets on royal paper.[49] Possibly there was indeed political remuneration behind this unusually large subscription; but if so, the student of *Jonathan Wild* is left with puzzling alternatives: either the fiction which Fielding published is less directly and extensively satirical of Walpole than most recent critics have assumed, or the novelist himself, either from negligence or ingratitude, failed to revise or remove those features which might seem to bite his subscriber's hand. Moreover, even if Walpole's generosity is to be seen as a form of political pay-off, there is nothing to connect it specifically with *Jonathan Wild* when it could easily be simply a general reward for Fielding's silence or even payment for breaking silence in a way pleasing to the minister, as in *The Opposition: A Vision.* Or it may well be the case, as Mr Amory has suggested, that Walpole's subscription and those of numerous of his former supporters are without much political significance at all. Subscriptions, he points out, were seldom a party affair, and in any event those paid for by the names on Fielding's list cannot as a rule be dated, much less broken down into "sides" reflecting diverse periods in the life of his political allegiances.[50]

Clearly, those who argue for a date of composition earlier than 1742 must base their conclusion on a number of questionable suppositions and assumptions, assumptions about the original political purpose of the satire and about the stages at which they think other parts of the book, mainly the Heartfree–Wild plot and Mrs Heartfree's travels, were added on. They must also accommodate the uncomfortable fact that some passages in the text, including an entire chapter, could not have been written before the summer of 1742. There is, however, another view of the work, one which the present editors share and which takes all these suppositions as unnecessary. Long ago Wilbur Cross argued that Fielding began *Wild* in the spring of 1742, not long after Walpole finally fell; it was in fact Walpole's defeat, Cross believes, that made complete the analogy between the two "great Men," and he goes on to support his case with some of the datable allusions I have already cited.[51] More recently Roy B. Friedman has argued at length against the received theory of composition, concluding that Fielding began the work in the spring of 1742 after finishing the revisions for the second edition of *Joseph Andrews* and probably completed most of it late in that year. The darker tone of *Wild* he explains by the painful circumstances of Fielding's life in those months, and the apparent allusions to Walpole he sees as entertaining readers of all stripes while forming a concrete reference point which the general vision of the book transcends.[52] And one might add to his comments that the general political cynicism of the whole work, as described above, seems incompatible with a partisan satire meant to contribute to a campaign to defeat a minister in power but fits very well with a retrospective comment on Walpole and all other great men who hacked and hewed each other in the political wrangles of the recent past.

Admittedly, such alternative arguments cannot be "proved" any more than can those which propose an earlier date. But they have the advantage of starting, at least, with the assumption that the work we have may be approached like other works, as a single, complete, and possibly coherent text, rather than supposing it constituted of different strata written at different times. Aesthetic, not textual, judgements sometimes seem to be at the root of the usual theory of composition: that is, since some sections strike the critic as "boring" or weak, they are presumed to have been added to pad out a briefer, sharper satire on Walpole-as-Wild, which was the presumed nucleus of the present book.[53] But there is simply no way of determining which parts of Volume Three of the *Miscellanies* were written early or late or whether they were in fact composed at various times. Some modern critical views of the novel, in fact, have stressed that the book is thematically unified and that the Heartfree episodes cannot be separated from the Wild episodes.[54] William J. Farrell, for example, after demonstrating convincingly that Fielding has in mind Plutarch's *Life of Alexander* in the Wild sections, finds it "very tempting" to see the juxtaposition of Wild and his foil Heartfree as similar to Plutarch's device of comparing "parallel lives."[55] Moreover, not only are there such links and connections between the two plots, but many disagree with the dismissive views of the episodes involving Mr and Mrs Heartfree from which the "strata" theory of composition seems to have arisen.

To be sure, a fair amount of critical disapproval has been expended on the characterization of the Heartfrees, especially Mr Heartfree, who has been regarded as lifeless and insipid. A few critics have even argued that Heartfree is deliberately made passive and colourless because of his role in the book's moral scheme. Fielding's "moral allegory" here, says Allan Wendt, involves depicting both Wild and Heartfree as human failures, the latter because his goodness and benevolence are incomplete. In Fielding's distinctions in his Preface between the great, the good, and the great and good, Heartfree would have the imperfection of goodness without greatness, of benevolence without the "Parts" or "Courage" needed for true greatness.[56] This criticism, however, has been forcefully answered by others, especially C. J. Rawson, who agrees that Heartfree's characterization is a failure but argues that however clumsily he is presented Fielding clearly intended him to be taken seriously as the positive foil to Wild's "greatness."[57] Regardless of the tripartite scheme of the Preface, Rawson argues, the "good and the great" category is unrepresented in the novel, and "It would be uncharacteristic of Fielding to write a work in which his positives are not prominently emphasized."[58] One may also point to a passage in the *Champion,* a serious moment in Fielding's essay proposing a "Hospital for Fools," which I think absolves men like Heartfree from the charge of being fools despite their inability to see through the Wilds of the world: "Honest and undesigning Men of very good Understanding would be always liable to the Attacks of cunning and artful Knaves, into whose Snares we are as often seduc'd by the Openness and Goodness of the Heart, as by the Weakness of the Head. True Wisdom is commonly attended with a Simplicity of Manners, which betrays a worthy Man to a tricking Shuffler, of a much inferior Capacity."[59] In short, there appears to be, in the case of Heartfree, no deliberate subversion of his virtues on the part of the author, though Rawson cites instances where authorial control seems missing and the character ends up seeming crudely sentimentalized.

One possible sidelight on Heartfree might make it very unlikely that Fielding intended any ridicule at the character's expense. For it was suggested long ago that, following a fairly frequent practice in his fiction, Fielding modelled the character on an actual figure whom he knew well, in this case the playwright George Lillo, author of *The London Merchant.*[60] Like Heartfree, Lillo was a reputable and successful jeweller and a man, according to Fielding's memorial tribute, with "the gentlest and honestest Manners, and, at the same Time, the most friendly and obliging."[61] Fielding, who had ridiculed critics of the *London Merchant,* in 1736 produced Lillo's *Fatal Curiosity* at the Little Theatre in the Haymarket; he also wrote the prologue, puffed the play in the *Daily Advertiser,* and the following year brought it on again to run with his own *Historical Register.*[62] Whether he also had this "plain and simple"[63] jeweller-playwright in mind when he created Heartfree, one cannot, of course, say with certainty, but it seems a reasonable speculation. One episode reported by Lillo's biographer, it is amusing to note, seems a bit like those scenes in the novel where Heartfree's debtors fail to pay him: to test the sincerity of a friend "who professed a very high regard for him," reports Thomas Davies, Lillo practised the "odd stratagem" of asking for money but refusing to give any security other than a note in his hand; the friend would not accept the terms, though Lillo's nephew did, and inherited the bulk of the playwright's estate.[64]

With Mrs. Heartfree many readers have been similarly unimpressed, sometimes viewing her extraordinary adventures as, at best, needless padding on Fielding's part, and, at worst, merely an unrelated burlesque of travel books and "triumph of virtue romances."[65] In Michael McKeon's view, Fielding really wishes us to find both her character and her story untrustworthy: "her self-reliance reminds us of no one so much as Wild himself."[66] One need not accept that extreme position to agree that some of the touches in her characterization seem gently humorous or humanizing, such as her dwelling on the compliments the Hermit makes to her beauty (IV. xii); and her adventures undeniably contain a great many "Incidents very surprising." Yet Fielding was most specific in the Preface to the *Miscellanies* in saying that only one chapter (IV. ix) of her narrative is "visibly meant as a Burlesque on the extravagant Accounts of Travellers," with the rest of the book staying "within the Rules of Probability."[67] Given her and her husband's roles as positive foils to the machinations of Wild, most critics have felt there is little reason to doubt that Fielding seriously intended Mrs Heartfree's travels to inculcate the providential theme she states herself (IV. xii).[68] The truth is that like all the characters in the work both Heartfrees are deliberately flattened in keeping with Fielding's satiric mode. Satire, of course, has no place for deep or full characterization, and as R. H. Hopkins has reminded us, *Jonathan Wild* should be approached not as a "second-rate novel" but a "first-rate satire."[69]

The most arresting features of the satire in *Jonathan Wild* have long been recognized as its tone and the particular quality of its irony. To some, Fielding's manner as he unmasks the pretences of false greatness has seemed unpleasant, acerbic, disturbing; a recent comment on the book, for instance, finds it "unsettling," with "a glimpse of apocalyptic nihilism at its heart."[70] Other modern criticism, however, has gone a good way toward qualifying that verdict, as commentators have pointed to Wild's clownish missteps amidst his villainy, to his farcical theatricality, to the comic play of the language in the work, and to the humour derived from Fielding's fictional control over a shocking world.[71] Nevertheless, despite such comedic elements and Fielding's obvious playfulness, as in his two chapters parodying travel books and proverb collections, overall *Jonathan Wild* is deeply cynical about the ways of greatness which are the ways of the world. From Wild's speeches and frequent "maxims" especially we receive a view of the world, at least of the political world, that seems coolly realistic and disillusioned about partisan politics and much else in human society.[72] We learn, of course, that there is no essential difference between high and low life, between ending on the block at Tower Hill or the gallows at Tyburn, that both styles of life require the same "Parts" and offer the same satisfactions (I. v); this parallel is crucial to the satiric framework. But Fielding's *Realpolitik* goes far beyond the analogue of statesman and thief. He has Wild make cynical and lengthy analyses of the social and economic structures of society, in which some are born to labour and a few others to enjoy the fruits of those labours, some (the "Base and Rabble") to use their hands and a few others to "employ Hands for their own Use only" (I. viii, I. xiv). One wonders if Fielding had noted a passage in those early essays in *Mist's* in which Wild is said to be planning a new treatise on the Laws of Nature and to be intending "to employ the ingenious Pen of the Author of the *Fable of the Bees* for that Purpose."[73]

And the cynicism continues beyond economics; we learn from another speech by Wild that "Honour" consists only in the word itself (I. xiii) and in yet another of his harangues that political principles and other ideological distinctions are only meaningless symbols, like so many hats, that enable knaves to prey on their victims all the better (II. vi). One of the most acerbic comments comes not from Wild but from the narrator, who is not only the vehicle for the irony (as a "whitewashing biographer" with "corrupt values and vocabulary") but also indirectly the authoritative and normative voice of the satirist.[74] In this instance (III. xi) our author-narrator, not content merely to describe the political system as a puppet-show where all figures are manipulated by a great-man–puppeteer, reaches the conclusion that the public, like the spectators at the show, are well aware that they are being imposed upon at those "Farces . . . which are acted almost daily in every Village in the Kingdom" and would have it no other way. The narrator concludes the image with a comment behind which one may detect some bitterness on Fielding's part: "He must have a very despicable Opinion of Mankind indeed, who can conceive them to be imposed on as often as they appear to be so. The Truth is, they are in the same Situation with the Readers of *Romances;* who, though they know the whole to be one entire Fiction, nevertheless agree to be deceived; and as these find Amusement, so do the others find Ease and Convenience in this Concurrence." Such comments, one may note in passing, are ironic at the expense of the whole political process, not of Sir Robert Walpole or Pulteney or any other particular politician; like some of the other remarks cited above, they would not likely have been made as part of a partisan campaign against any one government. Indeed, it is only with the speech of the "grave Man" in Newgate (IV. iii) that any positive programme, any "Change in our Manners," is ever recommended to the characters or the readers.

All these insights are delivered as speeches or as direct and explicit commentary. But for the most part, of course, the signal feature of *Jonathan Wild* is not direct comment but sustained irony. As irony it has not always struck readers as deft or subtle, since its principal device ("greatness" is good, "goodness" is silly and weak), involving a simple inversion of values, is reiterated, insistently and predictably.[75] But the heaviness of the main ironic framework should not be allowed to endanger or interfere with the reader's perception of the smaller ironies and comedic touches, some in Fielding's most assured novelistic manner. One thinks, for example, of Laetitia's plaintive cry after her fight with Jonathan, "Why B——ch,?" a query repeated even as her husband is about to be hanged; or Jonathan picking the Ordinary's pocket on the gallows and carrying his bottle screw out of the world. Touches like these have nothing to do even with the main theme of "greatness," much less with politics or Walpole. Small-scale satiric hits abound of the sort any reader of *Joseph Andrews* would have come to expect, as in the description of Wild's "Assurance": "not with that Aspect with which a pitiful Parson meets his Patron, after having opposed him at an Election, or which a Doctor wears, when sneaking away from a Door where he is informed of his Patient's Death . . ." (II. viii). Such asides, typical of Fielding's best fiction, do much to alleviate both the heaviness of simple ironic reversals (like those in the first chapter) and the darker tone of some of the speeches and set pieces.

Five years after publication of the *Miscellanies* Fielding expressed his doubts about irony. As he dropped his "mask" in the *Jacobite's Journal,* he declared that, however exquisite a tool it is for ridicule, no other sort of humour is "so liable to be mistaken" and thus prove so dangerous; "an infinite Number of Readers have not the least Taste or Relish for it." Moreover, he maintains, irony is little to the taste of the present age: "I am firmly persuaded, that if many of those who have formerly gained such Reputation this Way, were to revive and publish their Works *de novo,* they would have few Readers, and acquire but little Credit."[76] Though primarily designed as a comment on his devices in the *Journal,* his remark seems also an apt comment on the reception of *Jonathan Wild,* his most sustained ironic effort. For except for those immediately in his personal circle and a few random sneers by his later journalistic enemies in *Old England, Wild* seems to have attracted no more comment than the rest of the *Miscellanies.*

One of the odder exceptions to this rule is the reaction of George Bubb Dodington, Fielding's political patron, to whom he had dedicated the first edition of his poem "Of True Greatness," who subscribed for six sets of the *Miscellanies,* and who in Martin Battestin's view was in some sense the inspiration for Fielding's writing of the book.[77] According to Richard Cumberland, Dodington was in the habit of reading to the dowager Ladies Stafford and Hervey. "His selections however were curious, for he treated these ladies with the whole of Fielding's *Jonathan Wild,* in which he certainly consulted his own turn for irony rather than their's for elegance, but he set it off with much humour after his manner." The ladies, apparently, were good enough to pretend to be pleased.[78]

Another friend of Fielding's, Jane Collier, author and member of the Collier family of Salisbury with whom he had many connections, in her own ironic work *An Essay on the Art of Ingeniously Tormenting* (1753), cited "the behaviour of Jonathan Wild toward his friend Mr. Heartfree" as a prime example of "the interested use that is to be made of your friends."[79] And finally one may note the tone which Fielding's sister Sarah takes toward this work in an allusion in her novel *The History of the Countess of Dellwyn* (1759); about a selfish character she writes, "his whole Stock of Knowledge seemed to be centered in a few political Maxims, by which he constantly regulated his Conduct; altho' he had either read *The Life of Jonathan Wild,* or his native Genius was sufficient to form Rules very like those of that renowned great Man."[80] At least some of those closest to Fielding had sufficient "Taste or Relish" for this kind of writing to take pleasure in the mock-history of "that renowned great Man."

*Jonathan Wild* appeared in a Dutch translation in 1757 and in French in 1763; interestingly both translations were based on the original edition in Volume Three of the *Miscellanies* rather than on the revised separate publication of 1754, and neither translator makes any comment about possible political meanings. The preface to the Dutch translation quotes at length from Fielding's comments on Goodness and Greatness in his Preface to the *Miscellanies.* And the French translator, Christophe Picquet, left no doubt in his preface that he understood well the larger themes and the technique of the work he was translating: "L'Auteur, sous le voile de l'ironie, cherche à désabuser les hommes des idées fausses, & presque toujours dangereuses, qu'ils se forment communément de la grandeur."[81] The remainder of his comments stress the false greatness of figures like Alexander and Caesar as the main satiric objects of Fielding's novel.

Yet, despite such attention on the Continent, as with other pieces in the *Miscellanies* it has remained for later readers to ponder Fielding's style and purpose in this work, the only part of his *Miscellanies* that, for whatever reason, he saw fit to revise and publish in a later edition.[82] His choice seems understandable on thematic as well as artistic grounds; in the collection as a whole, *Jonathan Wild* reiterates and serves as the culmination of the overriding moral ideas of the other two volumes. "Greatness," here exposed with such consistent irony, appears a compound of grasping ambition, "assurance," sanctimonious hypocrisy, low scheming—in a word, of all those human evils Fielding attacks in his essays and satires in Volume One and in the *Journey from This World to the Next* in Volume Two, evils which of course he would continue to condemn in his later fiction and serious social tracts.

*Notes*

1. See "H. D. late Clerk to Justice R——," *The Life of Jonathan Wild, from his Birth to his Death* (1725), p. 37.

2. *Misc.* i. 9.

3. G. Howson, *Thief-Taker General: The Rise and Fall of Jonathan Wild* (New York, 1970), p. 284.

4. See Irwin, *The Making of Jonathan Wild*, pp. 32–4.

5. *Select Trials,* ii. 288. *Select Trials* appeared in four volumes in 1742, with the account of Wild located at ii. 212–88. This work is item 552 in the Baker list of Fielding's library. There were three issues of the edition of *Select Trials* in 1742, one printed by J. Applebee for George Strahan, Sam Birt, and other booksellers, another by Applebee for James Hodges, and a third (called "second edition") printed for L. Gilliver and J. Huggonson; except for the front matter these are all identical issues of the same edition, with no resetting of type. The Applebee issues were advertised in the *Champion* and other papers in April and May of 1742. The account of Wild is shorter but otherwise substantially the same as that in the 1734–35 two-volume edition of *Select Trials . . . at the Sessions-House in the Old-Bailey,* which was not in Fielding's library but which he may have seen. I am indebted to Dr Frederick G. Ribble for his help in identifying these various issues.

6. *Select Trials,* ii. 283 (font reversed). This poem originally appeared as part of a satirical print of 1725 called "The Funeral Procession of the Celebrated Jonathan Wild Thief-Taker General of Great Britain & Ireland"; see *Catalogue of Prints and Drawings in the British Museum. Division I, Political and Personal Satires,* No. 1751.

7. Quoted in *Select Trials,* ii. 239.

8. Sig. B. The author of the Introduction is unknown; "Charles Johnson" is the pseudonym used by Defoe, who died in 1731, for his *General History of the . . . Pyrates* (1724). The ESTC describes the 1734 volume as follows: "Consisting of adaptations of lives of highwaymen and others from 'the history of the lives of the most noted highwaymen . . . by Capt. Alexander Smith' interspersed with lives of pirates taken from the first volume of 'a general history of the pyrates' by Capt. Charles Johnson, i.e. Daniel Defoe." The Introduction included in the 1734 volume, however, is in neither the Smith nor the Defoe works.

9. "H. D.," *Life of Jonathan Wild,* p. 30.

10. Ibid., pp. iv–vi.

11. W. J. Farrell, "The Mock-Heroic Form of *Jonathan Wild,*" MP 63 (1966), 225.

12. Ibid. 222–3, and see below, p. 7 n. For another example of typical openings of biographies, cf. Peter Heylyn's *Cyprianus Anglicus: the History of Life and Death of Archbishop Laud* (1671), in Fielding's library (Baker, item 280), which opens: "To recommend unto Posterity the *Lives* and *Actions* of eminent and famous Persons, hath always been esteemed a work becoming the most able Pens" and follows with the instances of Plutarch and Diogenes Laertius (sig. [G1–G4]).

13. He quotes from Middleton's work at the end of the Preface to his *Enquiry;* see the comment by Malvin Zirker in his edition, p. 74 n.

14. See C. J. Rawson, *Henry Fielding and the Augustan Ideal Under Stress* (1972), pp. 148–51.

15. Cf. his reference to "one St. Luke" in *CGJ* 11 (8 Feb. 1752), p. 80. On these distinctions see B. A. Goldgar, "Fielding on Fiction and History," *Eighteenth-Century Fiction,* 7 (1995), 279–92.

16. Thomas Keightley, "On the Life and Writings of Henry Fielding," *Fraser's Magazine,* 57 (1858), 213.

17. Wells, "Fielding's Political Purpose," 54.

18. *Select Trials,* ii. 213.

19. *Common Sense, or The Englishman's Journal,* collected edn. (1739), ii, 279. The Wild/Walpole comparison appears also in one portion of the leader in *Common Sense* (11 Apr. 1741).

20. As reprinted in *GM* 9 (1739), 138–9.

21. Fielding's leader in the *Champion* (4 March 1739/40) mentions Wild briefly, but the context is non-political.

22. *Epilogue to the Satires, Dialogue ii,* l. 39.

23. *Misc.* i. 9.

24. H. K. Miller (*Misc.* i. 9 n.) reads this as a hint that some members of the triumphant Opposition are fit models for the portrait, but he provides no evidence for such a reading.

25. T. R. Cleary, *Henry Fielding, Political Writer* (Waterloo, Ont., 1984), p. 192; Wells, "Fielding's Political Purpose," pp. 4–6.

26. See Hollis Rinehart, "The Role of Walpole in Fielding's *Jonathan Wild,*" *English Studies in Canada,* 5 (1979), 420–31; in what follows I am much indebted to Rinehart's essay.

27. As reprinted in *LM* 11 (1742), 498–500.

28. Ibid. 559–60.

29. *LM* 12 (1743), 135–6.

30. Rinehart, "The Role of Walpole," 422.

31. See *GM* 12 (1742), 441.

32. "H. D.," *Jonathan Wild,* p. 32.

33. Rinehart, "Walpole," p. 426.

34. *Champion* (8 May 1740).

35. Rinehart, "Walpole," p. 423.

36. Wells, "Fielding's Political Purpose," 50; Irwin, *Jonathan Wild,* pp. 40–1; Cleary, *Henry Fielding,* pp. 195–6.

37. See *Misc.* ii, pp. xxiv–xxv.

38. H. Rinehart, "Fielding's Chapter 'Of Proverbs' (*Jonathan Wild,* Book 2, Chapter 12): Sources, Allusions, and Interpretations," *MP* 77 (1980), 291–6. See also p. 82, n. 6.

39. Cross, i. 410; in 1754 Fielding changed the adverb to "formerly." On his use of similar language elsewhere, see p. 87, n. 1.

40. See Battestins, pp. 310–16, 352–8. Similarly, efforts to date the composition of the text by Fielding's earlier use of images or jokes have been unsuccessful; see B. Goldgar, "The *Champion* and the Chapter on Hats in *Jonathan Wild,*" *PQ* 72 (1993), 447–8.

41. Cross, i. 410.

42. As another instance, though the image is admittedly commonplace, Mrs Slipslop's assault on Joseph Andrews (I. xi) is introduced with the simile, "as a voracious Pike, of immense Size, surveys through the liquid Element a Roach or Gudgeon which cannot escape her Jaws, opens them wide to swallow the little Fish"; the identical mock-heroic image figures in *Wild* in a simile about Mr Snap and other bailiffs waiting for their prey: "as the voracious Pike lieth snug under some Weed before the Mouth of any of those little Streams . . . , waiting for the small Fry which issue thereout" (I. xi. [67]). And the same pike appears later in *Wild,* as we are told that Nature sends good-natured men into the world "with the same Design as Men put little Fish into a Pike-Pond, in order to be devoured by that voracious Water-Hero" (II. i. [96]). Fielding also compares subtle knaves to pikes in the pond in the *Champion* (21 Feb. 1739/40).

43. Battestins, p. 281.

44. Ibid., pp. 281–2.

45. Keightley, "Life and Writings of Henry Fielding," 763; Austin Dobson, *Henry Fielding* (1907), pp. 103–6; Aurelien Digeon, *The Novels of Fielding* (1925), pp. 115–18; Cleary, *Henry Fielding,* pp. 192–3.

46. See M. C. Battestin, "Fielding's Changing Politics and *Joseph Andrews*," *PQ* 39 (1960), 39–55; B. A. Goldgar, *Walpole and the Wits* (Lincoln, Nebr., 1976), pp. 197–208; Battestins, pp. 317–24; and T. Lockwood, "Fielding and the Licensing Act," *HLQ* 50 (1987), 379–93. For a different interpretation, see W. B. Coley, "Henry Fielding and the Two Walpoles," *PQ* 45 (1966), 159–65, and Cleary, *Henry Fielding,* pp. 152–62.

47. Battestins, p. 285; this interpretation of the passage, which I endorsed in *Walpole and the Wits,* p. 198, now seems to me more questionable. Cleary, *Henry Fielding,* pp. 137–8, argues for *Grub-Street Opera* as the book referred to.

48. See Textual Introduction, pp. 204–7.

49. Battestins, p. 309.

50. See Mr Amory's Introduction to the List of Subscribers, pp. 296–7, and his essay "Virtual Readers: The Subscribers to Fielding's *Miscellanies,*" *SB* 48 (1995), 94–112.

51. Cross, i. 409–12.

52. R. B. Friedman, "Fielding's *The Life of Mr. Jonathan Wild the Great:* A Textual and Critical Study," Ph.D. thesis (City University of New York), 1982, pp. 143–99.

53. I owe this point to Mr Amory's suggestion.

54. See, e.g., A. Wendt, "The Moral Allegory of *Jonathan Wild,*" ELH 24 (1957), 306–20. Cf. R. H. Hopkins, "Language and Comic Play in Fielding's 'Jonathan Wild,' " *Criticism* 8 (1966), esp. 219–20.

55. Farrell, "The Mock-Heroic Form," 224.

56. Wendt, "The Moral Allegory," pp. 306–20. H. K. Miller also argues that Fielding is impugning Heartfree's "trusting simplicity"; see Miller, *Essays,* p. 47.

57. Rawson, *Fielding and the Augustan Ideal,* pp. 233–5.

58. Ibid., p. 235.

59. *Champion,* i. 296. Cf. Fielding's comment on Allworthy's apparent failure to understand fully the character of Thwackum, *TJ,* p. 135.

60. Digeon, *Novels of Fielding,* p. 121; Irwin, *Jonathan Wild,* pp. 73–4.

61. *Champion,* i. 313.

62. Thomas Davies, *Works of George Lillo, with Some Account of his Life* (1775), vol. i, pp. xvi–xvii; on the puffing, see Battestins, p. 206, and Robert D. Hume, *Henry Fielding and the London Theatre, 1728–1737* (Oxford, 1988), app. iv.

63. The phrase is Davies'; see his *Works of George Lillo,* vol. i, p. xvii.

64. Ibid., vol. i, p. xlvii.

65. Dudden, i. 478. Morris Golden, who finds both Heartfrees "faintly ridiculous," puts that view to use in an unpersuasive biographical reading of the novel; see his "Public Context and Imagining Self in *Joseph Andrews* and *Jonathan Wild,*" *JEGP,* 88 (1989), 507–8.

66. M. McKeon, *The Origins of the English Novel* (Baltimore, 1987), pp. 390–2. For a response to McKeon, see Treadwell Ruml, "*Jonathan Wild* and the Epistemological Gulf between Virtue and Vice," *Studies in the Novel,* 21 (1989), 117–27.

67. *Misc.* i. II.

68. On this point see Rawson, *Fielding and the Augustan Ideal,* pp. 258–9 n. 30; and Simon Varey, *Henry Fielding* (Cambridge, 1986), p. 39.

69. Hopkins, "Language and Comic Play," 215.

70. Ian Bell, *Literature and Crime in Augustan England* (1991), pp. 184, 189. Much earlier, Digeon had called the character of the book "at bottom purely anarchical"; see his *Novels of Fielding,* p. 127, cited by Rawson, *Augustan Ideal,* p. 227 n.

71. For the most insightful of such analyses, see Rawson, *Augustan Ideal,* pp. 101–71; Hatfield, *Fielding and the Language of Irony, passim;* and Patrick Reilly, "Fielding's Magisterial Art," in K. G. Simpson (ed.), *Henry Fielding: Justice Observed* (London, 1985), pp. 75–100. See also Hopkins, "Language and Comic Play," 213–28. On the role of theatre and dramatic allusions, see Rawson, *Augustan Ideal,* pp. 127–8; Varey, *Fielding,* pp. 39–41; and Alexander Pettit,

"What the Drama Does in Fielding's *Jonathan Wild*," *Eighteenth-Century Fiction*, 6 (1994), 153–68.

72.   On the darkness of the novel's tone, see the discussion by Digeon, *Novels of Fielding*, pp. 126–8.

73.   *Mist's Weekly Journal* (19 June 1725).

74.   The phrases are from Hatfield, *Language of Irony*, p. 208; on the narrator as normative figure, see Varey, *Henry Fielding*, pp. 41–2.

75.   See, e.g., John Preston, "The Ironic Mode: A Comparison of *Jonathan Wild* and *The Beggar's Opera*," *Essays in Criticism*, 16 (1966), 268–80; see also F. R. Leavis's dismissal of the work as a "clumsy piece of hobbledehoydom" when compared to the irony of Conrad's *The Secret Agent*, in *The Great Tradition* (London, 1948), pp. 209–10. But cf. Hatfield's analysis of Fielding's linguistic manipulation of his irony, in his *Fielding and the Language of Irony*, pp. 102–8.

76.   *JJ* 17 (26 Mar. 1748), 211.

77.   See Battestins, pp. 278–81.

78.   *Memoirs of Richard Cumberland* (1806; suppl. 1807), p. 146.

79.   J. Collier, *An Essay on the Art of Ingeniously Tormenting* (1753), pp. 138–9.

80.   Sarah Fielding, *The History of the Countess of Dellwyn* (1759), i. 282.

81.   *Histoire de Jonathan Wild le Grand*, trans. C. Picquet (Paris, 1763), vol. ii, p. v.

82.   On the nature of his revisions, see Textual Introduction, pp. 210–15.

# Fielding and the Instrumentality of Belief:
## *Joseph Andrews*

### MICHAEL MCKEON

As Martin Battestin has shown most fully, *Joseph Andrews* is dedicated to promulgating the two Christian virtues that are embodied in its two principal characters, Joseph and Abraham Adams. Chastity and charity may be understood, respectively, as analogous private and public modes of moral restraint, the Christian capacity to limit the power of the selfish and destructive human passions. Joseph's early resistance to Lady Booby, which is the narrative's most declaratory reaction against Richardsonian example, broadly represents to us the triumph of chastity as such. If Shamela is Pamela as she really is, stripped of her feigned innocence, Joseph is Pamela as she should have been, stripped of her self-indulgence. Joseph is a reproach to Richardson's progressive protagonist because, unlike her, he masters both his sexual and his social appetites. Although he deferentially models his behavior on his older sister's, we are made to sense the unwitting and ironic contrast when he writes to her, "I never loved to tell the Secrets of my Master's Family," instantly reconciling himself to leaving Lady Booby's service so as to "maintain my Virtue against all Temptations."[1] But despite Fielding's easily insinuated parallel between the social servitude of Joseph the footman and that of Pamela the lady's maid, the sexual difference is all-important. It is not just that, as Fielding admits, a man's "Chastity is always in his own power" (I, xviii, 87). By making the issue one of male chastity, he slyly avoids all the social ramifications of female chastity.

For Richardson's Pamela, the "religious" injunction to remain chaste is overlaid by a complex "political" requirement, and she has both more to lose and more to gain—a social transformation—as the potential consequence of a liaison with her better. For Fielding's Joseph the situation is, despite appearances, much simpler. Already in love with Fanny, he must do no more than control his momentary sexual desire (I, x, 46–47). Although to Lady Booby

Reprinted from Michael McKeon, *The Origins of the English Novel 1600–1740* (1987), by permission of the Johns Hopkins University Press.

he implies that he is chaste by virtue of being "the Brother of *Pamela*," to Pamela he writes that it is as much from Parson Adams's religious instruction as from her that he has learned "that Chastity is as great a virtue in a Man as in a Woman" (I, viii, 41, x, 46; see also xii, 53). And for Adams the principle of chastity, devoid of any social complexities, has the simple moral purpose of guarding against "the Indulgence of carnal Appetites" (IV, viii, 307). Of course succumbing to Lady Booby would bring some material reward. Adams knows that with the proper encouragement and education, Joseph might rise up the ladder of domestic service as his sister did (I, iii, 26). But the final great elevation, from service to gentility, is not within the power of Lady Booby to engineer. This is the lesson Mr. B. teaches his sister, Lady Davers, in *Pamela*. In *Joseph Andrews* Lady Booby ends up the counterpart, in this respect, of Lady Davers rather than of Mr. B., prevented from doing what Mr. Booby has done with Pamela not only by Joseph's resistance but also by her own obsessive fear that so far from raising him to her level, she has the power only "to sacrifice my Reputation, my Character, my Rank in Life, to the Indulgence of a mean and vile Appetite" (IV, xiii, 328). Lady Booby's echo of Parson Adams's religious teachings here clearly is not a sign that she, too, believes in chastity. Instead it suggests how effectively Fielding has managed, not to refute Richardson's progressive social ethics in the great contest between "industrious virtue" and "aristocratic corruption," but to defuse its social volatility through the stealthy reversal of sexes. Adrift from its moorings in female experience, Joseph's heroically passive resistance soon becomes rather silly;[2] and in a characteristically conservative turn, neither "virtue" nor "corruption" comes off very well in the contest. In fact, so far from occupying the center stage that it has in *Pamela*, in *Joseph Andrews* the encounter quickly shrinks into an attenuated frame within which questions of virtue are most efficiently propounded in terms of the problem not of chastity but of charity.

An English Quixote obsessed with the rule of Apostolic charity, not of romance chivalry,[3] Abraham Adams reminds us of both the madness of the *hidalgo* estranged from reality and the conservative wisdom of the utopian social reformer. Traversing the circuit to London and back again, he upholds the standard of good works against a cross-section of humanity whose complacency, hypocrisy, and downright viciousness announce, again and again, the absence of charity in the modern world. The traditional proponents of charity—clergymen like Barnabas and Trulliber—abhor Methodist reform for the wrong reasons and jealously defend their own material comforts against the needs of the poor (I, xvii; II, xiv). The inheritors of the feudal obligation of charity, the country gentry, are, if possible, even worse. One squire specializes in entrapping the needy with false promises of munificence. Having been tricked himself by this man, Adams then listens in horror to "true Stories" of how the squire has ruined several local youths, among them a Pamela figure and a hopeful younger son, by feeding their expectations of upward mobility and withdrawing his support only after they have become fully dependent upon it (II, xvi–xvii). Another squire is so corrupted in sensibility and education that he has become addicted to victimizing those who have come into his care. Adams protests that "I am your Guest, and by the Laws of Hospitality entitled to your Protection" (III, vii, 247), but the practical jokes culminate in a serious attack upon his traveling party and the abduction of Fanny as a prospective "Sacrifice to the Lust of a Ravisher." The rape is foiled by Lady Booby's steward, Peter Pounce, a "Gentleman" and burlesque progressive "gallant"—the chivalric protector as monied man— who "loved a pretty Girl better than any thing, besides his own Money, or the Money of other People" (III, xii, 268–69). But needless to say, the monied man soon evinces his own species of corruption, and the adventure ends on a conservative note with Pounce replicating the sins of the selfish gentry, reviling the poor laws and asserting that charity "does not so much consist in the Act as in the Disposition" to relieve the distressed (III, xiii, 274).

The paradigmatic instance of failed charity in *Joseph Andrews* is the early stagecoach episode, in which an entire social spectrum of respectable passengers refuses to relieve Joseph's distress until the lowest of them all, the postilion, gives him his greatcoat (I, xii). Later confirmed by the humble goodness of Betty the chambermaid and the mysterious pedlar (I, xii, 55; II, xv, 170; IV, viii, 309–10), this episode establishes the basic paradox that if charity involves giving something for nothing, only those with nothing are likely to be charitable. And the traveling lawyer is of course no more compassionate than anyone else. Throughout *Joseph Andrews* the law is seen as the secularizer of traditional institutions, possessed of at least the potential to civilize their social functions for the modern world. In the progressively oriented "History of Leonora," for example, the symbolic supplanting of sword by robe nobility is intimated by the rivalry between the dishonorable fop Bellarmine, an accomplished "Cavalier," and the sober Horatio, who, "being a Lawyer . . . would seek Revenge in his own way" (II, iv, 115). Most often, however, the authority of the law in the settlement of modern disputes works only to aggravate the old thirst for "revenge" by making it financially profitable. This Adams learns when the interpolated tale of Leonora is itself interrupted by the fistfight at the inn, and a litigious bystander advises the parson's antagonist that "was I in your Circumstances, every Drop of my Blood should convey an Ounce of Gold into my Pocket" (II, v, 121). Later on Mrs. Trulliber, seeing that her husband is about to strike Adams for calling him uncharitable and un-Christian, advises him instead to "shew himself a true Christian, and take the Law of him" (II, xiv, 168).

It is a typically conservative reversal that in *Joseph Andrews* the modern institution of the law tends not to civilize the bloody passions of anger and revenge but to corrupt them, to replace physical with financial violence. And in this respect the law is a distinct deterioration from the traditional peacekeeping institutions—like Christianity—that it is quickly displacing in the modern world. When Adams delivers Fanny from her highway ravisher, he does it in the chivalric spirit of a stout "Champion" in defense of an innocent "Damsel" (II, ix, 139). But when the case is brought before the justice it is quickly corrupted by the ambitions of everyone involved for some portion of the reward. The innocents are libeled as "Robbers," "Highwaymen," and "Rogues," and they escape only through the chance intervention of a local squire and the justice's extreme obsequiousness to gentility (II, x–xi, 142–43, 145, 148–49). And when Lady Booby wishes to foil the match between Joseph and Fanny, she has no trouble persuading Lawyer Scout and Justice Frolick to help her in circumventing the settlement laws. As Scout puts it, "The Laws of this Land are not so vulgar, to permit a mean Fellow to contend with one of your Ladyship's Fortune" (IV, iii, 285).

But if the modern purveyors of charity and justice are riddled with corruption, we are also justified in being skeptical about the efficacy of Adams's anachronistic ideals, and not simply because the parson's own means of fulfilling them are severely limited. As a comprehensive moral imperative, the rule of charity does not readily admit of fine ethical distinctions as to relative obligations and deserts, a problem of which the growing popularity of benevolist philosophies was making contemporaries aware.[4] The innkeeper Mrs. Tow-wouse is surely discredited when she exclaims to her husband, "Common Charity, a F———t!" (I, xii, 56). But her real point here is suggestively echoed later on by Adams's wife and daughter. Book IV opens with a sharp contrast between the reception of Lady Booby and that of Parson Adams on their return to their respective country seats. We are well aware of the total absence of feudal care in her ladyship, and Fielding's ironic portrait of her entry into "the Parish amidst the ringing of Bells, and the Acclamations of the Poor" is quickly followed by a sincere account of how the parson's parishioners "flocked about" him "like dutiful Children round an indulgent Parent, and vyed with each other in Demonstrations of Duty and Love" (IV, i, 277). As Mrs. Adams tells Lady Booby, her husband does indeed say "that the whole Parish are his Children," but there are children of his own on whose career prospects the parson has exercised less patriarchal care than on those of Joseph and Fanny. "It behoved every Man to take the first Care of his Family," she complains to her husband. However, Adams is oblivious, Fielding adds, persisting "in doing his Duty without regarding the Consequence it might have on his worldly Interest" (IV, xi, 321, viii, 307). There is certainly no calculation on the part of the parson, but is his virtue always untainted by his interest? Even the innocent Joseph knows how "an Ambition to be respected" can inspire acts of goodness, and Fielding has allowed us to observe how Adams's vanity can be manifested in the very denunciation of vanity (III, vi, 233, iii, 214–15). Fielding's latitudinarian beliefs are very close to the Mandevillian argument that the autonomous purity of virtue is a pleasing fiction. And although we clearly are not encouraged to see the parson's undiscriminating love of his neighbor as a stealthy self-love, nevertheless, to a real degree, the Apostolic and feudal role of charity is itself demystified in *Joseph Andrews* as a Quixotic social fiction.

By the same token, although Fielding surely strips modern institutions like the law and the gentry of their authority, at times the assault is moderated and the reigning fictions are allowed a certain instrumental utility. We have already seen this to be true of the law in *Jonathan Wild* and of gentility in *Shamela.* When Mr. Booby discovers that his brother-in-law has been ordered to Bridewell for, in Justice Frolick's sage words, "a kind of felonious larcenous thing," he is shocked by the triviality and brutality of the law. But the justice is happy to commit Joseph and Fanny to Booby's benevolent custody instead, easily discerning now, with the kindly lechery that often distinguishes Fielding's basically good-natured men, that Fanny's beauty deserves better than Bridewell (IV, v, 289–91). And at the end of the narrative, Booby calls to mind his own briefly normative incarnation in *Shamela,* becoming the true representative of feudal gentility by dispensing gifts of "unprecedented Generosity" and by entertaining the assembled company "in the most splendid manner, after the Custom of the old *English* Hospitality, which is still preserved in some very few Families in the remote Parts of *England*" (IV, xvi, 343, 341).

At such moments of affirmation, customary noblesse oblige and the hallowed system of the English law seem able to redeem themselves as the best scheme of social justice available, if also the only one. But this is not to say that they are also able to counter the endemic condition of status inconsistency—perhaps the more precise term for Fielding would be "status indeterminacy." In a central chapter of *Joseph Andrews,* Fielding characteristically affirms that social distinctions are merely formal, being determined neither by birth nor by accomplishments but by fashion (II, xiii, 156–58). "*High* People" are distinguished from "*Low* People" by the way they dress, and the great "Ladder of Dependance," of which social hierarchy consists, is a closely articulated chain of employments, each of which attends upon its next-highest neighbor and is attended upon, in turn, by the next-lowest one. The function of attendance is essentially the same; what differs is the level at which it is done. Thus social station is arbitrary: the relative placement of a Walpole or a Wild—of a Booby or a Slipslop (I, vii, 34)—is quite accidental. But if the ladder is a fiction in that its rungs are placed arbitrarily, the ladder itself is systematic and functional. And if there is no basis for affirming the justice of the present arrangement, there is no reason to suppose that any systematic alteration would be an improvement. To be sure, there are exceptions to the rule of status inconsistency. Fielding "could name a Commoner raised higher above the Multitude by superior Talents, than is in the Power of his Prince to exalt him," but he also "could name a Peer no less elevated by Nature than by Fortune" (III, i, 190–91; cf. III, vi, 235). The very ease with which exceptions to all rules can be enumerated seems to strengthen the implacability of the system itself, which continues remorselessly to grind out the present dispensation, certainly no better, but probably no worse, than any replacement for it might do.

Something akin to this quiet desperation must be the issue of any direct attempt to distill Fielding's stance on matters of social justice and reform—on questions of virtue—in *Joseph Andrews*. And it is strikingly discordant with the genial and confident exuberance of the voice that self-consciously suffuses so much of the narrative. How does his stance on questions of truth help palliate Fielding's social vision? Calling itself, on the title page and at various points throughout the narrative, a true and authentic history, *Joseph Andrews* deploys the range of authenticating devices and claims to historicity with which we have become familiar not only in Fielding's predecessors but also in his own earlier efforts.[5] His extreme skepticism is never really in doubt, but it is conveyed to us through a characteristic combination of parodic impersonation and self-subversive definition that undertakes the positing of a form by a series of contradictory negations. In Chapter I, for example, Fielding specifies his "History" as a biographical life; yet after a brief allusion to ancient Roman biographies, his chief instances of this form are several late-medieval redactions of chivalric romance (I, i, 17–18).[6] Moreover, two eminent modern examples are autobiographies that work, "as the common Method is, from authentic Papers and Records"; but these are none other than Cibber's *Apology* and *Pamela* (I, i, 18).

In the first chapter of Book III (185–91) Fielding picks up, where this early discussion left off, the account of what he means by "history," and now he is prepared to be more explicit in his epistemological reversals. Whatever "Authority" they may be accorded by the vulgar, books that bear the title "the History of *England,* the History of *France,* of *Spain,* &c." are really the work of "Romance-Writers." The skeptical reader is correct to judge them "as no other than a Romance, in which the Writer hath indulged a happy and fertile Invention," for it is in biography "that Truth only is to be found." Of course no one would deny that the aforementioned "histories" can be relied upon for the quantitative and topographical recording of isolated "Facts." "But as to the Actions and Characters of Men," the very same facts can be "set forth in a different Light." Biography is concerned with this more qualitative sort of truth. The "Facts we deliver may be relied on" because their truth is understood to be fully dependent upon the interpretive "light" in which they are "set forth." Biography aims at the truth of general nature and of universal types. A good example is the "true History" of Gil Blas or Don Quixote: the "Time and Place" of Cervantes' characters may well be questioned, but "is there in the World such a Sceptic as to disbelieve the Madness of *Cardenio,* the Perfidy of *Ferdinand* . . . ?"

It is clear enough that Fielding is seeking here to distinguish between a naively empiricist and a more "imaginative" species of belief. But he is also at pains to emphasize the crucial degree to which he is in accord with the empiricist perspective, and to distinguish his preferred sort of belief also from the sheer creativity of romance.[7] For he quickly adds, "I would by no means be thought to comprehend" in this preferred category "the Authors of immense Romances" or of *chroniques scandaleuses,* "who without any Assistance from Nature or History, record Persons who never were, or will be, and Facts which never did nor possibly can happen: Whose Heroes are of their own Creation." Both romancers and romancing historians, in other words, rely too much on a "happy and fertile invention." As a biographer, Fielding is "contented to copy Nature" and to write "little more than I have seen," aiming not at all to repudiate the evidence of the senses but to do full justice to its complexity. And the category "true History," in which he places *Joseph Andrews* at the conclusion of the chapter, provides a positive term for the complicated dance of double negation—neither romance nor history—in which his extreme skepticism has thus far consisted.

Another such category, of course, is "comic romance." Fielding's "Preface" to *Joseph Andrews* is as celebrated as it is in part because it so explicitly announces the fact that this is a project in epistemological and generic categorization, an effort to describe a "kind of Writing, which I do not remember to have seen hitherto attempted in our Language," and which "no Critic hath thought proper to . . . assign . . . a particular Name to itself" (3). Fielding's taxonomic procedure in the "Preface" is self-consciously imitative of Aristotle's, but only up to a point. For given the normative meaning of "history" in Fielding's redefinition of the term, the invidious Aristotelian distinction between "history" and "poetry" can hold no attraction for him. So despite its crucial importance in most of his other generic considerations, in what has become the most famous of all the term "history" makes no appearance whatsoever. Even so, "comic romance" is an appropriate substitute for "true history." Together these terms resuscitate the two generic categories Fielding's extreme skepticism has decisively discredited, and the adjectival addition in each case signifies that the naiveté of the original category has been corrected by (a Cervantic procedure) conjoining it more closely with its supposed antithesis.[8]

How does "romance" correct "history" in the body of *Joseph Andrews?* Most obviously, in the parodic and self-subversive deployment of the claim to historicity that I have already noted. But as in *Jonathan Wild,* all modes of self-conscious narration work here to subjectify the objective historicity of the narrative line. On the micronarrative level these reflexive intrusions are everywhere, and they are most amusing when Fielding's ostensible purpose is not to frankly advertise his control of the plot but on the contrary to underwrite a self-effacing authenticity.[9] On the macronarrative level, authorial intrusion amounts to a quite palpable interruption of the main action by apparently unrelated episodes. On such occasions, the challenge to the historical criterion of truth involves replacing the linear coherence of contiguity by—not chaos, but the alternative coherence of relations of similarity, which are simply too neat to be "natural." The most complex instance of this in *Joseph Andrews* occurs in Book III, when the "authentic History" of Fanny's rape (ix, 255) is interrupted by two successive chapters of static dialogue, first between the poet and the player and then between Joseph and Adams (x, xi). The first discourse, disclaimed as "of no other Use in this History, but to divert the Reader" (x, 259), concerns the power of actors to affect for good or ill the material that authors give them to work with. The second discourse, acknowledged as "a sort of Counterpart of this" (x, 264), debates the proper degree of human submission to "the Dispensations of Providence." And when at last we irritably return to Fanny's plight, we find that the "main plot" has really been continued rather than suspended by these analogous "episodes," since she was destined all along to be delivered by Peter Pounce (had we only had patience enough to submit ourselves to Fielding's narrative dispensations).[10]

Because *Joseph Andrews* is periodically punctuated by coincidental meetings that increasingly seem too neat to be natural—Joseph with Adams (I, xiv, 64), Adams with Fanny (II, x, 143), Joseph with Fanny (II, xii, 154–55), Fanny with Peter Pounce (III, xii, 269)—its entire plot gradually takes on the air of a "historical" line that has been charmed, by the magical intrusions of "romance," into a circle. Yet there is one coincidental discovery, Joseph's meeting with Mr. Wilson, that is different from these in that our intrusive author denies us the crucial knowledge needed to distinguish it from the random ongoingness of everyday history—the knowledge that Mr. Wilson is Joseph's father. (Thus our ignorance of our hero's lineal descent at this point preserves the impression of linear contingency.) We cannot say that we have not been warned—although the early clues are rather ambiguous. True, there have been "romance" intimations of Joseph's genealogical gentility in what we have heard of his external appearance (I, viii, 38–39, xiv, 61). But readers have long since become used to hearing such things said of progressive protagonists who possess "true," as distinct from inherited, gentility, especially in narratives that progressively insist, as here, that their heroes are capable "of acquiring Honour" even in the total absence of ancestry (I, ii, 21). In other words, Fielding's "romance" conventions are equally parodic, antiromance conventions, and they create in us the erroneous expectation of an empiricist and a progressive ending.[11]

So as his long-lost child, innocently returned to his place of birth, sits listening, Mr. Wilson concludes the history of his life with the only episode for which he cannot gratefully thank "the great Author," the theft of his eldest son by gypsies. Shortly thereafter the three travelers renew their journey. Joseph and Adams are soon lost in discourse about the rival claims of nature and nurture, until they find themselves all at once in "a kind of natural Amphitheatre," nature reworked by art, whose trees "seemed to have been disposed by the Design of the most skillful Planter . . . [And] the whole Place might have raised romantic Ideas in elder Minds than those of *Joseph* and

*Fanny,* without the Assistance of Love" (III, iii, 224, v, 232). Here the travelers rest, and here our own author, as though encouraging us to rest in his analogous design, informs us that Mr. Wilson plans to pass through Parson Adams's parish in a week's time, "a Circumstance which we thought too immaterial to mention before." And as a pledge of his good will Fielding ends this chapter by letting the reader in on what the next contains, "for we scorn to betray him into any such Reading, without first giving him Warning" (III, v, 233). Thus the narrative power of imposition is defused by being made explicit, and the incredibility of "romance" coincidence is gently softened into a benign and watchful disposition of the author. When Mr. Wilson's visit later turns out to coincide remarkably with other events to which it is intimately related, Fielding will remind us that we knew it was going to happen (IV, xv, 338), as though now encouraging us toward an instrumental belief in a palpable fiction in which, after all, we are already to this degree knowingly invested. The last chapter heading—"In which this true History is brought to a happy Conclusion"—finely balances the claims of history and romance contrivance, and its closing words pleasantly insist upon the present historicity of Fielding's characters, as if counting on us to know the sort of belief with which to honor that claim (IV, xvi, 339, 343–44).

It is tempting to say that questions of truth and virtue merge with the climactic discovery of Joseph's parentage. Certainly it is a scene of contrivance calculated enough to permit the ghosts of romance idealism and aristocratic ideology to be raised simultaneously. But the effect depends so fully on the delicate balance of our liaison with our author that the relation is most accurately seen not as a merging but as a subsumption of questions of virtue by questions of truth. Not that Fielding does anything now to discourage our (highly provisional) belief in the benevolent authority of the gentry and the law. Thus far he has led us to associate Joseph's social elevation—the overcoming of his status inconsistency—with the interested goodness of Mr. Booby, who not only improves the law of Justice Frolick but immediately thereafter has Joseph "drest like a Gentleman" (IV, v, 292). If anything, Mr. Booby's charity increases in the last episodes of the narrative. But of course the real agent of Joseph's upward mobility, Fielding's narrative procedure insists, is not noblesse oblige at all; it is the good will of our benevolent author. Social justice and the rule of charity are most dependably institutionalized not in the law or the gentry but in the patriarchal care of the narrator, who internalizes the charity of an imagined "old English hospitality."

The representatives of the archaic feudal order that one finds among Fielding's characters are plentiful enough, but they are hedged about with a suppositional aura that we detect also in the power of providence—in some respects analogous to the power of the old gentry in Fielding—largely because of the perpetual association of providence with the more manifest power of the author. Not that he would have us doubt for a moment the reality of divine justice. But the belief in it that Fielding argues for most energetically tends to be a well-rationalized and instrumental one. And meanwhile we are able to experience the palpable poetic justice of the narrator—why not call it providence?—who periodically intrudes into the daily life of story so as to ensure there what divine and human justice manifestly do not ensure in the world outside.[12] Fielding's subsumption of questions of virtue by questions of truth transfers the major challenge of utopian projection from the substantive to the formal realm. And a central reason for this, we may speculate, is the relative uncertainty of his commitment to the utopian institutions and communities envisioned by conservative ideology. Attracted, on the other hand, to the energy of the career open to talents, Fielding was appalled by the vanity and pretension of those who enacted that career with any success or conviction. Accordingly, what "happens" at the end of *Joseph Andrews* (and *Tom Jones*) is less a social than an epistemological event; not upward mobility but—as in the invoked model of *Oedipus* (IV, xv, 336)—the acquisition of knowledge.

The subsumption is anticipated in *Joseph Andrews* in its two most extended discussions of formal strategy, the "Preface" and the first chapter of Book III. In both discussions Fielding's extreme sensitivity to the analogous relation between questions of truth and questions of virtue leads him to exemplify the former by the latter. Thus we are told in the "Preface" that comic romance works through the discovery of affectation, as when we find someone "to be the exact Reverse of what he affects." And the exemplary cases of affectation are also cases of status inconsistency: a "dirty Fellow" who "descend[s] from his Coach and Six, or bolt[s] from his Chair with his Hat under his Arm"; or a "wretched Family" in whose presence we find an "Affectation of Riches and Finery either on their Persons or in their Furniture" (9). Later on Fielding qualifies his technique of representing universal types in biography by acknowledging that life admits of exceptions to the rule. And the exceptions singled out for comment are those elevated individuals whose social status is, surprisingly enough, consistent with their "superior Talents" and "Mind" (III, i, 190). The ease with which formal argument comprehends the substantive social problem in both of these passages, by treating as an exemplary case, prefigures the increasing facility with which Fielding's charitable narrator will tacitly compensate for the failure of social—and providential—mechanisms to justify our provisional credence, by mobilizing narrative's own more perfect versions of them. Fielding's reflexive narration permits the discursive argument of the instrumentality of a belief in what cannot be shown to be credible to infiltrate narrative form itself. And once acclimatized, it becomes an automatic and all-purpose gesture of reconciliation, an invisible thread of affirmation that is as unconditional as the fact of the narrative form into which it has been woven. Approaching it from a very different direction, Fielding meets Richardson at the nexus where moral and social pedagogy hesitate on the edge of their transformation into something else entirely, aesthetic pleasure.

*Notes*

1.   Henry Fielding, *The History of the Adventures of Joseph Andrews And of his Friend Mr. Abraham Adams. Written in Imitation of The Manner of Cervantes, Author of Don Quixote* (1742), ed. Martin C. Battestin (Oxford: Clarendon Press, 1967), I, v, 29–30, x, 47 (hereafter cited as *Joseph Andrews*). All parenthetical citations in the text and in the notes of this chapter are to this edition, and include book, chapter, and page numbers. While still in her service, Joseph hopes "your Ladyship can't tax me with ever betraying the Secrets of the Family, and I hope, if you was to turn me away, I might have the Character of you" (ibid., I, v, 29). When he later learns that Lady Booby "would not give him a Character," Joseph says that he will nonetheless always give her "a good Character where-ever he went" (ibid., IV, i, 279). On the importance of these matters of "character" in *Pamela,* see above, chap. 11. n. 18. On Joseph and Abraham as embodiments of chastity and charity, see Martin C. Battestin, *The Moral Basis of Fielding's Art: A Study of Joseph Andrews* (Middletown, Ct.: Wesleyan University Press, 1959), chaps. 2, 3, and passim.

2.   Many critics have observed this. However, it is worth noting that what is ludicrous is not male chastity itself but the spuriously social resonance it acquires in this particular encounter. On male chastity see above, chap. 4, n. 40.

3.   See the observations of Paulson, *Satire and the Novel,* 120.

4.   E.g., see Samuel Johnson, *Rambler,* no. 99 (Feb. 26, 1751), in *The Rambler,* ed. W. J. Bate and Albrecht B. Strauss, Yale Edition of the Works of Samuel Johnson (New Haven: Yale University Press, 1969), II, 164–69.

5.   E.g., see *Joseph Andrews,* I, ii, 20, xvi, 71–72; II, xv, 168; III, vi, 235, vii, 246, ix, 255; IV, v, 289, xvi, 339.

6.   In *Jacobite's Journal,* ed. cit., no. 13 (Feb. 27, 1748), 177–78, Fielding attacks Thomas Carte's *General History of England* as a "great Romance," compares it to these same popular romances, and advises that if published serially as they are, it should have as good a sale as "the inimitable Adventures of *Robinson Crusoe.*"

7.   The difficulty of the exercise is suggested by the fact that in another context Fielding used the story of Cardenio, Ferdinand, Dorothea, and Lucinda as an example of how Cervantes "in many Instances, approaches very near to the Romances which he ridicules": *Covent-Garden Journal,* ed. cit., no. 24 (March 24, 1752), I, 281. In the absence of a stable critical theory, to reject naive empiricism inevitably risks a return to its antagonist, romance idealism.

8.   Thus, just as Fielding distinguishes his own "true history" from the naive claim to historicity that he discredits, so here he distinguishes the "comic Romance" from the serious "Romance." And we would seem to be justified in identifying the latter with "those voluminous Works commonly called *Romances*" (*Joseph Andrews,* "Preface," 3–4), that is, with the French heroic romances that he later alludes to as those "immense Romances" and that he discredits for their idealist detachment from both nature and history (see above). As Sheridan Baker has argued, and despite modern critical practice, the significant generic term in the "Preface" is "comic Romance" and not the pedantically exhaustive synonym "comic Epic-Poem in Prose"; see Baker's "Henry Fielding's Comic Romances," *Papers of the Michigan Academy of Science, Arts, and Letters,* 45 (1960), 441.

9.   Contrast the following passages from *Joseph Andrews:* "to which likewise he had some other Inducements which the Reader, without being a Conjurer, cannot possibly guess; 'till we have given him those hints, which it may be now proper to open" (I, x, 47); and "Indeed, I have been often assured by both, that they spent these Hours in a most delightful Conversation: but as I never could prevail on either to relate it, so I cannot communicate it to the Reader" (II, xv, 168).

10.   Compare the technique of Cervantes (above, chap. 7, sec. I). The invasion of "historical" contiguity by "romance" similarity is especially pleasing when it occurs within an interpolated tale, which is already itself an interruption of the linear plot and which nonetheless

may lay claim to being integral with it. A good example of this in *Jonathan Wild* is the disruption of Mrs. Heartfree's travel narrative by Wild's marital outrage. The best instance in *Joseph Andrews* is the progressive plot of Leonora (II, iv–vi), which is accompanied by claims to historicity but interrupted by the conservative themes that arise during Adams's fistfight at the inn.

11.    In *Joseph Andrews* Fanny also has a "natural Gentility" (II, xii, 153), so much so that once on the road she is more than once taken to be a young lady of quality either run or stolen away from her parents (III, ii, 199–200, ix, 257).

12.    Thus the status of Fielding's narratives as expressions of a belief in a providentially ordered universe seems to me far more problematic—or, at its simplest level, far less interesting—than it does to Aubrey Williams, "Interpositions of Providence and the Design of Fielding's Novels," *South Atlantic Quarterly,* 70, no. I (Spring, 1971), 265–86; see also Martin C. Battestin, *The Providence of Wit: Aspects of Form in Augustan Literature and the Arts* (Oxford: Clarendon Press, 1974), chap. 5. See above, chap. 3, nn. 75–80. For Fielding's instrumental belief in divine justice see, e.g., above, n. 18.

# Joseph Andrews
# and the Failure of Authority

## CHARLES A. KNIGHT

The garrulous narrator of *Joseph Andrews* and his complex novel have been interpreted in terms of implicitly conflicting analogies describable alternatively as religious and political. According to the first, the apparent authority of the narrator stands for the authority of God, especially the Christian and incarnate God who acts in history.[1] The function of Fielding's fictions is thus to reinforce, by their comic conclusion, the reader's confidence in a universe controlled by a benevolent deity. The secular alternative sees narrative authority as analogous to political and legal control. The narrator's control over the actions of characters and the interpretations of readers stands for social control over personal behaviour. The narrator adopts or prefigures techniques like those of civil control. John Bender sees Fielding concerned with "the deployment of narrative as an authoritative resource." Narratives parallel the information systems that organize an urban society, "the densely stored, cross-referenced informational networks that characterize written accounting in the modern metropolis. . . . I count the realist novel as one of these systems."[2] The epistemic shifts implied by the closely sequential developments of the novel as a canonic genre, of lawyers' roles in presenting and arguing legal cases, and of the reforming penitentiary give particular importance to narratives: "not to possess a story, to be without narrative resources, is to lack a comprehensible character within the metropolitan order and to be subject to a reformation of consciousness."[3] These religious and secular versions of Fielding's narrative authority are both clearly analogies, although of different sorts. Both account for a limited range of material and shape the text to fit the terms of the analogy. My present concern is with a possible misfit between Bender's legal-political analogy and the text of *Joseph Andrews*. The secular analogy proposes suggestive connections (especially for *Jonathan*

Reprinted from *Eighteenth-Century Fiction* 4 (1992): 109–24, by permission of the publisher.

*Wild* and *Amelia*), but it represents the critic's assertion of an authority which, like the narrator's, is open to sceptical scrutiny about the limits of its utility.

Authority is the assertion of a claim to power and, because it is an assertion, it is both the subject and product of interpretation: "it is an attempt to interpret the conditions of power, to give the conditions of control and influence a meaning by defining an image of strength. . . . It is an interpretive process which seeks for itself the solidity of a thing."[4] But the urgency that governs this interpretive assertion often derives from the threat to authority or even from its collapse. In Fielding's case the values he could use in addressing a broader audience seemed uncertain, forcing him both to pretend to authority and to mock that pretence. And the new genre of the novel either required an authoritative statement of generic ancestry or served to undermine literary authority altogether. In *Joseph Andrews* the significant collapse of generic clarity portends broader failure. Three elements of *Joseph Andrews* seem to threaten its claim to narrative authority: the instability of its genre, the unreliability of its narrator, and the ironies of its ending.

## GENERIC INSTABILITY

Fielding's critical pronouncements on the genre of *Joseph Andrews* manifest his authority in several ways: he parodies Richardson to establish authority through contrast; he asserts the realism of his own material and thus the naturalness of his authority; he articulates generic terms that are familiar to readers and verify his authority by reference to tradition. His useful classical precedents lead to overlapping terms. Hence his Preface asserts that his novel is a "comic Romance" (from Scarron's *Roman comique*) that is in turn "a comic Epic-Poem in Prose," and he goes on to analyse these terms, especially "comedy."[5] His classifications seek to place the novel among the familiar and to account for its novelty. The Preface and the introductory chapters to the first three books trace the relationship of his new form to Homer's *Odyssey* and Fénelon's *Télémaque,* to French romance, and to histories and biographies.

But many readers suggest that the Preface is itself inconsistent and does not fit the novel. Michael McKeon observes that Fielding seeks to redefine genre with a "self-serving skepticism," especially regarding the terms "history" and "romance," which he seeks to recombine into different meanings, a pattern to which I shall return as a tactic of reading.[6] Walter Reed explores various senses of "romance" in European literature (senses which Fielding certainly knew); he notes that Fielding's elaborate generic classifications are themselves affectations (hence proper comic subjects) and that the Preface contradicts the text.[7] Fielding's protestation that "I have no Intention to vilify or asperse any one" (Preface, p. 10) is surely violated on the first pages by his attacks on Cibber and Richardson. The assertion is at odds with the novel's failure to remain circumscribed to a fictional world. Likewise, despite the recent claim that Adams "is designed as a universal type,"[8] early readers recognized him as Fielding's friend William Young, and several specific historical characters, perhaps including Fielding himself, appear by way of fictional representation or direct reference.[9] The character of Adams is certainly comic but not based on affectation, vanity, and hypocrisy, and Fielding's description of him as "a Character of perfect Simplicity" recommended by "the Goodness of his Heart" (Preface, p. 10) may seem too simplistic itself.[10]

Fielding's difficulty in asserting the authority of his genre lies both in the ungeneric nature of novels (the intractable form eluding Fielding's efforts to give it authoritative shape) and in the conflicting implications of the works to which he refers for his authority. For example, the title page proclaims that the novel is "Written in Imitation of the Manner of Cervantes, Author of *Don Quixote*." But *Don Quixote* attacks "romance" itself in ways that parallel Fielding's attack on Richardson, and its attack has serious implications for the mixture of genres and structures in *Joseph Andrews*.[11]

The reader becomes engaged by Joseph's love for Fanny as the romantic issue which the novel will resolve. The powerful comic narration and the force of Fielding's surprising movement from mockery of Joseph's chastity to sympathy with his real love give the romantic plot particular urgency for the reader, who is metaphorically making the marriage of Fanny and Joseph possible by reading the novel. The satisfaction that attends the fulfillment of their love, despite the manipulation that brings it about, gives the literal boy-girl plot a nearly mystic function.[12] The apparent authority of the narrator derives in part from his role in providing that comic conclusion.

Pulling against this purposeful romantic plot and the authority it bestows is an open, Cervantic structure that takes the form of a journey and, despite the recurrence of significant topics, includes episodes that make no apparent contribution to the romantic resolution. If Joseph is the hero of the romantic plot, Adams seems the centre of its Cervantic mode. Like Quixote, Adams seems unable to change, and his character shows its ambiguities and shortcomings in the changing contexts of his journey. His progress from London to Booby-Hall is, like the sallies of Don Quixote, built on repetition and variation, rather than on the linear movement of romance. Such a structure may advance primarily local meanings. Unlike the strongly significant romantic plot, it may be indeterminate, as is stunningly shown by the capacity of *Don Quixote* to survive conflicting views of its basic issues.

The Cervantic incidents of *Joseph Andrews* carry much of the novel's satire but establish a fragmentary narrative surface, especially in the central books. The reader's instinct, however, is to feel the romantic plot as a governing structure. The usual response to the most egregious interruptions of the novel, the three interpolated stories (II, iv, vi; III, iii; and IV, x), is to link them to the romantic plot by seeing them as related to thematic concerns, to the behaviour of the central characters, or to the reactions of those who hear them.[13] But such links are nearly impossible for the rapid pattern of minor interruptions. The merging of a romantic plot with an open structure may be a major advance on Cervantes,[14] but it presents a central critical problem because Fielding's various generic signals are only approximate rather than authoritative guides.

Although books I and IV of *Joseph Andrews* emphasize its romantic and parodic elements and books II and III its Cervantic journey, the romantic plot and open structure overlap. The romantic plot is modified by the opening parody of *Pamela* and by the literary artifices of the conclusion. Joseph becomes realistic by escaping from the romantic into the quixotic. His chastity ceases to be an abstract principle inculcated by Adams and exemplified by Pamela; his return to Fanny becomes the goal of his journey (I, xi). But when the lovers are reunited (II, xii) and Adams persuades them to marry properly (II, xiii), the journey's purpose is again redefined, only to be interrupted when the abduction of Fanny reveals the depth of Joseph's feelings (III, xi). Critics have proposed each event as a turning point, but all are stages in bringing the romance plot to its expected conclusion.[15] Moreover, scenes redefining the journey seem occasional (though they recur regularly near the end of each book), and their striking connection with the romance plot reminds readers that much of journey is not thus connected.

Romance in *Joseph Andrews* parodies the novelistic contrivance of *Pamela* and is an aristocratic answer to the Puritan, middle-class myth that confuses virtue with self-interest. But once this romance response is established, it is rendered problematic by its incapacity to meet the needs of ordinary experience (the need for money, for example). But "ordinary experience" is suspect because its demands are often products of arbitrary institutions or unreasonable conventions. Thus each generic shift is destabilized by the next pattern. The genres question at the moment they assert, and the assertion of power repeatedly seems a compensation for incapacity.

Traditional romance establishes characters by stereotypes. Thus the mixed genres of *Joseph Andrews* produce an inconsistency between stereotypical roles and actual behaviour. This gap is a formal equivalent to the distance between affectation and personality that Fielding identifies as central to his comedy. It allows Adams to appear as a comic character without the negative affectations of Mrs Slipslop, Peter Pounce, and Pamela herself. Adams not only acts in a way that is inconsistent with his professed principles, he also falls into inappropriate roles from romance; as a result romance itself is open to question as a dubious social affectation. (Throughout, the conventions by which readers interpret texts are proposed as equivalents to the social conventions satirized by the novel.) The shifting of generic characters also parallels the shifting of narrative voice that I shall shortly discuss, for its presence is often revealed by the disconcerting presence of stereotypical discourse.

The texture of these shifting stereotypes is shown by one of Fanny's infrequent excursions into speech. In book II, chapter x, after Adams has rescued her from violent attack, she is caught in an unusual lie about her affection for Joseph: " 'La! Mr. *Adams,*' said she, 'what is Mr. *Joseph* to me? I am sure I never had anything to say to him, but as one Fellow-Servant might to another.' " Adams accuses her of being dishonest to him or false to Joseph but tells her of Joseph's affection, without further inquiry, for he "never saw farther into People than they desired to let him." The narrator adds several sentences telling how Fanny, hearing of Joseph's misfortune, "immediately set forward in pursuit of One, whom, notwithstanding her shyness to the Parson, she loved with inexpressible Violence, though with the purest and most delicate Passion." The passage shows a quick sequence of readjustments, moving from Fanny's effort to deceive and Adams's failure in perception to the explanation of Fanny's statement by the conflict between her shyness and the violence (though refinement) of her passion. But it shifts again to a sudden consciousness of audience: "This Shyness, therefore, as we trust it will recommend her Character to all our Female Readers, and not greatly surprise such of our Males as are well acquainted with the younger part of the other Sex, we shall not give ourselves any trouble to vindicate." The narrator's intrusion seems designed to tell us that he need not intrude, but since we hope that even an intrusive narrator will supply useful information, we may combine this reference to social practice (which we have learned to regard suspiciously) with our surprise at the Slipslopian archness of Fanny's language to Adams, to conclude that the naturalness of her character does not prevent a significant social artifice (not entirely unbecoming to Pamela's actual sister), but redeemed by her true strength of feeling, much as Adams's naïveté is redeemed by his active goodness.

For much of the novel Fanny appears as the desirable heroine of romance—the worthy reward of Joseph's coming to maturity. Here she has been saved from rape not by the heroics of her lover but by the bravery of the comic parson, indeed the very parson whose sermons have been cited as a source of her lover's chastity. And the incident shows us a realistic Fanny—coy, deceptive, and passionate. Fanny has recognized Adams because he thought of Joseph and "could not refrain sighing forth his Name." The stereotypes of the romantic plot are all askew: Adams, not the hero, rescues Fanny; Adams, not the heroine, sighs out Joseph's name. The action progresses through such shifts among literary and social conventions.

The quixotic patterns of repetition and variation encourage readers to form subjective groupings according to topics. Many groupings are connected with travelling, such as the repetition of inn scenes, of hosts, of Adams's efforts to borrow money, and of debates on the topic of charity. The more such incidents accumulate, the broader seem their implications: for example, the professions (medicine, the church, the law, and innkeeping) function both to make money and to provide necessary human services, but service is repeatedly perverted by the profit motive. Once the reader has elicited this moral (surely early in the novel), it multiplies in its forms and in its impediments to the marriage of Fanny and Joseph. But as parallels extend, they grow complex in their implications and extend beyond the limitations of genre and the patterns of repetition and variation. The conflict of structures, the medley of generic signals, and the interruptions of interpolation, are replicated in narrative shifts that require frequent readjustment of the reader's expectations. *Joseph Andrews* seems not so much an indeterminate novel as a novel of determined instability.

The instability of authority in *Joseph Andrews* may be contrasted with the determination of legal discourse. The fitting analogy between novelistic and legal discourse may be that romantic fictions resemble legal procedures and that realistic ones contrast with them. Because it includes both romantic and realistic modes, *Joseph Andrews* has a dialectic rather than analogical relation to the law. John Bender argues that Fielding's novels parallel a shift in trials from the activist status of a judge who could use them as a devices of inquiry to the role of lawyers not only in cross-examining but organizing and conducting the cases for the prosecution and defence.[16] But legal argument in a trial by jury, whoever makes it, moves from the top downward. The jury is to determine the guilt or innocence of the defendant and must exclude information irrelevant to that determination. The role of detail is to confirm the presupposition that the defendant is innocent or to deny it beyond reasonable doubt.

But in realistic novels the procedure seems reversed. The discoveries made by the reader are not clearly defined but must themselves be discovered, and the text suggests various possibilities, some deliberately misleading. Because romantic plots are highly determined, their pattern is closer to jury deliberations, limited by rules of procedure, by the judge's charge, and by the questions to be answered. Romance resembles the movement of legal argument by defining initially the issues governing its structure. The more realistic and unstable the genre is, the less it resembles this basic process. *Joseph Andrews* is thus legally complex: its authoritative romantic conventions establish the reader's strong expectation that the novel will conclude with the marriage of Joseph and Fanny, but against that expectation it arrays both the uncertainties of interpretation and the dangers that emerge from the random but real world where unhappy endings are more common than happy ones.

Trial by jury assigns the factual determination of guilt or innocence to the jury, whatever the private opinion of the judge might be, and hence the judge's role differs from that of the omniscient narrator. The task of readers is to find out what the narrator already knows, and part of the complexity of *Joseph Andrews* lies in the tension between the narrator's revelations and the author's concealments. That fictions are the creations of authors and that authors overlap with narrators limit the comparability of narrative and judicial roles. These limits pertain even in an epistemology that sees all discourse as mental construct, for the "fiction" of novels differs from the "fiction" of law: judges and narrators, juries and readers know (or construct) evidence in different ways.

## NARRATIVE UNRELIABILITY

Because of the generic instability of *Joseph Andrews,* the narrator is tentative even when his tone is authoritative. At the beginning of book III, he contrasts unreliable historians with authoritative biographers (whom he equates with novelists). Histories supply contradictory testimony, "where Facts being set forth in a different Light, every Reader believes as he pleases, and indeed the more judicious and suspicious very justly esteem the whole as no other that a Romance, in which the Writer hath indulged a happy and fertile Invention" (III, i, pp. 185–86). "Biographers," in contrast, although unreliable on time and place (the only reliable information of historians), speak truly about people and values. This claim of narrative authority overstates the unreliability of historians and conflates historical fact with the subjective but universal truth of fictitious character, but it distinguishes between historical and fictional discourses, a distinction that the term "narrative discourse" overrides. This distinction points to a further one between the reliability and the authority of the narrator. The narrator takes responsibility for the text composed by the author, but given his unreliability, especially in providing generic terms for his novel, he may be particularly authoritative when irony itself implies meaning. The contrast of the artificial romantic plot of *Joseph Andrews* with its random realism is echoed by the shifting voice of a narrator who is both assertively ironic and disarmingly direct.

He frequently shifts from the surface of his story to reveal information needed to understand a character. The present, Fielding implies, is deceptive, and appearances cannot be deciphered without a narrator's privileged information. In the context of the romantic plot, temporal and causal shifts to the past are ambiguous: because they are shifts, they interrupt the forward movement of the plot; in so far as they are causal, they may contribute to the outcome (which actually does require revelations about the past, significantly not supplied by the narrator). We are encouraged by our trust in the narrator to accept such temporal shifts as unobtrusive and helpful. But shifts that reveal relevant information can easily shade into non-causal shifts where the narrator voices opinions not germane to his plot, and narrative shifts are so common in *Joseph Andrews* that we cannot consistently see them as signals to look for indirect meanings. Hence Fielding adopts a self-conscious irony that alerts us to interpretive caution, as in his description of Adams and Fanny in book II, chapter x. He directly states or ironically hints that narrative shifts require alert reading, and we move from feeling that the romantic plot organizes reading to a sense that it is guided by our conversational relation to the narrator.

But sometimes the text shifts laterally away from the central characters or from the direction of the action without the presence of the narrator. Such lateral shifts, lacking a trustworthy explanation and a reliable explainer, leave readers to their own resources and perhaps in some doubt about the relevance of a narrated incident. Usually the narrative surface is stabilized by the presence of a central character, and movements from one character to another as the centre of attention are plainly marked, often, in the central books, by changes in the mode of travelling or, in book IV, by quasi-dramatic entrances or shifts of scene. But at times the silence of the narrator gives lateral shifts the quality of Joycean epiphanies—sudden flashes of ambiguous revelation.

Despite their remoteness from the romantic plot and their questionable relevance to the characters, lateral shifts open the scope of the novel's satire by commenting on recurrent topics. As Ronald Paulson has pointed out, Fielding's satire uses the central characters as touchstones through whom others reveal their hypocrisy.[17] But, as Paulson goes on to note, the consequent interpretive process is complex: the narrator may be silent; the central characters are not strong interpreters; the explanation, as with the host of book II, chapter iii, may come from a character who fails the novel's satiric test. And some incidents, such as the hunters' conversation of book I, chapter xvi, seem completely random. Even when readers understand the significance of such instances, they are aware that, like the characters, they may be wrong. Occasionally such shifts defy efforts to incorporate them into a larger structure. (Robert Alter comments that the story of Leonard and Paul can be made relevant "only by the most determined overinterpretation.")[18]

Readers concerned about shifting and its relation to structural units may welcome the narrator's discussion of "Divisions in Authors" in book II, chapter i. But Philip Stevick shows appropriate frustration that this chapter is "so arch, so puzzlingly ironic, that it leaves quite unclear what Fielding meant to assert."[19] Walter Reed notes the "politicization of the republic of letters" in book II, chapter i, and its "figurative displacement of literary authority into the realm of commercial enterprise."[20] The most distinct moral of Fielding's playful similes is that frequent division slows the pace of reading, so that one will not "miss the seeing some curious Productions of Nature which will be observed by the slower and more accurate Reader." Since the novel's shifts imply that we must think diversely about our reading, Fielding's consciousness of pace leads one to question whether the structure of chapters suggests proper patterns in our thought. The parallels and contrasts framed by Fielding's manipulation of chapters seem to point towards meanings that we do not find. Fielding's narrative frames heighten gaps as well as connections. Chapters enforce patterns of interpretation without necessarily resolving the questions they create. Their manipulated irresolution may confirm our puzzlement.

The novel's tendency to spread beyond the narrator's explanations parallels the quarrel between reading and experience associated with the learned but credulous Parson Adams and is complicated by the fact that Adams, like Don Quixote, is a questionable reader.[21] His constant companion (until book II, chapter xii, where he accidentally throws it into the fire) is the Greek text of Aeschylus, but his treatment of it speaks more highly of his Greek than of his judgment. Careful reading of Aeschylus ought to correct his Pelagian belief in the goodness of human nature. He may be right that books articulate principles that guide individual perceptions, but he does not derive such awareness from his own reading of Aeschylus, whose companionship seems a whimsy. Yet even if we see Adams's position as dubious, we continue to read (and Fielding to write) a book.

The reading debate between Adams and the host in book II, chapter xvii juxtaposes familiar positions: experience is meaningless unless interpreted through the corporate knowledge expressed in print; learning may appreciate aesthetics regardless of content (as in Adams's reading of Homer) or may fail to apply the relevant generalities to experience (as in his reading of Aeschylus). Fielding sets forth a dichotomy only to contradict it: reading without experience is useless; experience without reading is dangerous. The debate reveals the narrowness of both positions, and truth lies in the unity of their partial truths. A proper reaction (as with the narrator's generic distinctions in the Preface) is to recombine the debated terms.

Trust in a benevolent authority and scepticism about an unreliable narrator imply a distinction of terms that modify each other throughout the novel. The variety of discourses achieved in such comic novels as *Joseph Andrews* depends not only on the dialectic between the narrator's voice and those of his characters but also on his capacity to shift according to the material he articulates, in contrast to the efforts of courts and bookkeepers to reduce disparate evidence to a useful single discourse.[22] Such special discourses as legal proceedings and double-entry bookkeeping were efforts to reduce ambiguity and to make unequivocal action possible. The "heteroglossia" of the novel has the opposite effect of heightening ambiguity to complicate discernment and judgment. Just as the looseness and variety of the novel imply the inadequacy of a single genre to organize human experience, a unified and consistent narrative procedure cannot articulate it. One possible explanation of the difference between Fielding the novelist and Fielding the magistrate lies not in his character or personal intentions but in the discourses through which he acted.

The cacophonies among the various languages adopted by the narrator and between the voice of the narrator and those of his characters echo the discordancies between the author's narrative roles and his personal intentions and the disharmonies among the various genres subsumed by the text or proposed as models for its readers. The noisy disorder is not merely random, for the same author is responsible both for the garrulous and shifting narrator and for the material that eludes his strategies of control. The narrator's struggles to control his text further replicate the author's ultimate difficulty in controlling its readers. The novel's resemblance to the Panopticon prison is rather different from that suggested by Bender.[23] While visual transparency allows guards to keep prisoners under surveillance and supervision, such openness also allows prisoners to communicate with one another. The simultaneous dialogues of many voices subvert the transforming purpose of impersonal and physical isolation.

## ENDINGS AND CONCLUSIONS

The openness that permeates the narrator's efforts to erect controlling structures for his fiction and that threatens to render his authority local and tentative is reinforced by the conscious manipulations that make the ending of the novel ambiguous. Fielding has been blamed for the aristocratic idyll that blesses the marriage of Fanny and Joseph by making Boobies of them.[24] But the ending concludes a plot that emphasizes the power of personal affection to engage characters in a world of risk. By the novel's end they have identified protected centres of experience, only to have them disappear. Mr Wilson has withdrawn from London to tend a farm. From that vantage point he is initially sceptical of Adams, Joseph, and Fanny and able to narrate the past from which his scepticism derives. But the "tragic" death of his daughter's dog (III, iv) reminds him that injustice is inescapable. Adams's counsels of Christian stoicism are undercut by his grief at the "death" of his son and by his wife's testimony that he is more caring than his doctrines imply. Indeed, Adams is preeminently the character whose activity derives from his commitment to others. But Joseph himself fails a similar test when the Pedlar who saved Jacky brings the news that Fanny is his sister.

Our discovery that the report of Jacky's death is false surely prepares us for a similar discovery in this case, but the news sets off a conversational sequence on Platonic love that nearly equals the poet-player and Adams-Joseph pairings (III, x–xi) in its elaboration; the Platonic-love conversations frame the "curious night-adventures" (IV, xiv) that are the novel's comic apogee. At the end of book IV, chapter xiii (p. 330), Pamela

> chid her Brother *Joseph* for the Concern which he exprest at discovering a new Sister. She said, if he loved *Fanny* as he ought, with a pure Affection, he had no Reason to lament being related to her.—Upon which Adams began to discourse on *Platonic* Love; whence he made a quick Transition to the Joys in the next World, and concluded with strongly asserting that there was no such thing as Pleasure in this. At which Pamela and her Husband smiled on one another.

The night adventures begin with Didapper pretending to be Joseph and proclaiming to what he thinks is Fanny that they are not siblings and can be lovers; it concludes with the innocent Adams explaining that he does not know whether Fanny is man or woman.

> As soon as *Fanny* was drest, *Joseph* returned to her, and they had a long Conversation together, the Conclusion of which was, that, if they found themselves to be really Brother and Sister, they vowed a perpetual Celibacy, and to live together all their Days, and indulge a *Platonick* Friendship for each other. (IV, xv, p. 335)

"Platonick Friendship" sounds suspiciously like the language of seduction ("vowed . . . to live together . . . and indulge"), even as it yokes Joseph and Fanny directly to Adams's Christian stoicism. Here the readers rather than Pamela and her husband smile. The perpetual celibacy of the lovers denies the force of their sexual passion. Joseph's brief but striking link with the naïveté of Adams on the issue of Platonic friendship makes it difficult to read the novel as an *Erziehungsroman* in which Joseph replaces Adams as moral guide. The evaluation of Adams's Christian stoicism now applies to Joseph's: for all its worthiness, it denies powerful and deeply human passions.

It seems a mistake to read the ending of *Joseph Andrews* simply as an aristocratic cop-out or as an affirmation of providence. The interpretive task imposed by the recombination of apparent opposites is the difficult reconciliation of the harsh real world to the romantic one concocted by the comic artist. "The rhetorical method of *Joseph Andrews* is a negative one—taking away comfortable alternatives rather than offering any really plausible ones."[25] The novel's shifting narrative makes the reader account for the conflicts manifested by its consciously constructed gaps. To argue that the comic artifice of the ending displaces the discordant reality of the middle books is to simplify the complexities of Fielding's art.

A proper understanding of Fielding's outlandishly happy conclusion may depend on a distinction between fiction and truth rather than a distinction between fiction and reality. Because fiction is not measured by the usual criteria of truth, the opposing elements of a fictional contradiction can both be affirmed, and their opposition remains as an implication of meaning. Fictional affirmation can imply statements that avoid the restrictions of ordinary language. A problem of discourse, as the reading debate between Adams and the host shows, is that speakers overstate their cases to make narrow points or to feed their vanity or to put down their antagonists. And individual speakers lack the variety and breadth of perspective that is possible in Fielding's fiction by virtue of its narrative shifts. As a satire of discourse *Joseph Andrews* repeatedly demonstrates the superiority of its own fictionality, which can simultaneously affirm truths and express reservations about them. The openness of the affirmative fictional structure allows conflicting statements to retain their meanings and provides an alternative to the confining tyranny of discourse. If the authority of the narrator derives from his responsibility for the romantic and comic plots, it also derives from his openness to the multiple meanings that undermine the conclusiveness of the ending itself. Ultimately the narrator's authority derives from his failure to be authoritative.

The difficulty of the analogy between novels and history lies in its literalness, in its tendency to deny the fictional nature of one of its terms. Fiction is itself a genre of uncertainty where each of the relationships that it subsumes—between what characters say and what they do, between the narrator's generic claims and his actual material, between the author's intentions and the readers' interpretations—is unstable and open to question. Hence it can be used only tentatively and approximately to locate cultural analogies. Rather than reflecting the connected roles of Fielding as both narrator and magistrate (a connection plausibly argued for *Amelia*),[26] *Joseph Andrews* may emphasize the difference. At the moment when Fielding's narrative authority reflects the need for social control, his parodic discourses proclaim his distrust of the vehicles of control and of the motives of those who seek it.

What makes the failure of narrative authority comfortable is the naturalness and universality of readers. Even if Fielding had not read book III of Hume's *Treatise of Human Nature* (1740), his narrative process shares its sense of moral sentiments, "so rooted in our constitution and temper, that without entirely confounding the human mind by disease or madness, 'tis impossible to extirpate and destroy them."[27] This sense of universal sentiment means that individual readers, however their interpretations differ in detail, share what is important in Fielding's novel (and do not find Joseph and Fanny unattractive or Adams hateful). It allows broad scope for an irony circumscribed by a belief that author and readers share a natural moral feeling—a belief that distributes authority between judicious readers and a judicial author.

*Notes*

1. Martin Battestin, *The Moral Basis of Fielding's Art* (Middletown, CT: Wesleyan University Press, 1959), as well as several articles on *Tom Jones* reprinted in *The Providence of Wit* (Oxford: Clarendon Press, 1974); see also Aubrey J. Williams, "Interpositions of Providence and the Design of Fielding's Novels," *South Atlantic Quarterly* 70 (1971), 265–86.

2. John Bender, *Imagining the Penitentiary: Fiction and the Architecture of Mind in Eighteenth-Century England* (Chicago: University of Chicago Press, 1987), especially pp. 139–98 (the quotations appear on pp. 139 and 140); John Richetti compares the narrative procedure of *Tom Jones* to "the workings of the Hanoverian-Whig oligarchy" in "The Old Order and the New Novel of the Mid-Eighteenth Century: Narrative Authority in Fielding and Smollett," *Eighteenth-Century Fiction* 2 (1990), 190.

3. Bender, p. 160.

4. Richard Sennett, *Authority* (New York: Vintage, 1981), p. 19.

5. Henry Fielding, *Joseph Andrews,* ed. Martin C. Battestin (Middletown, CT: Wesleyan University Press, 1967), p. 4. References are to this edition.

6. Michael McKeon, *The Origins of the English Novel 1600–1740* (Baltimore and London: Johns Hopkins University Press, 1987), pp. 404–5.

7. Walter Reed, *An Exemplary History of the English Novel: The Quixotic versus the Picaresque* (Chicago and London: University of Chicago Press, 1981), pp. 117–23; cf. Sheridan Baker, "Fielding's Epic-in-Prose Romances Again," *Philological Quarterly* 58 (1979), 63–81.

8. David Nokes, *Henry Fielding: Joseph Andrews,* Penguin Critical Studies (Harmondsworth: Penguin Books, 1987), p. 30.

9. Martin C. Battestin, with Ruthe R. Battestin, *Henry Fielding, A Life* (London and New York: Routledge, 1989), pp. 329–36.

10. For a reading of Adams as a character free of affectation, see, for example, J.B. Priestley, *The English Comic Characters* (London: Lane, 1925), pp. 106–27.

11. Discussions of the Cervantic characteristics of *Joseph Andrews* include Leon Gottfried, "The Odyssean Form: An Exploratory Essay," in *Essays on European Literature in Honor of Liselotte Dieckmann,* ed. Peter Uwe Hohendahl, Herbert Lindenberger, and Egon Schwartz (St Louis: Washington University Press, 1972), pp. 19–43; also Stephen Gilman, "On Henry Fielding's Reception of *Don Quijote,*" in *Medieval and Renaissance Studies in Honor of Robert Brian Tate,* ed. Ian Michael and Richard A. Cardwell (Oxford: Dolphin, 1986), pp. 27–38; and Reed, pp. 123–32.

12. See Jeffrey M. Perl, "Anagogic Surfaces: How to Read *Joseph Andrews,*" *The Eighteenth Century—Theory and Interpretation* 22 (1981), 249–70.

13. I.B. Cauthen, Jr, "Fielding's Digressions in *Joseph Andrews,*" *College English* 17 (1956), 379–82; Douglas Brooks, "The Interpolated Tales in *Joseph Andrews* Again," *Modern Philology* 65 (1968), 208–13; J. Paul Hunter, *Occasional Form: Henry Fielding and the Chains of Circumstance* (Baltimore: Johns Hopkins University Press, 1975), p. 152.

14. Reed, p. 130.

15. Dick Taylor, Jr, "Joseph as Hero of *Joseph Andrews,*" *Tulane Studies in English* 7 (1957), 91–109, regards II, xii as the central scene, where Joseph becomes more independent as a character, and Robert Alter sees Joseph's song as recapitulating "the action of the whole novel" (*Fielding and the Nature of the Novel* [Cambridge: Harvard University Press, 1968], p. 105); Joseph's emotional depth in III, xi is the turning point for Dianne Oslund, "Tied Back to Back: The Discourse between the Poet and Player and the Exhortations of Parson Adams in *Joseph Andrews,*" *Journal of Narrative Technique* 12 (1982), 191–200.

16. Bender, pp. 174–80.

17. Ronald Paulson, *Satire and the Novel in Eighteenth-Century England* (New Haven: Yale University Press, 1967), pp. 121–26.

18. Alter, p. 110.

19. Philip Stevick, *The Chapter in Fiction: Theories of Narrative Division* (Syracuse: Syracuse University Press, 1970), p. 25.

20. Reed, p. 134; James Cruise sees the displacement as sinister, in "Fielding, Authority, and the New Commercialism in *Joseph Andrews,*" *ELH* 54 (1987), 268–69.

21. Reed describes Adams as "a Quixote who is deluded by classical literature" and by a "neoclassical culture" (p. 126), but Adams fails to comprehend the potential conflicts between classical texts and his own principles, and hence is never informed by his reading of the classics.

22. "The comic style demands of an author a lively to-and-fro movement in his relation to language, it demands a continual shifting of the distance between author and language, so that first some, then other aspects of language are thrown into relief" (M.M. Bakhtin, *The Dialogic Imagination: Four Essays,* ed. Michael Holquist; trans. Caryl Emerson and Michael Holquist [Austin: University of Texas Press, 1981], p. 302).

23. For Bender "the penitentiary stages impersonal, third-person presence . . . so as to represent actual character and conscience as fictions capable of alteration" (p. 203).

24. This point is intriguingly made by Cruise (pp. 271–72), who finds the ending a narrative compromise undertaken to avoid moral compromise.

25. Hunter, p. 114.

26. Bender, pp. 180–96.

27. David Hume, *A Treatise of Human Nature,* ed. L.A. Selby-Bigge, 2nd edition; revised by P. H. Nidditch (Oxford: Clarendon Press, 1978), p. 474.

# Interpolated tales as Allegories of Reading:
## *Joseph Andrews*

JOSEPH F. BARTOLOMEO

In the opening chapter of Book 2 of *Joseph Andrews,* Fielding's narrator compares his chapter headings to "so many Inscriptions over the Gates of Inns . . .
informing the Reader what Entertainment he is to expect, which if he likes
not, he may travel on to the next."[1] To extend the metaphor, one could add
that few accommodations have proven less hospitable to wary and sometimes
wearied travellers through the text than the three interpolated tales: a "well
bred" (p. 102) young woman's history of Leonora, who abandons a worthy
fiancé for a fortune-hunting fop and loses both; Mr. Wilson's memoir of
degradation as a London rake and reformation as a married rustic; and young
Dick Adams's aborted story of a politic friend whose efforts to appease a
quarreling couple turn both husband and wife against him. These interruptive stories have long been maligned as superfluous or at best marginally relevant digressions, and an initial reading establishes their manifest inferiority—
in plot, style, and narrative voice—to the larger narrative in which they are
imbedded. Defenders have established various kinds of thematic significance
for the tales, regarding them as exempla of vanity and hypocrisy, vices identified in the preface as objects for ridicule,[2] as satiric, patently ironic revisions
of *Don Quixote,* Fielding's professed model,[3] or as implicit commentaries on
the courtship and marriage plots in the novel.[4] Others posit a dialogic relationship between the tales—as self-consciously "literary" artifacts—and the
disorderly world of immediacy in the novel proper.[5]

On a more broadly conceived epistemological level, J. Paul Hunter reads
the tales as models of the simplistic narrative and rhetorical conventions common to Fielding's contemporaries, with which the author implicitly contrasts
his own sophistication.[6] Hunter's interpretation rests on difference, and the
differences are undeniable, but I would argue that the similarities are more
significant, that the tales actually serve a paradigmatic function within a text

*Studies in the Novel,* vol. 23 (1991). Copyright by the University of North Texas in 1991. Reprinted
by permission of the publisher.

that purports to define, in both theory and practice, a new genre. All three foreground the complex, often problematic dynamics of presentation and reception, of writing and reading, inherent in prose fiction in general and in *Joseph Andrews* in particular. Through narrative compression they bring into sharp relief issues of authority, reliability, control, closure, misreading, and indeterminacy, concerns that continue to engage readers of this self-consciously experimental, initiatory novel.

Early novelists faced no problem more vexing than establishing authority for their texts in light of the commonly-accepted superiority of "truth," or at least fact, over fiction. The epistemological struggle over what Michael McKeon calls "questions of truth"[7] resulted in attempts to relate fiction *to* fact, to inform fiction *with* fact, and to disguise fiction *as* fact. Each of the narrators of the tales reflects a different, and ultimately deficient strategy for inscribing "truthfulness" on a narrative. The well-bred lady grounds the story of Leonora in the informed hearsay of an earwitness acquainted with the characters involved. She is prompted to tell the story when she passes Leonora's house, and in her concluding discussion of the fate of the rejected suitor Horatio, she uses the telling phrases "I hear" and "they say" (p. 129). Both the story itself and the manner of telling it, however, subvert the reportorial pose. Claims to documentary truth are rendered transparent by the romance-derived names of the characters and the stilted language they share with the narrator—language so different from that of the novel itself, as the opening of a letter to Leonora from her suitor Horatio illustrates: "How vain, most adorable Creature, is the Pursuit of Pleasure in the absence of an Object to which the Mind is entirely devoted, unless it have some Relation to that Object" (p. 105). The narrator's having "got by heart" (p. 105) several additional paragraphs of such inane sentiments, coupled with her ability to venture into characters' minds, reinforces the artificiality of her account. Even before the story occurs, Fielding's narrator suggests the dubious reliability of such reportage through a sarcastic conclusion about the probable complicity of a constable in the escape of a felon: "But notwithstanding these and many other such Allegations, I am sufficiently convinced of his Innocence; having been positively assured of it, by those who received their Informations from his own Mouth; which, in the Opinion of some Moderns, is the best and indeed only Evidence" (pp. 71–72). In the case of "The Unfortunate Jilt," whatever authority readers might impute to the narrator derives not from her historical veracity but from her frequently-mentioned good breeding, exhibited in her indulgent smiles at Parson Adams's frequent and often silly questions and her refusal to descend to the condemnatory invective of the prudish Miss Grave-airs, who peremptorily declares near the beginning of Leonora's story, "I never knew any of these forward Sluts come to good . . . nor shall I wonder at any thing she doth in the Sequel" (p. 104). Not coincidentally, both obvious breeding and bemused tolerance of absurdity have long been considered salient characteristics of the narrator of *Joseph Andrews* as well.

Mr. Wilson's narrative, like other first-person accounts, insulates the narrator from the necessity of providing a source for his facts, but his assessment and interpretation of those facts cast some doubt on his absolute reliability. Despite his habitual condemnation of his past conduct, Wilson often shades his own disreputable actions—particularly his selfish relationships with women—from the harshest interpretive light. After describing how an innocent woman he seduced became corrupted further by the town, and eventually stole his money and left him, he admits shamefully enough that he "had been the first Aggressor, and had done her an Injury for which I could make her no Reparation, by robbing her of the Innocence of her Mind" (p. 208), but concludes by focussing on the fate and faults of the woman: "I had been perfectly constant to this Girl, during the whole Time I kept her: But she had scarce departed before I discovered more Marks of her Infidelity to me, than the Loss of my Money" (p. 208). Deflecting attention and blame elsewhere and emphasizing his own victimization allow Wilson to mitigate his acknowledged faults.[8] As he recounts his next affair, an unconsummated one with a married coquette who initially encourages but ultimately rebuffs his advances, he recalls becoming convinced that "her Husband had the sole Possession of her Person, and that neither he nor any other had made any Impression on her Heart" (p. 210). With a straight face, completely oblivious to any irony in the statement, he simply moves on to recall his next affair, with the "Wife of a Citizen" (p. 211). Acknowledging that her husband loved her, he hastens to assure Adams that "it is a great Satisfaction to me that I was not the Man who first seduced her Affections from him" (p. 211). After they are discovered, Wilson is sued by the husband, comes to live with the now-divorced woman, and soon becomes disenchanted with her. The language with which the memoirist describes the conclusion of the affair captures both his desire to appear noble and long-suffering and his penchant for objectifying women: "At length Death delivered me from an Inconvenience, which the Consideration of my having been the Author of her Misfortunes, would never suffer me to take any other Method of discarding" (p. 211). Exculpatory remarks like these underscore a difficulty inherent in first-person narration: a lack of the distance required for reliable evaluation. Throughout the novel, characters like Lady Booby, Mrs. Slipslop, and the corrupt clergymen go even further than Wilson in rationalizing their conduct: were any of them to tell the story, it might resemble the largely first-person narrative that *Joseph Andrews* attacks for its self-serving casuistry, Richardson's *Pamela*. In his next novel, Fielding continues to exploit unreliable first-person narration, but now for more obviously thematic purposes. The two long digressive stories in *Tom Jones* are told by characters considerably less admirable than the reformed Wilson to auditors less naive than Adams. Tom rejects, in word and deed, the Man of the Hill's misanthropic conclusions, and Sophia rightly questions Mrs. Fitzpatrick's veracity. Acute interpretation of the skewed memoirs of characters whose experiences parallel their own, and therefore might normally encourage sympathy, reinforces the fundamental worthiness of the hero and heroine.

For Dick Adams, authority resides in the printed text from which he reads, making him truly his father's son. Parson Adams, who ignores Lady Booby's commands and repeatedly interrupts Dick to correct his errors, is "silenc'd by Authority" (p. 316) only when the boy defends a passage Adams considers "Nonsense" with the rejoinder, "It is so in the Book" (p. 316). Given his preference for books over experience, his belief that books are "the only way of travelling by which any Knowledge is to be acquired" (p. 182), it is hardly surprising that Adams epitomizes what McKeon terms "naive empiricism,"[9] an uncritical acceptance of the truth of any written record. While few empiricists were as naive as Adams, this impulse helps account for novelists' familiar practice of claiming merely to be editing a newly-discovered manuscript, a ruse satirized in the mock-praise of the author of *Pamela* as "an Historian who borrows his Lights, as the common Method is, from authentic Papers and Records" (p. 18).

The pursuit of narrative authority in the three tales, however crudely represented, anatomizes Fielding's own practice. His rhetorical maneuvering to endow his text with various kinds and levels of truthfulness leads him to adopt different and often contradictory poses. Prefatorial comments reveal a proudly self-conscious creator of the admittedly fictional "comic Epic-Poem in Prose" (p. 4) and a "biographer" who scorns representation of the particular in favor of describing "not Men, but Manners; not an Individual, but a Species" (p. 189). At other points, the same narrator adopts the roles both of the conventional historian, who makes fruitless inquiries into Joseph Andrews's ancestry, Slipslop's reasons for dismissing Fanny, or Adams's dinner menu at the Tow-Wouses' inn, and of the intimate friend to whom Joseph and Fanny shyly refuse to relate "a most delightful Conversation" (p. 168) that they had at an inn, and to whom Mr. Wilson writes, at the end of the novel, with the news that Fanny is pregnant. While the latter personae undoubtedly provide what McKeon calls "the parodic and self-subversive deployment of the claim to historicity,"[10] their uneasy coexistence with more "authorial" voices suggests an author wrestling with the difficulties surrounding narrative authority and belief that are schematized more emphatically in the individual tales.

Issues of manipulation and control, of the selection, omission, and timing of information, also connect the tales to the novel. Faced with the exigencies of a present, live audience and external events, the narrators of the tales find their control circumscribed and provisional. Extremely sensitive to the demands of her listeners, the young woman who tells Leonora's tale not only provides the details that Adams continually requests, but actually abides by a vote among her audience as to whether or not she should include the love-letters between Leonora and Horatio. Her party's arrival at an inn puts a temporary halt to her story, and she resumes it only after Slipslop requests her to do so. Mr. Wilson carries his indulgence to Adams even further: after making statements like "I will here desist" (p. 207) or "Now I made some Remarks, which probably are too obvious to be worth relating" (p. 214), he quickly reverses himself when Adams objects. His pliability suggests a lack of confidence about how to tell his own story, which is confirmed in his concluding statement to Adams: "Thus, Sir . . . I have finished my Story, in which if I have been too particular, I ask your Pardon" (p. 225). The irony seems more at Wilson's expense than at his instigation. A reader rather than a teller, Dick Adams can neither choose the details of his story nor prevent it from being interrupted, not by one of many leisurely stops at an inn, but by events that precipitate the climax of the novel, guaranteeing that the far less significant story of Leonard and Paul will remain unfinished. Yet the unknown original narrator of "The History of Two Friends," available only through the printed text, can and does decide when to elaborate and when not "to detain the Reader with minute Circumstances" (p. 316).

Language of choice and deliberation relates this narrator most directly to Fielding's, who frequently calls attention to his passing over details which "would not be very entertaining to the Reader" (pp. 159–60), not to mention his withholding of information—from characteristics of Slipslop and the "roasting" squire to Joseph's attraction to Fanny and ultimately to Joseph's true parentage—until the proper time. The key distinction between the confident narrator and the diffident teller derives from the different conditions surrounding writing and speech. Writers always remain absent from their audience, and absence confers an obvious degree of power to determine the shape and to regulate the pace of a text.

Readers confronting a completed text by an absent author retain considerable powers of their own, of course, the most basic of which is to stop reading and thus to leave the text as unrealized as the story of Leonard and Paul. Less drastically, reading also involves both voluntary and involuntary interruptions, figured in *Joseph Andrews* by the way in which the tales impede the progress of the main narrative and are themselves impeded by events or characters from that narrative. While few readers would imitate Adams, the arch-bibliophile who nonetheless hurls his beloved Aeschylus into the fire and runs for help when Fanny faints, we inevitably yield to the more mundane constraints of time and tired eyes. And unlike Adams, we also consciously choose to stop reading in order to evaluate, to question, and to reread. From the other side, many novelists anticipate and attempt to regulate interruptions by dividing their novels into books and chapters. In the famous discussion of this process in *Joseph Andrews,* Fielding extends the metaphor of the inn, with which I began, in order to address specifically the reader's role:

in this, as well as all other Instances, we consult the Advantage of our Reader, not our own; and indeed many notable Uses arise to him from this Method: for first, those little Spaces between our Chapters may be looked upon as an Inn or

> Resting-Place, where he may stop and take a Glass, or any other Refreshment, as it pleases him . . . As to those vacant Pages which are placed between our Books, they are to be regarded as those Stages, where, in long Journeys, the Traveller stays some time to repose himself, and consider of what he hath seen in the Parts he hath already past through: a Consideration which I take the Liberty to recommend a little to the Reader. (pp. 89–90)

Without commenting directly on this advice, Wolfgang Iser seems to use it as a point of departure, advising the reader to write in the margins, to help construct for himself the proper balance between the two unmediated poles represented in the text: naive virtue, as embodied in Adams, and cynical worldliness, as demonstrated by most of the characters with whom he interacts.[11] Yet for Iser and any reader-response critic, partnership in the configuration of meaning requires not only regular, programmed interruptions provided by the author, but also countless spontaneous interruptions initiated by the reader.

The preceding phrase is especially problematic in the context of this discussion, however, since the tales help to deconstruct the notion of a single, normative implied reader by illustrating diverse responses determined by character, circumstances, and acuity. At the most literal level, Dick Adams's faulty pronunciation—"Leo-nard" (p. 315) for Leonard and "East Indi-es" (p. 315) for East Indies—reveals misreading based on simple ignorance. A more elaborate pattern emerges in the idiosyncratic and quite conflicting reactions to the news that Leonora affected indignation at Horatio's initial declaration of passion and that he took her seriously:

> "More Fool he," cried *Slipslop*, "it is a sign he knew very little of our *Sect*." "Truly, Madam," said *Adams*, "I think you are in the right, I should have insisted to know a piece of her Mind, when I had carried matters so far." But Miss *Grave-airs* desired the Lady to omit all such fulsome Stuff in her Story: for that it made her sick. (p. 105)

All three continue to respond characteristically when told of Leonora's surprise at being discovered flirting with her new suitor, Bellarmine, by Horatio:

> "Poor Woman," says Mrs. *Slipslop*, "what a terrible *Quandary* she must be in!" "Not at all," says Miss *Grave-airs*, "such Sluts can never be confounded." "She must have then more than *Corinthian* Assurance," said *Adams*; "ay, more than *Lais* herself." (p. 113)

Although these responses have been correctly characterized as simplistic ones that "combine total subjectivity and conventional knee-jerk,"[12] they nonetheless illustrate the inevitability of variety in interpretation. In the principal narrative, Fielding wittily anticipates similar diversity, counterbalancing numerous references to "the" reader with divisions of the audience based on gender, intelligence, and personality. He acknowledges, among others, "sagacious" (pp. 36, 48), "good-natur'd" (pp. 10,324), "curious" (p. 20), "fine" (p. 89), and "heroick" (p. 238) readers, suggests that male and female readers might respond to Fanny's shyness differently, and predicts that "some few Readers" will find Adams's immediate disregard of his own advocacy of stoicism on learning of the apparent death of his son "very low, absurd, and unnatural" (p. 306). Through these divisions, as Hunter has observed, Fielding "both comprehends and excludes every real reader: we share and we opt out, and in no pattern that can be generalized for everyone."[13]

The text itself, moreover, is replete with characters who "read" other characters and events differently, based on their temperaments and preoccupations. And varied responses often demarcate levels of moral worth, nowhere more notably than in the reaction of several stagecoach passengers to the sight of the naked, beaten Joseph:

> The Postillion hearing a Man's Groans, stopt his Horses, and told the Coachman, "he was certain there was a *dead* Man lying in the Ditch, for he heard him groan." "Go on, Sirrah," says the Coachman, "we are confounded late, and have no time to look after dead Men." A Lady, who heard what the Postillion said, and likewise heard the Groan, called eagerly to the Coachman, "to stop and see what was the matter." Upon which he bid the Postillion "alight, and look into the Ditch." He did so, and returned, "that there was a Man sitting upright as naked as ever he was born."—"O *J-sus!*" cry'd the Lady, "A naked Man! Dear Coachman, drive on and leave him." Upon this the Gentlemen got out of the Coach; and *Joseph* begged them, "to have Mercy upon him: For that he had been robbed, and almost beaten to death." "Robbed," cries an old Gentleman; "Let us make all the haste imaginable, or we shall be robbed too." A young Man, who belonged to the Law answered, "he wished they had past by without taking any Notice: But that now they might be proved to have been *last in his Company;* if he should die, they might be called to some account for his Murther. He therefore thought it adviseable to save the poor Creature's Life, for their own sakes, if possible; at least, if he died, to prevent the Jury's finding *that they fled for it.*" (p. 52)

Here interpretation and morality merge: good reading is tantamount to "good-natured" reading, and the very absence of this quality in the passengers encourages its presence in readers of the novel, who can assume the role of the Good Samaritan at one safe but satisfying remove.[14]

Within the tales, the responses that matter most, and not only because they arise so frequently and intrusively, belong of course to Adams, a "circumstantial Teller of a Story" (p. 201) whose conduct ensures that others will follow his example. This self-styled wise interpreter repeatedly struts his classical learning and superior judgment, only to reveal amusing shortcomings. Searching frantically for his sermon on vanity, he responds to Wilson's assurance that he is cured of the passion by insisting that "for that very Reason . . .

I would read it, for I am confident you would admire it: Indeed, I have never been a greater Enemy to any Passion than that silly one of Vanity" (p. 214). Wilson merely smiles, but readers need not be so polite. Adams' pretensions are further deflated when his naiveté leads him to obvious misreadings. When Wilson recalls being confined for a month by his surgeon after escapades at Covent Garden, Adams replies, "I think . . . the Advice of a Month's Retirement and Reflection was very proper; but I should rather have expected it from a Divine than a Surgeon" (p. 206). And at Wilson's description of his arrest for debt by his tailor, Adams confidently observes that "this could not last long . . . for doubtless the Taylor released you the moment he was truly acquainted with your Affairs; and knew that your Circumstances would not permit you to pay him" (p. 219). In both instances, misinterpretation results from an innocence of the world that prompts condescending laughs from most readers, whose worldliness the elegant narrator both acknowledges and fosters. But as Iser aptly observes, a feeling of superiority to the foolish but virtuous Adams aligns readers with the "sophisticated" and seldom virtuous characters opposed to Adams, thereby entangling us in an internal moral and epistemological conflict.[15] Since Adams's follies never extend to fundamental moral judgments, the inarticulate groans with which he greets the news of Leonora's faithlessness, groans which the rest of the immediate audience purposely ignores, mark him as an uncompromising moralist whom readers, however compromised, cannot afford to dismiss.[16]

What allies Adams to readers of every stripe is the insatiable curiosity that prompts his countless questions. Many of his requests merely anticipate details that the tellers would surely have provided, such as the names of Horatio or Wilson. With others, though, it can be difficult to imagine, while suspending one's sense of the completed text, how much might have been revealed without his prodding. Would the young woman have described Bellarmine's wardrobe as "a Cut-Velvet Coat of a Cinnamon Colour, lined with a Pink Satten, embroidered all over with Gold" (p. 108) and a "Waistcoat, which was Cloth of Silver" (p. 108), a description that undeniably enhances our sense of his foppery? Wilson directly states his intention not to detail the results of his seduction of an innocent young woman, but Adams's insistence results in an effective if melodramatic portrait of the consequences of vice, analogous in many respects to Hogarth's "Harlot's Progress." The lack of such direct powers of compulsion, however, actually confers an advantage on readers of *Joseph Andrews,* who can use their imaginations, sharpened through encounters with Fielding's, to invent details that the narrator withholds, from the ending of the story of Leonard and Paul—should anyone be interested enough to bother[17]—to the substance of that intimate conversation between Joseph and Fanny. Adams, too, is deprived of a conclusion, when he allows Joseph to take his place in the coach and misses the end of Leonora's story, but Fielding's narrative demands place Adams under temporal and imaginative constraints with which no reader is burdened.

Fielding acknowledges the desire for information which we share with Adams by frequently calling attention to his manner of piquing, maintaining, and eventually satisfying his audience's curiosity. Several chapters conclude with language promising "to indulge the Curiosity of my Reader, who is no doubt impatient to know what he will find in the subsequent Chapters of this Book" (p. 92). Motives, moreover, are often revealed after actions: for example, the narrator discloses Joseph's love for Fanny as an explanation for his hasty departure from London and uses the occasion to generalize tellingly on his practice:

> It is an Observation sometimes made, that to indicate our Idea of a simple Fellow, we say, *He is easily to be seen through:* Nor do I believe it a more improper Denotation of a simple Book. Instead of applying this to any particular Performance, we chuse rather to remark the contrary in this History, where the Scene opens itself by small degrees, and he is a sagacious Reader who can see two Chapters before him. (p. 48)

Finally, the story is repeatedly interrupted at significant points with digressions, such as the parallel dialogues between the poet and the player and between Adams and Joseph that occur immediately after Fanny's abduction. Between the two dialogues, the narrator drops a tantalizing hint about an "Accident; which, if the Reader is impatient to know, he must skip over the next Chapter, which . . . contains some of the best and gravest Matters in the whole Book" (p. 264). Even more prominent as digressions, of course, are the three tales themselves, which we may read with impatience or ignore with risk.

An affinity between Adams and the reader extends to the minutest level of interpretation, defining individual words. A self-regarded authority on denotative reference, Adams must nevertheless ask Wilson for the contextual significance both of the phrase *"tied up"* (p. 215) in regard to literary patronage, and of a perplexing imported term: "Pray, Sir . . . What is a Coquette? I have met with the Word in *French* Authors, but never could assign any Idea to it. I believe it is the same with *une Sotte,* Anglicé *a Fool*" (p. 209). We cannot request definitions, but Fielding offers us helpful glosses of specialized terms like *"ride and tie"* (p. 94), a *"Whipper-in"* (p. 21), and *"Bird-batting"* (p. 141), and he also exploits multiple meanings for humorous and serious ends. A litigious guest, having heard that Adams initiated a fight with an innkeeper, suggests that the latter could *recover.* The innkeeper's response: "Recover! Master . . . Yes, yes, I am not afraid of dying with a Blow or two neither; I am not such a Chicken as that" (p. 121). More significantly, the selfish incipient capitalist Peter Pounce and Adams debate their different notions of the central moral concept of the novel, charity. Adams's Christian, benevolistic definition echoes one given earlier by Joseph, but, with characteristic irony, unheard by Adams, who "was fast asleep" (p. 235) at the time! From arcane usages to philosophical abstractions, Fielding's practice—and Adams's—underscore the importance, difficulty, and individuality of every interpretive act.

Adams's hermeneutic adventures and misadventures complement the unconventional heroism of his often foolish but always well-meaning behavior. His actions and reactions during the telling of the tales magnify stages within the interpretive process, in the same way as the telling itself magnifies dimensions of the writing process. By reducing writing and reading to their crudest, most elemental forms, Fielding alerts us both to the formal challenges faced by a pioneering novelist and to the stakes in and obstacles to good reading, within a novel which we must read actively and collaboratively. Confronted with a narrator who veers between sincerity and irony and whose reliability remains problematic, and a text continually offering conflicting interpretations of character and circumstance, we can incorporate the epistemological lessons of the tales in shaping and constantly questioning our responses. As instructive and sometimes amusing allegories of reading, the tales unmistakably endorse the sentiment with which the novel opens: "It is a trite but true Observation, that Examples work more forcibly on the Mind than Precepts" (p. 17).

*Notes*

1. Henry Fielding, *Joseph Andrews,* ed. Martin C. Battestin (Middletown, CT: Wesleyan Univ. Press, 1967), p. 90. All further references to this work appear parenthetically in the text.

2. See I. B. Cauthen, "Fielding's Digressions in *Joseph Andrews,*" *College English* 17 (1956):379–82. In Cauthen's view, Leonora, Leonard, and Leonard's wife embody vanity, Bellarmine and Paul hypocrisy, and the unregenerate Wilson both. In *The Moral Basis of Fielding's Art* (Middletown, CT: Wesleyan Univ. Press, 1959). Martin Battestin largely dismisses the first and last tales, but regards Wilson's story as an essential reflection on the worldly vanity that Joseph, with the help of Adams, has escaped (pp. 122–29).

3. See Homer Goldberg, "The Interpolated Stories in *Joseph Andrews* or 'The History of the World in General' Satirically Revised," *Modern Philology* 63 (1966): 295–310.

4. Goldberg contrasts the largely negative perspective on love and marriage in the tales with the celebrated love between Joseph and Fanny (p. 307), and Douglas Brooks, in "The Interpolated Tales in *Joseph Andrews* Again," *Modern Philology* 65 (1968): 208–13, sees the initial comparisons between the Leonora/Bellarmine affair and the Fanny/Joseph affair, and between Leonard's relationship with his wife and Parson Adams's with his, resolve into more significant contrasts.

5. See Robert Alter, *Fielding and the Nature of the Novel* (Cambridge, MA: Harvard Univ. Press, 1968), pp. 108–12, and Bryan Burns, "The Story-telling in *Joseph Andrews,*" in *Henry Fielding: Justice Observed,* ed. K. G. Simpson (Totowa, NJ: Barnes and Noble, 1985), pp. 119–36. Building on Alter's notion of the "contrasting textures" (p. 112) of the tales and the novel, Burns reads the tales as interruptive devices by which Fielding attempts to distance his readers from the incidents of the story in order to "encourage us teasingly to reconsider the implications of what we have seen, and the moral position of the work as a whole" (p. 127).

6. J. Paul Hunter, *Occasional Form: Henry Fielding and the Chains of Circumstance* (Baltimore, MD: Johns Hopkins Univ. Press, 1975), pp. 151–61.

7. Michael McKeon, *The Origins of the English Novel 1600–1740* (Baltimore, MD: Johns Hopkins Univ. Press, 1987), p. 20.

8. Wilson's status as a moral exemplar has already been questioned by Hunter, on the ground that he tells his story "with a relish that, in the liveliest parts, raises troubling questions about the relationship between repentance and nostalgia" (p. 152).

9. McKeon, pp. 21, 47–64.

10. McKeon, p. 405.

11. Wolfgang Iser, *The Implied Reader: Patterns of Communication in Prose Fiction from Bunyan to Beckett* (Baltimore, MD: Johns Hopkins Univ. Press, 1974), pp. 31–46.

12. Hunter, p. 159.

13. Hunter, p. 164.

14. The extent to which Fielding deludes the reader into believing that such benevolence is the result of his own reflection, while it in fact derives from rhetorical manipulations by the author, is a central concern in a recent essay by Nicholas Hudson. See "Fielding's Hierarchy of Dialogue: 'Meta-Response' and the Reader of *Tom Jones*," *Philological Quarterly* 68 (1990):177–94.

15. Iser, pp. 43–44.

16. In Hunter's view, the women who ignore his groans are "responders-within who . . . partly stand for us" (p. 158); following Iser, I would approach their supposed sophistication more warily.

17. According to Douglas Patey, the "story breaks because by now Fielding expects us, his readers, to have a sufficiently trained judgment to complete it for ourselves." See *Probability and Literary Form* (Cambridge: Cambridge Univ. Press, 1984), p. 204.

# Exemplarity and Excess in Fielding's Fiction

JONATHAN LAMB

> For precept must be upon precept, precept upon precept; line upon line, line
> upon line; here a little, and there a little.
>
> —Isaiah 28:10

Fielding's novels are full of scenes of failed instruction, of preceptors handing out maxims of self-control so unpersuasive that they fail even themselves to be convinced by them. This is Fielding's justification for writing fiction, for if precepts will not work, then examples might. He begins *Joseph Andrews* with the "trite but true Observation, that Examples work more forcibly on the Mind than Precepts."[1] In the dedication of *Tom Jones* he defines *example* as a "kind of picture, in which virtue becomes as it were an object of sight."[2] However, there are difficulties in substituting examples for precepts if the former are deployed (as they inevitably are in Fielding's novels) in the vicinity of preceptors who insist on reciting maxims of prudence and self-government that they do not care to follow. Rather than the smooth encounter of the probable fable with the decisive moral implied in Fielding's trite observation, a set of self-contradictions is spawned from what is itself a self-contradictory proposition: a precept in contempt of precepts. Such opposition between the mode of fiction and its point, exacerbated by scenes in which the drift is at odds with the professions of the teachers represented in them, pushes examples into uneconomic excess as much as it threatens precepts with irrelevance.

The problem of examples that will not redeem the rules they are designed to recommend is made more acute in Fielding's case by the many strong analogies between fictional and legal exemplarity that bind his duties as novelist to his job as magistrate. Poetic justice and real justice alike are served by examples sufficiently probable to justify the imposition of certain

Reprinted from *Eighteenth-Century Fiction* 1 (1989): 187–207, by permission of the publisher.

prescriptions. Fielding's search for a moral economy in the art of verisimilitude is closely matched by his search in the realm of penology for punishments that might perfectly exemplify the law and win the people to obey it. In tracing the difficulties he faced in these two related fields of fiction and law, I want to suggest that two texts mark the boundaries of his efforts to arrive at a theoretical solution to them—*Of the Remedy of Affliction for the Loss of our Friends* (1743) and *An Enquiry into the Causes of the late Increase of Robbers* (1751). I want also to show how his unsuccessful efforts to locate efficacious precepts in probable examples foster a kind of excess that repels and fascinates him, and that this excess constitutes the sublime in Fielding's writing. Finally, I mean to suggest that this joint-problematic is marked by three closely tied substitutions: excess for economy, possibility for probability, and particularity for universality.[3]

A favourite device of Fielding's is to reserve the swollen language of the mock sublime for the sentiments of his hypocrites—characters who pretend to exemplify certain impregnable attitudes. We are told of the "ineffable, incomprehensible Majesty" to which the Man of the Hill has devoted his high, important, and glorious studies (p. 431) and of the "vast elevation of thought, in purity approaching to angelic perfection" informing Captain Blifil's views of charity (p. 101). Having already decided that the Longinian sublime is bombast,[4] that is to say a waste of words and feelings inimical to the economy of exemplary writing, Fielding adapts it as the perfect signature of hypocrites, who never intend their expressions of concern, love, grief, and so on to come within the purview of practical altruism. The supererogations of heroic tragedy can be heard in Lady Booby's tormented reflections on love ("I will have those pitiful Charms which now I despise, mangled in my sight," p. 327) and in Miss Mathews's paean of vengeance: "Murder! Oh! 'tis Music in my Ears."[5]

Unfortunately, this manageable and satirizable excess is not the exclusive province of bad or weak characters. Mr Allworthy's maladministration of the law is notorious; subtler and more telling is his urging of the precept of forgiveness with so much energy that he disobeys it in proclaiming it: "He expressed, indeed, so much resentment against an unforgiving temper, that the captain at last pretended to be convinced by his arguments" (p. 85). This is the sort of embarrassing conflict associated with hypocrites like Square, who bites his tongue and curses with impatience half-way through a sentence on the contemptibility of pain; or Bridget Allworthy, who discourses in high terms against curiosity after listening at a keyhole (pp. 204, 71). The discovery that Allworthy can be equally immoderate and disobedient alerts the reader to the vulnerability of his preceptual set-pieces, such as his speech to Jenny Jones on sexual appetite or his reflections of the torment of a murdered conscience, neither of which is ever exemplified in the behaviour of the characters.

The collisions between rule and practice are even more pronounced in *Joseph Andrews*. In the twinned scenes of consolation, Adams's lessons of patience first of all fail to teach Joseph to reconcile himself to the ravishment of Fanny; then they fail to subdue the passions of the preceptor himself when it seems his son has drowned and they are recited back to him by his pupil. Adams takes this problem of preceptual improbability even further in his dialogue with the Roman Catholic priest. After exchanging the standard commonplaces on the contempt of riches, the priest asks Adams to lend him one and sixpence. Adams is unable to oblige because his half guinea has been stolen from him in the previous adventure; so he complains, "Was ever any thing so unlucky? because I have no Money in my Pocket, I shall be suspected to be no Christian" (p. 254). In other words his professed scorn for gold is credible only if he has some; yet gold in his pocket would render his professions meaningless. He seems poised on an intuition of the inevitable non-coincidence of certain actions with certain propositions, such as Fielding's own depreciation of precepts in a precept or Allworthy's resentment of resentment. Adams shows that an example is never quite continuous with a precept, even in cases where there is neither a deficiency of the will nor an intention to deceive. Captain Blifil's sublime of sententious excess, or Lady Booby's of tragic exclamation, is consistent with this pattern of absent or contradictory examples in so far as it arises from a disproportion between what is said and what is done. Furthermore, a destructive reflexivity that restricts exemplification to the self-contradictory instance (being resentful about resentment, say) seems to characterize this excess.

In *Amelia* the failure of precepts to coincide with practice shapes two of the great occasions of the novel. In Dr Harrison's conversation with the nobleman the irrelevance of classical maxims of government to the business of the modern British state is shown to be complete; and all that Harrison can hope from its citizens is enough hypocrisy to *pretend* they understand and believe the language of honour and honesty (pp. 460–61). Before this dialogue, Harrison's letter on the sin of adultery has been read out to an amused crowd at the masquerade, a rendezvous for the discourse of moral improvement as thoroughly inappropriate as those mentioned by Swift in *A Tale of a Tub*.[6] With the world at large oblivious to the laws of religion and moral integrity, it is no surprise to find characters in this novel unsustained by the precepts Harrison sets such store by. Like Adams, Harrison believes consolation to be the greatest challenge to Christian doctrine and, if it works, the greatest benefit that can be conferred on suffering humanity. He evolves a notion of jesting comfort, and tries to practise it when consoling the Booths for the loss of Amelia's fortune; but Miss Mathews tartly observes, "These are very pretty Things to read . . . but the Loss of Fortune is a serious Matter; and I am sure a Man of Mr Booth's Understanding must think so" (p. 140). She is quite right, for in a subsequent discussion of the usefulness of consolation for people mourning lost lovers and friends Booth puts the great sceptical question: "Do you really think, that any Meditations on the Shortness of Life will soothe their Afflictions? Is not this very Shortness itself one of their Afflictions?" (p. 350). Here is another case of destructive reflexivity—the terms of consolation being identical with those of the problem it is designed to remove—already exemplified in *Joseph Andrews,* where Adams and Joseph have tormented each other with emollient advice.

## JOBS IN PETTICOATS

Is my strength the strength of stones?

Job 6:12

At these moments of exemplary preceptual failure, when rules of conduct (and even language itself) cease to be adequate to experience, a space opens up in the novel which dialogue and narrative can no longer bridge. When Amelia hears simultaneously of Booth's assignation with Miss Mathews and his imminent duel with Colonel James, her cry of despair exceeds the competence of good doctrine and the rules of clear expression: "It is too much, too much to bear . . . O my Children! my Children! Forgive me, my Babes—Forgive me that I have brought you into such a World as this" (p. 491). Sometimes language fails entirely, and grief manifests itself in a silent agony "which exceeds the Power of Description " (*Amelia,* p. 346). At the level of dramatic action these crises are the clearest demonstration of the failure of consolation and of the irrelevance of precepts to the experience of extreme distress. They could be taken as the last proof of the priority of immediate, practical concerns over the formal methods of representing and directing them. At the level of narrative, they constitute a type of aposiopesis long admired by Fielding. In love scenes he has frequently resorted to the device as a way of disqualifying readers without sufficient practical experience of lovers' raptures from participating in those taking place in the story: "To paint the looks or thoughts of either of these lovers is beyond my power. As their sensations, from their mutual silence, may be judged too big for their own utterance, it cannot be supposed, that I should be able to express them: and the misfortune is, that few of my readers have been enough in love, to feel by their own hearts what past at this time in theirs" (*Tom Jones,* p. 646). This narrative idealization of exalted feelings is related to a pragmatism that has sometimes sported with the unaccountable: "I am not obliged to reconcile every matter to the received notions concerning truth and nature" (*Tom Jones,* p. 579).

But when narrative silence echoes inarticulate grieving, it is much harder to do without the reassurance of received notions. In the absence of such a criterion it is impossible, for instance, to tell the difference between the agonized repetitions that belong to real suffering and the threadbare strains of factitious sorrow. "My poor Jacky, shall I never see thee more?" cries Adams (p. 309); "I shall never see him more," exclaims Bridget Blifil (p. 116); and when Booth is leaving for the wars Amelia calls to him, "Farewel, farewel for ever: for I shall never, never, see you more" (p. 104). Feeling that exceeds the bounds of general prescription diminishes the efficacy of precepts and maxims not simply by the uneconomical discharge of energy and the repetition of inane formulas, but also by the conscious rejection of the world as an equitable sphere of action. Whether Bridget Blifil means what Amelia means when she calls out, she gestures so forcibly at her isolation (or particularity as John Gay would call it)[7] that she becomes impervious to the consensual wisdom of precepts at the same time as she rejects, in what amounts to an exclamation of incredulity, any wisdom that might possibly inhere in an experience she cannot concede is exemplary. Aware of the crisis in these scenes of grief but bereft of any alternatives, Fielding jettisons the aposiopesis of amorous excess in favour of the ethical economy of mollified sorrow, despite the fact that he has frequently shown it to fail. So forlorn lovers and distracted parents are reminded that "sublimest grief, notwithstanding what some people say to the contrary, will eat at last" (*Tom Jones,* p. 748). He writes an essay on purpose to encourage this unheroic compromise between the soul and the body, stuffed with the precepts he has found most useful in avoiding or lessening this particular form of excess.

These prescriptions for the good husbandry of sorrow, of making it familiar by anticipation and acceptable by recollection, and of dulling the keenness of loss by meditating on eternal reunions, form the basis of all the consolations we meet in his fiction. In topographical terms they are intended to cater for those who are neither "elevated Souls" operating at a "divine Pitch of Excellence" nor consigned to a state of mere activity he here calls "the abject Condition of a Fool"; and in temporal terms they are aimed not at "the first Agonies of our Grief" but at the habits formed before and after it.[8] By directing his remedy at the areas either side of the moment of loss, Fielding tries to encourage a shift from the strange to the familiar, from a sense of tragic uniqueness (on the sufferer's part at least) to an ethical community Dr Harrison is not afraid to call comic, being convinced that "there is no Calamity so great that a Christian Philosopher may not reasonably laugh at it" (pp. 104, 137). Fielding compares this strategy with the procrastinations of lovers, a displacement of attention from the thing itself to its antecedents and aftermath, for "it cannot be Death itself (which is a Part of Life) that we lament" (*Remedy,* p. 221). In an equation he will remember, consolation is matched against the customary, repetitious, and ritual aspects of privation; and it is generally seen to be unequal to them.

It seems likely that a sense of this impotence of consolation, its calculated dodging of the thing itself, rather than any faith in its efficacy in emergencies, is what impels Fielding to quote his wife's exclamations after the birth and then the death, six years afterwards, of their daughter. Her first: "Good God! have I produced a Creature who is to undergo what I have suffered!" Her second: "[My] Child [will] never know what it [is] to feel such a Loss as [I now] lament" (p. 224). Although he offers the second outburst as a specimen of Christian self-consolation exhibiting a wholesome immunity to the fear of death itself, plainly neither belongs in a preceptual economy of grief. In the first, Charlotte Fielding is astounded that her limitless suffering can be reserved for repetition in the life of her child; in the second, she says that death is better than life on those terms. In effect she makes the same election as Job when his sufferings are mocked into exemplarity by his comforters. Amelia Booth also laments that her children are destined for the unbearable excess of pain she is suffering: like Charlotte she complains against the repetition of unexemplary agony, and sees the uniqueness of her suffering as the only mercy. What both women struggle to articulate is their incredulity that experience of this peculiar intensity should ever be moralized or turned into a lesson. But this incredulity must remain inaccessible, and therefore incredible itself, to an audience that cannot accommodate a sense of pain in excess of the categories invented to account for it: that cannot believe in pain as waste. The mutual failure of belief isolates the suffering party almost as completely as Job is isolated by his refusal to allow the cant of his comforters any relevance to his case. Either as an "elevated Soul" or an "abject Fool," the awkward victim is removed to the anti-category of the sublime where ambiguity and reversal supplant the rules of energy-saving: where the high can border on the low, and love can become deadly or unclean.[9] The crisis of exemplarity in Fielding's scenes of consolation deepens when the afflicted person is a parent, and then most particularly when she is a mother. The excessive feelings of a parent, as Adams says, must be allowed a vent; but when the figure of a bereft and grieving mother declares for death rather than have her suffering rendered as a repeatable and probable item in the series of a moral history, she widens considerably the gap in Fielding's fiction that has opened up between productive comedy and the waste of pain. The arts of probable representation become the formal equivalent of the forces in her own life that are denying her a language of complaint. The more she speaks, the more they need to quell her. This explains why the worst enemy of Molly Seagrim and Mrs Partridge is Mr Allworthy, and why Dr Harrison does more to hurt Amelia than her would-be seducers.

In *Joseph Andrews* two mothers lose their children, Harriet Wilson and Gammar Andrews, and neither is allowed to complain until complaint is adaptable to the scheme of verisimilitude that apportions children to parents on grounds of probable narratives. Until then Harriet's grief has to make way for her husband's (pp. 224–25), and Gammar Andrews has to keep hers a secret, for fear her husband might reject the changeling she has been left with. The priority of masculine language and judgement is formalized in *Tom Jones,* where the men who deny women the right of complaining are magistrates, guardians of legal sentences and power. Western's brutality has reduced his wife to silence; Allworthy's standards of virtue oblige Bridget to hold her tongue and keep her motherhood a secret. Her letter to her brother, a narrative explaining the double loss of a child and of an idiom in which to complain of it, is never delivered to him and never reproduced in the larger story, which depends for its inception and resolution on the credibility of stories told by the surrogate mother, Jenny Jones, to Allworthy, the magisterial father-substitute.

In *Amelia* Mrs Bennet, an afflicted mother who has lost both husband and child, manages to tell her story. It is a tale that begins with the loss of her own mother down a well and ends with the destruction of her family circle; but it is clear from the occasion that gives rise to it, as well as from the circumstances of the plot and the manner of its narration, that it is not meant to be trusted. The excessive emotions that punctuate it, the implausible motivations of the characters, and the unaccountable shift from a tragic to a comic register at the end of it are designed to make it look like the seamy underside of Amelia's "true" story. Physically Amelia's double, Mrs Bennet is intended to be seen as a mirror-image, doing everything in reverse. But a tale that thwarts the worst possibilities in Amelia's story by embodying them has to be credible—to Amelia at least—if it is to succeed in averting its repetition. And if she is somehow contaminated as well as saved by her belief in it, it must be because the excessive feelings which shape it are not simply antithetical to her matronly passions, but are in a more complex state of alliance and sympathy with them than the principles of verisimilitude governing the main story. The cries of despair, the tears, and the agonies of grief which interrupt Mrs Bennet's account of her misery closely resemble the passages in Amelia's life where she gives "full Vent to a Passion almost too strong for her delicate Constitution," or bursts into "an Agony of Grief, which exceeds the Power of Description" (pp. 316, 346). The accompanying aposiopesis—"The Scene that followed . . . is beyond my Power of Description" (p. 316)—is in fact deeply ambiguous. As a gesture of sympathy, it echoes Amelia's heartfelt belief in what Mrs Bennet tells her; as an expulsion of a scene of bootless grief it belongs to the system of suppression that misplaces Bridget's letter, silences Mrs Wilson and Mrs Andrews, and intersperses signs of improbability among the circumstances of Mrs Bennet's story. Just to add to the ambiguity, Fielding has Mrs Bennet begin it with a paraphrase of the *Remedy,* two astoundingly inappropriate precepts on the subduing of grief whose ironic drift it is impossible to ascertain.[10] Perhaps he is once more showing how precepts are mocked by matters that do not conform to received notions; perhaps he is showing how unworthy of a story those matters are; possibly he is multiplying and emphasizing contradictions in order to master the excess they breed; or perhaps his story is tainted by the ambiguities it seeks to expel. At all events, he confounds the distinction between grief which is supposed to be probable, consolable, and economical, and that which is barely possible, scarcely credible, and disorderly.

In his excellent essay on the *Remedy,* Henry Knight Miller points to the "duality" or "antipodality" of Fielding's work, the frequent contradiction of favourite precepts in his characters' behaviour and even his own, as a conscious transgression of the rules of sexual difference as well as of comic economy (pp. 267–71). He takes a specimen from the *Journal* entry for 26 June 1754, where Fielding records his last farewell to his children in these words: "I was . . . to take leave of some of those creatures on whom I doated with a mother-like fondness, guided by nature and passion, and uncured and unhardened by all the doctrine of that philosophical school where I had learnt to bear pains and to despise death. . . . I submitted entirely to [Nature], and she made as great fool of me as she had ever done of any woman whatsoever."[11] In one sense Fielding is patronizing his sorrow by calling it womanish, like Booth, whose despair and madness at the thought of his family's vulnerability convert him, he says, into a woman (p. 333); in another, he is outlining some of the more curious effects on the underside of exemplary comedy, one of which is undoubtedly a species of abject transsexuality. Its simplest manifestation is in the cross-dressing of Colonel Bath, who, when he is not being the most punctual observer of the maxims of military etiquette, dresses in a woman's bed-gown and a dirty flannel nightcap and becomes "a very proper Object of Laughter" (p. 129). A more complex scene of the ridiculous loneliness of feminine suffering is obtained from reading the *Journal* immediately after *Amelia.* When Fielding, practically paralysed with dropsy and in considerable pain, is being slung aboard his ship like a carcass, he mentions how few of the sailors and watermen witnessing this "spectacle of horror" resisted the temptation to insult and mock his torment (*Journal,* p. 202). His feelings on the occasion are identical with Amelia's after her nose has been badly damaged, "When I lay, as I then imagined, and as all about me believed, on my Death-bed, in all Agonies of Pain and Misery, [and became] the Object of Laughter to my dearest friend" (p. 72). I want to trace another route to Fielding's and Amelia's "spectacle of horror" by considering the criminal on the gallows as cousin german to the speechless and grieving mother.

## YOUTHS IN CARTS

To whom, of what, or how shall I complain?

*The London Merchant*

The close links between literature and the law in Fielding's mind are indicated by the ease with which he can switch from propositions about exemplary art to ones about exemplary justice. In *Jonathan Wild* (1743), a piece straddling the categories of fiction and criminal history, the narrator writes enthusiastically of hanging as an event "exemplifying the last and noblest act of greatness." Prior to being exalted in this way, Wild is consoled by the Newgate Ordinary who enumerates the spiritual advantages accruing from "exemplary punishment" at the end of a rope (pp. 168, 166). Similar language is used in the pamphlet Fielding published in the same year as *Tom Jones* to justify the notorious execution of Bosavern Penlez. The riots which led to Penlez's offence (the theft of some linen) were such, he argues, "as called for some Example, and . . . the Man who was made that Example, deserved his Fate."[12] Two years later Fielding enters into a theoretically sophisticated discussion of the utility and aesthetics of exemplary punishment, *An Enquiry into the Causes of the late Increase of Robbers*. In it he quotes Sir Matthew Hale's rhetorical question—"Is not the inflicting of punishment more for example, and to prevent evil, than to punish?"—and glosses it like this: "The terror of the example is the only thing proposed, and one man is sacrificed to the preservation of thousands . . . so true is that sentiment of Machiavel, that examples of justice are more merciful than the unbounded exercise of pity."[13]

Here is Fielding once again being driven to defend examples in a series of precepts, and the reason is the same: namely, that a space has opened up between the prescriptive authority of the law and the sum of social practices (what he calls the *constitution* in the *Enquiry*) that is supposed to exemplify it. At large he detects an appetite for excess that overflows the ancient boundaries of the feudal order; and locally, in the case of Bosavern Penlez, he identifies a tendency among the public to make heroes of persons hanged for indulging this appetite. With punishment no longer automatically exemplary in the public eye, the law itself becomes infected with the excess it seeks to control by wasting the lives whose loss has ceased to be a merciful example of justice: "If therefore the Terror of this Example is removed . . . the Design of the law is rendered totally ineffectual: The Lives of the Persons executed are thrown away" (*Enquiry*, p. 166).

The economy of a penal example differs, of course, from a comic one. In the latter the example is simultaneously the practical embodiment of a precept and a model to be emulated: its success corresponds to its repeatability. But the example of a man being hanged for a felony relies for its success on the illusion of inimitability: the malefactor must appear as the final instance of the law's retributive power, an original never to be copied. The position is succinctly put by the judge to the criminal who complains that death is an excessive punishment for stealing a horse: "You are not to be hanged, sir, for stealing a horse, but you are to be hanged that horses might not be stolen" (*Journal*, p. 195). The example is aimed at satisfying the demands of neither vengeance nor equity, rather at convincing the public of the tragic continuity of prescriptive power with the suffering of its transgressor. The condemned person, therefore, functions at the juncture of law and credibility by giving legal process the lineaments of fatal destiny, and by personifying the consequence of all the future felonies his audience has just been persuaded never to commit. In terms of the economics of Benthamite penology, the capital investment in the death of a citizen returns the profit of a law-abiding public.[14] In generic terms this enhancement of value is achieved by turning a hanging into a tragedy (from the crowd's point of view) and an allegory (from the malefactor's): as the audience begins to believe in the poetic justice of its ineluctable close, the chief actor in the performance swells to meet the exemplary challenge, like the Reverend Robert Foulkes, who told his audience, before he was turned off for child-murder, "You see in me what Sin is."[15]

The case of Bosavern Penlez exhibits none of this symmetry. By reprieving a man tried for the same offence and by admitting the testimony of a notorious brothel-keeper, the law lost any illusion of immanence: there was no *fate* for Penlez to deserve, just the chance of partial justice to be endured.[16] And owing to the hostility of the Tyburn crowd it was with some difficulty that the sentence against him was carried out. At no point in this clumsy procedure (in which Fielding played a central role) did the young man either confess the crime of riot for which he was to be hanged, or acknowledge the justice of his fate.[17] His death was the theme of pamphlets and songs which, as Fielding complained, transformed a malefactor "into a Hero [who] . . . instead of remaining an Example to incite Terror, is recommended to our Honour and Admiration" (*A True State,* p. 3). By construing his execution as a sacrifice to a capricious and vengeful law, the public underlined its real expense and at the same time reduced its apparent value to nothing. In refusing to believe in the tragic inevitability of his death, they likewise reduced Penlez to a human dimension, dignified by suffering but far from being a personification in a penal allegory. Fielding's pamphlet is meant to repair the breach in exemplarity which, like the slippage between precepts and experience in his fiction, lets pain run to waste and permits feelings to bloom into excess; but the task of restoring verisimilitude to a burst illusion demands more than the forensics of *A True State*—it needs the poetics of the *Enquiry*.

The route to this solution covers the same terrain, and takes up roughly the same amount of time, as Fielding's efforts to fit consolation into schemes of comic probability in his fiction. His difficulties in both departments arise from people who refuse to suffer in the right way. These rebarbative victims cry out at the wrong moment in the wrong words, or remain silent when they should be eloquent, or accuse providence and the law when they ought to be accusing themselves.

In terms of genre, the unexemplary criminal's perception of his or her place in the juridical economy constitutes a shift from Dennis's schematic conception of the tragic moral, which reflects an equitable distribution of rewards and punishments, to Addison's less prescriptive notion of the tragic upshot as one where virtue and goodness are often left to welter in temporal misfortunes.[18] This is analogous to the alternating allusions in *Amelia* to the comic economy of *The Beggar's Opera* and (when Amelia fears her husband's jealousy) to the tragic excess of *Othello*. Basically it amounts to a revision of the standards and purposes of probability. If the criminal is bereft of an Addisonian role (denied a sympathetic audience such as the sailors who attended Penlez to his death, let us say) and at the same time refuses a Dennisian one (confessing the crime, asking the good people to take warning by this ignominious death, and so on), then two alternatives remain. One is abandonment to carnival, where tragic dignity is shed in favour of unexemplary antic laughter at ruin and death, like Swift's clever Tom Clinch. The other is an entry upon the spectacle of horror, a scene of isolation without generic status, where all that is heard is the mockery of those who might have sympathized. This degree of abjection is experienced by Amelia, Fielding, and (as I mean to show) Jonathan Wild.

Like *The Beggar's Opera, Jonathan Wild* is a story that tests the relation of probability to exemplary justice by playing with different endings. In the first hanging scene the innocent Heartfree strives to meet his obligations as Dennisian tragic hero by receiving consolation and saying goodbye to his loved ones with composure and magnanity: "I will bear all with patience," he informs Friendly, as he is about to console his wife with the promise of their reunion in heaven (p. 138). The Addisonian possibilities are outlined in the narrator's anticipation of the reader's desire that this unlucky pair might, "by dying in each other's arms, put a final period to their woes." The carnivalesque opportunities of such dying are hinted at by the man who says that Heartfree has got his ten minutes with a woman at bargain rates. The laughter of the bystanders that greets Mrs Heartfree's frantic question ("Tell me, somebody who can speak, while I have my senses left to understand, what is the matter?") marks the beginning of agonized isolation.

All possibilities are cancelled with the news of a reprieve, whereupon the narrator steps in to justify the verisimilitude of this device: "Lest our reprieve should seem to resemble that in the *Beggar's Opera,* I shall endeavour to shew [the reader] that this incident, which is undoubtedly true, is at least as natural as delightful; for we assure him we would rather have suffered half mankind to be hanged, than have saved one contrary to the strictest rules of writing and probability" (p. 140). It is the same boast that is going to be made, rather more plausibly, in *Tom Jones,* where various alliances are made between ideas of improbability and scenes of hanging;[19] but here it is evidently meant less as an effort to persuade the reader than as a counterpart to what the narrator says when no reprieve arrives for the great man, Wild. He urges the sacrifice of the strictest rules of writing and probability to ensure that rogues hang. The historian is invited to "indulge himself in the licence of poetry and romance, and even do a violence to truth, to oblige his reader with a page . . . which could never fail of producing an instructive moral" (p. 172).

The irony of these two positions is controlled by a double feint, one at history, the other at fiction. The facts of Wild's story are all true, authenticated in official records and corroborated in the many narratives of his life and death. To imply that these are false while asserting the contrary of the factitious scene of Heartfree's farewell is to set up an ironic symmetry between what is credible and what is just. Heartfree's efforts on behalf of a probable exemplary narrative demand, therefore, that he be "probably" rescued in the nick of time; while Wild's ending, being offensive to these principles, loses its entitlement to probability and poetic justice. It does not matter that Wild's death, cursed by a crowd which he curses in turn, is a pretty accurate rendering of what actually happened: lacking any vestige of an instructive moral it must first be excluded from Fielding's system of poetic justice and generic differences before it can be assimilated to verisimilitude and the law. This explains Fielding's preoccupation with *The Beggar's Opera,* a play which ends improbably in a *maxim* after cleverly juggling with the relations of poetic to human justice in terms of a *moral.*

Half-relying on this precedent, Fielding tries to transform probability from a quality his narrative aims to embody to an item in a series of variable equations. In these, the addition of probability (in the form of an assertion or quantum) to the story of a virtuous man and woman in distress equals comedy instead of tragedy—an equation dominating the comic economy of the novels. Contrariwise, the removal of probability from the narrative of a comic villain (or a villain in what purports to be a comedy) ensures a hanging and an instructive moral as it were by default. In what amounts to a rewriting of *The Beggar's Opera,* Fielding is suggesting that Gay got these equations the wrong way round by breaching probability to *save* a criminal instead of to execute him.

*A True State of the Case of Bosavern Penlez,* published the same year as *Tom Jones,* bears the imprint of his lost confidence in the probability equation. Although he is retailing "the real Truth of this Case" from circumstances "known only to myself, and a very few more" (p. 54), the lifeless heap of privileged corroborative statements makes no headway against the public's buoyant faith in a different story, arising from three palpable lies Fielding believed Penlez to have told him about how he came by the linen. From Fielding's angle, no better proof could be had of the public's gullibility and of a criminal talent for plausible narratives. The figure of Penlez-hero, enjoying the same esteem as an unexemplary character such as Macheath, blots out the ironies

Fielding had invested in the life and death of Wild. Penlez restores ambiguity to terms like "greatness" and "exalted ends," and he makes the equation of malefactor and improbability itself improbable: a reflexive feat which, as we have seen, often attends an unexemplifiable precept.

That Fielding had solved this judicio-literary problem by 1753 is evident from his account of a case almost perfectly the reverse of Bosavern Penlez's, *A Clear State of the Case of Elizabeth Canning.* It concerns a young woman who disappeared for several weeks, and who, when she showed up, told an amazing story of abduction, imprisonment, and starvation in a disorderly house at Enfield Wash, on the outskirts of London. Many people found this story hard to believe, for not only was it vehemently contradicted by her supposed abductors, but also crucial motivations and corollaries were missing from it— why was she not raped, or forced to see company, instead of being starved; why did it take her so long to escape, and how had she the energy to accomplish it? In the end she was transported for perjury (see Zirker, pp. xciv–cxiv). Fielding, who had heard her testify under oath and was much impressed by her candour, set himself the task of answering these objections in a remarkable double critique of the principles of evidence and verisimilitude. Having schooled his audience to the admissibility of bare possibilities by means of a complete reversal of the probability equation,[20] he then asks them to consider the double injury their disbelief inflicts on her.

> An innocent young creature, who hath suffered the most cruel and unheard of injuries, is in danger of being rewarded for them by ruin and infamy; and what must extremely aggravate her case, and will distinguish her misery from that of all other wretches upon earth is, that she will owe all this ruin and infamy to this strange circumstance, that her sufferings have been beyond what human nature is supposed to [be] capable of bearing.[21]

In this effortless formulation of the paradox of wasted pain, Fielding condenses the predicaments of all the characters in his novels—mostly mothers—whose lack of a credible idiom of complaint has left their misery distinct enough to be the object of mockery and disbelief.

His sudden intuition of the injurious and misogynist aspects of probability owes something to the discoveries he made while writing *Tom Jones* and *Amelia;* but its clarity and force are derived from the *Enquiry.* Why a paper on the most effectual way of hanging criminals should teach Fielding to sympathize with the silence of female injury is a paradox explained by the disarrangement of his probability equation. In the *Enquiry* he makes a sharp division between the innovations he wants to allow in criminal trials, and those he wishes to introduce into procedures of execution. In the first he argues for the maximization of the opportunities of criminal narrative, maintaining that the evidence of accomplices ought to be admitted, even where there is no corroborating proof, provided their testimony is (like all good stories) "connected and probable," and delivered "with every Circumstance of Probability" (*Enquiry,* p. 160). The jury will be the audience, sole arbiters of the credibility of the tale. The drift of Fielding's logic is plain. Since knaves have thriven so well on the arts of probability, why not give them the chance to narrate one another to death? But once the belief of the audience has been won and the sentence passed, the criminal is to be stripped of everything that might offer consolation during the moments of passage. Directed by the watchwords Celerity, Privacy, and Solemnity, the officers of justice will empty the crowded space depicted in the eleventh plate of *Industry and Idleness* in order to subject their victim to a series of terrible privations—the loss of time, light, colour, noise, and company, and, worst of all, the loss of the circumstances and the idiom in which a counter-narrative, a complaint, or even an execration might be uttered.

This is where Fielding applies himself to the aesthetics of terror. As "the great business is to raise terror," he affirms on Homer's and Milton's authority how well it is excited by events which are sudden and fell. As for the terror of a hidden death, Horace's *Art of Poetry,* Duncan's murder in *Macbeth,* and a paraphrase from Montaigne's *Essays* are used to show that violence obscured by walls or ritual is more disturbing than a clear sight of it: that "It is not the Essence of the Thing itself, but the Dress and Apparatus of it, which make an Impression on the Mind, especially on the Minds of the Multitude" (p. 170). It is odd how nearly these ideas of raising terror recall in mirror-form those of the *Remedy,* where Fielding shifted attention from "Death itself" to the manner of dying in order to show that "Death is not that King of Terrors . . . he is represented to be" (pp. 221–23). And it is uncanny how closely they anticipate those of Burke's *Enquiry,* published six years later, especially the analysis of the sublime impact of the combined ideas of death, power, privation, and obscurity.[22]

Although Fielding is drawing heavily on the poetics of tragedy for his penological sublime, the tragedy he now has in mind has nothing to do with Dennis's moral allegory, for the malefactor is no longer in a position to exemplify anything, terror having replaced the conventions of public confession and repentance. The exclusion of a sympathetic audience likewise puts the Addisonian tragedy of popular heroism out of the question. Rather than a performance linking actor and audience in the probable exemplification of a precept or a law, Fielding is opting for a mysterious pageant of death, the ceremonious elaboration of its "Dress and Apparatus," whose primary effect is calculated for a lonely victim who will scarcely be able to believe what is happening. Fielding has in mind the private torment and inarticulate excess usually negatively defined by comic economy in his novels, but which Elizabeth Canning has taught him how to exploit. It is as if, in clearing the space of Hogarth's eleventh *Industry and Idleness* plate, Fielding found that he had swept away everything exemplary—the Bible in the felon's hand, the two clergymen, the marginal gloss, and even the unimprovable carnival of the crowd—leaving only the figure of the woman, a sort of coarse Madonna clutching a story that no one will attend to, who stands for the intensity of feelings that never find a proper language or channel in his fiction—who stands in effect for the very punishment he now seeks to define and impose.

This is Fielding's solution to the problem of negative reflexivity in perceptual discourse. The *Enquiry* is the *Remedy* back to front; it is a manual on how to remove every shred of comfort from people about to die in order to re-establish the principles of good economy. Excess will solve the problem of excess: waste shall waste waste. It is astonishing that the completion of the project of penological thrift is owing to Fielding's intuitive grasp on the double weight of female grief, "put in Execution"[23] not as consolation but as a refinement of capital punishment. There is no doubt that he perfectly understood the kind of pain he was recommending. Having witnessed his wife's despair, and having imagined the isolated agony of Amelia and Elizabeth Canning, he has peculiar authority for his observation that "Nothing can, I think, be imagined . . . more terrible than such an Execution" (p. 171). It tempts the reader to restore the dangerous ambiguity of sublime abjection that Fielding thinks he has managed to divide between suffering women, as worthy of pity, and criminals, as deserving none. It can be done, I think, by returning to the scene of Fielding's last farewell. Raised on a machine not unlike a gallows because his health has been fatally broken in service to the public among the criminal classes of London, he beholds a circle of faces utterly devoid of pity. In that moment he experiences the pain of a woman in circumstances that uncannily resemble the exalted and improbable end of Jonathan Wild, who was also rendered incredulous by the public's ingratitude. Fielding makes his own contribution to the economy of poetic justice by being condemned to suffer the pain he had himself devised. *Schadenfreude,* however, is not an option for readers who owe their scepticism about such an economy, and the prescriptive system underwriting it, to Fielding's staging and restaging of its bankruptcy.

*Notes*

1. *The History of the Adventures of Joseph Andrews,* ed. Martin C. Battestin (Oxford: Clarendon Press, 1967), p. 17. References are to this edition.

2. *The History of Tom Jones, a Foundling,* ed. R. P. C. Mutter (Harmondsworth: Penguin, 1988), p. 37. References are to this edition.

3. This argument plainly follows the main outlines of John Bender's. Briefly, his thesis revolves around the centralizing tendency that dominates equally the reformism of eighteenth-century penologists and the realism of the novelists. The panoptic structure of the new prisons is matched in the novel by such an efficient processing of information that a fiction which is transparent upon the real and whose moral truths are self-evident is (or ought to be) possible. He accounts for the failure of Fielding's panoptic novel (*Amelia*) in terms of a crepitation of the old and the new that disturbs and complicates this narrative aim. I will be suggesting that this

disturbance is present from the beginning of Fielding's experiments in fiction, and that Field-ing's penological interests clarify a contradiction at the core of his thinking about genre and verisimilitude. References are to John Bender, *Imagining the Penitentiary: Fiction and the Architec-ture of Mind in Eighteenth-Century England* (Chicago: University of Chicago Press, 1987), pp. 139–200.

4.   "What can be so proper for tragedy as a set of big-sounding words, so contrived together as to convey no meaning? which I shall one day or other prove to be the sublime of Longinus" (Preface, *The Tragedy of Tragedies* in *Eighteenth Century Plays* [Dent: Everyman, 1954], p. 168). The joint foundation of Fielding's literary principles in Scriblerian satire and Aristotle's poetics makes him especially alive to the bad economy of the transports recommended by Longinus. For a fine analysis of these economic differences that is applicable to Fielding, see Marc Shell, *The Economy of Literature* (Baltimore: Johns Hopkins University Press, 1978), pp. 90–105.

5.   *Amelia,* ed. Martin C. Battestin (Oxford: Clarendon Press, 1986), p. 43. References are to this edition.

6.   "You may preach in Covent Garden against foppery and fornication . . . against pride, and dissimulation, and bribery, at White-Hall: you may expose rapine and injustice in the Inns of Court Chapel: and in a city pulpit be as fierce as you please against avarice, hypocrisy and extortion" (*A Tale of a Tub* in *Jonathan Swift,* ed. Angus Ross and David Woolley [Oxford: Oxford University Press, 1984], p. 85). Swift is showing how the currency of the dis-course of moral reproof is the inverse of its effect: how difficult it is not to write satire, and how little difference it makes. It is the negative form of Fielding's proposition, but one which Har-rison's experiences (especially his conversation with the noble lord) reinforce. Having men-tioned masquerade, it is fit to own here how often this argument will border Terry Castle's remarkable chapter on *Amelia* in *Masquerade and Civilization* (London: Methuen, 1986), pp. 177–252. In starting with the implied order of exemplified precepts, however, I am not simply approaching the question of disorder from the top, as opposed to the carnivalesque bot-tom of masquerade, so that I can arrive at the same conclusions. Although the contradictions I examine in Fielding's work do open onto the area of uncanny confusions, excess, and generic instability Castle identifies as the sublime of masquerade (which she goes on to relate to the infoliated moral and structural cruxes that form the anti-allegory of *Amelia,* [pp. 53, 246]), I want to show that carnival, like perceptual discourse, contributes to the generic failures consti-tutive of this confusion, rather than functioning as its last instance or as the figural other of transparent, "programmatic" writing (p. 189). If programmes such as the *Remedy* and the *Enquiry* are read in this way, they can be incorporated as "examples" of disorder and excess instead of marking the boundaries of it.

7.   Throughout *The Beggar's Opera* lovers are accused of considering their pleasure and pains to be "particular."

8.   *Of the Remedy of Affliction for the Loss of our Friends* in *Miscellanies,* vol. I, ed. Henry Knight Miller (Oxford: Clarendon Press, 1972), pp. 217–18. References are to this edition. See also Miller's commentary on the *Remedy* in *Essays on Fielding's Miscellanies* (New Jersey: Prince-ton University Press, 1961), pp. 228–71, and Ian Donaldson, "Cato in Tears: Stoical Guises of the Man of Feeling," in *Studies in the Eighteenth Century,* ed. R.F. Brissenden (Toronto: Univer-sity of Toronto Press, 1973), pp. 377–95.

9.   The sort of sublime I am trying to approach here is outlined by Jean-Pierre Ver-dant, "Ambiguity and Reversal: On the Enigmatic Structure of *Oedipus Rex,*" *New Literary His-tory,* 9 (1977–78), 475–501, and more fully explored in terms of abject mothers by Julia Kris-teva, *Powers of Horror: Essays in Abjection* (New York: Columbia University Press, 1982), pp. 1–132.

10.   "I will not tire you, dear Madam, with Repetitions of Grief; I will only mention two Observations which have occurred to me from Reflections on the two Losses I have mentioned. The first is, that a Mind once violently hurt grows, as it were, callous to any future Impressions

of Grief; and is never capable of feeling the same Pangs a second Time. The other Observation is, that the Arrows of Fortune, as well as all others, derive their Force from the Velocity with which they are discharged: For when they approach you by slow and perceptible Degrees, they have but very little Power to do you Mischief" (p. 271). See Terry Castle's superb analysis of the contradictions in this whole scene, *Masquerade and Civilization,* pp. 215–22.

11.   *Jonathan Wild, {and} The Journal of a Voyage to Lisbon* (London: J. M. Dent, 1932), p. 201. References to both works are to this edition.

12.   *A True State of the Case of Bosavern Penlez* (London, 1749), p. 52.

13.   *An Enquiry into the Causes of the Late Increase of Robbers, and Related Writings,* ed. Malvin R. Zirker (Middletown, CT: Wesleyan University Press, 1988), pp. 166–67. References are to this edition. A useful survey of the mutuality of law and literature, with special emphasis on Fielding, is given by David Punter, "Fictional Representation of the Law in the Eighteenth Century," *Eighteenth-Century Studies,* 16 (1982), 47–74. For a more theoretical consideration of the tradition linking law to poetics, see Kathy Eden, *Poetic and Legal Fiction in the Aristotelian Tradition* (Princeton: Princeton University Press, 1986).

14.   See Leon Radzinowicz, *A History of English Criminal Law* (London: Stevens and Sons, 1948), I, 383–86. In his paraphrase of Bentham he sets out the following equation: "If the punishment is to be economic it is . . . necessary to increase as much as possible its apparent value, thus allowing its real value to be reduced. . . . It is the apparent value that influences the conduct of individuals and gives the profit; the real value constitutes the expense." For Fielding's part in the discussions and reforms of the penal system in the early 1750s see Radzinowicz *passim;* J. M. Beattie, *Crime and the Courts in England 1660–1800* (Oxford: Clarendon Press, 1986), p. 371 ff., and Hugh Amory, "Henry Fielding and the Criminal Legislation of 1751–52," *Philological Quarterly,* 50 (1971), 175–92. An influential theorization of the shifts in penological thinking that were taking place in eighteenth-century Europe is to be found in Michel Foucault, *Discipline and Punish,* translated by Alan Sheridan (New York: Vintage Books, 1979), pp. 73–131. It is significant, however, that Foucault plays no part in John Bender's argument, although he is generously saluted at the beginning of it for his analysis of the relation of discourse to power. I suspect the reason for this is that in England the actual practice of the law and its libertarian justifications form a much less symmetrical division between the theatre of state vengeance and the mathematics of deprivation than that described by Foucault as characterizing pre-revolutionary and post-revolutionary France.

15.   Charles Johnson, *A General History of the Lives and Adventures of the Most famous Highwaymen, Murderers, Street-Robbers, etc* (London, 1734), pp. 316–17; cited in Lincoln B. Faller, *Turned to Account: The Forms and Functions of Criminal Biography in Late Seventeenth and Early Eighteenth Century England* (Cambridge: Cambridge University Press, 1987), p. 61.

16.   In an ironic anticipation of the argument of the *Enquiry,* Fielding's anonymous opponent in the pamphlet war over Penlez accused him of deserting the maxim of equal and impartial exercise of the laws, a breach that is particularly damaging, he argues, "when the Partiality is seen, to run with too staring a Bias in Favour of the Rich, in Contra-distinction to the Poor" (*The Case of the Unfortunate Bosavern Penlez* [1749], p. 42; quoted by Malvin R. Zirker in his Introduction to the *Enquiry,* p. xliv).

17.   For a good account of the Penlez case see Peter Linebaugh, "The Tyburn Riot against the Surgeons," in *Albion's Fatal Tree* (Harmondsworth: Penguin, 1975), pp. 89–100. The most authoritative treatment of the case as it affected Fielding is now Malvin R. Zirker's, *Enquiry,* pp. xxxii–lii.

18.   In his essay, "To the Spectator, upon Poetical Justice," Dennis makes use of the *sorites:* "For what Tragedy can there be without a Fable? or what Fable without a Moral? or what Moral without poetical Justice? What Moral, where the Good and the Bad are confounded by Destiny, and perish alike promiscuously?" In his "Remarks upon *Cato,*" he defines negatively the true Aristotelian tragedy: "As the Action of this Tragedy cannot be Allegorical, because it is not Moral, so it is neither General or Poetical, but Particular and Historical." *The*

*Critical Works of John Dennis,* ed. Edward Niles Hooker, 2 vols (Baltimore: Johns Hopkins University Press, 1943), II, 19, 45.

19.  For example, "We had rather relate that he was hanged at Tyburn (which may very well be the case) than forfeit our integrity, or shock the faith of the reader" (p. 678). The improbable repentances of heroes in the last acts of modern comedies are, suggests the narrator, to be compared with those at Tyburn, "a place which might, indeed, close the scene of some comedies with much propriety, as the heroes in them are most commonly eminent for those very talents which not only bring men to the gallows, but enable them to make an heroic figure when they are there" (p. 366). There is a very detailed discussion of this scene, exploring its connections with *The Beggar's Opera,* in Bender, pp. 151–57. He argues that Fielding arranges the conflict between Wild and Heartfree "as a combat between variant novelistic accounts of material circumstance," with Wild representing the distorted presentation of evidence and the "good magistrate," who acquits Heartfree, using the clear and panoptic processing of real facts which is to become the narrative ideal of *Amelia.* But as the most fascinating part of Bender's argument turns on the uncanny resemblances between Wild and Fielding as thieftakers, it seems hard to reject a conclusion which becomes inescapable by the time of *Tom Jones,* which is that the villains develop and improve the identical arts of verisimilitude being used by the narrator. See Susan P. McNamara, "Mirrors of Fiction within *Tom Jones:* The Paradox of Self-Reference," *Eighteenth-Century Studies,* 12 (1979), 372–90.

20.  In a very lucid assault upon Fielding's position, Allan Ramsay makes the point Fielding himself would have made ten years before: "To bring a fact within the compass of possibility, there is nothing required but that it should not contradict itself; but to make it probable, it is likewise required that it should not be contradictory to ordinary experience; for in proportion to the several degrees in which it is removed from common experience, it acquires an appearance of falshood, and to entitle it to belief, must be supported by evidence apparently true, to as great or greater degree than the fact which it means to prove, is apparently false. This . . . is the general and leading principle in all enquiries concerning probable evidence." (*A Letter Concerning Elizabeth Canning* [A. Millar: London, 1752], pp. 5–6).

21.  *Enquiry,* p. 310. The same problem of injustice upon injury (*tort* upon *dommage*) has recently been theorized by the French philosopher Jean-François Lyotard. He calls it the *differend,* and, like Elizabeth Canning's aggravated case, it occurs when "the plaintiff is divested of the means to argue and becomes on that account a victim. . . . A case of *differend* between two parties takes place when the 'regulation' of the conflict which opposes them is done in the idiom of one of the parties while the injustice suffered by the other is not signified in that idiom." And like Fielding, Lyotard relates the silence of an idiomless injury to the sublime: the challenge of a feeling in excess of all modes of presentation. See J-F. Lyotard, "The *Differend,* the Referent, and the Proper Name," and David Carroll, "Rephrasing the Political with Kant and Lyotard: From Aesthetic to Political Judgments," in *Diacritics,* 14 (Fall, 1984), 5, 83.

22.  *A Philosophical Enquiry into our Ideas of the Sublime and the Beautiful,* ed. J. T. Boulton (London: Routledge and Kegan Paul. 1958), pp. 60–71.

23.  A telling phrase used by Booth when he promises Harrison to abridge the agony of parting by not saying goodbye to Amelia (p. 105).

# Patterns of Property and Possession in Fielding's Fiction

## JAMES THOMPSON

Henry Fielding's *Tom Jones* (1749) tells the history of a number of lost objects which range from the foundling protagonist and his patrimony to wives, daughters, a muff, and several bank notes. The most prominent story of errant money begins with the £500 Squire Allworthy gives to Tom (p. 310), which he subsequently loses (p. 313).[1] Black George appropriates the money (p. 314), and passes it on to Old Nightingale, in whose hands Squire Allworthy recognizes it (p. 920), and so it is presumably restored to Tom, the natural or rightful owner (p. 968). We are treated in similar detail to the fortunes of the £200 which Squire Western gives to Sophia (p. 359), who also loses her money (p. 610). Her wallet is found by a beggar who passes it on to Tom (pp. 631–35), and who, in turn, restores it to its proper owner: "I know the right Owner, and will restore it her . . . the right Owner shall certainly have again all that she has lost" (p. 634)—a promise which emblematizes the narrative of lost property in the novel. Partridge, of course, repeatedly urges Tom to spend the hundred pounds (pp. 675–76, 679, 711), but Tom restores it to Sophia whole: "I hope, Madame, you will find it of the same Value, as when it was lost" (p. 731).

In good Aristotelian fashion, the peripeteia in this tale of economic wandering coincides with Allworthy's recognition of his original bills: Old Nightingale, the financier or broker, announces:

> "I have the Money now in my own Hands, in five Bank Bills, which I am to lay out either in a Mortgage, or in some Purchase in the north of *England*." The Bank Bills were no sooner produced at Allworthy's Desire, than he blessed himself at the Strangeness of the Discovery. He presently told *Nightingale,* that these Bank Bills were formerly his, and then acquainted him with the whole Affair. (p. 920).

Reprinted from *Eighteenth-Century Fiction* 3 (1990): 21–42, by permission of the publisher.

This scene is one in a long series of recognitions, of Mrs Waters, Partridge, Tom's ancestry, his goodness, each in its own way a classic anagnorisis. But this recognition of money is by far the most curious, for it is difficult to say what, exactly, is being recognized here. Is it some true identity, ownership, or value which these bills reflect or retain and which, in the economy of plot, must be revealed and recognized? How does Allworthy recognize his notes, and, moreover, why has Fielding interpolated these little tales of monetary loss and restoration? The monetary subplot in *Tom Jones* reflects a conservative desire to stabilize cash and paper credit, and to represent and contain currency within traditional patterns of property and possession; a desire which is determined by a specific stage in the development of money. That is to say, in a view we could characterize as "late feudal" (following Ernest Mandel), Fielding domesticates cash transactions and commodities by inscribing them in a traditionally fixed, hierarchical (and agricultural) economy, where real property is the essential model for all other types of property, especially currency.[2]

Another way to put this is to say that Fielding represents cash transactions in the traditional comic form of the "lost and found": objects, characters, and values are lost, temporarily separated from their rightful owners, so that the comic plot can eventually reassert order by restoring lost objects to their owners, as if possession were a transcendent relation, unaffected by the vicissitudes of time, accumulation, and profit.[3] *The History of Tom Jones, a Foundling* opens with the discovery of a "lost" object, an infant, and the plot of the novel is concerned with the process of restoration, returning the infant to his family and thereby restoring the heir to his inheritance.[4] But the protagonist is only one of a multitude of objects lost and found in the novel; children, estates, wives, jobs, reputations, even a kingdom follow the same lost and found pattern, in which a temporary, unworthy claimant is foiled and the object is inevitably returned to its rightful owner: nothing is finally lost in *Tom Jones.*[5] Here we will focus on one representative example of this ordering pattern, the loss and restoration of money, for Fielding observes a kind of comic rule of conservation, under which it is finally impossible to lose anything.[6] The story of money in *Tom Jones* is bound up with the nature of currency in the period and its inherent instability, and so we need to understand the situation of currency in eighteenth-century English society before we can understand its function in Fielding's fiction.

The monetary system in eighteenth-century England was far more unstable than anything we are accustomed to now. To conservative observers such as Alexander Pope, Jonathan Swift, and Henry Fielding, this instability must have accentuated their hostility to a cash nexus, the growing dependence on short-term credit and public debt.[7] In Pope's *Epistle to Bathurst,* for example, paper credit exacerbates all of the dangerously changeable, movable, fluid qualities of money, as opposed to the stability and constancy represented by land and the hereditary estate, a metonym for genealogical and possessive continuity.[8]

> Blest paper-credit! last and best supply!
> That lends Corruption lighter wings to fly!
> Gold imp'd by thee, can compass hardest things,
> Can pocket States, can fetch or carry Kings;
> A single leaf shall waft an Army o'er,
> Or ship off Senates to a distant Shore;
> A leaf, like Sibyl's, scattered to and fro
> Our fates and fortunes, as the winds shall blow.
>                                    (lines 69–76)

Pope's and Fielding's hostility must be understood in the context of the social impact of paper money in early modern Europe, the significance of which Fernand Braudel explores: "If most contemporaries found money a 'difficult cabbala to understand,' this type of money, money that was not money at all, and this interplay of money and mere writing to a point where the two became confused, seemed not only complicated but diabolical. Such things were a constant source of amazement."[9] More suggestively, Marc Shell explores the correlation between language and money as representation:

> money, which refers to a system of tropes, is also an "internal" participant in the logical or semiological organization of language, which itself refers to a system of tropes. Whether or not a writer mentioned money or was aware of its potentially subversive role in his thinking, the new forms of metaphorization or exchanges of meaning that accompanied the new forms of economic symbolization and production were changing the meaning of meaning itself.[10]

The purpose of this paper is not simply to identify the notes in Nightingale's hands, but rather to explore one dimension of the historicity of Fielding's discourse by focusing on his representation of money and value; that is, to connect Fielding's narrative with a particular stage in the development of money.[11] Tracing similar forms of representation of value through Fielding's fiction, we can discern a consistent resistance to capital.

The story of eighteenth-century English currency, in terms of both economic practice and economic theory, turns on three interrelated factors: the rapid expansion of the economy; the establishment of mechanisms for credit on which that expansion was predicated; and the shortage of government-issued currency—copper, silver, and gold coins. Until 1797 coin was the only legal tender in England, and yet a vast number of financial transactions had to be carried on by other means. Because silver fetched a higher price in the Far East and on the continent than the price established by statute for the English Mint, newly minted silver coins, and later gold and copper as well, were culled from circulation, melted down, and shipped abroad as bullion—an illegal, but profitable and therefore common practice. The long-term history of a coinage always follows an endless cycle of issue, eventual debasement from wear, clipping, and counterfeiting, leading to the necessity of large scale recoinage. In this period, however, recoinage (in 1696–98 and 1773–74, as well as the devaluation of the guinea in 1717) had little or no effect on the number of coins in circulation, precisely because the new, heavier coins were the readiest targets for melting, following Gresham's Law that "bad money drives out good." The result of such culling and melting was a severe and chronic shortage of coin of the realm throughout the century.[12] What coin remained in circulation was disastrously debased: in 1777, the government found that a sampling of £300 in silver, which ought to have weighed 1200 ounces, weighed 624 ounces.[13]

In theory, currency was based on its "intrinsick" value as precious metal, but this theory bore little or no relation to practice because the silver coinage was both severely debased and entirely inadequate to the volume of circulation. Lord Lowndes claimed in *A Report containing an Essay for the Amendment of the Silver Coins* (1695) that "the Moneys commonly currant are Diminished near one Half, to wit, in a Proportion something greater than that of Ten to Twenty two." Light silver "when offered in Payments, is utterly Refused, and will not Pass, and consequently doth not serve the end or Purpose for which it was made." He goes on to describe the social disruption caused by inadequate coinage, a disruption which is essentially a crisis in the concept of value:

> In consequence of the Vitiating, Diminishing and Counterfeiting of the Currant Moneys, it is come to pass, That great Contentions do daily arise amongst the King's Subjects, in Fairs, Markets, Shops, and other Places throughout the Kingdom, about the Passing or Refusing of the same, to the disturbance of the Publick Peace; many Bargains, Doings and Dealings are totally prevented and laid aside, which lessens Trade in general; Persons before they conclude in any Bargains, are necessitated first to settle the Price or Value of the very Money they are to Receive for their Goods; and if it be in Guineas at a High Rate, or in Clipt or Bad Moneys, they set the Price of their Goods accordingly, which I think has been One great cause of Raising the Price not only of Merchandizes, but even of Edibles, and other Necessaries for the sustenance of the Common People, to their great Grievance.[14]

The monetary system maximized instability and as a consequence suffered chronic shortages and periodic crises, with increasing frequency towards the end of the century.[15] In all senses, this was a transitional system, neither realist nor nominalist, or both realist and nominalist, based neither on bullion nor on paper money. Such contradictions are evident everywhere in the pamphlet literature, much of which argues against lowering the value of money—recoinage by way of debasement—by insisting on the "intrinsick" value of precious metal. Locke's influential argument in *Some Considerations of the*

*Consequences of the Lowering of Interest and the Raising of the Value of Money* encapsulates all the contradictions of eighteenth-century monetary theory: silver has both real and imaginary value, and intrinsic and extrinsic value. Silver coins are indistinguishable in value from an equal amount of bullion, for value is based solely on quantity, but value is also based on quality (fineness), and both quantity and quality are in turn guaranteed by the authoritative stamp which functions as a pledge to insure its weight and fineness. In short, silver money is a physical, material object that has value, but that value is based on conventional agreement: precious metals have no real inherent value, but are accepted only by custom and contract:

> Now Money is necessary to all these sorts of Men as serving both for Counters and for Pledges, and so carrying with it even Reckoning, and Security, that he, that receives it, shall have the same Value for it again, of other things that he wants, whenever he pleases. The one of these it does by its Stamp and Denomination; the other by its intrinsick Value, which is its *Quantity.*
>
> For mankind, having consented to put an imaginary Value upon gold and Silver by reason of their Durableness, Scarcity, and not being very liable to be Counterfeited, have made them by general consent the common Pledges, whereby Men are assured, in Exchange for them to receive equally valuable things to those they parted with for any *quantity* of these Metals. By which means it comes to pass, that the intrinsick Value regarded in these Metals made the common Barter, is nothing but the *quantity* which Men give or receive of them. For they having as Money no other Value, but as Pledges to procure, what one wants or desires; and they procuring what we want or desire, only by their *quantity,* 'tis evident, that the intrinsick Value of Silver and Gold used in commerce is nothing but their *quantity.*[16]

The inherent value of silver is a point which Locke never tires of repeating: "*Silver, i.e.* the *quantity* of pure Silver separable from the alloy, makes the real *value* of Money. If it does not, coin Copper with the same Stamp and denomination, and see whether it will be of the same value" (p. 145). And then, in answer to the question, why then do we not simply exchange in bullion, by weight, he answers simply that it would be inconvenient, for it is hard to tell the difference between fine and mixed silver.[17] Despite its function as pledge, in *Short Observations on a Printed Paper Intituled, For encouraging the Coining Silver Money in England, and after for keeping it here* (1695), Locke dismisses the value of the stamp: "the Stamp neither does nor can take away any of the intrinsick value of the Silver, and therefore an Ounce of Coined standard Silver, must necessarily be of equal value to an Ounce of uncoined standard Silver" (p. 2). The fundamental argument here is a tautology— silver is silver: "it will always be true, that an Ounce of Silver coin'd or not coin'd, is, and eternally will be of equal value to any other Ounce of Silver" (p. 10). In 1757, eight years after Fielding's *Tom Jones* appeared, we find the same insistence on permanence and immutability of silver coins, and the same language of real, inherent and intrinsic worth in Joseph Harris's *An Essay upon Money and Coins:* "Money . . . differs from all commodities in this, that, as such, its value is permanent or unalterable; that is, money being the measure of the values of all other things, and that, like all other standard measures, by its quantity only; its own value is to be deemed invariable." Along with the emphasis on immutability, we find the same hostility to paper: after a consideration of the physical properties money should have—scarcity, immutability, easy divisibility, ability to be tested for fineness, resistance to wear—he argues against experimentation with paper money:

> We see that some of our plantations, make a shift without any money, properly so called; using only bits of stamped paper, of no real value. But, wherever that material, which passeth as or instead of money, hath not intrinsic value, arising from its usefulness, scarcity, and necessary expence of labour in procuring it; there, private property will be precarious; and so long as that continues to be the case, it will be next to impossible for such people, to arrive at any great degree of power and splendour.[18]

Yet a mere twenty years later, Adam Smith could claim that "the substitution of paper in the room of gold and silver money, replaces a very expensive instrument of commerce with one much less costly, and sometimes equally convenient. Circulation comes to be carried on by a new wheel, which costs less both to erect and to maintain [*i.e.,* as fixed capital, which he has been examining] than the old one." When he writes of bank notes, paper and silver specie, it is to assert their fundamental equivalence: "these notes come to have the same currency as gold and silver money, from the confidence that such money can at any time be had for them."[19]

> The gold and silver which circulates in any country, and by means of which the produce of its land and labour is annually circulated and distributed to the proper consumers, is, in the same manner as the ready money of the dealer, all dead stock. It is a very valuable part of the capital of the country, which produces nothing to the country. The judicious operations of banking, by substituting paper in the room of a great part of this gold and silver, enables the country to convert a great part of this dead stock into active and productive stock; into stock which produces something into the country. The gold and silver money which circulates in any country may very properly be compared to a highway, which, while it circulates and carries to market all the grass and corn of the country, produces itself not a single pile of either. The judicious operations of banking, by providing, if I may be allowed so violent a metaphor, a sort of wagon-way through the air; enable the country to convert, as it were, a great part of its highways into good pastures and cornfields, and thereby to increase very considerably the annual produce of its land and labour. The commerce and industry of the country, however, it must be

acknowledged, though they may be somewhat augmented, cannot be altogether so secure, when they are thus, as it were, suspended upon the Daedalian
wings of paper money, as when they travel about upon the solid ground of gold
and silver.[20]

There is not a simple continuum of monetary theory from Locke to Smith;
rather, Locke, Harris, and Smith exemplify positions taken throughout the
century. And even if Smith's view appears to be sharply divergent from those
of the earlier two writers, the seeds of that view are implicit in the deep contradictions found throughout Locke's economic theory.

The suspicion and hostility to nominal or paper currency evident in
Locke and Harris were shared by other writers throughout the century. But,
as a consequence of the constant dearth of coin, merchants, manufacturers,
bankers, and employers regularly had to resort to the use of various forms of
scrip or symbolic money, from metallic tokens stamped with the emblem of a
shop's guild to elaborate systems of paper money, all issued by small, private
institutions.[21] (In order to protect the monopoly of the Bank of England,
banking laws limited banks to no more than six partners.) Business was trans-
acted in negotiable, interest-bearing securities in addition to coin of the
realm.[22] Of the various forms of paper credit—the bill of exchange, promissory note, and the cheque—bills of exchange were the most common. Bills of
exchange had been used in foreign trading since the thirteenth century, but
they come into use in the second half of the seventeenth century in inland
trade and with third parties as the bearer.[23] Many of these changes can be
traced to the increased volume of commerce, and the need for new methods
of payment and, in turn, new mechanisms of banking. English banking followed Italian and then Dutch innovations, starting with goldsmiths who paid
interest on money deposited with them, in turn lending it to others, often the
Crown, at a higher interest.[24] Credit currency develops from these practices,
as goldsmith's receipts eventually become negotiable notes payable to an
anonymous bearer, and as goldsmiths take on what we now consider to be
bankers' functions. Bank bills derive from bills of exchange: the Bank of England issued bills under their seal (their sealed bills were discontinued in 1716),
and cash notes, signed by the cashier, with blanks for names and amounts.
Bank notes were engraved forms with blanks for amount and bearer. Often
part was drawn off, and noted on the back, but the note could still be
endorsed off to a third party or discounted by a broker; that is, the broker
would buy the bill before it was due at a price less than its face value. It is the
bill brokers who become the first commercial bankers, discounting bills for
provincial customers. By and large, money circulated from agricultural districts, through London, to manufacturing districts by means of bills of
exchange, not bank notes. Country bank notes or cash notes circulated in the
agricultural districts, while bills of exchange circulated in the manufacturing
districts.[25]

To return to Henry Fielding's *Tom Jones,* what are the notes which Allworthy recognizes? They are referred to at one point as "five bank bills" and as "bank bills" (p. 920), and at another point as "the 500*l.* Bank-Notes" (p. 968). According to the *Oxford English Dictionary,* "bank-note" and "bank bill" were used synonymously, though it is clear from the dictionary's examples that both referred to interest-bearing bills. Under "bank bill," the first definition is "bank note," and the second is "a bill drawn by one bank upon another payable at a future date, or on demand, synonymous with *banker's draft.*"[26] Allworthy's notes cannot, of course, be government-issued currency, which was not issued until well into the nineteenth century. His notes are unlikely to be a country bank's notes, for there were very few provincial banks in operation in the first half of the eighteenth century. They are unlikely to be bills of exchange, for those circulated largely in manufacturing districts, and less commonly in agricultural districts. Rather, they are more likely to be bank notes or bills drawn on a London bank. (In sending him off to make his fortune, Allworthy presumably would have given Tom his most negotiable paper.) They are unlikely to be Bank of England notes, for those circulated almost exclusively in London and not in the provinces. The best guess is that they are in the form of a cash note, from a smaller, West End bank of the sort that catered to the gentry, such as Hoare's or Child's.[27]

Unlike the anonymous and interchangeable paper money issued by the post-absolutist state, bills in Fielding's day would be individually identifiable as a consequence of the individualized nature of paper money in the eighteenth century, which not only held the name of the drawer and the bearer, but often a number of intermediary bearers who had endorsed it.[28] It is entirely possible to read the history of a bill or note in its endorsements—the various hands through which it passed. Paper money is not government issued, neither anonymous nor impersonal in this period, but is something which can be "told" and narrated. These are identifiable, distinguishable objects whose history can be read from their surfaces, much like a novel. This fact gives a significant clue to the function of money in Fielding's fiction.[29] A readable bank note has obvious uses in Fielding's romance plot of discovery, a plot which asks if money can (re)make the man.

The threat of the transformative or generative power of money runs throughout Fielding's novels, particularly in the anonymity promoted by journeys, during which strangers are trusted on the strength of their money. Parson Trulliber is a prominent example of trust contingent upon cash in *Joseph Andrews,* as is the first landlady in *Tom Jones:* "this was one of those Houses where Gentlemen, to use the Language of Advertisements, meet with civil Treatment for their Money" (p. 407); those who have money are assumed to be gentlemen.[30] Peter Pounce in *Joseph Andrews* is Fielding's archetypal money man, the servant turned master, all by means of credit and interest.

Pounce's fortune is accumulated by usury (legally defined at the time as any rate of interest above 5 percent):

> [Pounce] used to advance the Servants their Wages: not before they were due, but before they were payable; that is, perhaps, half a Year after they were due, and this at the moderate *Premiums* of fifty *per Cent*, or a little more; by which charitable Methods, together with lending Money to other People, and even to his own Master and Mistress, the honest Man had, from nothing, in few Years amassed a small Sum of ten thousand Pounds or thereabouts. (p. 38)

Old Nightingale is Peter Pounce's counterpart in *Tom Jones:* "He had indeed conversed so entirely with Money, that it may be almost doubted, whether he imagined there was any other thing really existing in the World; this at least may be certainly averred, that he firmly believed nothing else to have any real Value" (pp. 771–72). These hostile portraits of Pounce and Nightingale serve to deny the generative power of money. In like manner the money which Lady Bellaston gives Tom (p. 718) cannot change his nature even though it may temporarily transform him into a town beau. Much the same thing may be said of charity: when Tom gives money to Mr Enderson, the "highway-man" (p. 680), the money enables Enderson to live up to his natural class or station—it does not transform him into something he is not. Enderson may be said to exemplify for Fielding the worthy poor, those whose lot is improved by charity. Black George, on the contrary, exemplifies the unworthy poor, those on whom Tom's charity is wasted, leaving them in unimproved squalor. Either way, money cannot change the nature of the individual; rather the cash nexus is invariably pictured by Fielding in such a way as to deny its efficacy.

In all these scenes of exchange in *Tom Jones,* Fielding expresses a tradi-tionally conservative hostility to the potential of liquid assets, to their danger-ously enabling capacities, to which Marx later also draws attention:

> Do not I, who thanks to money am capable of all that the human heart longs for, possess all human capacities? Does not my money, therefore, transform all my incapacities into their contrary? . . . The overturning and confounding of all human and natural qualities, the fraternization of impossibilities—the *divine* power of money—lies in its *character* as men's estranged, alienating and self-disposing *species nature*. Money is the alienated *ability of mankind*. That which I am unable to do as a man, and of which therefore all my essential pow-ers are incapable, I am able to do by means of *money*. Money thus turns each of these powers into something which in itself it is not—turns it, that is, into its *contrary*.[31]

It is just these alchemical properties of money that Fielding is at such pains to negate, and the negation points to a curious, if not contradictory, conjunction of two languages or two stories in *Tom Jones*. As Braudel observes: "uneasiness [with new systems of bank notes and paper credit] was the beginning of the awareness of a new language. For money is a language . . . it calls for and makes possible dialogues and conversations; it exists as a function of these conversations."[32] Fielding's purpose in *Tom Jones* is to transform this new language, these new dialogues and conversations of accumulation and profit, and the transformations which result from them, back into the old dynastic language of the stable hereditary estate.

One way to account for this fundamental difference in the representation of credit is *not* simply in terms of political affiliation, that is, by seeing Fielding as a conservative Whig, allied by family to the landed aristocracy and their agricultural interests;[33] rather, we need to see Fielding responding to a highly transitional or contradictory stage in the currency system and in the English economy itself. In the *Grundrisse*, Marx argues that money passes through three stages of development, in which it functions first as a measure of value, and secondly as price or a universal equivalent or medium of exchange. In the second stage, money comes to represent accumulation or treasure, that is to say, wealth itself. Finally, in the most complex system of development, money comes to be posited in exchange *per se*, not merely as the measure of accumulated wealth, but rather as a means of wealth, as capital. The following passage encapsulates the complex dialectical relation among these three successive but interrelated stages and functions of money:

> Only with the Romans, Greeks, etc. does money appear unhampered in both its first two functions, as measure and as medium of circulation, and not very far developed in either. But as soon as either their trade, etc. develops, or, as in the case of the Romans, conquest brings them money in vast quantities— in short, suddenly, and at a certain stage of their economic development, money necessarily appears in its third role, and the further it develops in that role, the more the decay of their community advances. In order to function productively, money in its third role, as we have seen, must be not only the precondition but equally the result of circulation, and, as its precondition, also a moment of it, something posited by it. Among the Romans, who amassed money by stealing it, from the whole world, this was not the case. It is inherent in the simple character of money itself that it can exist as a developed moment of production only where and when *wage labour* exists; that in this case, far from subverting the social formation, it is rather a condition of its development and a driving wheel for the development of all forces of production, material and mental.[34]

At issue, then, is Fielding's response to and representation of a stage in the development of money, specifically capital—what Marx calls "money in process" for "capital is a not a thing but a social relation between persons, established by the instrumentality of things."[35] In order to see this instrumentality in *Tom Jones*, we need to look at Fielding's earlier and later fiction, first *Jonathan Wild* and then *Amelia*, both narratives with considerably more economic detail than Fielding's master work.

Like many Augustan satirists, in *Jonathan Wild* (1743), Fielding shows his central character as a parodic or inverted capitalist. Wild and his gang are presented as capital and labour, the gang leader exploiting the labour of others. In such a scheme, money is the motor of human activity: "Having thus preconceived his scheme, he [Wild] saw nothing wanting to put it in immediate execution but that which is indeed the beginning as well as the end of all human devices: I mean money" (p. 80). Wild is a successful exploiter: as the narrator puts it, "a prig [thief] to steal with the hands of other people" (p. 168). Fielding also plays with the other dimension of capital, its capacity to make money from money, so that Wild cheats a whole series of people one after another, profiting from each of them. Theft then serves Fielding as a kind of laboratory economy, a miniaturization of an exchange system. It also serves as the ironic frustration of capitalist exchange, for theft is a zero-sum game, one in which money moves around, through various forms of thieving, cheating, and pickpocketing, but the value remains constant (as in the card-sharking scene, pp. 72–76). In this microeconomic system, thieves prey upon one another in daisy-chain fashion, all cheating one another and negating each other's effects: "Bagshot and the gentleman intending to rob each other; Mr Snap and Mr Wild the elder meditating what other creditors they could find out to charge the gentleman then in custody with; the count hoping to renew the play, and Wild, our hero, laying a design to put Bagshot out of the way, or, as the vulgar express it, to hang him with the first opportunity" (p. 76).[36] Like *Tom Jones,* this narrative comically traces the return of goods to their rightful owners, though here it is Wild who plays the role of an inverted providence by orchestrating the return of possessions to their original owners: "Wild, having received from some dutiful members of the gang a valuable piece of goods, did, for a consideration somewhat short of its original price, re-convey it to the right owner" (p. 169). As a fence, Wild deals in commodities and exchange value, for stolen objects are of no use either to thief or fence: their only value lies in exchange. The perpetual frustrations of Wild present the criminal/capitalist as the essence of unproductive labour, involved in an elaborate but useless exchange system which ultimately produces no increase in value.

Many of the narrative functions of loss and recovery work in the same way here as in *Tom Jones;* the central objects purloined and eventually returned are the jewels which Wild steals from Heartfree.[37] In *Amelia,* the casket which Amelia gives to Booth has the function of the muff or wallet in *Tom Jones* (that is, it is both a possession and a kind of romance love-token). Like *Tom Jones* again, in *Amelia* the plot turns on the theft of an inheritance by a sibling. In its representations of economic exchange, *Amelia* is Fielding's most interesting novel, for it portrays a world almost totally ruled by money; Amelia's is a world where money talks and where the most basic needs and rights are denied to the poor. In *Tom Jones* we watch the movement of bills, but in *Amelia* we trace the journey of debts, in particular the climactic use of

Booth's gambling debt to Trent, which is sold to the lecherous Lord (pp. 432, 438, 472, 492). In Fielding's last novel desire and justice are caught in a cash nexus, for "justice" is bought and sold with perjured witnesses, and bodies are for sale in prostitution; in short things are for sale here that should not be for sale, just as there is no equal access to basic human rights (as is the case with Mrs Bennet's first husband, denied burial rights by his creditors). Booth before the Justice of the Peace and in Newgate is powerless without money: injustice *per se* is thematized in *Amelia*. The negotiations with various suitors over Amelia's hand in marriage illustrate the point—precious things are to be had for money. These issues come to the fore early on when Miss Mathews announces that she has not enough money in her pocket to pay the lawyer Murphy to save her life: life itself in the form of life-saving service is available only for money.

Furthermore, money and the power it represents are inevitably exploitive here, where the rich prey upon the poor; as Dr Harrison puts it, where they "prey upon the Necessitous" (p. 355), or, as the narrator puts it, where "a Set of Leaches are permitted to suck the Blood of the Brave and Indigent; of the Widow and the Orphan" (p. 477). The narrator says of the nobleman who is promoting Booth's commission in the army in order to gain sexual access to Amelia, "This art of promising is the Oeconomy of a great Man's Pride, a sort of good Husbandry in conferring Favours, by which they receive ten-fold in Acknowledgments for every obligation, I mean among those who really intend the Service: for there are others who cheat poor Men of their Thanks, without ever designing to deserve them at all" (p. 203). Exploitation functions as a gross inversion or parody of the deference and obligation which Harold Perkin called the glue that held the Old Society together.[38] When a "great man" receives "ten-fold," we can see a kind of capitalization of hierarchical obligation; similarly, the political satire at work throughout *Jonathan Wild* of course indicates that Robert Walpole has capitalized political patronage, turning political deference and obligation into a cash nexus. Colonel Bath, Booth says, "hath oppressed me, if I may use that Expression, with Obligations" (p. 368), while Booth defines "Obligations, as the worst kind of Debts" (p. 236).[39] In Fielding's attack on the decadent aristocracy in *Amelia,* social obligation has become explicitly financial, transformed into a kind of social capital deployed to oppress the lower classes.[40]

In the first half of the eighteenth century Defoe recognized and celebrated money as capital, as an instrument for creating wealth, not just as wealth itself, but Fielding refuses to show the reproduction of accumulated capital in criminal hands. Black George has instructed Old Nightingale to "lay out [the £500] either in a Mortgage, or in some Purchase in the North of England" (p. 920), but Fielding has constructed his story so as to resist or repress the possibility of turning cash into capital. The notes remain inert and non-transformative, and Black George's act does not lead to accumulation but remains simple theft. Recognized and recovered by Allworthy, the notes remain safe, stable, unchanging property, much like a landed estate, suspended within the patriarchal system of continuity. The new language of money has its analogue in the language of the new form of the novel; Defoe's novels are stories of new dialogues, social mobility, and personal development, individual changes that are achieved by way of financial accumulation, profit, and class transgression. The conjunction of these two languages of real and monetary property, then, can be understood in generic terms. It has been argued that *Tom Jones* is a hybrid form, a comic epic in prose, a romance, a satire; its mixed form can be seen most clearly in relation to the economic base of the culture.[41] In his *The Theory of the Novel* Georg Lukács distinguished between the epic, which tells the history of an unchanging community, and the novel, which takes the outward biographical form of the history of a problematic individual. *Tom Jones* combines the residual with the emergent, vestiges of the epic with elements of the new form of the novel, for it concerns the story of Squire Allworthy's estate just as much as the story of the titular hero.[42] From the Lukácsian point of view, the title and outward biographical form mask the fact that the true protagonist of *Tom Jones* is Paradise Hall.[43] Tom's becoming a worthy steward to the estate is but part of the larger history, the possessive and genealogical continuity represented by the dynastic estate itself.[44]

To the very end of his life Fielding displayed a consistent resistance to the notion of free-flowing capital. In his Introduction to *The Journal of a Voyage to Lisbon,* Fielding observed of his income as Bow Street Magistrate:

> I will confess to him [the reader], that my private affairs at the beginning of the winter had but a gloomy aspect; for I had not plundered the public or the poor [in his capacity as magistrate] of those sums which men, who are always ready to plunder both as much as they can, have been pleased to suspect me of taking: on the contrary, by composing, instead of inflaming, the quarrels of porters and beggars (which I blush when I say hath not been universally practised) and by refusing to take a shilling from a man who most undoubtedly would not have had another left, I had reduced an income of about £500 a year of the dirtiest money on earth, to little more that [*sic*] £300. (pp. 189–90)

The taint of dirty money here is adduced from the immoral conditions of the job, the *Amelia*-like conditions of bribery and exploitation, and such immorality adheres to the money. Such a persistence of immorality, even after the money changes hands, is quite unlike the laundering of money that goes on in Defoe's novels where money is rootless, without meaningful genealogy, and so is always "clean." Stolen objects, such as the bank note in *Colonel Jack* or the watch in *Moll Flanders,* carry no taint of their history: giving her son a gold watch at the close of her story, Moll adds, "*I did not indeed tell him* that I had stole it from a Gentlewomans side, at a Meeting-House in *London,* that's by the way."[45] In *Tom Jones,* Jacobite rebellions, runaway wives, daughters, rogue nephews, and the cash nexus of London[46] momentarily threaten the stability of landed property, but the transcendence of possession extends beyond land to cash itself in Fielding's epic, harnessing, domesticating, or declawing the threat of cash, paper credit, unbridled accumulation, and universality of exchange value—in short, early market capitalism and commodity. Those intermediate systems of sealed bills and bills of exchange, with their assertively individualized appearance, similarly can be seen as provisional mechanisms which evolved to control the treacherously fluid capacity of paper money. After anonymous Bank of England notes become legal tender in 1797, rightful possession would never again be so easily recognized or so easily restored.

## Notes

1.    Quotations from Fielding's fiction are from the *Wesleyan Edition of the Works of Henry Fielding*, ed. Martin Battestin: *Tom Jones* (1975, reprinted Middletown, CT: Wesleyan University Press, 1983); *Joseph Andrews* (1967); *Amelia* (1983, reprinted 1984); *Jonathan Wild*, ed. David Nokes (Harmondsworth: Penguin Books, 1982); *The Journal of a Voyage to Lisbon* in *The Works of Henry Fielding*, ed. William Ernest Henley (1902, reprinted New York: Barnes and Noble, 1967), vol. XVI. Page references are to these editions.

2.    Ernest Mandel, *Late Capitalism*, trans. Joris de Bres (London: Verso, 1978). Samuel L. Macey characterizes Fielding's attitude towards money as "aristocratic" (*Money and the Novel: Mercenary Motivation in Defoe and his Immediate Successors* [Victoria, B.C.: Sono Nis Press, 1983], p. 122.) Michael McKeon writes of "Fielding's profound distaste for monied culture" (*The Origins of the English Novel* [Baltimore: Johns Hopkins University Press, 1987], p. 503).

3.    Fielding's comic order has been discussed in terms of Providence. See Aubrey Williams, "The Interpositions of Providence and the Design of Fielding's Novels," *South Atlantic Quarterly* 70 (1971), 265–86 and Martin Battestin, *The Providence of Wit* (Oxford: Clarendon Press, 1974). Henry Knight Miller connects the persistence of romance form (cycle and return) with providential thematics (*Henry Fielding's "Tom Jones" and the Romance Tradition* [Victoria, B.C.: University of Victoria, 1976], especially chap. 2, pp. 22–41). What appears as transhistorically romantic to Miller I argue has peculiar historic specificity, for the comic interpositions of providence work to support a late aristocratic concept of property. On the differences between Fielding's and earlier providential plots, see Leopold Damrosch, Jr, "*Tom Jones* and the Farewell to Providential Fiction," in *Henry Fielding, Modern Critical Views*, ed. Harold Bloom (New York: Chelsea House, 1987), pp. 221–48, reprinted from *God's Plot and Man's Stories* (Chicago: University of Chicago Press, 1985). See also John Bender, *Imagining the Penitentiary* (Chicago: University of Chicago Press, 1987), pp. 186–87.

4.    Homer O. Brown, in "*Tom Jones:* The Bastard of History," *boundary* 2 7 (1978), 201–33, observes that Tom remains a bastard and therefore ineligible to inherit the estate. He is a "genealogical aberration" (p. 207), a disruption of the dynastic narrative. Similarly, Brown sees the allegorical or metonymic function of the Jacobite rebellion of 1745 in *Tom Jones* as "history as order" (p. 224). From Coleridge to its most classic statement in R. S. Crane ("The Plot of *Tom Jones*" [1950], reprinted in *Essays on the Eighteenth-Century Novel*, ed. Robert D. Spector [Bloomington: Indiana University Press, 1965], pp. 92–130), the favourite word used in all sorts of descriptions of the novel and its plot is "order" or "ordered." Studies of Fielding's thematics are similarly filled with concern for the "whole," as in Damrosch: "Fielding's poetics

finds significance in the whole, and is committed to showing how everything is interconnected. This narrative epistemology is reflected in the world of social relationships" (p. 236). So too, Paul Hunter opens his discussion of Fielding's elaborate patterns of symmetry with the observation that "Viewing *Tom Jones* is a little like viewing the eighteenth century as a whole" (*Occasional Form* [Baltimore: Johns Hopkins University Press, 1975], p. 167). The fragility of this totalizing order, at least for the later Fielding, is explored by C. J. Rawson in *Henry Fielding and the Augustan Ideal under Stress* (London: Routledge and Kegan Paul, 1972). Terry Castle also explores the subversion of apparent order in *Amelia* in *Masquerade and Civilization* (Stanford: Stanford University Press, 1986), pp. 177–252. Here, I am interested in exploring both the economic dimensions of the fictional order, and the historical forces it is arrayed against.

5. A similar conservation or continuity is apparent in Fielding's psychology: see John S. Coolidge, "Fielding and 'Conservation of Character,' " in *Modern Philology* 57 (1960), 245–59. Similarly, Patricia Meyer Spacks argues that Fielding's characters are not subject to transformation: "The characters in eighteenth-century fiction show less capacity for essential change than we like to believe is possible in life, and the limited possibilities for change they have depend upon external kinds of learning about the world outside themselves." *Imagining a Self* (Cambridge: Harvard University Press, 1976), p. 7.

6. Brian McCrea in *Henry Fielding and the Politics of Mid-Eighteenth-Century England* (Athens: University of Georgia Press, 1981) focuses on "the central role of property in Fielding's political and social writings" (p. 201), which he characterizes as Lockean: the purpose of the state is to protect property: "Fielding was unequivocal and unsparing in his defense of property" (p. 203). "His political career is understood, most truthfully, as one instance of the transformation of Whiggism from a revolutionary political philosophy that challenged royal authority to a conservative political philosophy that protected the values and interests of a property-owning elite" (p. 207).

7. For the history of these developments, see P. G. M. Dickson, *The Financial Revolution in England: A Study in the Development of Public Credit 1688–1756* (London: Macmillan, 1967).

8. See Earl Wasserman, *Pope's Epistle to Bathurst* (Baltimore: Johns Hopkins University Press, 1960), for a thorough discussion of economics in the poem.

9. Fernand Braudel, *Capitalism and Material Life 1400–1800*, trans. Miriam Kochan (New York: Harper and Row, 1973), p. 358.

10. Marc Shell, *Money, Language and Thought: Literary and Philosophical Economies from the Medieval to the Modern Era* (Berkeley: University of California Press, 1982), pp. 3–4.

11. Fredric Jameson offers a suggestive model for this connection between money form and fiction: "The art-novella, then, may be governed by the experience of money, but of money at a specific moment of its historical development: the stage of commerce rather than the stage of capital proper. This is the stage Marx describes as exchange on the frontiers between two modes of production, which have not yet been subsumed under a single standard of value; so great fortunes can be made and lost overnight, ships sink or against all expectations appear in the harbor, heroic travellers reappear with cheap goods whose scarcity in the home society lends them extraordinary worth. This is therefore an experience of money which marks the form rather than the content of narratives; these last may include rudimentary commodities and coins incidentally, but nascent Value organizes them around a conception of the Event which is formed by categories of Fortune and Providence, the wheel that turns, bringing great good luck and then dashing it, the sense of what is not yet an invisible hand guiding human destinies and endowing them with what is not yet 'success' or 'failure,' but rather the irreversibility of an unprecedented fate, which makes its bearer into the protagonist of a unique and 'memorable' story" ("The Ideology of the Text," in *The Ideologies of Theory, Essays 1971–1986* [Minneapolis: University of Minnesota Press, 1988], I, 52). For other relevant studies of literature and economics, see Max Novak, *Economics and the Fiction of Daniel Defoe*

(Berkeley: University of California Press, 1962); Walter Benn Michaels, *The Gold Standard and the Logic of Naturalism* (Berkeley: University of California Press, 1987); John Vernon, *Money and Fiction: Literary Realism in the Nineteenth and Early Twentieth Centuries* (Ithaca: Cornell University Press, 1984); and Roy R. Male, *Money Talks: Language and Lucre in American Fiction* (Norman: University of Oklahoma Press, 1981).

    12.    T. S. Ashton writes that "in 1773, coin of the realm was hardly obtainable" (*An Economic History of England: The Eighteenth Century* [New York: Barnes and Noble, 1955], p. 186).

    13.    C. R. Josset, *Money in Britain: A History of the Currencies of the British Isles* (London: Frederick Warne, 1962), p. 112.

    14.    William Lowndes, *A Report containing an Essay for the Amendment of the Silver Coins* (London, 1695), reprinted in John R. McCulloch, ed., *A Select Collection of Scarce and Valuable Tracts on Money* (1856, reprinted New York: A. M. Kelley, 1966), p. 233. Josset confirms Lowndes's picture (pp. 112–13).

    15.    "Banking statutes do appear to have maximized instability. . . . English banks remained small, with six partners or fewer, and unincorporated. Yet, in their operation (in great contrast with most continental states) no public control was exerted on the extent of their note issues, their cash ratios, their reserves, cheque transactions or expansionist credit policies. Thus, instability was maximized" (Peter Mathias, *The First Industrial Nation: An Economic History of Britain 1700–1914* (London: Methuen, 1983), p. 36).

    16.    John Locke, *Several Papers Relating to Money, Interest and Trade* (1696, reprinted New York: A. M. Kelley, 1968), p. 31. This volume contains: *Some Considerations of the Consequences of the Lowering of Interest and the Raising of the Value of Money* (1691); *Short Observations on a Printed Paper Intituled, For encouraging the Coining Silver Money in England, and after for keeping it here* (1695); and *Further Considerations concerning Raising the Value of Money. Wherein Mr. Lowndes Arguments for it in his late Report concerning "An Essay for the Amendment of the Silver Coins," are particularly Examined* (second edition, 1696). Page numbers refer to this collection of pamphlets.

    17.    "The *Stamp* was a *Warranty* of the publick, that under such denomination they should receive a piece of such weight, and such a fineness; that is, they should receive so much silver. And that is the reason why counterfeiting the Stamp is made the highest Crime, and has the weight of Treason upon it: Because *the Stamp is the publick voucher* of the intrinsick value" (Addenda to *Some Considerations,* pp. 146–47).

    18.    Joseph Harris, *An Essay upon Money and Coins* Part I, 1757, reprinted in McCulloch, pp. 372 and 374.

    19.    Adam Smith, *The Wealth of Nations,* ed. Edwin Cannan (Chicago: University of Chicago Press, 1976), pp. 309, 310.

    20.    Smith, p. 341.

    21.    As Sir Albert Feavearyear puts it in his history of English money, "Roughly speaking, paper money of all kinds in the first half of the century stayed within the sphere occupied by cheques today. Outside that sphere coin alone was used" (*The Pound Sterling: A History of English Money,* 2nd ed. [Oxford: Clarendon Press, 1963], p. 160).

    22.    According to T. S. Ashton, "Some of these including exchequer bills, navy bills, and lottery tickets (as also the short-term obligations of the East India Company, the Bank of England, and the South Sea Company) could be used to settle accounts between individuals, and may perhaps, therefore, be thought of as falling within the somewhat shadowy boundaries of 'money' " (pp. 177–78). The transition towards "true" paper money in circulation by the end of the century (that is, as we currently understand paper money) involves the gradual purging of the interest-bearing functions of these notes (Feavearyear, pp. 117–18). As Ashton puts it, "By means of a bill, purchasing power could be transferred by one man to another under conditions of repayment plainly set forth and generally understood. Unlike the coin or bank note, the bill could be sent from place to place without danger of theft. It could pass from hand to hand without formality other than endorsement, and each person who put his name to it

added to its security. Any holder could get coin or other currency by discounting it: as a security it was highly liquid" (p. 185).

23. Feavearyear, p. 101.

24. See Ernest Mandel, *Marxist Economic Theory,* trans. Brian Pearce (London: Merlin Press, 1962), pp. 242–70.

25. Feavearyear, p. 159. See pp. 161–67 for the circulation of bills of exchange. There is an excellent discussion of the history of bills of exchange in Braudel, pp. 367–70.

26. Under *bank note,* the definition reads as follows, "a promissory note given by a banker: *formerly* one payable to bearer on demand, and intended to circulate as money." Under *note,* we find, "a bank-note, or similar promissory note passing current as money," from 1696. Under *bill,* we find: "(more fully Bill of Exchange) A written order by the writer or 'drawer' to the 'drawee' (the person to whom it is addressed) to pay a certain sum on a given date to the 'drawer' or to a third person named in the bill as the 'payee.' "

27. See Dickson, pp. 437–44, for a detailed discussion of Child's Bank, an example of private London bank catering to the aristocracy.

28. Feavearyear notes that bills under £1 were prohibited in 1775: "in 1777 an Act was passed which provided that all notes of 20s. or of any amount greater than 20s. and less than £5 should specify names and place of the abode of the persons to whom or to whose order they were payable. Further, they were to bear a date not later than the date of issue and to be made payable within twenty-one days, after which period they would cease to be negotiable" (p. 174).

29. For an intelligent discussion of Fielding's use of detail, see Lennard Davis, *Factual Fictions: The Origins of the English Novel* (New York: Columbia University Press, 1983), p. 205 and note.

30. See James Cruise, "Fielding, Authority, and the New Commercialism in *Joseph Andrews,*" *ELH* 54 (1987), 253–76 for an extended discussion of Fielding's hostility towards commercialism and the cash nexus.

31. Karl Marx, *The Economic and Philosophical Manuscripts of 1844,* ed. Dirk J. Struik (New York: International Publishers, 1964), pp. 167–69.

32. Braudel, p. 328.

33. For a good overview of politics in Fielding, see Morris Golden, "Fielding's Politics," in *Henry Fielding, Justice Observed,* ed. K. G. Simpson (Totowa: Barnes and Noble, 1985), pp. 34–53. For McCrea, in *Henry Fielding and Politics,* the issue of Fielding's politics is explicitly biographical: how Fielding's family connections mediate his political position and so on. Both these studies focus on the contradictions between praxis and theory, between political patronage and association, between conservative and progressive political stances, inherent in the unstable nature of Whiggism at mid-century, issues that come out of Bertrand Goldgar's influential *Walpole and the Wits* (Lincoln: University of Nebraska Press, 1976). Straightening out the interrelations among political service and patronage, loyalty, and ideology is a continuing project in Fielding studies. The most detailed study is Thomas R. Cleary, *Henry Fielding, Political Writer* (Waterloo: Wilfrid Laurier University Press, 1984).

34. Karl Marx, *Grundrisse,* trans. Martin Nicolaus (Harmondsworth: Penguin Books, 1973), p. 223. The whole "Chapter on Money" (pp. 113–238) is relevant, particularly pp. 226–38.

35. Karl Marx, *Capital,* 3 vols. ed. Frederick Engels, trans. Samuel Moore and Edward Aveling (New York: International Publishers, 1967), I, 154 and 766.

36. Crime as unproductive labour or negation is encapsulated in Fielding's description of Newgate: "all Newgate was a complete collection of prigs, every man behind desirous to pick his neighbour's pocket, and every one was as sensible that his neighbour was as ready to pick his: so that (which is almost incredible) as great roguery was daily committed within the walls of Newgate as without" (pp. 203–4). Compare this with Mrs Heartfree's conclusion:

"THAT PROVIDENCE WILL SOONER OR LATER PROCURE THE FELICITY OF THE VIRTUOUS AND INNO-CENT" (p. 203).

37. Fielding's hostility to capital is apparent in the fact that only the disreputable know how to exploit the tricks of credit here (p. 90): the count obtains one of the jewels, sells it, raises money on that cash, which he then uses as a deposit for the rest of Heartfree's jewels—making money on money: "so he paid him the thousand pound in specie, and gave his note for two thousand eight hundred pounds more to Heartfree." They then attack Heartfree and steal the cash back from him, after which the cash is stolen by the prostitute Molly Straddle. Wild offers the jewels to Lætitia Snap, but they turn out to be paste, substituted by the Count. The jewels reappear with the Count in Africa (pp. 192–93) and are returned eventually to Heart-free (p. 203). So too, Heartfree recognizes a bank note (one of the Count's) stolen from him the previous day, just as in *Tom Jones* (p. 99); Heartfree endorses it over, it is stopped (because the Count has disappeared and will not make good on it) and, as the endorsee, Heartfree is held for the debt and jailed.

38. Harold Perkin, *The Origins of Modern English Society* (1969, reprinted London: Rout-ledge, 1985), pp. 17–62.

39. There are negative suggestions of the generative or reproductive capacity of capital, in that Booth cannot borrow money without having some to start with (p. 122). In keeping with Fielding's "late feudal" outlook, money in this novel is still part of a zero-sum game, for it changes hands by theft or misappropriation or coercion (primitive accumulation), but there is no new money produced. It is only old, familiar, known money that appears, disappears, and reappears in the course of the narrative, just as in *Tom Jones*.

40. It could be argued that Fielding's obsession with prostitution in *Amelia* is con-nected with capitalization, as in the central contrast between the good wife, Amelia, who pro-tects her virtue at all cost, and Mrs Trent. Amelia is explicitly termed Booth's "Treasure" (p. 382) compared to Colonel Bath's worthless wife or Colonel Trent's wife, who is a commod-ity to be traded, a prostitute. In this respect, *Jonathan Wild* seems very much like a satiric ver-sion of *Amelia*, since the central contrast is also one between honour (a nostalgic aristocratic virtue) and its commodification or capitalization, between the good wife and the whore, Mrs Heartfree and Lætitia Wild. Like Amelia, Mrs Heartfree's adventures consist of a sequence of resisting would-be rapists. For these issues of gender, see April London, "Controlling the Text: Women in *Tom Jones*," *Studies in the Novel* 19 (1987), 323–33.

41. Sheldon Sacks, *Fiction and the Shape of Belief* (Chicago: University of Chicago Press, 1964), remains the best discussion of the variety of forms in *Tom Jones*. The issue of form is related to the more general matter of the historicity of his discourse, and the question of how it is inscribed in the cultural field of the 1740s and the 1750s. In other words, what do Fielding's narratives tell us about the dialectic between romance and novelistic discourse? There are at least two senses of "history" as story and reality that need to be worked out here: See John F. Tinkler, "Humanist History and the English Novel in the Eighteenth Century," *Studies in Philology* 85 (1988), 510–37. See also John J. Burke, Jr, "History without History: Henry Fielding's Theory of Fiction," in *A Provision of Human Nature*, ed. Donald Kay (University: University of Alabama Press, 1977), pp. 45–63. McKeon's *Origins of the English Novel* is the fullest and most successful attempt to resolve Fielding's place in both romance and novelistic discourse.

42. Georg Lukács. *The Theory of the Novel*, trans. Anna Bostock (Cambridge: MIT Press, 1971). My application of Lukács is dependent upon J. M. Bernstein's excellent study of Lukács's novel theory in *The Philosophy of the Novel* (Minneapolis: University of Minnesota Press, 1984).

43. The ending sentence of *Tom Jones*, with its emphasis on the estate and its depen-dents, condenses Fielding's Tory myth of genealogical continuity and economic conservatism: "And such is their Condescension, their Indulgence, and their Beneficence to those below them, that there is not a Neighbour, a Tenant, or a Servant, who doth not most gratefully bless

the Day when Mr. Jones was married to his Sophia." It is no accident that in *Pamela* and in *Sir Charles Grandison* Richardson felt obligated to track the newlyweds much further before the family history could be safely and sensibly concluded. *Pamela* ends, not with the marriage of Pamela and Mr B or with the reconciliation of Mr B and his sister Lady Davers; instead, the whole narrative is stretched out in order to end with a triumphant return to the paternal estate. So too, Smollett's *Roderick Random* closes with a return to the dynastic estate and a similar show of affection, deference, and dependence by the servants. As a measure of what has changed by the end of the century, we may compare these endings with Sir Walter Scott's *Waverley,* where the estate returned to at the end is pitifully fragile, only recently recovered, and only partially restored.

44. By contrast, Defoe's novels speak a completely different economic language, and present the cash nexus, paper money, and credit in an entirely different light. Rather than being threatened by the alchemical, transformative powers of money, Defoe's characters are explicitly made rich by its properties: that is to say, for Moll, Colonel Jack, and Roxana, mastery of the credit system is the *sine qua non* of success in the material world. The most instructive example of paper credit in Defoe's fiction is Colonel Jack's £94 bank note, the accumulation of his early years of theft. Once Jack passes into the New World, that note loses all connection with its illicit origin; indeed the £94 note becomes a sign of Jack's gentility, surety to his new master that Jack is not, in fact, a transported criminal, but rather an innocent who has been abducted to Maryland by an unscrupulous sea captain (Daniel Defoe, *The Life of Colonel Jack,* ed. Samuel Holt Monk [London: Oxford University Press, 1970]). For the drawing up of the bill see pp. 76–77, and for its function in Maryland, see pp. 124–25. In short, the note in Defoe serves in all its enabling capacity, transforming Colonel Jack from a common criminal into a respectable citizen, which is exactly what Fielding prevents the £500 note from doing for Black George in *Tom Jones.*

45. *Moll Flanders,* ed. David Blewett (Harmondsworth: Penguin Books, 1989), p. 422.

46. In Jane Austen's *Mansfield Park* (1814) Mary Crawford recites "the true London maxim, that everything is to be got with money." R. W. Chapman, ed., *The Novels of Jane Austen* (London: Oxford University Press, 1923), III, 58.

# Controlling the Text: Women in *Tom Jones*

## APRIL LONDON

That *Tom Jones* and *Clarissa* represent two contrary possibilities of narrative has long been critical orthodoxy: the one, "masculine," architectonic, and expressive of the primacy of collective ideals; the other, "feminine," involuted, and shaped by the imperatives of private feeling. More recent focusing of feminist attention on *Clarissa* has reinforced these truisms, suggesting tacitly through neglect that Fielding's novel did not contribute to "the complex network of power/knowledge relationships that shaped [the] then inarticulate 'femininity' into words and gestures."[1] Yet *Tom Jones,* in part through its allusive references to *Clarissa,* can be seen as central to the literary and cultural transition marked by the feminization of discourse in the eighteenth century.[2] For both Fielding and Richardson this transition is made possible by the adaptation of a key metaphor, that of property, which the early novel consistently set in apposition to its exploration of the female self.

The appeal of property as metaphor lay in part in its inclusiveness as an explanatory model for the relations that especially interested contemporary authors. Property, the guarantor and permanent reflection of public order, is sustained and defined by individual propriety; the common root of the two words attests to the inextricable relation between material fact and behavioral code. More pertinently, both law and ideology in the eighteenth century imposed a virtual identification between women and property.[3] To consider female limitations and potential in the novels of Richardson and Fielding, then, involves understanding how their narratives adapt metaphors of property. Such an analysis suggests that in the body of *Tom Jones* Fielding plays with the multiple meanings of property, undercutting the equation of female and helplessness, to offer versions of power unconstrained by gender which are then apparently contradicted by the final reassertion of Sophia's subordination as an aspect of the novel's happy ending. This seeming discontinuity between Sophia's role in the text proper and in its conclusion is a function of her transformation from character into a metaphor of those property relations

*Studies in the Novel,* vol. 19 (1987). Copyright 1987 by North Texas State University. Reprinted by permission of the publisher.

that underlie Fielding's version of the ideal order his narrative finally endorses. To examine the process of that transformation is to move toward a fuller awareness of what constitutes "femininity" in the early novel.

Fielding himself invites a coupling of *Tom Jones* and *Clarissa* by building into his own work a structure of pointed allusions to Richardson's text. These allusions are most insistent in the presentation of Sophia and they first become obvious in Western's gleeful response to the news from his misinformed sister that Sophia loves Blifil:

> I was never more rejoiced in my Life: For nothing can lie so handy together as our two Estates. I had this Matter in my Head some Time ago; for certainly the two Estates are in a Manner joined together in Matrimony already, and it would be a thousand Pities to part them. It is true, indeed, there be larger Estates in the Kingdom, but not in this County, and I had rather bate something, than marry my Daughter among Strangers and Foreigners. Besides, most o' zuch great Estates be in the hands of Lords, and I heate the very Name of *themmum*. (pp. 276–77)[4]

Western's confounding of the physical and metaphorical meanings of the estate leads him to assume that private emotion will yield to the imperative of dynastic continuity. To him, the ascendancy of property demands that the physical proximity of the estates will be extended to the union of Sophia and Blifil; their marriage will confirm an alliance already present in nature. Western's sentiments here correspond to James Harlowe's approval of the "*noble settlements*" (I, p. 59)[5] Solmes would bring to his marriage with Clarissa. The squire's closing allusion to the "Lords," however, suggests the differing political and finally ethical orientations of Fielding's novel. In *Clarissa,* the threat of Solmes and the Harlowes is filtered to the reader primarily through the consciousness of the heroine. The epistolary form, in heightening this relentlessly private focus, also serves to translate the political issues of obedience, subordination, and self-determination into the context of individual feelings. Refusing mastery by an alien authority is thus rendered as Clarissa's sexual repulsion toward the "odious" Solmes; the divided impulses that follow from the unjust demands of a just authority become her mixed emotions about resisting paternal rule. In *Tom Jones,* however, familial threat does not become internalized but remains objectified in the Western brother and sister, who are placed not in a private but rather a public context, with their actions depicted not in relation to the politics of repression, but of party. Western, we are told, was "twice a Candidate in the Country Interest at an Election" (p. 272); his sister, in turn, delights in parading her Court "knowingness" in literature, politics, and love. Brother and sister, then, parody two political responses which, as H. T. Dickinson notes, "came to dominate political arguments in the early Hanoverian period,"[6] supplanting the earlier division between Tory and Whig.

The identification of the Westerns with narrowly defined party interests goes hand in hand with the references to *Clarissa;* the final result of this counterpointing of political extremism with literary precedent furthers Fielding's undercutting of the tragic dimensions of *Clarissa* while advancing his advocacy of a more temperate version of authority. Through a structure of allusion and analogy the power that the Westerns attempt to wield emerges as a comic instance of the power exercised familially by the Harlowes and individually by Clarissa and Anna Howe. The parallel scenes of the two novels thus seem designed in part to locate the characters in relation to the crucial issue of authority and its sources. To the absolutist Westerns and Harlowes power derives from their hierarchically validated roles as parents; to Clarissa and Anna power is vested in the right of individual choice. Only Sophia, Fielding suggests, assumes a median course between acceptance of authority and assertion of integrity and so becomes the model not only for Tom's accession to virtue but also for the just political state founded on the rule of property which the novel will endorse as the alternative to the autocracy of the gypsies and Jacobites.

Given that in the eighteenth century "the structure of authority . . . arose from property,"[7] it is appropriate that in both novels the occasion for the testing of power should be the daughters' relation to their parents' acquisitiveness. The first act of disobedience for both Sophia and Clarissa, the refusal to enter into a marriage that would enlarge the family's estates, thus provokes an equivalent response, a denial of freedom of movement. When Western discovers that Sophia is in love with Tom, he, like the Harlowes, confines his daughter to her room. Mrs. Western, perhaps echoing Anna Howe's feminism, declares that "*English* Women . . . are no Slaves" (p. 320), and has Sophia released. Yet Mrs. Western is finally neither a feminist nor an advocate of Sophia's cause. Searching for an analogy to convey her thoughts on the ideal relationship of women to men, Anna comments to Clarissa that

[t]he suiting of the tempers of two persons who are to come together is a great matter: and yet there should be boundaries fixed between them, by consent as it were, beyond which neither should go: and each should hold the other to it; or there would probably be encroachments in both. To illustrate my assertion by a very high, and by a more manly (as some would think it) than womanly instance. If the boundaries of the three estates that constitute our political union were not known, and occasionally asserted, what would become of the prerogatives and privileges of each? The two branches of the legislature would encroach upon each other; and the executive power would swallow up both. (I, pp. 340–41)

Mrs. Western adopts a similar, although characteristically inflated and regal, comparison, but argues to the opposite end:

It is the Honour of your Family which is concerned in this Alliance; you are only the Instrument. Do you conceive, Mistress, that in an Intermarriage between Kingdoms, as when a Daughter of *France* is married into *Spain,* the Princess herself is alone considered in the Match? No, it is a Match between two Kingdoms, rather than between two Persons. The same happens in great Families, such as ours. (p. 335)

Mrs. Western's grandiloquent extension from familial to political to international contexts finds its rationale in a reading of the estate that places a premium upon its conceptual significance: estate as a condition of place in the hierarchy and source of the "Honour" which accrues to those who marry prudentially. She also inverts her brother's reading, most obviously by reversing his rabid dislike of "Foreigners," but equally by seeming to empty "place" of its physical connotations. In the end, of course, although one reads the estate in material terms and the other in emblematic terms, the course of action prescribed is identical; both demand that Sophia marry the loathed Blifil.

Both of the Westerns also make use of a logic that tends toward their own glorification and demands unconditional obedience of the person to whom it is directed. This narcissism masquerading as moral principle links the Westerns to the Harlowes, but having suggested the parallel Fielding carefully neutralizes the threat they pose to Sophia by focusing on the comic resonances of paired antitheses. The Westerns' apparently contrary interpretations of "estate" thus function as a reflexive parody of responses to property, an impression confirmed by their relation to other exemplary figures of an even more extreme nature.[8] Just as Fielding directs attention here to interpretations of the female estate, and not to the experience of that estate, so too, when presenting Sophia's escape, does he emphasize her adherence to a code of decorum, and not her inner struggle. In both instances, the sorts of complex ethical questions that surround Clarissa's ultimate emergence as tragic figure are precluded by the displacement of emotion. Clarissa, "all amaze and confusion, frightened beyond the power of controlling" (I, p. 484), is tricked by Lovelace into fleeing her home. Sophia's escape, in contrast, is represented as the "discharge [of] her Duty" (p. 559), and it is successful because she, "with all the Gentleness which a Woman can have, had all the Spirit which she ought to have. When, therefore, she came to the Place of Appointment, and, instead of meeting her Maid, as was agreed, saw a Man ride directly up to her, she neither screamed out, nor fainted away" (p. 559).

Fielding's glance at Richardson's heroine here seems intended not only to mark out for praise Sophia's confidence, but also to imply that the man she encounters remains a neutral figure because she has not left herself open to the influence of a Lovelace. The details of her plan of action before and after the elopement further emphasize her peculiar blend of integrity and deference and so again work to suggest that Clarissa's being "frightened beyond the power of controlling" is a function of an imperfect sense of self and an exaggerated passivity in the face of masculine power. Sophia, like Clarissa, is faced with the threat of an imminent and undesired marriage, but her reaction to Honour's flurried news of her father's intentions is a model of the prudential response to crisis: she solicits "advi[c]e" (p. 349), is then "wrapped in Contemplation" (p. 350), and finally announces she has "come to a Resolution" (p. 350). Her ultimate decision to place herself under the protection of her aunt nicely balances calculated rebellion with obedience. Knowing that Lady Bellaston "looks upon the Authority of a Father in a much lower Light" (p. 350) than she does, Sophia determines to take advantage of her aunt's guardianship "till [her] Father, finding [her] out of his Power, can be brought to some Reason" (p. 351). She will, in other words, reject her father's authority in fact without rejecting it in spirit. Fielding's structuring of the novel at this point supports his presentation of Sophia as the self-conscious controller of her own history. The account of her decision to elope is thus followed by thirty-six chapters tracing Tom's adventures on the road to Upton, where he "resolved never more to abandon the Pursuit of" (p. 554) Sophia. Only after Tom is firmly established as the unfaithful questor does the *"History {go} backward"* (p. 554) to follow Sophia's escape and parallel journey to Upton, where she renounces Tom after discovering his affair with Mrs. Waters. Continuing her journey to London, Sophia thus becomes the initiator (physically and morally) of action, while Tom assumes the more conventionally female position of dependency.

These gestures in the direction of *Clarissa,* along with subsequent twists in the plot allowing Sophia a measure of autonomy, suggest another of the functions of the allusive structure of Fielding's novel. For ultimately it is Sophia's ability at once to resemble and essentially to differ from Clarissa which marks her virtue. Fielding repeatedly brings Sophia close to Richardson's heroine only to reveal some resource peculiar to those who exemplify his understanding of integrity, a resource which is then translated into purposive action. Conversely, the *Clarissa* echoes cling to such dissolute figures as Mrs. Fitzpatrick. When the latter would not comply with her husband's wish to sell her "little Estate . . . he confined [her] to her Room, without suffering [her] to have either Pen, Ink, Paper, or Book; and a Servant every Day made [her] Bed, and brought [her] Food" (pp. 599–601). Helped by money provided by an ignoble Lord, Mrs. Fitzpatrick bribes her keeper and journeys to London where she becomes her rescuer's mistress.

The difference between a Sophia on the one hand, and a Mrs. Fitzpatrick on the other, ultimately depends upon the ability to recognize and act upon the sense of "Duty" which earlier assured Sophia's presence of mind. This ability suggests a coincidence of individual virtue and communal values and so raises a number of questions about the origin of these qualities, the means by which they are instilled, and the political and economic structures which assure their efficacy. The conventional answer to this questioning of the relation between female self and social order would center on the concept of hierarchy, that divinely ordained system which in the Augustan frame of values places property over money, reason over passion, and men over women. Yet in *Tom Jones,* scrutiny of the relative power exercised by men and women yields a surprising conclusion: it is the female characters who embody the choices offered to the protagonist and who thus determine not only the course of the novel's action but also the form of its ending. As in Richardson's novels, women here are identified with property, but unlike many of Richardson's women, they seem initially to escape the imposition of a full equivalence with the cluster of values that follows the conventional blurring of a metaphorical and literal reading of the female estate. As Carole Fabricant has demonstrated, such blurring and the subsequent presentation of women as quiescent and therefore inherently victims is also common in contemporary poetry.[9] Lady Bellaston, the concupiscent and assertive seductress, is clearly one example of Fielding's contravention of this norm.

Lady Bellaston arranges for Lord Fellamar to rape Sophia and then greets his hesitancy with a rhetoric that neatly conflates the "Masculine" (III, p. 195) Mrs. Sinclair's verbal aggression with Lovelacean libertinism:

> Are you frightned by the Word Rape? Or are you apprehensive _____? Well, if the Story of *Helen* was modern, I should think it unnatural. I mean the Behaviour of *Paris,* not the Fondness of the Lady; for all Women love a Man of Spirit. There is another Story of the *Sabine* Ladies,—and that too, I thank Heaven, is very ancient. Your Lordship, perhaps, will admire my Reading; but I think Mr. *Hook* tells us they made tolerable good Wives afterwards. (pp. 794–95)

Lady Bellaston's machinations are principally directed, however, not against Sophia but toward Tom, for as the narrator informs us, "[s]he was indeed well convinced that *Sophia* possessed the first Place in *Jones's* Affections; and yet, haughty and amorous as this Lady was, she submitted at last to bear the second Place; or to express it more properly in a legal Phrase, was contented with the Possession of that of which another Woman had the Reversion" (p. 748). Martin C. Battestin notes in his commentary on this passage that "[i]n the laws of property, a reversion is the returning of an estate to the rightful owner after it had been temporarily granted to the use and possession of another" (p. 748, n. 1). It is entirely appropriate that the narrator should here employ a metaphor conventionally associated with female passivity. For what seems merely an incidental equation of Tom and property is, in fact, part of a continuous subtext of allusions placing the hero's actions in a context that eighteenth-century novels considered typically feminine. Most obviously, Tom has throughout responded to others' actions, actions initiated by women. Even his expulsion from Paradise Hall, though pronounced by All-worthy, follows from Bridget's withholding of information. If it were simply a question of Tom's being manipulated by powerful women, of his being made to act out a role more often assumed by the other sex, this novel's values could be seen to accord with the more usual fitting of action to gender. Tom's weakness would then be no more than a comic version of Lovelace's control by Mother Sinclair and her minions; it would be an index of his "fallen" state. But female power, although most richly evoked in negative terms as an expression of carnality, also has its positive embodiment in the person of Sophia. It is she against whom Tom continually measures his flaws, and it is the pursuit of her as a form of wisdom that allows his concluding restoration. Yet Sophia is not presented as a static ideal, and the "discharge of her Duty" acquires potency precisely to the degree that it serves as an active model of the virtue to which Tom aspires. To this end, Sophia's adventures in London are carefully counterpointed to Tom's in order to keep alive the possibility of integrity surmounting circumstance, a possibility questioned by Tom's own yielding to the numerous temptations he encounters.

Additional weight is given to Sophia's critical acumen by the narrative implications of her role as interpreter and arbiter of Tom's history. In this role she uses sources both oral (the maid Susan at Upton) and written (Tom's letter proposing marriage to Lady Bellaston), sifts the evidence, and finally delivers a sentence of banishment on her erring lover. Her magisterial act echoes Allworthy's earlier pronouncement, but while the latter's judgement is undercut by subsequent events, Sophia's is not. If such interpretive abilities suggest a place in the narrative as surrogate reader, her relationship to the narrator marks out a complementary status as author manqué. The "perfect Intimacy" (p. 157) which the narrator initially wishes to encourage between the reader and Sophia—the "Idea of Female Perfection" (p. 154)—is soon paralleled in his own relation to her; and while at crucial moments he distances himself from Tom, the congruity between narrator and paragon becomes more insistent as the novel moves toward its conclusion. Ultimately, the narrator's determination to affirm order through closure is made dependent on Sophia's willingness to "save" Tom.

The coincidence of redemption and closure has temporal implications that follow from the narrative illusion of a natural consonance among beginning, middle, and end. Allworthy's conciliatory speech to Tom at the end of the novel presents the imagistic (and ethical) antithesis to this consonance. He begins with the warning that "Villainy . . . when once discovered, is irretrievable; the Stains which this leaves behind, no Time will wash away;" he then moves to a spatial representation of vice: "Where-ever [the Wretch] turns his Eyes, Horror presents itself; if he looks backward, unavailable Repentance treads on his Heels; if forward, incurable Despair stares him in the Face; till, like a condemned Prisoner, confined in a Dungeon, he detests his present Condition, and yet dreads the Consequence of that Hour which is to relieve him from it" (p. 960). The inverted relation of this rhetoric to that used in contemporary topographical poetry is made clear by Allworthy's conclusion; in renouncing "Error," Tom exchanges the "confinement of the dungeon" for a "Prospect" in which "Happiness seems in [his own] Power" (p. 961). The "deep Sigh" with which Tom greets this pronouncement mutely acknowledges, however, that just as Adam needed Michael to make meaning of the prospective vision in *Paradise Lost,* Book XI (the tacit reference for much eighteenth-century topographical poetry), so, too, does he require Sophia. Michael, the "heavenly instructor," who "future things canst represent as present" (XI, lines 870–71), reconciled Adam to his fallen state by allowing him to glimpse the progress of human time. The exchange between Sophia and Tom when they meet at Squire Western's offers a comic version of this intersection of the providential and the fallible. Sophia initially responds to Tom's pleas for mercy with the comment that "Time alone" (p. 972) will prove his penitence. She is then pushed to name a trial of twelve months—"an Eternity" (p. 974), according to Tom; and finally, under the cover of obedience to her father, she agrees to marry him next day. Sophia's transformation in this scene from distant moral exemplar to acknowledged lover, from adherence to an "eternal" notion of justice and mercy to engagement with such worldly institutions as marriage, exemplifies the absorption of the ideal into the material that distinguishes the novel's ending.

This final conciliation of seemingly opposed qualities accords with J. Paul Hunter's reading of Tom as "the new man of mid-century English society, a citizen, altogether unsure of his identity for a long time but ultimately sure of a rightful place as heir and proprietor of a large, and resonant, estate. Like princes of the past, he must be prepared for his high responsibility by education and experience."[10] Such a summary statement as this needs only the qualification of Sophia's pivotal role as catalyst. For not only does she control Tom's education and experience throughout the body of the novel, she also allows the completion of his identity as proprietor. Tom's "rightful place" is, in fact, achieved when Western resigns both "his Family Seat, and the greater Part of his Estate, to his Son-in-law" (p. 981). The closing emphasis on Tom's redemption surrounds the image of the estate with resonances that are almost entirely beneficent. A more particularized description of the connotations of property ownership in mid-century is suggested by Blackstone in the famous second volume of his *Commentaries,* "Of the Rights of Things": "There is nothing which so generally strikes the imagination, and engages the affections of mankind, as the right of property; or that sole and despotic dominion which one man claims and exercises over the external things of this world, in total exclusion of the right of any other individual in the universe."[11] The terms in which Blackstone details the rights conferred by property, "sole and despotic dominion," are reminiscent of those used by Fielding in his satire of autocracy in the gypsy episode of *Tom Jones* as well as in his anti-Jacobite writings in *The True Patriot* and in pamphlets written between 1745 and 1749.[12]

Neither Fielding nor Blackstone, of course, considered this version of "dominion" as unnatural or undesirable; in their view, property as a "thing" devoid of personality ensured stability and checked individual aspiration as effectively as did, at a higher level, the constitutional form of monarchy. Under property's impress, and acting in conformity with the role its dominion imposes, Tom assures his status as citizen hero. Sophia, as one of those "external things of the world" that "one man" possesses "in total exclusion of the right of any other individual in the universe," is correspondingly diminished as she becomes part of the property relations that now define her husband. In direct proportion to the confirming of his identity through his worldly estate is the nullification of hers. The imagery conveying Sophia's accession to this new place in the social structure suggests that Fielding sees the transition in essentially positive terms. At the party on the evening preceding their marriage, we are told that Sophia "sat at the Table like a Queen receiving Homage, or rather like a superiour Being receiving Adoration from all around her" (pp. 977–78). The shift from "Queen" to "superior Being" attests to the erasure of her personality since it emphasizes not only her passivity but also her relinquishment of any independent title. Her transfiguration has much in common with the nineteenth-century paradigm of the Angel in the House; she too achieves her apotheosis as a secular "Being" by "produc[ing] [Tom] two fine Children, a Boy and a Girl" (p. 981). Such productivity, of course, again aligns her with the cluster of values that surrounds land in the eighteenth century: symmetry, stability, continuity.

The subsumption of female by male through the agency of the "natural" right of property and the "affections it engages" is common to all of Fielding's novels. In *Joseph Andrews* and *Amelia,* the heroines similarly provide funds for the purchase of the estates to which the contented couples retire, and in both this provision allows Fielding to mark out the limits of female power within his moral universe. For, quite clearly, as the examples of Fanny Goodwill, Sophia Western, and Amelia Booth suggest, virtuous women are given power in order that they may renounce it by the willing ceding of their property, metaphorically and literally considered, to the control of their male partners once the latter have revealed themselves as prudential. While Clarissa Harlowe mourns the need to be "given up to a strange man; to be engrafted into a strange family; to give up her very name, as a mark of her becoming his absolute and dependent property" (I, p. 153), Fielding's heroines celebrate their ability to contribute to the maintenance of a hierarchy that denies them as individuals, but offers them instead secular canonization as "superiour Beings." Relinquishing the possibilities of character, they are absorbed into the ethic of property relations, becoming metaphoric attributes of the constitutional order Fielding defends.

*Notes*

1.   Sue Warrick Doederlein, "Clarissa in the Hands of the Critics," *Eighteenth-Century Studies* 16 (1983), 403.

2.   In "The Rise of Feminine Authority in the Novel," *Novel* 15 (1982), Nancy Armstrong locates in the eighteenth century the origins of a "development of a distinctively feminine mode of literature . . . [with] many of the distinctive features of a specialized language for women" (p. 133). John Sitter, *Literary Loneliness in Mid-Eighteenth-Century England* (Ithaca and London: Cornell Univ. Press, 1982), similarly attests to the "flight from history in mid-century poetry" toward "the feminine image used as a symbol of retreat from the harsh world of traditionally male history." His analysis of Fielding's novelistic career echoes these evolutionary terms: "after two 'masculine' novels, Fielding attempts to create a heroine" (pp. 219, 131, 190).

3.   For a summary view of this relation, see Mary Poovey, *The Proper Lady and the Woman Writer: Ideology as Style in the Works of Mary Wollstonecraft, Mary Shelley, and Jane Austen* (Chicago and London: Univ. of Chicago Press, 1984), pp. 10–14.

4.   Henry Fielding, *The History of Tom Jones,* ed. Martin C. Battestin (Middletown, CT: Wesleyan Univ. Press, 1975). Subsequent references are to this edition.

5.   Samuel Richardson, *Clarissa* (London: J. M. Dent & Sons, 1962). Subsequent references are to this edition.

6.   H. T. Dickinson, *Liberty and Property: Political Ideology in Eighteenth-Century Britain* (London: Methuen, 1979), p. 92.

7.   Douglas Hay, "Property, Authority and the Criminal Law," in *Albion's Fatal Tree: Crime and Society in Eighteenth-Century England,* ed. Douglas Hay, Peter Linebaugh, and E. P. Thompson (New York: Pantheon, 1975), p. 25.

8.   Western, for example, stands as the most benign of a series of male authorities who equate females with property. The series includes Captain Blifil, who was "greatly enamoured . . . of Mr. *Allworthy's* House and Gardens, and of his Lands, Tenements and Hereditaments; of all which the Captain was so passionately fond, that he would most probably have contracted Marriage with them, had he been obliged to have taken the witch of *Endor* into the Bargain" (p. 67); it also includes his son, for whom Sophia's "Fortune and her Person were the sole Objects of his Wishes, of which he made no Doubt soon to obtain the absolute Property" (p. 295).

9.   Fabricant, "Binding and Dressing Nature's Loose Tresses: The Ideology of Augustan Landscape Design," *Studies in Eighteenth-Century Culture,* ed. Roseann Runte (Madison: Univ. of Wisconsin Press, 1979), pp. 109–35.

10.   Hunter, "Fielding and the Disappearance of Heroes," in *The English Hero,* 1660–1800, ed. Robert Folkenflik (Newark: Univ. of Delaware Press, 1982), p. 139.

11.   Blackstone, *Commentaries on the Laws of England,* 12th ed. (London: 1793–95), II, p. 2.

12.   See Thomas R. Cleary, *Henry Fielding Political Writer* (Waterloo: Wilfred Laurier Press, 1984), pp. 207–72.

# Virtues of Authority in *Tom Jones*

## Eric Rothstein

Perhaps no English novel bears so many visible marks of intention as *Tom Jones*. It has overt statements from a reliable narrator. In its dedication it announces a didactic purpose; and part of this purpose, in turn, depends on teaching the virtue of discretion or prudence, which itself depends on judicious action. In managing the plot of *Tom Jones* the narrator himself enjoys a full command of prudence or its equivalent, an ability to assess the future. As a retrospective narrator, he is *in* the future: what is to come for the characters and reader has already come for him. Finally, to go with these other modes of intention—self-aware commentary, didactic purpose, theme and practice of prudence—he calls attention to a fourth type, the creation of a new, well-calculated aesthetic form. He discusses it, he provides a high degree of visible coherence and design, and he often alludes to other works of literature in a way that locates his own. Of course these marks of intention legitimate Fielding's novel as the novel of a man who knows what's what and what he's up to. Such a man of judgment can teach others, as Fielding says he wishes to do, for didacticism entails the teacher's authority to discriminate those who possess (know, believe, practice) "true" learning from those who do not, and the more sharply so when writings are esoteric or audiences balky. Although *Tom Jones* is exoteric, it does find or invent two balky audiences, the school of reptile critics who hiss an unorthodox "history" and the flock of fools and knaves within Fielding's novel who shun or betray the virtues he praises. No wonder, then, that the narrator—"Fielding," as I shall call him, on my axiomatic assumption that he represents Henry Fielding—flaunts his authority and wields a powerful irony, setting "good" readers, who practice what he preaches, apart from aesthetic and moral reptiles. Visible intention helps create Fielding's authority to do this; but the authority does not always help to fulfill the claims of intention.

The narrator's control and unshakable confidence let him partake of two modes of authority, paternalism and autonomy. Richard Sennett's analysis of

Reprinted with permission from "Virtues of Authority in *Tom Jones*," by Eric Rothstein, *The Eighteenth-Century*, vol. 28 (1987): 99–126, Texas Tech University Press. Also by permission of the author.

these two modes, to which I am indebted, describes the first of them, paternalism, as an offer of intimacy and protection to those who are deferent.[1] This
"egoistic benevolence" of paternalism generates a contradiction: "There is a
promise of nurturance made . . . [but] the essential quality of nurturance is
denied: that one's care will make another person grow stronger" (69, 82).
This contradiction, I will argue, appears in Fielding's treatment of those who
depend upon him, his readers and "all the Personages of this History[, whom
I regard] in the Light of my Children" (857).[2] As to the second mode of
authority, autonomy, Sennett discusses it partly in terms of self-possession and
self-sufficiency, and of the disciplinary tool of shame (84, 92–95). Self-possessed and armed with satire that can threaten his readers, Fielding insists on
his self-sufficiency as "the Founder of a new Province of Writing, . . . at liberty to make what Laws I please therein" (77), as a man always in control,
bound by only voluntary constraints, needing the approval of no one. Like
paternalism, autonomy has its contradictions, which I will trace in Fielding's
treatment of rivals inside and outside his novel proper. Among rivals are,
first, figures who have social authority (Allworthy and the patrons to whom
Fielding dedicates *Tom Jones*), second, the reader (to whose authority as judge
Fielding responds in the first paragraph of *Tom Jones*), and, third, other literary
works and genres—parts of a canon prior to and independent of this novel—
which he uses and transforms. Simply to underscore my argument, I shall discuss each of these largely in terms of one or more specific visible marks of
intention.

## 1. Figures of Social Authority, and "Reliable" Statements about Them

In the Dedication to *Tom Jones,* Fielding speaks in his own person, sincerely—
at least one is supposed to suppose that a dedication is sincere. But a printed
dedication also frames a novel, surely one as deliberate as *Tom Jones.* In com-
plimenting his patron Lyttelton, as he lavishly and elegantly does, Fielding of
course compliments himself, for whom but the worthy would a patrician of
high moral quality and aesthetic judgment egg on, support, and praise? Lyttelton suggested the novel to Fielding, helped him live while writing it, acted
as model for Allworthy's benevolence, and now has "commended the Book
. . . warmly." Fielding not only puffs himself through another's noble lips, he
also insists on his own rights over Lyttelton, whose modesty he overrides:
"Notwithstanding your constant Refusal, when I have asked Leave to prefix
your Name to this Dedication, I must still insist on my Right to desire your
Protection of this Work." In that any social compulsion on Fielding stays
invisible, he displays his own autonomy too: Lyttelton's "Benefactions" to

him are to be read as disinterested and Fielding appears to speak only from gratitude, asserting his "Right to your Protection and Patronage" only when he no longer really needs them, i.e., as soon as the completion of his book offers him too the chance to be disinterested. As with various other forms of repayment, like potlatches or reciprocated invitations to dinner, "the *presentation,* the manner of giving, must be such that the outward forms of the act present a practical denial of the content of the act."[3] In this case, the manner of giving provides both Lyttelton and Fielding with not only each other's praise but also the guise of not needing anybody's praise (because each is inherently a man of merit, as the praise from the other man confirms).

The beneficiaries of this rhetoric, Fielding and Lyttelton, therefore seem to be acting perfectly freely, autonomously, on the basis of independently shared values that also qualify them for their paternal roles. These values include generosity and discernment, immediately plain in their generosity to each other, their discernment of each other's virtues. Beyond that, Lyttelton as patron propagates virtue and the arts; Fielding offers his new and inventive novel for the promotion of virtue among "Mankind" (7). Throughout this novel appears, in the narrator's shrewd voice, Fielding's version of Lyttelton's aesthetic and moral discernment. And of course the values that Fielding shares with his patron—discernment, benevolence, only obliquely making the exercise of one's virtues public—all become major themes within the novel.

Two general points seem to me of interest here. One is a paradox of rank: Fielding admits his patron's superiority and yet emerges his patron's essential equal, thus raising his own authority. The overt statements of intention which constitute a dedication, then, are in a certain sense ironic. They say, "I defer," but mean something else. The second point of interest is the use of analogy, in which Fielding becomes a type of Lyttelton. Moreover, because Lyttelton is outside the text, he cannot perform for us the actions that would embody his normative authority, but Fielding, who succeeds and to some extent supplants Lyttelton, can and does perform such acts for us, in writing his artistically and ethically successful novel. This use of analogy in turn not only boosts Fielding's authority, it also gives a clue as to the handling of that benevolent fumbler, Squire Allworthy, who should fit into the analogical sequence Lyttelton/Fielding/Allworthy, moving from the real world to the authorial world to the world depicted in *Tom Jones.*

Like the patron Lyttelton and the independent, fatherly Fielding, Allworthy in the novel is beholden to no one, is not prey to the compulsions of power, sex, money, or approval; like them, he protects others through a social and paternal power of judgment. But Fielding's treatment of this apparent analogue has always puzzled critics. As Henry James Pye remarked in 1792, "The author is at great pains to inform us frequently that [Allworthy] is . . . a man of sense and discernment, with a benevolence almost angelic," but he is "really drawn . . . [as] the dupe of every insinuating rascal he meets; and a dupe not of the most amiable kind, since . . . the consequence of his pliability is oftener the punishment of the innocent than the acquittal of the guilty; and in such punishment he is severe and implacable."[4] If Fielding has allowed Lyttelton's superiority in a way that in fact makes him Lyttelton's equal, he implies Allworthy's equality in a way that in fact makes Allworthy his inferior. Indeed, even if Allworthy were simply an amiable "dupe," in Pye's words, the interested reader could not rely on him as on Fielding. Moreover, by the mode of *Tom Jones,* readers enhance the narrator's authority through their active, complicit responses to hints, irony, and playfulness in his voice, while they can only be passive before Allworthy's earnest homilies. But the demotion of Allworthy goes well beyond this.

In discussing Allworthy, I shall take for granted that the "good Man" is gullible and wrongly self-confident. Obviously his trust is betrayed by everyone—his sister, his nephew, his guests and friends, his lawyer, doctor, and servants, and ipso facto himself—betrayed by nearly everyone, that is, except the only person, Tom, whom he blames bitterly and exiles for just such betrayal. Seeing these faults, the narrator and numerous others after him have smiled that Allworthy is too laudably innocent himself to see evil in others. Taken seriously, the excuse is incoherent: if an innocent heart must produce a gullible head, even in an experienced, well-read magistrate, then by logic a sagacious head like those of Allworthy's presumed analogues, Fielding and Lyttelton, must have a guilty heart as its partner. Taken as a means of mitigation, special pleading for Allworthy's private failings still ignores the degree to which he bungles the public function that Fielding parades for him. One may bypass his public role of patron where, while Lyttelton fosters the voices of a Fielding and a Thomson, Allworthy (as far as Fielding chooses to show us) feeds a nest of singing Blifils. More telling is his conduct as Justice of the Peace.[5] Since Lyttelton was helping Fielding ascend to this very office during the writing of *Tom Jones,* Fielding probably had fresh in his mind what was expected of JPs. The important, landed men of affairs whom he thanks as patrons in the Dedication, Lyttelton, Ralph Allen (vestryman, councilman, mayor of Bath), and the Duke of Bedford (Lord Lieutenant of Bedfordshire), presumably did too.

One such expectation, especially of rural JPs, was a paternal care for the community; hence Theodore Barlow, in 1745, praised committing "the Security of the Peace . . . not to Strangers, who can ill distinguish between the Oath of the Honest Man and the Knave, but to such whose Knowledge of their Neighbours enables them to make a proper Judgement of the Testimony produced before them."[6] Allworthy, of course, "ill distinguishes" such oaths even from his own friends and relatives, but I suspect a country reader in the 1740s would have been surprised too by his ignorance of the community. He commissions the egregious Wilkins as his Bow St. runner to interrogate the servants and villagers about Tom's parentage, while he withdraws to his study (45); he does not recognize the name of his annuitant Partridge, married to his ex-scullion (82, 97), and is "perhaps the only Person in that Country who had never heard of" the Partridges' fight (97). Having heard of Jenny Jones's learning, he misjudges her virtue, since he intends to marry her "to a neighbouring Curate" (50); Bridget proves shrewder. Appropriately, although one of the justice's most vital functions was to arbitrate community disputes (Landau, 173–75), we never see Allworthy doing so. How could he?

After having introduced his good man as an earnest, well-meaning, but detached JP, Fielding continues with a logic of spoiled expectations: Allworthy repeatedly violates the law and its principles. For example, when Allworthy judges Partridge on Mrs. Partridge's testimony, he violates "the great Wisdom and Sagacity of our Law, which refuses to admit the Evidence of a Wife for or against the Husband" (100). He also ignores a rule of reasonable doubt in failing to ask about other likely candidates for impregnating Jenny, for since "there was in the same House a Lad near Eighteen" intimate with Jenny, "it by no means followed, of Necessity, that *Partridge* must have been [the infant's] Father" (102). Allworthy justifies his verdict by declaring "that the Evidence of such a Slut as [the absent Jenny] appeared to be, would have deserved no Credit; but he said he could not help thinking that had she been present, and would have declared the Truth, she must have confirmed what so many Circumstances . . . did sufficiently prove" (101): if the circumstances had proved the case "sufficiently," as they do not, then of course Jenny's "declar[ing] the Truth" would have "confirmed" it—that is a tautology—but, also of course, Allworthy is wrong about the "Credit" to be given Jenny's evidence (as the novel goes on to show, despite her real "sluttishness"), just as he is about her testimony on Partridge's guilt.

Richard Burn's standard guide for the perplexed JP says, "It is a general rule, that hearsay is no evidence,"[7] but in the next case we read of, the good man condemns Black George on Blifil's hearsay, "without any Opportunity to defend himself" (148). Next—like father like daughter—in violation of no fewer than three explicit laws, Allworthy sends Molly Seagrim to a house of correction for being pregnant with a bastard. Because she refuses his demands to inculpate the father (although it was not "lawful . . . to compel any woman, before she shall be delivered, to answer any questions relating to her pregnancy"), Justice Allworthy illegally commits her before she gives birth, and does so on his sole authority despite the law's calling for two justices to examine the accused as well as to sign the order (see Burn, s.v. "Bastard," 125, 127, 135). With some additional sarcasm about how poorly and with what class bias Bridewells rehabilitate even the guilty (cf. 59–60), Fielding remarks that Allworthy "exceeded his Authority a little in this Instance. And, to say the Truth, I question, as here was no regular Information before him, whether his Conduct was strictly regular" (192). Then the good man releases her for the wrong reason, Jones's intercession, though the narrator has earlier assured us that Allworthy was "not in the least affect[ed]" by intercession but only by "any Doubtfulness of the Fact, or any Circumstance of Mitigation" (102–03). Here neither a "Fact" of bastardy nor a mitigating circumstance exists. Allworthy also assumes, falsely and without evidence, that by sleeping with Molly, Tom has "corrupt[ed] and ruin[ed] a poor Girl." In this case, he is first illegally harsh, then inconsistent: he did not consider her "a poor Girl" who had been "corrupted" by someone else when her demeanor towards him, in refusing to betray Tom's name to him, prompted him to "sacrifice" her "to Ruin and Infamy . . . in a *Bridewel*" (59). And finally, when this magistrate banishes his foster son, he breaks the legal principle that a court indictment had to "have a precise and sufficient certainty" and set forth "the offense itself . . . with clearness and certainty" so that the accused might "fully understand his charge."[8] Instead the defendant "hardly knew his Accusation," for Allworthy "out of Modesty sunk every thing that related particularly to himself, which indeed principally constituted the Crime," namely, having "filled the House with Riot and Debauchery " while Allworthy's life was at its most endangered. To cover his own motives, Allworthy credits hearsay testimony from a deponent whom he himself believes unreliable, Squire Western, about Tom's "base and barbarous" attempt to "steal away" Sophia (310, 306, 308).

If Allworthy's gullibility compromises his autonomy by showing him damagingly dependent on others, his parental function is compromised by his repeated difficulty in understanding the rules and logic of evidence, reasonable doubt, presumption of innocence, and legal procedures when acting officially as a magistrate or, even more important for the novel, when making judgments as a private citizen with education and experience as a magistrate. Before the climactic exile of Blifil, he makes negative judgments every single time for the wrong reasons, solemnly put forth and socially justified. With each such judgment the quality of his justice worsens, moreover: Jenny and Partridge confess but Partridge recants; the shady Black George happens to be innocent of the crime, habitual poaching, for which he is condemned unheard; Allworthy violates laws in committing Molly and his own principles in releasing her at Tom's intercession; and he wholly reverses right and wrong when he exiles Tom and slanders him thereafter.

Yet Fielding shields Allworthy instead of bathing him in satire according to the usual method in this novel. What seem to be—and in one sense *are*—direct, straight-faced narrative assertions about the "good Man" also enlarge the textual effect of irony, an irony of strained, unexplained, special privilege which has less to do with Allworthy's merits than with his relation to Fielding as a figure of benign authority. Effects that are plainly ironic elsewhere in *Tom Jones,* such as the narrator's advocacy of an untenable position (see, e.g., his praise of Harriet's affair with the Irish peer [616–17]), are reshaped so as to deflect judgment from Allworthy. For example, in the process of excusing the Squire's detachment from his community, Fielding explicitly applies to Allworthy the maxim "that by attending to the Conversation at a great Man's Table, you may satisfy yourself of his Religion, his Politics, his Taste, and indeed of his entire Disposition" (98). Elsewhere he would follow this with a punch line to make us laugh at a witty judgment, for as a matter of fact the models of religion, politics, taste, and disposition we hear at that table are only the Blifils, Thwackum, Square, and Squire Western. Yet here Fielding does not offer the punch line but diverts us to Partridge's trial, so that judgment of Allworthy on this matter loses force. Let me offer another example. Fielding praises Allworthy's neglect of minor illness, but then shows the neglect aggravating the illness badly and by allusion compares Allworthy with a famous pagan suicide, Cato (240–41). The sequence, which seems to be leading to criticism, is now deflected with a little eulogy of Christian fortitude and divine reward for the "faithful Labourer." This topic in turn suggests another irony, however, between God's proper reward for merit and Allworthy's complacent bequests to the unfaithful and unmeritorious (243–44). Yet this irony too is deflected, as Fielding focuses on the greedy, ungrateful legatees, not the duped testator. Repeatedly defined by this style of deflected blame, Allworthy gets a reward proper to his character and decorum, an irony of benignant (though for Fielding also deliberate) misjudgment from his fellow magistrate.

Most of the criticism of *Tom Jones* defers to such unexamined narrative authority by hastening, like the narrator, to pardon such faults in Allworthy as are made plain. This invited skewing of judgment has four useful effects. First, the narrator, who elsewhere does not hold his sarcastic tongue, establishes his own benevolence by going the benevolent man one better. For Fielding to erect such a prominent ethical sanctuary qualifies other judgments and assures favor, too, for Tom, also good but erratic. Allworthy, then, acts for Fielding in the plot not principally by being his spokesman and efficient agent but by failing to be; as the generous reader's generous patron, Fielding fills Allworthy's visibly empty shoes, assisting Tom and Allworthy himself. Second, because "Fielding himself clearly condescends to . . . Allworthy,"[9] he removes any center of reliable authority within the novel besides himself, and does so, third, while pretending a relation of equality or deep respect for the person over whom he shows himself superior. In this procedure we have an analogue to his handling of Lyttelton, and an undermining of a visible mark of authorial intention—the "reliable" statement—by the drive for authority. Fourth, he distinguishes himself as one who can grasp and adapt the law, the laws of human nature and of "history" writing, in contradistinction to Allworthy's damaging naiveté and fallings-off from the civil and criminal law he has sworn to uphold. Fielding thus legitimates his own law-making, his de jure as well as de facto authority.

## 2. READERS' AUTHORITY: DIDACTICISM, PRUDENCE, AND DESIGN

So far I have advanced the idea that Fielding develops authority by using a sort of irony in his overt statements about other figures of virtue. Saying one thing, effecting another, he harvests for himself the allworthiness within the history and inherits a mantle from Lyttelton and his other patrons. Through this same irony in regard to other visible marks of intention, he extends his authority over readers whom he appears to be treating as equals, just as with Allworthy. The first two chapters, where reader gets acquainted with narrator, show the process at work. For instance, Fielding begins the book proper by genially stepping down from the praise of famous friends into the subservient role of innkeeper, unlike a patron or "Gentleman who gives a private or eleemosynary Treat" (31). He proposes equitably to forestall the readers' "Right to censure, to abuse, and to d—n their Dinner without Controul" by encouraging their free choice through "a Bill of Fare" (31). But my hypothesis predicts that Fielding will reassume the role of patron and will refuse the reader the equality of free choice, let alone the superiority of sitting in judgment or of being catered to by right.

Thus his menu, when it appears, announces only that he plans to serve up "Human Nature," a "Bill of Fare" as unhelpfully vague as are a great many of the "particular Bills to every Course which is to be served up in this and the ensuing Volumes" (32). In fact, Fielding concedes that "the Excellence of the mental Entertainment consists less in the Subject, than in the Author's Skill in well dressing it up" (33). But that "concession" neatly abrogates advance choice. Only after eating what Fielding chooses to put on his table d' hôte can the reader, lacking a Guide Michelin, judge skill. By such maneuvers, Fielding gets to the end of the chapter not bound to bills of fare and his readers' personal taste, but matching the freedom of a certain great chef de cuisine—surely the source of "private or eleemosynary Treat[s]"— who goads the flagging appetite and "is supposed to have made some Persons" keep eating "for ever" (34). As Fielding ascends from plain public host, eager to please, and becomes a manipulative cuisinier, he grows in jovial disdain for the reader who is to be "rendered desirous to read on for ever" by being fed a "hash and ragoo" of human nature, spiced "with all the high *French* and *Italian* Seasoning of Affectation and Vice which Courts and Cities afford" (34). The free choice welcomed at the start of the chapter, next annulled by the vagueness of the "Bill of Fare," at the end reappears degraded to a predictable avidity to gourmandize on scandal. And while he shrinks the reader's rights to pick and criticize, the self-possessed Fielding exercises his own such rights by his raillery at innkeepers ("we have condescended to take a hint from these honest Victuallers"), Bristol aldermen ("well learned in eating"), epicures, shops that claim to stock Bayonne ham and "*Bologna* Sausage," and the nobleman's chef ("This great Man," "the great Person"), who is himself presumably French and therefore a countryman to "Affectation and Vice."

The next chapter takes up the narrative with a similar structure, from mutuality to mastery. First, the generous narrator: he offers his reader free choice (Chapter 1) and launches into an enthusiastic description of Allworthy (Chapter 2). But just as he reneges on his implied submissiveness in Chapter 1, so he goes on the attack in Chapter 2, with sarcasm about Allworthy's sister Bridget. As he ends Chapter 1 in dominance, needling the reader (not even a deviant reader), so he ends Chapter 2 with an assertion of his own will and a flouting of "pitiful Critics" (37) who presume to judge him. This judgment upon critics derives, by analogy and juxtaposition, from his—and our— judging the judgmental Bridget, who "would often thank God she was not as handsome as Miss such a one, whom perhaps Beauty had led into Errors, which she might have otherwise avoided" (36). Bridget endorses the rules (Prudence) to mask her incapacity and frustration (at not being wooed); so, Fielding thus hints, do those critics who blame his popular, beautiful, apparently wandering novel. Since he has already drawn the reader into sneering at the fictional Bridget, his analogy between her and the real critics now draws the reader into scorning them. Indeed, his sudden, exuberant ferocity makes one feel it would be risky not to. But this attack on critics is to cow us and wow us and herd us where he wants us, not to make us his equals, as the complex, anecdotal irony of the previous paragraph about Bridget seemed flatteringly close to doing.

Chapter 1 ends with us led by our appetites, not our judgments. Chapter 2 ends with our judgment of the novel driven by fear of Fielding's loud scorn, and our judgment of Bridget driven by our appetite for malice. Bridget, Fielding says, is now past "an Aera, at which, in the Opinion of the malicious, the Title of Old Maid may, with no Impropriety be assumed" (35). Of course by palming off on somebody else—"the malicious"—the irony of making "Old Maid" a "Title" eagerly "assumed," Fielding lets us enjoy gratis the malice of the comment. We enjoy the comment gratis, too, because we rightly guess that Fielding would not jab at a sympathetic spinster. He thus enables us to rationalize malice (the comment about all unmarried women over thirty) into just deserts. The same kind of thing happens in the next sentence: "She was of that Species of Women, whom you commend rather for good Qualities than Beauty, and who are generally called by their own Sex, very good Sort of Women—as good a Sort of Woman, Madam, as you would wish to know" (35–36). Unspecified people's politeness ("you commend" what commendable qualities there are) turns into a sneer (beauty, not "good Qualities" would be the trait naturally to be commended if it could be), then into dismissive cattiness ("very good Sort of Women"). But Fielding lets us, too, look down on Bridget because she is plain, by making clear through irony that she, too, would rank beauty over good qualities if her own looks let her dare to, and by locating the cattiness, like the sarcasm of "the malicious," not in him or us but in a female voice summoned up ad hoc to express it. The paragraph as a whole mocks doing the right thing (ranking beauty low, being prudent, the trained bands' going on duty) for the wrong reason, but allows us to do the right thing (laugh at Bridget) for the wrong reason, idle malice. In short, Fielding protects us from having to own up to our snideness, which then has full play. We appreciate the favor—but what is one to say about the moral intentions of a book that proceeds in this way?

What is one to say, too, about the freedom of the reader in a book that trains us to employ certain modes of reading—irony and analogy—which are designed to lead us into error as well as knowledge? Let me detail one example, again from the first few chapters of Book I: the doubling of Bridget and Deborah Wilkins, whose resemblance tickles us so much that it distracts us from guessing their difference. In Wilkins, Fielding provides a postmenopausal woman of 52, physically and occupationally a maid, to help us brand Bridget, who is in fact neither old nor maid. Bridget's hypocritical sexual virtue in Chapter 2 reappears in Chapter 3 as the property of Wilkins, who in turn adds to it vanity, callousness, and a hypocritical compliance with the wishes of Allworthy, "under whom she enjoyed a most excellent Place" (41); in Chapter 4 identical vices recur once more in Bridget, who allegedly contemns dress and adorns herself only "in Complacence to" her brother, whom she seldom contradicts though she "would wish she had been blest with an independent Fortune." In keeping with this closely followed analogy, the maid expects her mistress to vote for posting baby Tom, "as a kind of noxious Animal, immediately out of the House," and indeed both ladies describe the baby's mother with the same terms, "Hussy," "Slut," "Strumpet" (40, 44–45). Thus Fielding blinds the reader to the clues of Bridget's maternity. In Chapter 5 Bridget's kissing the baby and giving "Orders . . . so liberal, that had it been a Child of her own, she could not have exceeded them" seem merely to counterpoint Wilkins's simulated raptures over "the dear little Creature" (46). In Chapter 7, when Wilkins swears to wring the baby's father's name from Jenny, Bridget censures her "Curiosity," saying that even "her Enemies could not accuse her of prying into the Affairs of other People" (56). But since we know she "frequently" eavesdrops on Allworthy's judicial examinations (55), we pounce on her hypocrisy, answered by more of the same from Wilkins, and miss the double deceit by which Bridget hides her maternity through hinting the truth about it. My point is not that Fielding cleverly conceals his surprise ending—all novelists try to—but that he makes us conceal it for him, using the very skills at analogy and irony which he has taught us by example and encouragement. Of course he does not get blamed for co-opting our labor in this way, for during the first reading of *Tom Jones* we are naively congratulating ourselves on our collusion with him; on later readings we relish along with him an irony that no longer impugns us.

Fielding thus secretly exploits the interpretative smugness he prompts in us as first-time readers. We gain neither prudence nor charity as a result, since he keeps us from discovering this irony till the denouement, when all our judgments of the characters have been made and we can no longer become more tolerant of them by reflecting upon our own folly. But Fielding gains authority: he displays his autonomy by ironizing even our docility to his method, while, father-like, he protects us from being hurt by our induced, hidden ignorance. He also mimics both the irony and the protection by parading his own ignorance—for instance, when he says that he does not know why Allworthy was in London during Bridget's last trimester of pregnancy (38)—and his own swaggering overconfidence. We see his irony about himself as playful, since we know he knows the truth, but in catching that irony we miss irony of a different sort at our expense, for misjudging both the plot and Fielding's compact of mutuality with us.

The better a reader of *Tom Jones* one is, the better one grasps *Tom Jones,* for no character assessment backfires; but the better a reader of *Tom Jones,* the worse one grasps it too, for one's faithfully practiced skills preclude many possibilities, some of which, like Bridget's motherhood, turn out to be true. As the example of Bridget and Wilkins suggests, furthermore, Fielding gains community with the reader by sacrificing some complexity of moral judgment. The self-satisfaction of the reader is insured by her or his being trained always to pick the most cynical interpretation of behavior from the offered choices. Take an instance deliberately plucked from its context: "Whether a natural Love of Justice, or the extraordinary Comeliness of *Jones,* had wrought on *Susan* to make the Discovery, I will not determine" (553). Who does not know which of the two has "wrought on *Susan*" despite Fielding's wink of restraint? The charitable guess is invoked only for fun and a satiric tsk of moral assessment. Wittily prompted to be a polished cynic, the reader assumes his or her own authority, being in the know about human nature, never being a patsy for pretenders, keeping aloof and morally superior. But we pay for the pleasure of elitism by making automatically and reductively the only judgments that Fielding lets us make, seemingly unprompted, on our own.

Loyal and erratic readers alike, then, end up multiply misled when they try to share in the authority that the laws of the novel—the regularities that underline analogy, irony, and tone—make them think they can share. Analogy, irony, tone, and law are exquisitely used means of Fielding's control; and our response to them confirms our camaraderie with Fielding and lets us maneuver through his world by emulating his style and bearing, but *never* his independence as the wielder of fancy, the breaker and maker of "rules," the discoverer of paradox. *Tom Jones* gives the reader less actual freedom of interpretation and moral stance than any other major eighteenth-century novel because its narrator's power of grouping and exclusion is the most compelling of any. And as we have little autonomy and little power to judge "Fielding," so our experience of reading gives no weight—and therefore, I should say, no importance—to our decisions. Misled by the narrator (or narrative) we fall into error, but never suffer for it. The exhilaration of touring the microcosm with the paternal Fielding and the comic tone that shunts aside any fear of real disaster make this a novel of the continuous present, not a novel that makes one fear a dark future, a mighty stimulus for prudence, "the Duty," Allworthy says, "which we owe to ourselves" (960).

Prudence, freedom, and weight given to decisions—since these are devalued in us, they are rarely valued in the characters. The blots on Allworthy's public reputation, for example, come solely from his *worthier* actions. When he says he expects to meet his wife in heaven, his neighbors think him mad, impious, or fraudulent (35). His care of baby Tom leaves him suspected of fathering a bastard and making a scapegoat of its mother (58–59). He is accused of rigor and cruelty toward the Partridges (103), of having been "as arrant a Whoremaster as any within five Miles o'un" (by Western; 190), of being a hypocrite about money (277), and of having sent Jones "away Pennyless, and some said, naked from the House of his inhuman Father" (311). In each case, even that of the Partridges' sentence (once he had passed his unjust verdict), he is guiltless, blackened, and essentially unhurt. Whereas his "virtue itself 'scapes not calumnious strokes," in the words of *Hamlet,* a play to which we shall return, the squire's real injustices and naivetés pass without soiling his reputation or damaging him in any essential way.

Some adoring critics have singled out Sophia as prudence in the flesh, mostly because she alone sees through Blifil but also because her name means "wisdom" (not "prudence") in Greek. No one to my knowledge has followed this logic sedulously enough, however, to argue just as (im)plausibly for the honor of her gossipy maid Honour: if "Virtue and Innocence can scarce ever be injured but by Indiscretion" (7), then *Prudentia* really does have worldly honor at her side. But as to Sophia Western, she so often displays scant *phronesis*—prudence—that to allegorize her name risks irony, imprudently. (I suspect she is a Sophia, like George II's grandmother, mother, and sister, merely to link her with the Hanoverians for whom loyal Tom prepares to fight.)[10] This young Sophia rides by night, dressed in a gold-laced habit, through an England infested with thieves, such as attack her aunt, the Old Man of the Hill, and Jones, and such as almost attack and strip her (649); her maid Honour, a female Partridge, reveals her identity on the road. Sophia entrusts herself to a strange man to conduct her to Honour. She deliberately leaves her muff in her young lover's bed; he almost goes to jail as a result. Her comportment leads her—with dangerous potential—to be mistaken for the Pretender's mistress, the morally and politically tainted Jenny Cameron, and she at last moves in with the demirep Lady Bellaston, whose moral character she cannot detect and who plots her rape. Like Allworthy, but unlike the reader, she has so little "perspicacity of moral *vision,*" the faculty that "alone permits [one] to perceive the truth behind appearances and to proceed from the known to the obscure,"[11] that on the hearsay of "Landlords and Servants," she indicts the man she loves of traducing her name in public, "an Offence," as Fielding says, "foreign to his Character" (732). Despite her demand near the end of the novel that Jones serve a probationary period, her love takes over from her gestures toward prudence (and surely we approve). Her vanity takes over too, for she yields directly to fine sentiments and flattery, bound in a crude argument from Jones's self-interest: her beauty and mind are such, Jones exclaims, that no one could ever be unfaithful to her (983). In short, Fielding shows Sophia as courageous, resilient, lovely and loving, endangered, pure of heart, and—as a woman with a Hanoverian name—loyal. But not as reliably prudent. Nor does he illustrate prudence by situating her where some prudent course is clear.

Fielding of course could hardly make Allworthy and Sophia prudent when the reader, nestled within Fielding's wisdom, still lacks foresight. Besides, by its display of power, flair, and freedom, too, I suggest, Fielding's authority diminishes prudence and the consequences of imprudence in *Tom Jones*. Prudence depends on the probable, on acting in terms of likely consequences. Thus Obadiah Walker defines *prudence* in terms of (1) sagacity (penetration into things by skill in interpreting signs), (2) weighing of circumstances, and (3) "*Providence,* or prevision of futures, what may, and what may not, most probably fall out; which is the height of human wisedome."[12] The idiom of *Tom Jones,* with its hierarchy of narrator/reader characters, frustrates all three of these, sagacity, the weighing of circumstances, and prevision. Most clearly, it frustrates sagacity, for although *Tom Jones* gives the good characters an active love of virtue, which is the base for making good judgments, it denies to these characters the reader's skill (thanks to Fielding) in assessing dispositions to behavior, i.e., probabilities. Neither the characters nor we can guess sagaciously how these probabilities actually will come into play, something only Fielding knows, and knows as fact, not conjecture.

Fielding's emphasis on spontaneous virtue, the nature from which the good characters' goodness springs, partially frustrates Walker's second criterion, the weighing of circumstances. No one weighs when Tom dashes, armed with "an old Broad-sword," to save the Old Man from "two Ruffians" with pistols (447), or dashes, armed with an "Oaken Stick," to save Jenny Waters from Northerton, "without the least Apprehension or Concern for his own Safety" (496, 495), or shares his money with the highwayman Enderson, in defiance of Partridge's proverbial warning (681), some version of "Save a thief from the gallows and he will cut your throat" (Tilley T109). The same applies a fortiori to Tom's immediate, "instant," or "hasty" rescues of Sophy's bird (160), Sophy (200), the Merry Andrew (649), and Nightingale (702). In every case, risk (imprudence) augments the virtue. How could it be otherwise, when Fielding—although he, sagacious, knowing, and provident, is not imprudent—must present himself as freely taking risks, defying "rules," trusting his own *intuitive* judgment, displaying autonomy with a flair? In the narrative of *Tom Jones* spontaneity is not always good but good always arises spontaneously.

Finally, the idiom of *Tom Jones* frustrates Walker's third part of prudence, the "prevision of futures," for the story has so many improbabilities, so many coincidences and strokes of fortune, that some of the very critics who believe that Fielding is teaching prudence have also argued that he is dramatizing the workings of divine providence. The dramatization of providence entails improbabilities, hence a kind of argument from miracles or an argument from design. In "real life," of course, human prudence and divine providence need not clash if providence works through second causes, "seen" through prevenient faith, but in novelistic life, providence becomes evident only when it works by "wonderful Means" as "the Lord disposeth all Things" (943, 942). To the extent that *Tom Jones* lends itself to be read as dramatizing providential action, then, the case for human prudence, an art of probability, weakens. Weak it is, because Fielding has everything to gain if we read the text as legitimated by an outside normative force with which he ably allies himself. And this force exhibits itself as *both* a lawlike order of nature, probable, *and* an order of providential intrusion, improbable. The both/and applies whether or not *Tom Jones* is theologically charged. If it is, Fielding represents God by both maintaining regular order (the Newtonian position in the Clarke-Leibniz debate) and butting in to insure that this microcosm is sunny. If it is not, he impersonates "God" to naturalize—to employ only in disguised form—the conventions of happy-ending romance. In any case, his own creative authority and ethical authority increase under the (factitious?) divine light. Only through his appearing both to administer the plot and to do so "naturally" does he wield the rights of a law-giving, nurturing figure, a proper "Parent" to "the Personages of [his] History" (857). Nature therefore involves enough probability to keep the story lifelike and apparently useful to us, but, thwarting Walker's "prevision of futures," enough improbability to keep Fielding in charge while we and the characters, however much we may choose goods over evils, can never reliably "determine the proper and effective means of achieving the one and avoiding the other."[13]

Does Fielding then recur to prudence, about which he now and again editorializes throughout the novel, merely to affirm his own moral orthodoxy and the value of control, such as he himself epitomizes? What about Tom, who does suffer from imprudence and who seems to learn better sense as the novel progresses? The answers to both these questions respond to the line of argument I have offered. Prudent action implies freedom to choose, and since Fielding presents himself as historian, not puppeteer, his characters must give the illusion of having free will. He keeps his credentials as historian, then, by stressing, through prudence, that events move predictably (causally, with verisimilitude) and that characters choose freely. These are half-truths, but the more reason then to proclaim them true. Only in a law-governed, verisimilar world does his public authority—his accountability, his moral teaching—have meaning. But that world must also appear as comic, whose decorum accepts Fielding's paternal and detached tone. Where can this tone and the characters' freedom, which is to say their comic fallibility, intermesh? Not very well with Allworthy and Sophia, because no social or generic convention approves a friendly, amused superiority toward the follies of worthy magistrates or maidens. Very well with Tom, though, as a type of the scapegrace whose pains are part of a rite of passage. Youth's antics always elicit some version of this tone, in Roman comedy, in Waugh and Fitzgerald, in modern Deans of Students, as in Fielding.

And, as in Fielding, youth generally learns a prudence of avoidance rather than of planning, the more complex exercise of Obadiah Walker's criteria, sagacity, deliberation, and foresight. Tom very rarely looks to the future. His good acts have good motives, in G. E. M. Anscombe's sense of "the spirit in which an act is performed," but beyond the immediate future, not "intentions," which Anscombe relates to "the end to which the [act is] a means—a future state of affairs to be produced by" it.[14] If one takes "prudence" to be the proper exercise of Anscombe's "intention," none of the virtuous characters in *Tom Jones,* except, of course, for Fielding, displays it. Tom's rejection of the rich, lusty, and religious widow Arabella Hunt, who asks him to marry her, may serve as a test case, plainly its function. Here Tom, far from being Walker's prudent man, rebuffs all future considerations in favor of "the Voice of Nature, which cried in his Heart" (826–28). And this is as wise a criterion as any. Like the reader, Tom has freedom to choose in that he has no impediments, but cannot exercise any broader freedom in that the novel has no knowable principle for gauging the weight and consequentiality of any act. Like the reader, he has only very short-range "intentions," in Anscombe's sense.

Reducing "prudence" to learned avoidance in Tom, thereby professing a limited code of free will and responsibility, also helps closure in *Tom Jones.* Toward the end of the novel, Tom's rejection of other women, his good resolutions for the future, his submission to divine judgment, and his "recognition" that he, not Fortune, has brought ills upon him (894; 909; 916) complete his character in a way that social norms compel the reader to approve. Moreover, these statements also announce his sense that he has free will and that his exercise of it is important. Tom ceases to be Fielding's foster child and becomes his own man, an effect that complements his ongoing "growth," i.e., his being allowed to talk and understand others in an increasingly sophisticated way while on the road. Rejection of other women, good resolutions, and other acts of prudence—still avoidance rather than planning, still "motive" without "intention"—stabilize the situation with which the novel ends, for this kind of prudence is a virtue of cautious regularity that slows and simplifies change. When we need not have the actual (boring) experience of a judicious Tom, we can comfortably wish him judicious to help guarantee the happy ever after that we hope he has. This ending, with its providential, non-prudential "consequences"—character witnesses, plots discovered, Sophia gained—presents an analogue to the reader's final recognitions of narrative truths (and the truth of her or his relation to the narrator) while *Tom Jones* plies her or him with narrative rewards. Moral considerations come into play here, in that Tom and we get our rewards because he and we are generous; but this does not involve much moral learning.

### 3. The Authority of Genres: What Literary Allusion Intends

With a virtuoso play of styles and tones, *Tom Jones* redefines the autonomous, procreative genres that enter it. I am thinking, for example, of oedipal tragedy (Tom's "incest" and "parricide"), epic, the pastoral romance, Terentian comedy and comédie larmoyante (the Nightingale-Nancy episode), spiritual autobiography (the Old Man's tale), and history.[15] I have been arguing, in keeping with this redefinition, for an ironic inflection of the romance pattern and the didactic tone. By "ironic" I do not mean that Fielding attacks romance and didacticism any more than he jabs Homer with Molly Seagrim's reeking pitchfork by choosing to sing her battle with the "*Somersetshire* Mob" in "*Homerican* Stile." Rather, he employs the voice of didacticism, of the romance, of the *Iliad,* a multitude of voices from a multitude of positions. In *Tom Jones* the genres that Fielding visits for these voices become tokens of his comprehensiveness (but only tokens, incapable of providing his vaunted originality and his personal commentary). They also become agencies of knowing, because a genre is a dispositional structure, inclined with high probability to do certain things and requiring in turn to be regarded in a certain way (their decorum). In this sense they are just like the characters in *Tom Jones,* and one might expect to find the same kind of limits placed upon their authority, which Fielding filches from them in part by marking them as mere Art. Since in mimetic theory nature fathers the established genres, Fielding's "real life," represented by his verisimilar manufacture, takes precedence over literature that chronologically precedes the artifact *Tom Jones.*

The efficacy as well as the authority of characters and genres has its limits made clear. Fielding's characters, H. K. Miller has shown, descend from stock types, Tom the *adulescens,* Allworthy the *senex* and deceived king, Thwackum and Square the evil counsellors, and so forth.[16] Such stock types, given local habitations and names, become constitutive regularities of the novel within which they are also, self-consciously, appropriated—might I say "paternalized"?—and transcended. Though the actual characters, transposed into the "real life" of *Tom Jones,* take on complexity, their ancestral ethos also acts as a mode of limitation upon them. So too with stock genres, which are in part to the narrative as the characters are to the story. We readers share the genres with Fielding, since he and we alike have read others' books, and we assess events correctly with the help of whichever genre a section of *Tom Jones* invokes. Yet Fielding takes over generic patterns, as with patterns of characters' behavior, by exercising his freedom in completing them. As visible, discrete modes, they have something of the independent solidity of his characters, but their autonomous logic, like the characters', leads to their being inadequate to the "real life" with which Fielding tests them, and so he corrects or revises them.

As Fielding brings these genres under his own authority, he limits the degree to which we can make predictions from them. For instance, the adopted Tom may seem to double Oedipus, incestuous and parricidal, in that he sleeps with his supposed mother, Jenny, and nearly kills with his sword the man, Fitzpatrick, who has been living "as Husband and Wife" with her (909). But when the agent who abandoned him returns to reveal his real parents' names and the name of the villain to blame for the plagues, Tom ends up not eyeless and exiled but cleared and at home. And if tragedy is excess in one direction, comedy is excess in the other. Terence's *Adelphi* and Shadwell's adaptation of it in *The Squire of Alsatia* make the harsh father eat crow before the leniency of the uncle, his brother. Fielding (mis)reproduces this plot with the Nightingale brothers. First we have the imitation: the harsh father of young Nightingale violently opposes his son's marriage to poor, pregnant Nancy Miller, but the lenient brother, who himself chose a wife for love, expresses "the utmost Satisfaction" at this marriage (775). Then comes the reversal: in Terence, the happy ending has father and uncle both virtuous; in Fielding, the happy ending has them both greedy and amoral, for the father resists "much Perswasion" from the uncle and Tom, and the uncle, a "good Gentleman" with whom "*Jones* fell into Raptures," turns out to be like his brother, callous, worldly, and headstrong (777, 779–80, 814). Though the elopement of the uncle's daughter follows the Terentian model and the episode has a Terentian tone, we readers of Terence cannot thereby predict the outcome any better than the too easily enraptured Tom.

Still earlier in *Tom Jones,* the Old Man of the Hill offers a spiritual autobiography, a narrative of sin, suffering, and redemption whose potential validity as a type Fielding registers by underlining several analogies between the Old Man's and Tom's histories, and of course by the allegory of "Old Man." After the Old Man sojourns with the world (in the form of theft and fraud), the flesh (a perfidious mistress), and the devil (the "very diabolical" Sir George Gresham), a sudden stroke of providence, seconded by his "Humanity," restores him to his own flesh and blood (his father), to the worldly classical authority of "true Philosophy," and to the "divine Wisdom" of "the Holy Scriptures". Now he burns for salvation, that of a would-be suicide, of a nation menaced by self-destruction through Popery, and finally of his own soul, as he enters the contemplative, religious life on which he spins a rhapsody for Tom (483–85). One might expect this orderly allegorical story to be as exalted as the "very steep" Mazard Hill on which the Old Man lives (the name is Fielding's coinage, presumably from "mazard" = "head"), but no, "the Good Man of the Hill" (497) has become so much a misanthropic ingrate that he placidly lets the "good Angel" Tom, agent of Heaven (448; 496), plunge headlong, unarmed, into unspecified danger, and does not follow with his gun to help. Just as a specific literary model, *Oedipus,* is rewritten to end with the fulfillment of not the oracle's prophecy but Fielding's, so a literary type, spiritual autobiography, is rewritten to end with Fielding's, not God's, preservation of Tom, who needs and who heeds no warning tales. And, as the analogical method prevents as well as aids the reader to fathom what is going to happen, so does the reference to other genres.

A more detailed example may open this matter further. In Book 16, Chapter 5, are heard voices from two genres. One "voice" is that of *Hamlet,* which Tom, Mrs. Miller and her daughter, and Partridge go to see, a father/ brother/son play like *Oedipus, Adelphi,* and Southerne's *The Fatal Marriage.* The other voice is that of Partridge's comments, "the simple Dictates of Nature, unimproved indeed, but likewise unadulterated by Art" (852), with their ancestry in Cervantes and Addison. The handling of this episode repeats the pattern I have described for authority and grouping. Thus Tom ostensibly invites Partridge to come as "one of the Company," but really as a rustic sideshow from whom he expects "to enjoy much Entertainment" (852). By this pretense, Tom in fact colludes with Fielding and us to (in Erving Goffman's useful pun) excollude Partridge.[17] Fielding shares Tom's joke by bettering it—ironic ingenuity is not Tom's forte—in choosing *Hamlet,* which pivots on a play within a (commented upon) play, shown to supposed equals with designs on one another: Claudius and Partridge the watchers are themselves to be watched by the dispossessed heirs to whom they stand in dubious fatherhood. Playing Hamlet, Garrick attracts praise because he is so natural, just as Hamlet advises the actors to be, and just like the Partridge, he of "the simple Dictates of Nature," who mirrors Garrick's and Hamlet's responses. The novel specifically remarks on Partridge's and Garrick/Hamlet's responses to the ghost of the replaced father and to the perfidious, remarried mother, more figures from the history of Tom Jones. (At least Tom's mother's marriage to Blifil would have been a remarriage if the discerning Allworthy had not swallowed as sincere her prudish first refusal of young Summer [942].) Like Partridge, moreover, both *Hamlet* and *Tom Jones* ask who is an actor and who not.

Fielding's magnificently ingenious repetition and variants of *Hamlet*'s multiple framings (in Goffman's sense) top Shakespeare by going him one— or several—better. And some of the cognitive content at which they hint also excolludes Tom, Fielding's and our own ally in the original excollusion of Partridge. This silent irony toward his coworker resembles what we readers suffer when we are relishing our skill at ironic discrimination about Bridget. For instance, while grinning at Partridge's naiveté Tom does not know what we do, that the schoolmaster's lesson, *"Nulla fides fronti* is, I find, a true Saying"

(855), not only calls up Hamlet's own schoolboy tic (or irony) about setting down in his "tables" that "one may smile and smile and be a villain" (I.v.107–8), but also hints at the parallel between the younger brother Blifil and the younger brother Claudius, each a hypocritical auricular poisoner who has dispossessed a brother and a nephew. Blifil duly reappears in the next chapter at his doting uncle's ear. Here, on a level of knowledge above Tom's, we follow all the nice matchings of *Hamlet* and *Tom Jones* that Tom can, and some that Tom cannot or may not. The development of the plot encourages us to keep following these matchings. After *Hamlet* ends Tom gets a summons from Mrs. Fitzpatrick, as a summons from Gertrude comes to Hamlet after *The Mousetrap;* the heroes' swords then lay low the spies, Fitzpatrick and Polonius. As a somewhat displaced parricidal theme operates here in both texts, so, later, does the theme of incest—not, of course, from any protofreudian reading of *Hamlet,* but because the closet scene labels Gertrude incestuous, as Tom thinks his "mother" Jenny was with him (cf. the possible incest with Tom's real mother, 138–39).

At last, of course, Fielding evades colluding with us too. Through all these partial parallels we add further context to our assessment of the characters, and we admire the cleverness of the book; but no more than Tom can we foresee, as Fielding does, how the events in *Hamlet* predict those in *Tom Jones.* Stabbing and incest, yes; further exile, then a return so that the enthroned can be overthrown, yes; boomeranging plots, as on Rosencrantz and Guildenstern and on Laertes, yes; a little space for philosophizing before the denouement, yes; but a mad maiden, a poisoned cup, a Fortinbras, no. The parallels with Shakespeare's great tragedy enlarge Fielding's authority while they cost him not a bit of his freedom. No comparison between two resembling but non-identical texts can be pursued forever, but here Fielding's virtuoso sporting with *Hamlet* is so much in view as to exhibit his freedom and, therefore, cast doubt on any predictive analogy for *Tom Jones.*

Shakespeare's *Hamlet,* staged by Garrick, commented upon by Partridge who is, so to speak, "staged" by Tom, who—with the play and its audience—is staged by Fielding: as I have remarked, Shakespeare's *Hamlet* is also excolluded by multiple designs. Fielding does this without direct, damaging challenge, for he mutes the competition between his novel and Shakespeare's play. *Tom Jones* competes only with a random performance, a kind of optimal but imperfect actualization of the great tragedy, in which it cannot compel its audience as Fielding's performance compels his. The joint efforts of Shakespeare and Garrick in fact entertain less than Tom's debut as impresario: "*Partridge* had afforded great Mirth . . . to all who sat within hearing, who were more attentive to what he said, than to any Thing that passed on the Stage" (857). Because Shakespeare had to delegate powers to actors, a loud Claudius and a clumsy grave digger can expose the surplus of ill art behind the feigning of nature. As Fielding, who keeps us readers on such a tight rein knows, delegating one's authority is dangerous; that is a lesson taught by the mishaps of everyone who does so, Squires Allworthy and Western, Dr. Blifil, his crafty nephew, Lady Bellaston, everyone but Lyttelton, who can delegate his powers to Henry Fielding. In his grip, it is we, who know how shrewd we are, who validate *Tom Jones*'s fidelity to nature, while *Hamlet* is left to be validated by the "natural" Partridge, who can do so only where events in Elsinore mesh with his independent experience.

The effect of *Hamlet* in *Tom Jones* is still further diffused in that Partridge singles out issues that Fielding brings up elsewhere, dangerous luxury (852), ghosts, hypocrisy and bad acting, and the wicked mother/wife. The *Hamlet* scene merely collects them in fixed form, as a summary though not an agent of action in the verisimilar world of his novel. To begin with, Partridge's simple commentary itself echoes his earlier interruptions of the Man of the Hill's tragic narrative, which parody the Man's mixture of cynicism and folly and Tom's openness. As to the themes of the *Hamlet* scene, dangerous luxury, hypocrisy, and erring wives appear in Cibber's *The Provok'd Husband; or, A Journey to London,* which Tom and Partridge see on their own journey to London. Like the Covent Garden *Hamlet,* the performance of Cibber's play calls attention to itself as staged artifice, here by being a puppet show (though with "Figures . . . as big as the Life" [639]). And like *Hamlet,* this mock-life needs the supplement of "real life": with didactic intent that Tom and the others discuss, the puppeteer has cut the "low" plots, a number of which have analogues in *Tom Jones.* The real-life supplement to this sanitized *Provok'd Husband,* then, is the unexpectedly public sexual affair on stage where the maid Grace is discovered with the little Merry Andrew (640) after the performance meant to be public has ended with a marriage between a virtuous Lady Grace and wise, witty John Manly.

More doubling of *Hamlet* and insistence on supplementing art with "real life" occurs when Sophia reads another stage tragedy, Southerne's *The Fatal Marriage: or, The Innocent Adultery,* with doings of a hamletian cast, wicked non-father (a father-in-law), wicked scheming, usurping brother, and man returned from the dead. While melancholy Sophy sits showering her bosom with tears, Lord Fellamar breaks in for the purpose not of innocent adultery but of guilty rape. As it appears in *Tom Jones,* then, *Hamlet* loses its privilege of greatness. It keeps snagging on the conditions of its performance and, far from being unique, merely knits themes from analogous presentations earlier in the narrative. Like those other presentations it seems less full, less "true" than Fielding's history. Expectably, then, the logic of tragic fate in the epitome of tragedies, in Fielding's time the most often performed of Shakespeare's, is repealed by the divinity Fielding who shapes Tom's rough-hewn ends.

On this reading, *Tom Jones* frees itself from the tyranny of the preestablished, whether the authority of prior literary works, the conditions of narrative that make prudence possible, or figures of social power. Fielding proffers his own world alone as the "real," the measure of propositions about ethics and "human nature" (in that his readers, so his didactic claims insist, can project its patterns of action to their everyday lives).[18] As a work of art, it dispels the rule of rules in favor of the rule of taste, in keeping with much aesthetic thought of its time. And taste, a matter of finesse and connoisseurship in judgment, requires a tone of urbanity, of a wisdom filtered from much experience, of a nice balance between involvement and distance. *Tom Jones* provides just that tone. Taste also centers in an individual will able to legitimate its choices, to bring others to assent to its normative authority. By the circular axiology of norm and self, socialization and individual production, Fielding must affirm social, moral, and literary canons so that we trust him and he must also exploit or transcend these canons so that we have nothing to trust unmediated by him. Hence comes the feeling that *Tom Jones* is at once remarkably new and remarkably conservative.

As I have suggested, the techniques by which Fielding legitimizes his authority lead to an extension of his irony. His actions as narrator very often mean more—and often something else—than he says they mean, with the "more" or "something else" in service to his self-interest, just as with the characters' actions on which he slyly comments. And many of his actions as narrator function best when the reader does not really know what they mean. *Tom Jones,* that is, requires that we accept from Fielding "legitimate" versions of the same conduct, like deceit, that he prods us to condemn from the characters. No wonder that from the time of its writing to the present, different readers have emerged from the mystifications of *Tom Jones* with different notions of its didactic effects, some finding prudence and mutuality, others a sentimental, lax complaisance. The strategies of this novel can be pinned down better than can the ends they served in the literary culture that Henry Fielding had a share in creating and that created the narrator "Fielding." Both didacticism and the maintenance of authority are historically plausible goals for the 1740s, and in *Tom Jones,* as I have argued, the rights and roles of each are remarkably slippery. Yet an exact assessment of ends is what should—in theory—be pointed to by the visible marks of intention with which I began. Authorial intention, so one supposes, identifies its goals to others.

I began by identifying certain visible marks of intention in *Tom Jones:* the narrator's voice, the didactic purpose, the theme and practice of prudence, the coherent design of the novel. Each of these consistently establishes authority, Fielding's autonomy and paternalism, but does so at cost to the narrator's actual reliability, the actual teaching of prudence, and the sense of mutuality to which the novel pretends. Or, more exactly, at cost *if* one is an "ideal reader" of *Tom Jones,* for whom the most consistent, economical explanation of textual effects best explains moral effects. But "ideal readers" are themselves fictions in the service of certain notions of text, which are not keyed to affectivity or heterogeneous moral response. The published criticism suggests that Fielding's authority is such as to make many actual readers, including ones both learned and penetrating, suppress the effects that I have been highlighting. The novel may therefore produce its express intentions, moral and affective, in a way that suggests the poverty of describing the "intentions" of *Tom Jones* from its author's avowals, its internal coherence, or its conflicting aims. By the same token, one can hardly evaluate Fielding's statements of intention, which may be largely true without their offering much in the way of interpretative or structural coherence. And there is certainly room to discount them as self-serving, as subverted by other, deeper intentions, or simply as too general and orthodox to take into account the conditions and needs of the 1740s and this elaborate novel. One might even argue that the blurring of ends and means, the assertion and denial of the same codes, add an illusion of depth and complexity to *Tom Jones,* that the authority of the narrator is enhanced in part by his shallowness of intention, though these very intentions legitimate his authority in the first place. By the standards of readers who long for a consistent, morally weighty novel, in any case, both *Tom Jones* and their own responses to it may disturbingly illustrate Gresham's Law.

*Notes*

1. *Authority* (New York, 1980).
2. Page references to *Tom Jones* come from the Wesleyan edition, ed. Martin C. Battestin and Fredson Bowers, 2 vols. (Middletown, Ct., 1975).
3. Pierre Bourdieu, *Outline of a Theory of Practice,* tr. Richard Nice (Cambridge, 1977), 194.
4. Henry James Pye, excerpt from *A Commentary Illustrating the Poetic of Aristotle,* in *Henry Fielding: A Critical Anthology,* ed. Claude Rawson (Harmondsworth, Mx., 1973), 190.
5. Adrian A. Roscoe's "Fielding and the Problem of Allworthy," *Texas Studies in Literature and Language* 7 (1965): 169–72, offers a penetrating discussion of some of the lapses I shall mention, only to conclude with a social-democratic variant of the Allworthy-as-naïf excuse: his "Allworthy is a good man in a particularly bad system" of squirearchy (172). Can this be? The superior analogues to Allworthy, in Fielding himself and his patrons, show us readers clearly— before Allworthy ever swims into our ken—what standards we may justly apply within this very "system."
6. Quoted from *The Justice of the Peace: A Treatise* in Norma Landau, *The Justices of the Peace, 1679–1760* (Berkeley, 1984), 344. Landau's excellent study develops the paternal metaphor for the JP.
7. *The Justice of the Peace and Parish Officer,* 8th ed. (London, 1764), s.v., "Evidence."
8. William Blackstone, *Commentaries,* 11th ed. (London, 1791), 4:306, 323.
9. John Sitter, *Literary Loneliness in Mid-Eighteenth-Century England* (Ithaca, 1982), 193.
10. This is noted in an article that also shares with mine an interest in analogy and the motif of paternity, Homer Obed Brown, "*Tom Jones:* The 'Bastard' of History," *Boundary* 2, 7 (1979): 201–33; the Hanoverian "Sophia" is on 211. On allegorizing "Sophia" or Sophia, Leopold Damrosch, Jr., offers wise cautions in *God's Plot and Man's Stories: Studies in the Fictional Imagination from Milton to Fielding* (Chicago, 1985), 278–79.

11.    Martin C. Battestin, "Fielding's Definition of Wisdom: Some Function of Ambiguity and Emblem in *Tom Jones,*" *ELH* 35 (1968): 191.

12.    Cited in Douglas Lane Patey, *Probability and Literary Form: Philosophic Theory and Literary Practice in the Augustan Age* (Cambridge, 1984), 63; cf. Patey's citation from Hobbes, 335n3.

13.    Battestin, "Fielding's Definition of Wisdom," 191.

14.    G. E. M. Anscombe, *Intention,* 2nd ed. (Oxford, 1963), 18–19.

15.    My model here resembles not the psychohistory of Harold Bloom but the history of "imitation" explored by Howard D. Weinbrot, though without the tone of good sportsmanship he perceives. See, e.g., " 'An Ambition to Excell': The Aesthetics of Emulation in the Seventeenth and Eighteenth Centuries," *Huntington Library Quarterly* 48 (1985): 121–39, and his accounts of Pope's Horace in *Alexander Pope and the Traditions of Formal Verse Satire* (Princeton, 1982).

16.    Henry Knight Miller, *Henry Fielding's "Tom Jones" and the Romance Tradition,* ELS Monograph Series No. 6 (Victoria, 1976), 66–71.

17.    "Excolluding" is one of the cluster of ideas central to his *Frame Analysis: An Essay on the Organization of Experience* (New York, 1974), where, in fact, he discusses the various reframings of events in *Hamlet,* 183.

18.    "[L]egitimating world-views or ideologies . . . remove the . . . validity claims of normative structures from the sphere of public thematization and testing," writes Jürgen Habermas. *Tom Jones* provides an ideological variant: it thematizes and tests such claims within a verisimilar "sphere," one that therefore seems to be "public" but, as I have been arguing, is not. *Legitimation Crisis,* tr. Thomas McCarthy (Boston, 1975), 19.

# Masquerade and Allegory: Fielding's *Amelia*

## Terry Castle

$A$gain one must begin with an irony: that the moralistic impulse—the impulse toward complete rhetorical transparency—is if anything stronger in *Amelia* than anywhere else in Fielding's fiction. It is palpable from the start: in the dedication to Ralph Allen, Fielding baldly announces the purpose of his fiction will be "to promote the Cause of Virtue, and to expose some of the most glaring Evils, as well public as private, which at present infest the Country." The metaphor of exposure is significant. For Fielding indeed seems to have conceived *Amelia* along the lines of the anatomy or satiric allegory. Already, in the peculiar opening books, one finds he is as much concerned here with "unmasking" and enumerating contemporary vices as with developing a coherent mimetic action. The glaring evils glare indeed. From the start *Amelia* displays an element of hypertrophied didacticism, the artistic effects of which have often been calculated.[1]

The fact raises the interesting possibility that it may indeed be the work in which the conscious allegorizing tendency is strongest, where there is a surplus of didactic intention, that also shows the most revealing counterdidactic impulses. As the will toward didactic control over the reader intensifies, as an author strives more and more to make his or her fiction an entirely accountable ethical paradigm—the perfect allegorical *kosmos*—so an antithetical tendency, a submerged will toward scandal and impertinence, may intensify. The human need to embarrass oneself is most pressing when the embarrassing gesture is out of the question. One result may be a disruptive or uncanny episode. Certainly in the case of Richardson, the strain of writing an unambiguously "good" book in *Pamela,* Part 2, seems to have unleashed a certain subversive (and unintentional) mischief in the central sections of that novel. The fact that the scenery of the carnivalesque—the ultimate sign of moral and metaphysical chaos—is so prominent in these otherwise hidebound fictions suggests, again, the explosive working out of a previously suppressed alternative content.

Excerpted from *Masquerade and Civilization* by Terry Castle with the permission of the publishers, Stanford University Press. © 1986 by the Board of Trustees of the Leland Stanford Junior University.

In any event, at least for its first half *Amelia* displays an intense, seemingly inescapable didacticism. So insistent is this "instruction," the moralist's obsessive revelation of human guile, that one has little sense in the opening books of any real plot or forward narrative momentum—only of a somewhat desultory textual movement, like Booth's perambulations around the prison yard, from one scene of iniquity to another. Virgilian echoes notwithstanding, Fielding's formal procedure here is not so much the elaboration, in the classical sense, of a single unified action, but the satiric projection of a series of discrete moral set pieces. Like those disparate images in the World Upside-Down prints of the seventeenth and eighteenth centuries (donkeys flaying men, fishes in the sky), the narrator's cynical anecdotes create an impression of semantic overdetermination, for the ultimate meaning each conveys is the same. Human life is topsy-turvy, and the wise person remains perpetually on guard against its outrages.

Of necessity Fielding establishes his narrative persona early—that of the confidant, or the discloser of secrets. He takes it on himself to explicate the fictional world for his readers, to be our moral watchdog, to uncover what the world hides from view. He will illuminate the dark truth behind appearances. Addressing the reader in the second chapter of Book I, he writes that his "usual Manner" will be to "premise," or disclose in advance, "some things which it may be necessary for thee to know." The reader in turn is cast as the recipient of privy information, one who learns the truth. The process of reading is figured as a privileged movement from exteriority to interiority. The narrator will lead us, he implies, from outside to inside, toward a certain hidden content. Thus those multiple chapter headings early in *Amelia* promising a penetration of surfaces, and entry into a realm of truth: "Containing the Inside of a Prison" (I, 3); "Disclosing Further Secrets of the Prison-House" (I, 4); and the title of the chapter in which Miss Matthews is introduced, "Containing . . . some Endeavours to prove, by Reason and Authority, that it is possible for a Woman to appear to be what she really is not" (I, 6).

The truth of course is disillusioning: a logic of inversion governs the world of appearances. Things are not what they seem; everything masquerades in fact as its opposite. Whatever is, one may be sure, is wrong—the antithesis of what it might be, in an ideally ordered human community. The world of *Amelia,* like that of the "Essay on the Knowledge of the Characters of Men," is indeed a "vast Masquerade," a panorama of deception, the *mundus inversus* itself.

The logic is apparent immediately. Justice Thrasher's court, before which the hapless Booth is brought in Book I, is a cruel, almost Brechtian parody of justice—the allegory of a corrupt society, where evil is rewarded and good maligned. One soon grasps the pattern: a serving girl on an errand for her mistress is charged with soliciting and treated like a common whore; a badly beaten man is imprisoned for supposedly assaulting an unscathed accuser; Booth himself is punished for trying to rescue an innocent man from a gang of street bullies. We learn to expect the inevitable reversal of our expectations, and the fulfillment of a dark, continuous moral irony.

This pattern of reversal is expressed even more strikingly in the prison scenes that follow. Here the overthrow of normal human relations is complete. The prison yard—into which the reader, like Booth, is also, as it were, abruptly thrown—is a scene of nightmarish alienations, a surreal walled garden in which corruption and hysteria flourish. No one in this carnival of misery is what he or she seems: human affect, as in an anxiety dream, is shockingly misleading. Robinson, the Methodist "Philosopher" who befriends Booth in the yard, is really a pickpocket; a pretty girl with "Innocence in her Countenance" turns out to be a streetwalker, and discharges a volley of oaths at the confused captain (I, 4). Ordinary social relations are parodied. Women, Blear-Eyed Moll among them, assail male inmates with sexual overtures, and beat them when they refuse (I, 3). A homosexual prisoner, "committed for certain odious unmanlike Practices, not fit to be named," is given "various Kinds of Discipline" by a group of prostitutes (I, 4). Moral sympathies are consistently violated. While incorrigible malefactors seem to flourish in the prison—Moll, perversely, is one of the "merriest Persons" to be found there—the innocent, falsely incarcerated, waste away. Emblematic vignettes convey the prevailing malignancy: a "little Creature" Booth sees crying in one corner of the yard has been imprisoned by her father-in-law, a grenadier, for allegedly doing him "bodily Harm"; elsewhere, a starving young woman and her father languish, charged with stealing a loaf of bread (I, 4).

The prison scenes, one could say, are a generic cue to the reader. They situate us immediately in the anti-world of satire and condition a certain generic expectation about what is to follow. We learn here what is, in the inverted world of the anatomy or moral allegory, a familiar mode of interpretation: to distrust the appearance, to anticipate the eventual exposure of any simulacrum of goodness. Fielding's narrator trains his reader in the ways of suspicion. The result is that, at least at the outset, we may experience a paradoxical intellectual complacency, even an ennui, in the face of this "Universal Satire on Mankind." Its revelations follow a predictable hermeneutic pattern; its somber didactic message is nothing if not overdetermined.

One irony of the situation, to be sure, is that the reader's moral schooling is in no way matched by that of Booth himself, who is the focus of interest in these sections. He remains the epistemological naïf, perpetually fallible and perpetually surprised by each new example of chicanery he encounters. By the time Miss Matthews appears the disparity is well established: the reader, thanks to Fielding's incriminating clues, cannot help but suspect her; Booth, however, does not. Her odd demeanor, oscillating between she-tragedy posturing and comic coquetry, raises no question in his mind—or not, at least, until it is too late. Polite conversation between them resolves into sexual conversation; and thus begins the emotional entanglement that will produce so much difficulty for Booth in *Amelia*'s remaining books.

Booth's muddled passivity in the face of "snares" may be taken, however, as yet another generic cue, for it resembles in many respects the exemplary naïveté of the allegorical hero. Booth's very vacuousness—his curious lack of presence or of distinct moral personality—connects him with the cipherlike characters of traditional allegory: Everyman, Spenser's Red Cross Knight, Christian of *Pilgrim's Progress*. His "wavering" spiritual condition (I, 3) is symptomatic of a larger indefiniteness in his nature; he represents a kind of unbounded or free-floating textual energy. Such indistinctness conditions in turn the expectation again that *Amelia* itself will be a narrative structure of a certain familiar and highly formulaic type: the *psychomachia,* or battle of vice and virtue. In the first books of *Amelia* Fielding sets the stage for such a battle by suspending his hero between two worlds: that of Miss Matthews, the embodiment of lassitude and corruption; and that of Amelia, representative of moral purity and the domestic virtues. The crucial question at this stage is in fact the classic question of allegory: whether Amelia (whose name itself suggests the possibility of active goodness) will be a sufficiently potent force in the fictional world to draw Booth definitively into the camp of the virtuous, or whether her own virtue will in turn succumb, disastrously, to the schemes of the vicious. She loses her first skirmish in absentia, when Booth copulates with Miss Matthews in the prison. But we still await with some curiosity the outcome of this confrontation between virtue and vice, and the effect Amelia's actual presence will have on Booth's embryonic, imprecise moral nature.[2]

In subsequent books, when Amelia is in fact introduced and we mark the true extent of the troubles, financial and otherwise, besetting the Booths' marriage, the implicit allegorical pattern persists. Again, for approximately the first half of the novel, we have little sense of any underlying teleological narrative concern, other than this vague battle between the forces of good and evil. What we might call the basic embedded issues in Fielding's plot— whether, for example, Amelia and Booth will ever witness a true change in their fortunes and escape poverty—tend to get lost in a welter of discontinuous, fragmentary episodes: the "exquisite Distresses" the Booths are somewhat bathetically made to undergo. Like hero and heroine, Fielding's reader is caught up in this world of painful, disarming accident: we confront incidents with no apparent connection to one another, except that they confirm, in emblematic terms, the intolerable hypocrisy of human society and the cruel impostures that innocence must endure.

Thus the claustrophobic, circumscribed picaresque of Books III through VI, containing Booth's account of his courtship of Amelia, and their subsequent postmarital London travails. All the moral pathology associated with the little world of the prison recurs in that larger human community through which Booth and Amelia so guilelessly move. The couple are close prisoners in a metropolis of evil, the full scale of which they only intermittently perceive, if they perceive it at all. Most significant is what the reader sees and they cannot: the degree to which they are deceived and imposed upon by virtually everyone they encounter. Hypocrisy is global: from Amelia's "glavering" sister Betty, who feigns compassion for her disenfranchised sibling, to Monsieur Bagillard at Montpelier (the first of many "Friends" of the Booths with designs on Amelia's virtue), to the sinister London trio made up of Colonel James, Mrs. Ellison, and the circumspect, nameless "noble Peer." Each of these characters is in varying degree unmasked by Fielding's narrator: that is, we are apprised of their real natures—or seem to be—well in advance of the Booths themselves. Thus long before the captain or his wife becomes suspicious, for instance, of the villainous peer, the reader has already had a multiplicity of ironic clues about his character, including the barely veiled secret of his lust for Amelia. We are subject to continuous moral and emotional disillusionment, even in excess of that disillusionment suffered by Amelia and Booth themselves, for we can perceive what they so demoralizingly cannot—that their reverses are part of a larger, insidious syndrome, a consistent absence of authenticity in the realm of human relations. "Friend" and "Enemy," the narrator will observe later, are "often synonymous in the Language of the World" (IX, 2). But even before this piece of bleak commentary, the lesson has been instilled to depressing excess. We come soon enough to scrutinize the fictional landscape with cynicism, even paranoia, as again and again seemingly benevolent characters are exposed as maligners, pimps, and deceivers.

I made an analogy earlier between Fielding's formal method and the World-Upside-Down plate; the technique here, as well as Fielding's theme, could again be described as iconographic. The narrative in these early scenes, already spasmodic, has a tendency to stop altogether whenever Fielding is concerned to frame a particularly egregious instance of moral or ontological chaos. The result is a static, almost pictorial set piece, as in the unnumbered "Additional Chapter" in Book V.[3] Here one of Amelia's children develops a fever, only, it seems, to allow the narrator a satire on doctors and apothecaries. Arsenic and Dosewell are World-Upside-Down figures: the doctor turned poisoner, a satiric inversion of the familiar kind. Fielding admits the episode is not strictly necessary: "some Readers will, perhaps, think this whole Chapter might have been omitted." Yet, he maintains, it justifies itself by its instruction: "though it contains no great Amusement, it may at least serve to inform Posterity concerning the present State of Physic." One senses the satiric topos—"the present State of Physic"—taking precedence over the dynamics of narrative, forcing the fiction again into the characteristic mode of the visual anatomy, complete with caricatured, essentially pictographic illustrations of vice and folly.

At other times the satiric impulse produces simple uncanniness: what one might call a freezing of the freakish or discontinuous image. An example occurs during Booth's visit in Book III to Major Bath at Montpelier, where Booth finds his friend dressed, "whimsically enough," in "a Woman's Bed-

Gown and a very dirty Flannel Night-Cap." We already know Major Bath, "a very aukward, thin Man, near seven Feet high," as a kind of *miles gloriosus,* whose discourse "generally turned on matters of no feminine kind, war and martial exploits being the ordinary topics of his conversation" (III, 8). Bath tells Booth that his remarkable costume is due to the fact that he is nursing his ailing sister (and he is indeed warming a posset for her), yet this peculiar explanation hardly seems to account entirely for his strange appearance. One suspects—for the episode is otherwise unmotivated—the scene is meant to bring to mind again the stereotypical imagery of the World Upside-Down. Like the death-dealing doctor, the "warrior in skirts" is a conventional motif in World-Upside-Down engravings, deriving perhaps from ancient stories of Hercules and Omphale, but suggestive in any case of those sexual and social reversals characteristic of the *mundus inversus.*[4] The spectacle of the ordinarily martial Bath in transvestite deshabille likewise has its pictorial aspect: it too tends to stop the narrative flow, almost in the manner of a cinematic freeze-frame. (It is worth noting that the moment was selected for representation by *Amelia's* early illustrators. In the Henley edition, with engravings by Rooker and Corbould dating from 1793, the scene is the frontispiece to Volume I.) But it also points up again the generalized topsy-turvydom of the fictional world. Bath's travesty is a specimen of aberrance—comical enough, yet indicative too perhaps of other even less explicable inversions in *Amelia's* moral landscape.

Among the many similar instances of inversion and bathos in the first half of *Amelia,* one species of reversal is especially worth noting, for as we shall see it has an obvious relevance to the matter of the masquerade. One might call the phenomenon the transvaluation of pleasure. It particularly affects the pleasures of sociability, and it makes sense given the pervasive fictional atmosphere of betrayal and exploitation: in a world where no one may be trusted, one expects little in the way of true human community. But the negativity with which Fielding here treats even the most minor form of collective pleasure—whether it be the shared meal, the game, or more inclusive public entertainment—is unremitting. It is indeed the "Party of Pleasure," the human grouping or institution designed purely for enjoyment, that seems, in *Amelia's* dark world, to produce the direst and most ironic consequences. Much of the demoralizing effect of Fielding's novel has undoubtedly to do with this pervasive thematic syndrome: that ordinarily refreshing occasions, the lightest of festivities and amusements, are represented as having nothing but sinister ramifications. For the reader, as for *Amelia's* characters, there is no apparent escape, even temporary, from what one might call the code of disappointment, the oppression and tawdriness of the quotidian.

Just as the hypocritical individual is a dangerous simulacrum of affection and good will, so in Fielding's novel the pleasures of society are an equally dangerous simulacrum of delight. Their real function here, it seems, is to bring about pain and havoc. Nor does it make any difference whether one seeks one's pleasure in the anonymity of the crowd—at seemingly benign public places—or in a more intimate domestic setting. In a public space, such as the pleasure-garden, one is vulnerable to random, absurdly violent assaults—the meaningless brutality of strangers. When Booth and Amelia, seeking a brief respite from trouble, take a walk with their children in the park in Book IV, their son Billy is inexplicably attacked by a passing foot soldier with a bayonet, and saved only by the timely intervention of Booth's associate Sergeant Atkinson, who happens to be walking by. The episode has an ostensible significance in Fielding's plot—it reintroduces Atkinson, and later establishes the Booths' relationship with Mrs. Ellison, who offers Amelia a "restorative" when they return to their lodgings—but the violence here may nonetheless seem in excess of any narrative demand. Not surprisingly, the scene is almost immediately adduced to illustrate the requisite moral lesson: that the most "trifling adventure," even a stroll in "the green Fields of London," is capable of producing, in the narrator's words, "the most unexpected and dreadful Events" (IV, 7). A similar point will be made later when Amelia, walking in Vauxhall Gardens with Dr. Harrison, is physically assaulted by two rakes and made the butt of lewd jokes, to her pain and vexation (IX, 9).

The private pleasure party, held in the safety of one's own home, turns out to be no less problematic. Indeed, a less than pious reader might well be moved to laughter by the sheer number of times in *Amelia* that the most horrific disasters attend upon a scene of domestic celebration. Everything encompassed by the concept of "Civility" in the novel, all the ordinary pleasures of social existence, seem tainted by ill fortune. The pattern is set from the start, beginning with Miss Matthews's prison account of her history. Here one learns that a series of "musical Evenings" given by Miss Matthews's father prompted her first fatal attraction to Cornet Hebbers, for whose attempted murder she has been imprisoned. She was subsequently seduced and ruined by him, she tells Booth, when she became intoxicated at the festivities held in honor of her sister's wedding (I, 8). Likewise, in Mrs. Bennet's retrospective narrative a few books later (during which she also gives Amelia a crucial warning about the dangers of the masquerade), the same dysphoric syndrome is at work. The death of her own mother, relates Mrs. Bennet, resulted from an innocent family "Festival," Mrs. Bennet's sixteenth birthday party. Not wishing to disturb the servants, her unfortunate parent went by herself to refill a teakettle at a well, and promptly fell in and drowned. Misery everywhere supplants joy: the pathetic discovery once made, Mrs. Bennet tells Amelia, the family's "high degree of Mirth" evaporated, and they fell together into "the most bitter Agonies of Despair" (VII, 2).

The same principle of transvaluation operates, less melodramatically perhaps but still insistently, in those scenes of domestic sociability in which Booth and Amelia themselves engage. Meals taken with acquaintances, visiting one's neighbors, simple attempts at gaiety and friendly intercourse—all seem to produce the most troubling complications. Booth's memorable dinner with Miss Matthews in the prison, with its parody of domestic arrangements, is exemplary in this regard, but it is only the first of many such perverse parties. For Booth, later evenings spent with "Friends"—Captain Trent, for instance—lead to irksome problems: on one occasion, he loses all of his and Amelia's remaining money gambling with Trent and others, who have of course been set up to entrap him (X, 5).

But even the seemingly most structured forms of social intercourse have their dangers. Of the varieties of domestic civility represented in *Amelia,* none is so insidious finally as that genteel entertainment Booth refers to at one point as the *partie quarrée,* the private pleasure party, usually held in one's own lodgings, consisting of two married (or otherwise related) couples (III, 9). The heterosexual quartet is the characteristic social configuration in the fictional world. Scenes involving actual quartets recur throughout *Amelia,* beginning with that sociable foursome in Montpelier made up of Booth, Amelia, Major Bath, and his sister Miss Bath. But often too one may have the sense of a "latent quartet" structuring the novel's fictional situations, as in the prison scene itself, where Amelia and Cornet Hebbers—the absent sexual partners of Booth and Miss Matthews—are in a sense the missing members of an implicit and highly significant *partie quarrée.*

The most important feature of the *partie quarrée* is its moral instability. This instability is paradoxical, for the figure itself suggests a certain ideal geometry of social relations. It squares, so to speak, the virtues of fidelity and fellowship. Nothing might seem more decorous (as indeed it seems to the Booths) than a neatly symmetrical relation between two legitimate couples. That stylized occasion around which the *partie quarrée* forms—the shared meal, the hand of cards, the evening of conversation—appears to represent an idealized fusion of distance and intimacy, politesse and candor. But such decorum is fragile, as is the shape of the figure itself. For throughout *Amelia,* as one might expect in a fiction where adultery is so prominent a theme, the *partie quarrée* repeatedly dissolves into a problematic, disorderly cluster of transgressive psychological and sexual relations. Rather than affirming licit bonds, it threatens them by providing the opportunity for the formation of new and morally subversive connections between the very members of the couples that compose it. The image in little of civilized exchange, it contains the seeds of its own destruction.

In the Booth/Bath *partie quarrée* the potential for disaster is mostly implicit, yet even here the figure of the quartet is associated with a certain amount of moral chaos. After the Booths and Baths have spent a number of evenings in each others' company, Monsieur Bagillard, who has himself had designs on the heroine, accuses Major Bath of trying to seduce her and cuckold Booth under the guise of friendship. One result—for Bath denies the charge—is a bloody duel between him and Bagillard (III, 9). More important, the reader is apprised of an intrinsic danger in the pattern of sociability itself: the adulteration of legitimate relations is a constant possibility.

Later versions of the configuration confirm the threat. The foursome made up of Booth and Amelia and Colonel and Mrs. James (who is of course the former Miss Bath) contains a doubling of subversive cathexes: Colonel James hopes to seduce Amelia, and Mrs. James harbors a covert passion for Booth. Even more sinister is the *partie quarrée* organized by Mrs. Ellison (the Booths' landlady) and her supposed cousin, the Noble Peer. Pretending friendship (the Peer has claimed he will use his influence to help Booth), they invite the Booths to dine on several occasions. Later, however, in the crucial seventh book of the novel, the reader learns along with Amelia that such hospitality has from the start been a ruse. Some previous tenants in the Ellison house, Mr. and Mrs. Bennet, were treated to similar niceties; but there the *partie quarrée* was simply one step in the Peer's elaborate scheme, abetted by Ellison, to rape Mrs. Bennet. A similar fate has been planned for Amelia. The ritualized exchange of civilities thus is not an end in itself, but part of a malevolent secret plot against virtue. And again, the reader is forced to confront the pervasive moral brutality of the fictional world, where even the most innocent-seeming of domestic pleasures reveals a hidden, maladive, even obscene instrumentality.

The representation of the masquerade—the most expansive and theatrical of social festivities—is linked to the *partie quarrée* on a number of levels. The formation of the sinister foursome at Mrs. Ellison's, midway through the fiction, sets up the first reference to the masquerade: once the requisite number of evenings have been passed in sociability, the Peer proceeds to the next stage in his nefarious scheme, which is to present Amelia with tickets for a masked assembly at Ranelagh (VI, 5). In turn Mrs. Bennet is led to reveal to the heroine her own tragically instructive history. But thematic connections are also palpable. With its tendency to dissolve into a morally unregulated, adulterous human unit, the *partie quarrée* has a proleptic symbolic relation to the masquerade crowd itself, which represents unregulated sociability in its most demonic form. There, of course, the transgressive relationship will be all. In one sense the masquerade is simply the pleasure party universalized. Its characteristic locale, the assembly room, both parodies and magnifies the domestic salon; its systematic travesties but give outward form to the pervasive hypocrisy of everyday life. It summarizes, in effect, the *liaisons dangereuses* implicit in the most ordinary-seeming of human exchanges.

Not surprisingly, the masquerade figures first in *Amelia* as a sort of extenuation of the *partie quarrée*—as yet another example, though perhaps the most diabolical to date, of pleasure transmogrified. We are clearly meant to interpret it as another type—the emblem even—of malevolent sociability. One hardly has a chance to do otherwise, in fact: almost as soon as going to the masquerade becomes a narrative possibility, the Peer's invitation prompts a flood of didactic comment within the fictional world. The masquerade itself is unmasked in the customary way, as an image of false delights.

Indeed, the manner of the masquerade's unmasking might seem to preclude its representation. The point of Mrs. Bennet's crucial masquerade confession, after all, will be to prevent Amelia from making the same mistake she did—to keep the masquerade from being part of Amelia's own history. But even before this interesting intervention, there are other attempts to keep the masquerade from happening. Booth himself is suspicious of the Peer's invitation for once, though mainly because he has had hints from Colonel James regarding the Peer's reputation as a rake. The captain is sufficiently moved to animadvert on the masquerade in the conventional manner. When the devious Mrs. Ellison presses the Peer's tickets on Amelia, exclaiming what a "delicious Place" the masquerade is ("Paradise itself can hardly be equal to it"), Booth forces his wife to refuse the gift. Later he explains that a masquerade ticket is "perhaps the very worst and most dangerous" thing a woman may receive from a man, for "few Men make Presents of those Tickets to Ladies without intending to meet them at the Place." Amelia objects that he has nothing to fear from her virtue, but he continues: "The Snares which might be laid for that Innocence, were alone the Cause of my Apprehension. I feared what a wicked and voluptuous Man, resolved to sacrifice every thing to the Gratification of a sensual Appetite with the most delicious Repast, might attempt" (VI, 6). Though none of the Peer's stratagem has yet been confirmed, Booth (and Fielding) inscribe the masquerade with a familiar ethical significance: it is the preeminent site of "Snares," the place where plots against virtue are inevitably set in motion.

The exchange has an ironic aspect, not only because of Booth's morally problematic status as an adulterous husband, but also because he does in fact later relent and give Amelia permission to go to Ranelagh with Mrs. Ellison. This gesture in turn, however, provokes a new burst of anti-masquerade discourse. Fielding somewhat crudely prepares us for some revelation: when Amelia announces to the landlady that she will be going after all, Mrs. Ellison's mysterious, learned friend Mrs. Bennet (also present) turns unaccountably grave. Later, while Ellison extols "the extreme Beauty of the Place and Elegance of the Diversion," Mrs. Bennet becomes "extremely melancholy" and casts looks "of no very pleasant Kind" on the speaker (VI, 8). One is hardly surprised when she turns out to be the author of that anonymous poem in the next chapter warning Amelia of a "dreadful Snare" laid for her "under a Friend's false Pretence." It is her story, of course, related in Book VII, that will demystify the masquerade once and for all—or at least, for a time, may seem to.

In itself the point of Mrs. Bennet's melodramatic "masquerade tale" is clearly didactic. It is intended to alert Amelia to the danger she is in, and this it does by exposing the masquerade as the culminating event in a preexisting plot against innocence—a plot in which Mrs. Bennet has already to her sorrow been ensnared. The masquerade has been the symbolic end point, the climactic scene, in Mrs. Bennet's own disastrous history: she now relates this history precisely so that Amelia will not have to reenact it. Her story, one might say, is paradigmatic, but in a negative sense: it is meant to obviate its own repetition.

For all its subsequent outrageousness, this story is also highly conventional. Certainly Mrs. Bennet's account bears many resemblances to those salacious tales of masquerade disaster popular in eighteenth-century periodicals and in works like Haywood's *The Masqueraders: or, Fatal Curiosity* (1724). Fielding appears to have borrowed many of the standard lurid features of such tales without much modification.[5] Thus the early events of Mrs. Bennet's life—her upbringing, her marriage to the impoverished cleric Mr. Bennet, their move to London and into lodgings at Mrs. Ellison's—are but prologue to her sexual ruin at the hands of the dastardly Peer. Like Amelia, it turns out, Mrs. Bennet was treated to the hospitality of Mrs. Ellison and the Peer; like Amelia too, she was given masquerade tickets. And true to that function stereotypically ascribed to it in the exemplary tales, the masquerade facilitated her downfall. Attending without her husband (who had been sent on a spurious mission by the Peer), she found herself "intoxicated with foolish Desires, and liable to every Temptation." Temptation included the obsequious attentions of the Peer, in whom she was secretly proud to perceive a "Passion." Having given up "the Outwork of her Virtue" by being at the masquerade in the first place, Mrs. Bennet agreed to let the Peer accompany her home. He offered her a glass of drugged punch; she swooned and was raped (VII, 7). As in conventional tales of masquerade seduction, this gothic violation produces a horrific domestic coda: Mrs. Bennet tells Amelia how she was infected with a "Pollution" that she in turn passed to her husband, who thus discovered her (unintentional) lapse from wifely virtue. He reviled her and then succumbed to the infection. Their only child likewise died soon after (VII, 9). All this, Mrs. Bennet concludes, was the result of her single tragic error—the demonic "Residue" of that one "fatal Night."

The main point of Mrs. Bennet's story is that her suffering has been the result of a "long, regular, premeditated Design" against her, and that the same trap is now being laid for Amelia. This scheme, which can be repeated with an unlimited number of victims, is characterized by the strategic manipulation of public as well as private diversions. It is now revealed, for example, that an oratorio Amelia attended earlier with Mrs. Ellison was also part of the Peer's design: a gentleman in a "rag Coat" there who engaged them in polite conversation was the Peer himself, in disguise and hunting (with Mrs. Ellison's help) for new victims (IV, 9). Mrs. Bennet was marked for her own destruction in identical circumstances. But the masquerade, the exemplary scene of delirium and danger, is the public amusement most suited, obviously, to the realization of private schemes; thus it serves as a stage for the worst part of the Peer's plot, the actual entrapment of the victim. As in Richardson's sequel to *Pamela,* one detects an implicit negative hierarchy of diversions here: the masquerade is worse than the oratorio, for its intoxications are active and participatory rather than merely specular (or auditory). As its acolytes give themselves over to the occasion—indeed, are absorbed by it—they become the actors in a larger drama of vice and abandon.

Mrs. Bennet's salutary tale has its intended impact: Amelia listens with horror and immediately sends back the tickets. This unmasking of the Peer's plot likewise has a profound narrative impact: it seems to prevent the plot of sexual ruin from becoming the plot of *Amelia* itself. By this timely exposure Amelia herself is exempted from the role of victim. Her paragon status is preserved and her innocence instructed—all without any direct (and one suspects indelibly compromising) experience of the masquerade and its dangers. She is granted a license *not* to reenact the masquerade's classic scenarios of manipulation, disequilibrium, and degradation. Like a narrative *cordon sanitaire,* Mrs. Bennet's history mediates between Fielding's heroine and disaster, separating her from a melodramatic realm of plot and machination, violence and despair.

Such is also perhaps the ultimate extension of Fielding's allegorical method in *Amelia.* Just as the masquerade represents the most dangerous fictional evil to date—imposture in its most devastating and worldly guise—so Mrs. Bennet's tale represents the allegorical gesture of truth-telling in its most potently altruistic form. Mrs. Bennet is a heroine of knowledge, one who has foresuffered all, precisely that Amelia herself should not suffer. By pointing to the evil hidden behind the facade of delight, she replicates the narrator's own gestures of moral revelation. The logic of reversal holds once more: the ultimate scene of pleasure is in fact the ultimate scene of ruin. Like everything else in the fictional world, the masquerade itself wears a mask. But Mrs. Bennet's history removes the mask; it isolates the masquerade's intrinsic pathology and nullifies its secret destructive power.

Her disclosure carries a special, even exaggerated force not only because the masquerade pretends to a more seductive pleasure than any other form of diversion (paradise itself does not seem equal to it), but because her words prevent the most dire-seeming of possible events in the fictional world: the compromising of the one exemplar of unconditional virtue *Amelia* has provided. By preserving the heroine's unambiguously pure status, Mrs. Bennet's intervention also appears to preserve the shape of Fielding's *psychomachia.* Amelia is free here to remain what she has been—the embodiment of uncomplicated virtue and a moral beacon to Booth. Her symbolic role, essentially that of the type, is unimpugned by incident. Thus Mrs. Bennet's exposition of the *carnaval moralisé* effectively protects the allegorical status quo. It seems to mitigate against plot on every level; it stays any potential unmotivated, unprecedented, or irrational narrative development; and it confirms the fiction's underlying satiric and anatomizing tendency. The reader's function, consequently, also seems to remain the same: to be a passive receptacle for instruction. Like the heroine, Fielding's reader is again made here the recipient of a discourse at once pedagogic and ostensibly therapeutic—the beneficiary of an unmasking that is both specific and universally suggestive.

None of which makes any less bewildering the next (one is tempted to say first) event in Fielding's novel: a masquerade. The discontinuity here is shocking, as though the logical ground on which the fiction were founded had suddenly shifted. From the recollected or mediated representation of the masquerade, *Amelia* makes a startling leap to the thing itself when "Amelia," Booth, and the Jameses together depart for the Haymarket in Book X. And as it does in eighteenth-century fiction generally, this second, more immediate masquerade scene will have its dramatic and disarming effect on virtually every character in the novel. What to make of this perplexing turn of affairs?

Little in the way of new incident occurs before the Booths' strange expedition. Books VIII and IX of *Amelia* are for the most part listless and diffuse, as though the fiction were not entirely sure where it was going, and the episodes here are altogether reminiscent of earlier ones. Booth is arrested again for debt and subsequently released; he and Amelia are forced to remove their things from Mrs. Ellison's; Colonel James is seen brooding again over Amelia, for whom we already know he harbors a secret passion. Likewise there are two perfunctory and predictable satiric set pieces: Booth's encounter with the foolish author at Mr. Bondum's (VIII, 5), and the conversation between Dr. Harrison and the hypocritical clerics (IX, 10). By contrast the abrupt return of the masquerade as a narrative possibility—in the first chapter of Book X, when Colonel James presses tickets on the beguiled Booth—manages both to seem gratuitous and to provide a subtle relief. It makes no sense in didactic terms, for what more does one need to know of masquerades? Such a twist seems to negate the impact of Mrs. Bennet's emblematic history and contradict the implicit allegorical rhythm to which the reader is accustomed. But it also has a cathartic, if irrational, narrative potential. It heralds intrigue of a sort that has so far been missing. We do not entirely regret the disappointment of our expectations, or the implied swerve away from didacticism—baffled though we may be.

Which is not to say that the reader of *Amelia* does not speculate, even here, on the impulses motivating such a surprising narrative development. Fielding's second invocation of the carnival world forces us to look again at his first, including Mrs. Bennet's lugubrious masquerade tale, in a different way. The results are both compelling and unsettling. For reviewed in the light of this subsequent plot turn, *Amelia*'s initial representation of the masquerade no longer seems quite as transparent, allegorically speaking, as it did at first. We notice in retrospect a peculiar quality, even an illogicality or solecism, attaching to Mrs. Bennet's dysphoric revelations, not to mention a vaguely troubling ambiguity in her character itself. That Fielding's narrative should turn back with such apparent perversity toward the compromising world of the masquerade—after giving every indication it would not—may strike us as less completely shocking, if not less odd, when we reflect that an unacknowledged instrumental potential has been associated with the masquerade from the outset. It is implicit in Mrs. Bennet's history, and in the circumstances that succeed her catastrophe. The more we think about it, in fact, the more uncanny Mrs. Bennet's ostensibly lucid disclosures are likely to seem, as indeed she does herself.

The problem has to do with the matter of "Consequences" and the fact that Mrs. Bennet's history seems to admit more of these, paradoxically, than she herself allows. The problem manifests itself first as one of tone. Immediately following Mrs. Bennet's account of her ruin at the hands of the Noble Peer, for instance—a story so horrific that it sends Amelia into a faint at one point and Mrs. Bennet herself into a "violent Convulsion Fit" (VII, 8)—the conversation takes a sudden, puzzling shift to a gossipy and giddy discussion of the virtues of Sergeant Atkinson. (He has made a brief, inexplicable appearance in Mrs. Bennet's apartments during the conversation between the two women.) Mrs. Bennet is soon gaily teasing Amelia with the fact that she has another secret to tell her—that "no Woman" in fact has "so sincere, so passionate a Lover" as Amelia has in the sergeant (VII, 10). This news is succeeded, rather troublingly, by the information that Mrs. Bennet and the sergeant are now married to one another, hence his appearance in her rooms and her knowledge of his secret feelings. Mrs. Bennet (now revealed as Mrs. Atkinson) concludes her disclosures with a bit of sentimental philosophizing: she is not at all bothered by the sergeant's infatuation for Amelia, for "there is no greater vulgar Error than that it is impossible for a Man who loves one Woman ever to love another." Indeed, she continues, "it is certain that a Man who can love one Woman so well at a Distance" (and such passions only reside "in very amorous and very delicate Minds") "will love another better that is nearer to him."

We might be tempted to see Mrs. Bennet's marriage simply as another of those apparently meaningless twists of happenstance with which *Amelia* is filled, were it not that it transforms our sense of her story so ambiguously. For she is revealed here as something more than just the "destined Sacrifice" or exemplary victim of the masquerade. She has moved irresistibly toward a comic transcendence of her own tragedy. Contrary to that unhappy ending seemingly implied in her history, the masquerade has not in fact been fatal to her at all, either in body or in spirit. Rather it has produced, paradoxically, what we can only regard as an amelioration of her fortunes. Through the complex chain of circumstances it initiates (which includes, it must be admitted, the death of her first husband), the masquerade has resulted in Mrs. Bennet's marriage to the one character in *Amelia,* apart from Amelia herself and to a much lesser extent Dr. Harrison, who approaches paragon status. Her "ruin" is thus distinguished by the acquisition of this new and unimpeachable husband, the company of friends, financial comfort, and the freedom to enjoy her scholarly pursuits. Even as she recounts it, then, Mrs. Bennet might be charged with triumphing over her sensational and ghastly history.

The paradox here is implicit: no one calls attention to it within the fictional world, nor does Fielding's narrator. (Indeed, beginning with the scene of Mrs. Bennet's disclosures, the narrator tends to withdraw, and explicit moral commentary, so prevalent before, diminishes.) Yet this presentation of consequences subtly undermines the allegorical logic that until now has shaped the pattern of meaning in Fielding's novel. If in some mysterious way the masquerade is responsible for Mrs. Bennet's present happiness, then the prevailing logic of moral reversal no longer holds: the masquerade can no longer be said simply to represent evil in the guise of pleasure, for it has in fact produced pleasure. It cannot be glossed merely as the quintessential scene of vice, for though it has led Mrs. Bennet into an involuntary union with vice, in the person of the Noble Peer, it has also led her into a union with virtue, in the person of Sergeant Atkinson. The masquerade topos thus begins to lose some of its emblematic lucidity even as it ceases to reproduce a purely negative teleology on the level of plot. Through its association with an enigmatic realm of consequences—all of which belie any wholly malignant agency—the masquerade becomes, allegorically speaking, inscrutable. It can no longer be adduced for the purposes of any truly coherent "Instruction"; it is no longer merely the uncomplicated public image or social reification of the deceitful nature of appearances. Its meaning as moral sign, in short, has been made ambiguous.

This ambiguity has its corollary in the realm of character. If the masquerade becomes, with Mrs. Bennet's subsequent revelations, suddenly undecodable according to the logic with which we are familiar, so too does Mrs. Bennet herself. It is no coincidence perhaps that the character in *Amelia* most profoundly intimate—in every sense—with the world of the masquerade (she will play an uncanny part in the novel's second masquerade scene too, of course) should also be the first major character in the fiction to resist moral recuperation in simple allegorical terms. She is as peculiarly fluid and discontinuous a textual presence as the carnivalesque occasion with which she is associated. Mrs. Bennet's duality is most obvious in the primitive symbolic realm of onomastics: no sooner is she introduced and her history related than her name changes, as it were, when she announces her marriage to the sergeant. The disconcerting effect of her shift in identity is intensified by the narrator's self-conscious manner of handling it. "The Tea being now ready," he writes coyly, "Mrs. Bennet, or, if you please, Mrs. Atkinson, proposed to call in her Husband" (VII, 10). (I shall reinscribe the textual discontinuity by referring hereafter to Mrs. Bennet as Mrs. Atkinson also.) The shift here in the realm of reference replicates the essential irony of her history: that one does not know whether to regard her, in some deeper way, as the "unfortunate" Mrs. Bennet or the "fortunate" Mrs. Atkinson. Just as she is at once the victim of catastrophe and the embodiment of survival, Mrs. Atkinson is at once the same and different from herself: she is, indeed, Mrs. Bennet *and* Mrs. Atkinson.

But Mrs. Atkinson's nature is also morally ambiguous, as the previously noted exchange with Amelia suggests. Here the reader is torn between baffling perceptions of her. On the one hand, she has performed an admirable service for the heroine by saving her from the Peer's salacious scheme. On the other, with her remarks about Sergeant Atkinson and his love for Amelia, she seems to articulate a subversive emotional potential—the possibility that one married person might indeed love another, without moral stigma. In a novel where husbands conspicuously pimp for their wives, and vice versa, such a suggestion is charged and unsettling, even though Mrs. Atkinson may appear to speak only of platonic attachments between persons who are otherwise paragons. That it is her own husband whose affection for Amelia she reveals makes her contention all the more problematic: any potential *partie quarrée* in the fictional world involving the Booths and Atkinsons might seem to be compromised even as it formed. At the same time that Mrs. Atkinson preserves Amelia from coercive adultery at the hands of the Peer, she implicitly raises the possibility of another, subtler form of adultery—one the more dangerous, perhaps, for ostensibly being of the emotions only. Mrs. Atkinson has the curious, fleeting aspect here of the sentimental agent provocateur, even as she retains in other respects all the moral prestige and heroism associated in *Amelia* with the unraveler of secrets and teller of truths.

The narrator, significantly, gives the reader no clue about how to place Mrs. Atkinson in any larger moral or metaphysical scheme—or at least, no clues that are not contradictory. From this point on she will remain a strangely unclassifiable presence. She commits a number of violations of decorum: she drinks too much (as we learn several times); she has an unfeminine interest in learning and the classics (we see her arguing with the insufferable Dr. Harrison); her marriage to the sergeant, for all his virtues, is a kind of *de haut en bas* affair (he is of a lower rank than she), and by it her own social status is made problematic. She seems to represent World-Upside-Down energies, in that she embodies certain kinds of chaos and intractability the narrator has elsewhere castigated. Yet Mrs. Atkinson is never definitively unmasked by the narrator—certainly not in the way, say, that Mrs. Ellison is, or the Noble Peer himself. She is never merely dismissed, either in moral or in narrative terms. The narrator remains mute about her essential character, if indeed she can be said to have one; the reader sees only her contradictory affect in action. True, she is often surrounded by a vaguely suspicious aura. The figure of the sexually compromised bluestocking condenses, after all, two disparate eighteenth-century visions of nightmare femininity. At the same time, despite temporary idiosyncrasies, her good will toward the Booths is indisputable, thus distinguishing her from other, more palpably evil characters in *Amelia*. Likewise she is much loved by the noble sergeant himself, whose judgment is simultaneously, if somewhat provocatively, validated by his affection for Amelia. Mrs. Atkinson's increasing prominence in Fielding's fiction (after she tells Amelia her story, her narrative role becomes more significant) is an indication of an intensifying ambiguity in *Amelia* itself. Even here, Mrs. Atkinson personifies a potentially counterallegorical tendency in the work, just as the masquerade might be described as the tropological manifestation of this same tendency.

When *Amelia* reverts to the world of the masquerade, then, in Book X, however abrupt this narrative turn may otherwise appear, one is not altogether surprised that Mrs. Atkinson should figure so noticeably in the succeeding, highly paradoxical action. She is an insistent presence; her role in the fiction is so important that she seems temporarily to draw attention away from Amelia herself, whose place she literally takes, in a complex and suggestive piece of substitution, on the night of the masquerade. Mrs. Atkinson is the heroine of Fielding's second masquerade tale, just as she was of his first. But for a time she is also in a curious way the heroine of *Amelia* itself. For the second masquerade plot in which she participates is so compelling—and its consequences so crucial in every way to Fielding's novel—as to become indistinguishable, ultimately, from the plot of the fiction itself.

That *Amelia*'s second masquerade will be of a different order than its first is obvious from the start. To begin, one notices the utter lack of any didactic preface to the occasion; here, the all-important gift of tickets (which usually seems to evoke in archetypal terms the Edenic gift of the apple) elicits no flood of protective or otherwise inhibiting commentary. True, Amelia, because she already distrusts Colonel James, suspects the motives that lie behind his present to the Booths, and asks Dr. Harrison for advice about how to avoid the occasion. But Dr. Harrison's views are uncharacteristically liberal. Though he admits he thinks the diversion "of too loose and disorderly a Kind for the Recreation of a sober Mind," he also somewhat oddly sees little harm in her going, as long as she goes with her husband (X, 1). Booth too, despite his previous vociferous complaints against masquerading, is here so infatuated with the idea of obliging his friend Colonel James (whose designs on his wife he has no notion of) that he forces Amelia to agree to accompany him. Out of desperation Amelia turns, interestingly enough, to Mrs. Atkinson. All the reader knows at this point is that the latter resolves upon some scheme, for she tells Amelia not to fear: "two Women will surely be too hard for one Man" (X, 1). Indeed, like the heroine herself, the reader can do little here but be swept toward this imminent saturnalia—a saturnalia of narrative, as it were, as well as of persons. For Fielding's masquerade scene is nothing if not a hyperelaboration of incident—an eruption of complicated and enigmatic events, none of which seems contained by any textual gloss or obvious didactic frame.

The movement into complexity begins in the second chapter of Book X, with a mobilization of the *partie quarrée*. As though by convulsion the Booths and Jameses depart in an unexplained haste for the Haymarket. The unstable grouping of the quartet lasts only as long as the journey, however: upon arrival all four are immediately separated from one another and absorbed into the masquerade crowd. The ensuing scene is one of conundrum and chaos. Indeed, the reader of *Amelia,* looking to discover "What Happened at the Masquerade" (Fielding's ironic chapter heading), might well be baffled, for it is by no means clear what is actually happening at all. The representation of the masquerade signals a regression into secrecy: not an unmasking, but a masking of meaning itself.

The effect of mystification is not achieved through any extended description of sartorial phantasmagoria. Unlike comparable scenes in *Pamela,* Burney's *Cecilia,* or even Fielding's own satire *The Masquerade,* there is little here in the way of conventional masquerade *adynata*—few descriptions of specific costumes or of amusing or uncanny characters in the masquerade crowd. Rather the feeling of imbroglio arises almost entirely from the depiction of unaccountable or troubling exchanges between characters who otherwise should not be meeting (again) in the fictional world. Virtually every major character in *Amelia* seems to be here. Besides "Amelia" and Booth and Colonel James and Mrs. James, the Noble Peer, Miss Matthews, and Colonel Bath are all in the crowd—purely by coincidence, it seems, for their appearances are not otherwise motivated. (Captain Trent will later be revealed to have been at the masquerade also, disguised as a sailor; and one might say that Dr. Harrison is present at least symbolically, for he is the author of a pious letter on the sin of adultery that is circulated and mocked by members of the crowd.) One has the sense of a problematic conclave: a potentially dangerous rencontre of just those characters who, according to all narrative decorum, should have remained apart.

Which is not to say that everyone knows who everyone else is. Some do; some only think they do. A series of puzzling encounters ensues. We see "Amelia" deep in intimate conversation with an unknown domino; Booth is besieged first by a woman in a blue domino, then by a shepherdess. Colonel James searches for his wife (who is wearing a black domino) but cannot find her anywhere in the room; when he approaches the woman he believes to be Amelia (with the intention of seducing her), he is startled when she claims quite bluntly not to know him. That the identities of at least some of these cryptic personages are revealed during the course of the evening only makes matters even more perplexing for the reader; the domino "Amelia" allows to make such "fervent Love" to her is "no other than her old Friend the Peer," while the shepherdess with whom Booth banters (and whom he promises to meet at her lodgings the next day) is of course Miss Matthews. Fielding's characters, half-concealed, half-known to one another, like the mysterious companions of dreams, seem to perform in an inexplicable, scandalous dance—a kaleidoscopic pattern of union and reunion, turn and return.

In the face of this proliferation of perverse couplings, the reader cannot help feeling apprehensive about the future of Fielding's narrative. For all the counterindications in Mrs. Atkinson's history, the allegorical association between carnival and doom may still linger. Several possible catastrophes suggest themselves. Booth seems to hover on the edge of a profound recidivism: his meeting with Miss Matthews bodes nothing but ill for his moral state. The promise she extorts from him to visit her (under the threat of exposing their liaison to the masquerade crowd) is a parody of the classic masquerade assignation, but even so it portends a revival of their intimacies and a renewed threat to his marriage. Still more ominous is the strange meeting between "Amelia" and the hated Peer. Her flirtatious behavior with him is sinister and shocking. We see her greet him with "bewitching Softness" as her "Paramour," as though she were inviting the very violation he once before intended for her. One is forced to confront the possibility that the plot of masquerade rape and humiliation may repeat itself after all in *Amelia,* with the heroine this time the foolish victim.

Particularly striking in this chapter is the phenomenon to which I referred earlier—the disappearance of Fielding's ordinarily intrusive, truth-telling narrator. The familiar voice of the fiction, the perpetrator of exposés, is missing here, even as the reader's desire for information grows. We feel our grasp on *Amelia*'s characters slipping, especially in the heroine's case. She is acting "out of role." Yet we are given no inside view, no explanation for her behavior or anyone else's. We see only externals, the mask and not the face. Fielding's often pedantic narrator, the discloser of secrets, is replaced by one who revels in them: an impervious, sly, purposely mysterious authorial voice, aiming to increase our bafflement rather than alleviate it. In this he succeeds, yet at the cost of a breach of trust; for that estrangement, the reader feels, is a betrayal, in which we are excluded from the realm of truth and cast into one of charade and alienation.

To be sure, Fielding does return to the inside view soon enough, in the next chapter, "Consequences of the Masquerade, Not Uncommon nor Surprising" (X, 3). Yet the unmasking that takes place here is in many ways the most unsettling of any so far. For here one learns of that crucial feminine stratagem played out at the masquerade—Mrs. Atkinson's impersonation of Amelia, who it turns out was not there at all. The ruse is revealed when the Booths and Jameses return home: "Amelia" whimsically rushes indoors ahead of everyone, and has already removed her mask and domino when they come in. Later, when Booth asks his wife to name the person at the masquerade with whom she had been conversing so long, she announces, "I never was at one in my Life." Amelia then reveals that when the party departed for the Haymarket, she pretended to forget her mask, ran briefly back into the house, and handed her costume to her friend. Mrs. Atkinson emerged wearing it, as well as the mask, and deceived everyone thereafter by speaking only in a "mimic Tone." Booth has thus been imposed upon, along with Colonel James and the Noble Peer.

So too in a sense has the reader. Whether or not one has had an inkling of the substitution all along (the physical resemblance between Amelia and Mrs. Atkinson has been pointed out by several characters in the fiction earlier), the fact remains that for the first time Fielding's narrator has seemingly gratuitously withheld a piece of important information in the interest of narrative surprise. Looking back at the first account of the departure for the masquerade in the preceding chapter, one finds no mention there of Amelia's swift return to the house: this is explained only later. Technically speaking, the narrator has not lied, for in retrospect one notices that the description of the masquerade evening contains no direct assertion that the woman who appears to be Amelia is in fact she. Fielding is careful not to have Mrs. Atkinson make any false assertions about her identity during the scene; every statement she makes in response to the Peer's questions applies to her own situation as much as to Amelia's. Yet one might charge the narrator with a certain hypocrisy—an intention to mystify and dupe the reader. Given the narrative persona we are accustomed to, such an imposition cannot help but seem radical and inexplicable. In the most literal way possible, the narrator has abdicated suddenly from the role of unmasker. Much in the manner of the masquerade itself, he leaves the riddle of identity intact, in what may seem a perverse way.

This abdication has further troubling implications. Most important, the reader has no clue how to interpret the moral meaning of Amelia's and Mrs. Atkinson's ruse. Is it not suspiciously like the other examples of deception and role-playing in the fictional world, all of which have been insistently condemned? And what agreement has Mrs. Atkinson reached with the Peer? Granted, Dr. Harrison draws a limited moral lesson from these morning-after revelations: he suggests to Booth that he was foolish to make Amelia go to the masquerade in the first place—it being a scene of "Riot, Disorder, and Intemperance, very improper to be frequented by a chaste and sober Christian Matron" (X, 4)—and approves Amelia's stratagem. (What his opinion of Mrs. Atkinson is, he does not say.) But these remarks do not defuse the sense that the heroine has become, if not the actual perpetrator, the accomplice to an act of hypocrisy of the most theatrical sort. She has had her ostensible reasons, of course, though we notice even here that nothing especially dire seems to have happened as a result of this particular masquerade. She might be forgiven her lapse from integrity on the grounds that she feared worse from the masquerade, even though in this case none of its stereotypical threat has been realized. But for the first time, if only in a muted way, a certain moral ambiguity begins to shade the character of Amelia herself. Like the narrator, she is implicated here in inauthenticity, if not its actual embodiment. Most important, the masquerade has elicited this odd engagement with duplicity—the heroine's first technical lapse from paragon status.

This moment of self-alienation (for one might say Amelia is not herself here) is only one of the masquerade's destabilizing side effects, however. One must look again at the large and curious matter of its consequences, for these the narrator now turns to, rather than any retroactive moral interpretation. Chapters 3 and 4 are both entitled "Consequences of the Masquerade." The repetition is suggestive: it implies a new interest in story over allegory—the place of the masquerade in a larger causal sequence rather than its significance as a topos. Likewise, it suggests the narrator's own new and contradictory role: if he is less and less the elucidator of moral secrets, he is more and more a relator of "Consequences," of a chain of events. He now shows what things follow rather than what things mean. He approximates, in short, the neutral voice of narrative itself. But in that case, one may still wonder, what *are* the consequences of the second and decidedly undisastrous masquerade in *Amelia?*

As in the case earlier of *Tom Jones,* one might speak loosely of two sorts of consequences (though the two are obviously inextricably related on a deeper level): the effect the representation of the masquerade has on *Amelia*'s plot, and the effect it has on character. One could make a similar distinction between the narrative consequences of the masquerade scene—its structural function—and what one might call its epistemological or ideological consequences. On a multiplicity of levels, both kinds of consequences turn out to be liberating.

As far as Fielding's plot goes, this masquerade holds out nothing, ironically, but comic ramifications. There is little ambiguity about this, even of the sort seen earlier in the fiction's first masquerade scene. There, to be sure, Mrs. Atkinson derived certain compelling rewards from her masquerade venture, but only at the cost of a powerful and toxic humiliation, her sexual violation. Here, the pattern of loss followed by gain—of a fortunate fall—is for the most part superseded. It is no longer necessary, it seems, to fall in order to gain.

The new dispensation is most vividly apparent, interestingly enough, in the fate of Mrs. Atkinson herself. Fate is perhaps too ominous a term for it, for from this point on her narrative destiny may be visualized even more clearly than before as a steady, elegant upward curve. If her first masquerade was a kind of "exquisite Distress"—productive, in an oxymoronic way, of benefits as well as sufferings—her second is an unalloyed fulfillment of comic possibility. One might call it a rewriting of her first, for Mrs. Atkinson here revises, so to speak, that dysphoric "masquerade tale" written for her the first time around by the Noble Peer. She inverts the fictional pattern of manipulation by entrapping him in a "plot," a scheme of comic revenge.

The reader first learns of this ruse, again, after it has already succeeded, when Sergeant Atkinson inexplicably receives a letter with an officer's commission from the Peer several days after the masquerade. Mrs. Atkinson then explains to Amelia (who is puzzled because she gets a letter from him too) that while pretending to be Amelia at the masquerade, she informed the Peer that if he wished ever to have her "good Opinion," he had first to perform a favor for a certain "worthy Woman" whom he had previously gravely injured (X, 8)—meaning, of course, Mrs. Atkinson herself. The full story of Mrs. Atkinson's conversation with the Peer now comes out: he has agreed to use his influence on behalf of the sergeant in exchange for a renewal of intimacies with the woman he supposes to be Amelia. The letter Amelia receives is a request that she join him at a fashionable assembly.

Granted, the revelation of Mrs. Atkinson's trick creates a minor disturbance in the fictional world—an argument with Amelia, who is embarrassed at having been compromised in the eyes of the Peer (X, 8). This tiff, rendered more as farce than as a serious dispute (Mrs. Atkinson, we learn, has "taken a Sip too much that Evening"), produces a temporary estrangement between the Booths and the Atkinsons, but is subsequently mitigated when Mrs. Atkinson herself meets with the Peer, explains her ruse, and exonerates Amelia.

The force of the stratagem, however, is unaffected by these subsequent developments. The fact of the commission holds: the Peer does nothing to revoke it even after learning how he has been deceived. And the sergeant, like a male Pamela, quickly advances professionally and socially to the rank of captain—Booth's own rank—and the coveted status of gentleman. The change is radical, and best of all, permanent. Mrs. Atkinson's masquerade ruse thus works what one might call a carnivalesque alteration in the fictional world itself. Sergeant Atkinson's transformation is a classically carnivalesque metamorphosis from underling to master, and yet here it takes hold in the realm of ordinary life.

One could say that Mrs. Atkinson rewrites the melodramatic masquerade tale of the past—the tale of female humiliation and abuse—along the redemptive lines of stage comedy. By one scintillating hoax she alters the genre of her own history. No longer the degraded heroine in a trite and pathos-ridden story, she has become the resourceful protagonist in a witty comedy of retribution. The significance of the masquerade itself—the scene of the drama—is likewise utterly changed. No longer is it that clichéd world of sordid abuses and sexual disaster, masculine pathology and female victimization, found in contemporary sentimental fiction. Mrs. Atkinson's second masquerade is more like that represented on the eighteenth-century comic stage: a realm of fortuitous exchanges and ultimately happy metamorphoses. In popular comedies like Griffin's *Masquerade,* for example, Fielding's own *Miss Lucy in Town,* and Cowley's *Belle's Stratagem,* the masquerade is always surreptitiously linked to profitable consequences—marriages between thwarted lovers, the proper transmission of inheritances, the hoodwinking of villains, and so on. Mrs. Atkinson's "belle's stratagem" replays the comic pattern. The treatment she accords the Noble Peer—who is hardly harmed by her ruse, but only exposed as fatuous—notably resembles the light-hearted punishment meted out to foolish or corrupt characters in masquerade farces. If Mrs. Atkinson has here metamorphosed into a different kind of heroine, the Peer has also changed type from the debauched and repulsive ogre of the masquerade tale to the silly, obsessed, yet finally benign comic dupe of the masquerade play. The generic transformation is total.

We will return to the question of whether a generic shift of the kind registered in Mrs. Atkinson's history also occurs at this point in *Amelia* itself, that larger history in which Mrs. Atkinson's revisionist story is embedded. It is enough to say here that the shape of Amelia's narrative destiny repeats that comic curve demonstrated first by her double at the masquerade—as though Mrs. Atkinson's fortuitous experience were in some sense the signal for the imminent happy transformation of Amelia's own prospects.

Though Amelia paradoxically is not even present, the masquerade may again be held responsible for this second, even more dramatic narrative transformation. Prime among the masquerade's consequences, ultimately, is the most compelling comic turn in Fielding's plot: the restitution of the heroine's lost fortune. This is not to say that the masquerade is merely one of those "imperceptible Links in every Chain of Events" mentioned by the narrator in the first chapter of Book XII, "by which all the great Actions of the World are produced." Granted, it is possible to view the occasion in retrospect as simply one link among many leading to the Booths' final happiness, one more element in *Amelia*'s secret comic design. When, in the bailiff's house at the end of the novel, Amelia joyfully learns of her purloined legacy, Dr. Harrison's comment that "Providence hath done you the Justice at last which it will, one Day or other, render to all Men" (XII, 7) invites the reader, along with the heroine, to reflect on the entire chain of ostensible accidents that have produced her good fortune—including the masquerade—and gloss them all as analogous elements in a transcendent providential telos.

The invocation of Providence can be demystified, however. One may treat it in turn as a trope for plot itself—a figure concealing authorial, rather than supernatural, design. When we consider the implicit design of Fielding's narrative, the special role of the masquerade—its particular indispensability in the matter of the heroine's reward— becomes strikingly apparent. Above all it functions as a locus of intimacy, a topographical (and textual) hub, toward which disparate characters are drawn, and out of which is formed a highly motivated, highly influential, yet still minimally plausible human pattern. This preliminary, supposedly accidental convergence of characters is necessary, it turns out, for every subsequent and increasingly charged development in Fielding's plot, which now tends with intensifying purposiveness toward its comic conclusion. After the masquerade, and as a result of its gratuitous-seeming exchanges, *Amelia* begins to lose much of the randomness previously characterizing it (and symbolized always in Booth's hapless peregrinations), and displays for the first time a narrative momentum. The masquerade scene is in fact the crux of Fielding's narrative—a dense, agglutinative kernel of human relations, out of which the heroine's comic destiny is engendered.[6]

It is impossible to imagine the plot of *Amelia,* and that concluding happy conjunction of characters at the bailiff's house in Book XII, without the prior fateful conjunction of characters at the masquerade. The ironic providentiality of the masquerade is in no way undermined by the fact that the two most significant "accidental" meetings it occasions—between Booth and Miss Matthews and Mrs. Atkinson and the Noble Peer—seem hardly conducive, as we noted earlier, to any good result for the heroine. Neither of these potentially destructive encounters fulfills its negative promise. Booth's masked recontre with his former paramour, for instance, during which he makes a promise to visit her at home, sets up his subsequent agreement to dine with her when they meet a few days later in the street (XI, 7). He had intended to renege, but on meeting Miss Matthews again, he is forced to honor his word. Yet fortuitously, on his way home from this very assignation (during which, we note, he resists Miss Matthews's attempts at sexual blackmail and decides to confess at last his affair to Amelia) Booth is again arrested, ending up in the same bailiff's house to which Robinson, who knows the secret of Amelia's fortune, will also be brought. In circuitous yet integral fashion, Booth's attendance at the masquerade thus prompts what will turn out to be the most auspicious, as well as the last, of his many incarcerations. When Dr. Harrison and Amelia subsequently visit him in prison, the clergyman is recognized by the stricken Robinson, who is then moved to confess his part in the cheat practiced on Amelia by her sister and the lawyer Murphy. Not only does Booth's masquerade encounter not lead to the expected renewal of sexual intimacies with Miss Matthews—the opposite in fact—but it is also curiously instrumental in putting Booth in the place he needs to be, in order for the novel's most important moment of disclosure to take place.

An equally fortunate and necessary set of consequences attends upon Mrs. Atkinson's meeting with the Peer—for Amelia. The revelation of the trick played on the Peer, as I mentioned before, precipitates a temporary estrangement between the Booths and the Atkinsons. The result here is that the sergeant, whose emotional reactions earlier have been somewhat histrionic, falls into a melancholy fit, with accompanying fever, and seems to be on his deathbed. He calls for Amelia (who is at this moment reconciling with his wife), reveals his love for her, and presents her with a miniature of herself, which he now confesses he stole from her at the time of her marriage to Booth, purely out of sentimental ardor (XI, 6). This is the very miniature that, after Amelia pawns it to raise money for Booth (XI, 8), is examined by Robinson, who is pawning clothes in the same shop. He recognizes Amelia from her picture, is told of her desperate circumstances, and falls into a state of remorse that will precipitate his confession to Dr. Harrison in Book XII.

With Robinson's cathartic utterance (which depends as much on this second sequence of consequences as on the first), the two subplots resulting from the masquerade—the Booth/Matthews and Atkinson/Peer entanglements— merge into a single euphoric story line. Amelia becomes an heiress, Booth is released from prison, and together they return to Amelia's country estate, now revealed as rightfully hers.

Thus the "fatal" masquerade is not merely one of any number of elements in *Amelia* obscurely contributing to the heroine's ultimate reward; it conditions the very plot of reward itself. It permits that initial proliferation of intrigue on which every subsequent link in the novel's chain of circumstance depends. As with the similar episode in Richardson's sequel to *Pamela,* the paradox is that within the fictional world the masquerade itself has the aspect of an insufficiently motivated, even unmotivated occurrence. The fact that Booth and "Amelia" end up at the Haymarket is from one perspective the least plausible, least rational development in Fielding's novel. It is not governed by any prevailing didactic economy; it is not justified by any established allegorical principle. It is not necessary finally, except that it is necessary to the narrative itself. Though seemingly unmotivated, *Amelia*'s masquerade scene nevertheless motivates all that follows. Its fateful couplings both provoke and anticipate the revelatory meetings of the final book; its unstable transactions condition the most significant fictional transaction of all, the transformation of Amelia's own history from one of grief to one of joy.

The rewarding turn of *Amelia*'s plot after the masquerade represents a final rebuke to the moral logic that in the novel's early books seems so insistent and at times even oppressive. With the revelation of the masquerade's fortunate consequences, its allegorical legibility (already in question following Mrs. Atkinson's ambiguous story) is permanently obscured; its significance has become paradoxical and indeterminate. The meaning of Fielding's central moral image, the *carnaval moralisé,* is destabilized at the very moment when the masquerade itself becomes a destabilizing instrumental force within *Amelia*'s fictional world.

It is important to define this process of destabilization—here enacted in relation to the image or topos—because it also repeats itself so exactly on the level of character in *Amelia.* One may speak of the transformation in rhetorical terms: the figure controlling meaning in the novel after this point is no longer the antithesis but the oxymoron. The case of the masquerade is paradigmatic. What before was only hinted, now is plain: one can no longer interpret the masquerade simply as the antithesis of what it seems to be, that is, as the scene of vice that masquerades as the scene of pleasure. Its real meaning is no longer derived simply by reversing its apparent meaning, for the two sorts of meaning have become strangely indistinguishable. Of course, the reader of *Amelia* can never forget the reputation of the textual masquerade, just as Fielding's eighteenth-century readers would have been unable to forget the actual masquerade's stereotypical association with danger and licentiousness.

One cannot ignore the allegorical weight the topos has previously been made to carry. Rather, its new significance—that of euphoric agency—is super-added upon the old. The masquerade is now somehow both the stereotypical source of evil and a mysterious instrumental force for good. It cannot be made to seem other than paradoxical. Like the oxymoron, it fuses two contra-dictory sorts of meaning, producing a kind of semantic jamming in Fielding's fiction—a doubling of interpretative possibilities.

One witnesses a similar shift from the antithetical to the oxymoronic mode of signification in the realm of character. It is as though the moral destabilization of the masquerade figure—what one might call its ideological overdetermination—triggers a similar outbreak of ambiguity in the world of Fielding's characters. After the masquerade the moral typology of character on which *Amelia* has been implicitly founded, though never collapsing entirely, becomes distinctly unstable. By the end of the fiction it is maintained only precariously. One sees a breakdown (or near-breakdown) of that hierar-chy of types so essential earlier to the underlying fictional pattern of the *psy-chomachia*. Fielding's cherished dichotomy between knaves and paragons may no longer seem so resolutely preserved; indeed, as though by some extra-logical symbolic process, the best and the worst now appear to merge with one another in curious ways. After the enigmatic, transforming occasion of the masquerade, one might say, character itself is carnivalized.

More and more of Fielding's characters begin to resemble Mrs. Atkin-son—to approximate her doubleness and moral ambiguity. I spoke earlier of her indefinite hybrid nature—the ways in which she is repeatedly associated with the World Upside-Down, the adulteration of categories, mediation between opposites. To borrow a phrase from Natalie Davis, she is the "disor-derly woman" of Fielding's novel—a mercurial affront to rigid metaphysical and social classifications. From the start she has transcended Fielding's ordi-nary moral schema, for she acts inconsistently—sometimes purely in her own interest, sometimes in the interest of others, sometimes in an idiosyncratic combination of the two (the masquerade ruse). Contrasted with *Amelia*'s other, more clearly defined allegorical types, Mrs. Atkinson seems a more plausible character in many ways; at certain moments she even seems briefly to anticipate the more problematic "mixed" characters of nineteenth- and twentieth-century realistic fiction.

Granted, the reasons why Mrs. Atkinson seems particularly plausible have to do with our own conventions of what constitutes a realistic represen-tation of character. The notion of character as dualistic and contradictory, rather than monolithic and morally uniform, is a particularly modern idea. Though obviously a philosophical theme now and then earlier (one thinks of Pope's *Essay on Man*), the idea of the moral and emotional inconsistency of the individual has drawn special impetus from Freudian theory and the develop-ment of psychological concepts of ambivalence and unconscious motivation. We have internalized a model of behavior that incorporates contradiction.

Nonetheless it is possible to speak of Mrs. Atkinson, loosely, as a mimetic rather than an allegorical character: she displays what is to us a familiar ambiguity.

It is precisely this kind of ambiguity that now manifests itself in even the most obdurately fixed of *Amelia*'s types, as if the fiction itself were lapsing from allegory into a subtler mimetic mode. We have already noted the odd beneficence of the Noble Peer after the night of the masquerade: his apparent willingness to let Sergeant Atkinson keep his officer's commission, and the lack of any vengefulness or hostility directed at Mrs. Atkinson or Amelia. Such complacency, suggesting a mitigation of pure villainy, exemplifies one sort of characterological complication in the latter half of *Amelia:* the unexpected improvement of the knave. After the masquerade scene the novel's vicious characters, its ubiquitous hypocrites and debauchees, are no longer quite so vicious. Besides the Peer there are other examples of sudden, inexplicable benignity. After Colonel James's attempt to seduce Amelia fails (he does not even find her at the masquerade), Colonel James too lapses into stoic, inoffensive calm. He seems to have lost his desire for the heroine entirely. The frighteningly Machiavellian aspect of his character recedes, or at least becomes indistinguishable from a certain jaded savoir faire, and he becomes merely something of a psychological enigma: a cryptic, intelligent, at times strangely attractive presence in the fictional world. (He is infinitely more witty than the tiresome Booth, and alone among Fielding's characters in *Amelia* possesses a certain indefinable chic.) He retains his ambivalent status as Booth's friend until the end.

Most important, however, *Amelia*'s happy denouement itself depends on a crucial suspension of knavery. The thief Robinson is a compelling example of the supposedly incorrigible villain who suddenly performs an unaccountably virtuous act. With his timely prison confession he temporarily exempts himself from the ranks of hypocrites—those who keep their secrets—and assumes the implicit prestige of the truth teller. That Robinson later reverts to crime and is hanged (after the action of the novel ends) does not erase the effect of his noble gesture, or the momentary moral complexity that here attaches to his otherwise repellent character.

If after the crux of the masquerade Fielding's villains seem oddly less villainous—and in some cases remarkably helpful in the working out of the Booths' happy destiny—one sees the opposite change in his ostensibly good characters. If the knave is improved, the paragon, as in *Pamela,* is compromised. The most significant embodiment of this syndrome is of course the heroine herself. I have already described Amelia's disconcerting participation in Mrs. Atkinson's masquerade ruse as an early sign of ambiguity in her character. Amelia allies herself with the secret-keepers here, entering if only for a moment the realm of the charlatan and the opportunist. Granted, as we saw, she has good reasons. But for the sake of preserving her virtue, conceived here only in the limited modern sense of sexual purity, she forgoes virtue in the archaic sense, the sense implied in the ancient concept of *virtus*. She allows her essence, as it were, to be divided: she both is and is not that "Amelia" whom Booth accompanies to the masquerade.

On the phantasmic level the impersonation here is the paradigmatic indication of the underlying tendency toward the destabilization of fixed character. It is an enactment, in the most literal way possible, of the nonuniformity of the individual—the carnivalesque dream of the double body. Amelia's secret is her second "body"—the body of masquerade—with access to privileges and pleasures not available to the first. Yet this secret, though primary, is not her only secret, nor is the masquerade the only time when the paragon displays unsuspected, even aberrant depths to her nature.

If Amelia deceives Booth in the matter of the masquerade, purposely veiling knowledge in the classic manner of the hypocrite, she later deceives him again, though for what at first seem justifiable reasons. She is conspicuously silent, for instance, about Colonel James and his subtle designs upon her (IX, 6). Once more, her putative motive is good: she wishes to preserve Booth from dueling with the Colonel on her behalf. But her action is also vulnerable to the most subversive and cynical of interpretations—that she unconsciously courts Colonel James's adulterous attentions. We need not interpret her action this way—indeed, only the most perverse reader would—but even so, the gesture of secret-keeping inevitably produces complexities that implicate the paragon in a questionable moral realm.

Even when she gives up her secret, the heroine's role playing is unsettling. Witness the revelation in Book XII that Amelia has known of Booth's infidelity with Miss Matthews all along. When he confesses his transgression, she admits that she has had a letter with a "feigned Name" on the subject, but has forborne saying anything about it. "Here, my Dear," she exclaims, "is an Instance that I am likewise capable of keeping a Secret" (XII, 2). The reader is taken aback by this disclosure. It is of course another example of the narrator's hypocrisy, since he has led us to believe that Miss Matthews's letters to Amelia—for Matthews is indeed the author of the betraying letter—have miscarried. More important, Amelia too is suddenly revealed by her own admission as a person who is as able to deceive as any. That such a revelation jars is a testimony to the degree to which the emblematic aspect of her character has been emphasized earlier. On some level we have believed her, like those automatons of virtue in traditional allegory, incapable of disingenuousness.

Perhaps the most striking instance of the compromising of the paragon takes place in the memorable chapter—one of the most interesting in all of Fielding—following the masquerade, when Amelia visits Sergeant Atkinson on his supposed deathbed (XI, 6). Like Colonel James's machinations, the details of their charged exchange will be kept a secret from Booth by the heroine—here with very good reason, for her role in this scene is distinctly problematic. This meeting of paragons begins with a preliminary compromising of

Sergeant Atkinson. He confesses that he did in fact steal the miniature of Amelia, set in gold and diamonds, discovered to be missing so long ago. In his wife's conversation with Amelia, the reader has had hints already of his motive: not greed, but a desire to possess "that Face," the image of the woman he loves. "If I had been the Emperor of the World," he passionately begins—until Amelia, in deep embarrassment, stops the outpouring. Not only is the sergeant suddenly exposed as a thief, though of a decidedly senti-mental kind; he is also the purveyor of a hidden, disturbing, incorrigibly adulterous passion. Amelia is profoundly affected. When he asks to kiss her hand before she calls his wife, she becomes flustered and engages in hysterical disavowal, "carelessly" reaching out her hand while murmuring in confusion, "I don't know what I am doing." She betrays every sign, albeit in the crudely conventional style of eighteenth-century popular fiction, of inwardly recipro-cating his transgressive desire. Following this visit with the sergeant she is in such a state of disorder that she sheds "plentiful" tears and has to drink "a great Glass of Water" to calm herself.

Matters are now further complicated by the shocking commentary made here by *Amelia*'s narrator, who takes it upon himself, paradoxically, to unmask the heroine herself. "To say the Truth," he writes, "without any Injury to her Chastity, that Heart, which stood firm as a Rock to all the Attacks of Title and Equipage, of Finery and Flattery, and which all the Treasures of the Uni-verse could not have purchased, was yet a little softened by the plain, honest, modest, involuntary, delicate, heroic Passion of this poor and humble Swain." Like anyone whose chastity is not "hewn out of Marble," he concludes, Amelia here felt a "momentary Tenderness" in spite of herself—at which Booth, "if he had known it, would perhaps have been displeased."

I say shocking, for despite all its understatement and euphemism (we note the string of hygienic adjectives describing the sergeant's passion), the narrator's gloss on the scene does not entirely avoid its morally subversive implications. Indeed, in a larger literary context we are tempted to admire the passage's uncharacteristic liberality and insight. However stylized, it is probably the most sympathetic, least ironic representation of female desire in all of Fielding's fiction. In a way quite remarkable for Fielding, the scenario here may even bring to mind later highly psychological novelistic depictions of sentimental adulterous passion—Rousseau's *La Nouvelle Héloïse,* for exam-ple, or Goethe's *Die Wahlverwandtschaften.* As later eighteenth-century novel-ists were to realize, it was precisely the exquisite, "modest," most sublimated adulterous passion that carried the most revolutionary implications, both for society and for the shape of narrative itself. In Amelia's subtle, palpitating "Tenderness" for the sergeant, there are foreshadowings both of a more exact-ing psychological realism and of those transgressive plots of desire and con-summation characteristic of the later *roman larmoyant.*[7]

Which is not to say, again, that Fielding represents any actual trans-gression on Amelia's part, but only to say that such a narrative development now seems possible in the fictional world in a way that it did not before. The sergeant miraculously recovers, of course; he and his wife are reconciled with the Booths, and later, at the very end of the novel after the happy discovery of Amelia's fortune, the *partie quarrée* is reconstituted. The Atkinsons make a three-month visit to the Booths' country estate—the first visit, the narrator implies, of many more to come (XII, 9). The reader cannot help being left uneasy, however, and not just because of the dubious reinstitution of the novel's primary geometrical figure of adulterous sociability. The secret passion between Amelia and the sergeant is simply left unneutralized (the narrator never refers to it again), and our conception of the heroine has been profoundly altered. Her erotic invulnerability has in fact been the characterological basis on which the logic of *Amelia*'s allegory has depended. Yet as a result of that emotional éclaircissement with the sergeant, she is abruptly revealed to us as one likewise responsive to illicit passion, likewise vulnerable to paradoxical depths of emotional experience. However obliquely, the reader is invited to imagine an alternative future for Fielding's heroine, one characterized not by unwavering fidelity to Booth and the ineffable complacency of the paragon, but by the divisive patterns of erotic discovery.

This, then, is the most radical consequence following upon the masquerade: its exemplary disruptions anticipate a disruption in *Amelia*'s code of character itself. Most important, even the heroine is affected by the tendency toward destabilization. It is she, indeed, who is likely to seem least "like herself" after the event, and most liable, as we have seen, to atypical, amorphous action. If she seems here less the pure creature of allegory, less the representative of a didactic idée fixe, one suspects that this is because the masquerade itself—with which her narrative destiny has been so intimately connected— has already violated the novel's reductive allegorical pattern. Amelia's unprecedented moral fluidity is but a realization of the masquerade's adulterating influence on the fictional world—and the mysterious power of the figure to insinuate, in the place of moral certainty, a tropology of ambiguity and complexity.

*Notes*

1. Few modern readers have agreed with Cleland's judgment (in the *Monthly Review,* Dec. 1751) that *Amelia* delightfully "puts Morality into action," insinuating "its greatest truths into the mind, under the colours of amusement and fiction." Hunter, chap. 9, comments on the impoverishing artistic effect of *Amelia*'s hypertrophied didactic impulse.

2. On the *psychomachia* as a fundamental pattern of symbolic action in allegory, and the paratactic nature of allegorical narrative structure, see Fletcher, pp. 151–61.

3. This extra chapter appears in the Henley edition of *Amelia* only.

4. On the "warrior in skirts," see Kunzle. On the relevance of the Hercules/Omphale story to Tom Jones's sojourn with Lady Bellaston, see Ek.

5.   Other examples of the subgenre are Haywood's story of Erminia, *Female Spectator,* I, 32–33; and the anonymous article "Affecting Masquerade Adventure" in *Gentleman's Magazine,* Dec. 1754.

6.   An analogous crux in *Tom Jones* is the scene at the inn at Upton, where Fielding first exploits a cultural locale associated with accidental meeting (the lodging place) to strategic narrative advantage. One is tempted to speculate on the way in which certain generative cultural sites often seem necessary to plot in just this way. Inns, hotels, and other places of temporary residence, ballrooms, decks of ships, train carriages, and so on, are all part of a conventional topography of plot—a set of places where actions may indeed "take place." Each is a physically circumscribed yet public realm in which disparate characters may plausibly (and apparently randomly) be thrown together in a way that ultimately produces a significant or patterned result. One thinks of Mann's sanatorium, Elizabeth Bowen's hotel in Paris, or the inn on the river in *The Ambassadors* to which James, in the crucial scene in that novel, fortuitously brings Strether together with Chad and Madame Vionnet. In film iconography, the association between public places and plot is if anything even more insistent than in fiction. Classic examples include the Garbo/Barrymore *Grand Hotel,* the Marx Brothers' *Day at the Races* and *Night at the Opera,* and any of a number of Hitchcock films—*Lifeboat, The Lady Vanishes, Strangers on a Train.*

7.   Calling attention to this scene, Hagstrum writes of Amelia's response: "Such is the way to a *coeur sensible.*" Hagstrum sees *Amelia* as being ultimately more coherent than I do— "an important novel of controlled sensibility"—yet also takes into account the revolutionary and potentially disruptive elements in Fielding's treatment of love and desire (pp. 180–85). Though the influence of Richardson on the *roman larmoyant* tradition has been much discussed, this very fact, one suspects, may have obscured to some extent those few yet potent fictional moments when Fielding also somewhat paradoxically prefigures this same tradition.

# Fielding's *Amelia* and the Aesthetics of Virtue

ALISON CONWAY

Amelia's nose rarely provokes comment in today's readings of Fielding's last novel, but in 1751 it featured importantly in the novel's critical reception and demise.[1] Beaten "all to pieces" early in the narrative, the broken nose immediately became the target of Fielding's detractors, who pointed to the iconographic link it established between Amelia and the disreputable Blear-Eyed Moll. As Frederick Blanchard has suggested, "The reputation of the pure and womanly Amelia, owing to the unfortunate slip about her nose, was reduced to that of a common strumpet."[2] Fielding attempted to defend his heroine by admitting his error in forgetting to repair her nose, but to no avail; the damage was done: "As we take into account the incessant scurrility which was directed at the ill-starred heroine, Dr. Johnson's assertion to the effect that the sale of *Amelia* . . . was spoiled by that 'vile broken nose,' is to be seen, in the main, a statement of actual fact."[3]

Since the eighteenth century, Fielding's "favourite Child" has fully recovered from the scandal that initially overwhelmed her. In Fielding criticism Amelia has been identified as "the ideal wife," "the embodiment of moral courage," and "the ethical center of the novel";[4] feminist critics also have viewed Amelia as singularly virtuous, though they are less enthusiastic about the ideas behind Fielding's characterization of his heroine. Patricia Meyer Spacks, for example, argues that Amelia represents a male fantasy of female subjectivity governed by "unchanging structures of feeling": "Amelia in her fidelity and changelessness has a mythic aura, as though she existed outside of time."[5] For the most part, however, critics today tend to ignore Amelia; certainly she has never since held popular attention as strongly as she did in 1751. While those critics who do discuss Amelia perhaps best assess Fielding's intention when they define her as an ideal, the questions raised by the novel's early detractors are worth pursuing. Though Fielding took care, in his revisions of the text, to add a few sentences which repaired Amelia's nose, its initial beating remains a curious component of the narrative. The battered

Reprinted from *Eighteenth-Century Fiction* 8 (1995): 35–50, by permission of the publisher.

nose generates an ambiguity of character which critics are more inclined to grant to Mrs Bennet/Atkinson and Miss Mathews.[6] I will suggest here an answer to the riddle of Amelia's nose while addressing a larger question: in what terms does Fielding, author of *Shamela,* conceptualize a woman of virtue in the context of a moral universe which has become irredeemably compromised? Furthermore, what does Fielding's response to the aesthetic challenge he posed himself reveal about the final stages of his career as a novelist? For while the London setting informs, in part, the moral bleakness of the novel, the difficulty of constructing a heroine whose virtue might influence the world around her seems, finally, to have defeated Fielding. The terms of the critical drubbing *Amelia* received—Bonnell Thorton published a mock advertisement for a novel entitled *Shamelia* in the *Drury-Lane Journal*[7]—must have confirmed the suspicions Fielding had articulated earlier in his career, and he promised, in 1752, to "trouble the World no more with any Children of mine by the same Muse."[8]

The status of Amelia's nose as a visual sign of uncertain meaning links the questions raised by Fielding's last work to the hermeneutical issues raised by the eighteenth-century novel. Advocates of the novel believed fiction could generate social sympathy and moral virtue; its detractors claimed that the novel only worked to encourage illicit desire and transgressive behaviour. The refusal by critics to read Amelia as a virtuous heroine is suggestive of a wider interpretive problem encompassing all eighteenth-century novels, even Richardson's *Clarissa*. Novelistic anxiety over questions of meaning are pronounced in *Amelia* and are framed by the representation of female subjectivity. I will trace Amelia's characterization in order to suggest how it emblematizes problems of interpretation and fiction, and how it symbolizes the ability of the eighteenth-century novel to move simultaneously in two directions, towards moral stasis and towards desire. As we shall see, these concerns are most intensely focused on a portrait of the broken-nosed heroine, a miniature Amelia that circulates in the world of the novel just as *Amelia* circulates in the world outside.

Fielding's decision to focus his narrative on the plight of a virtuous woman probably was motivated by his admiration of *Clarissa* and, more generally, by the rise of the "feminine" novel.[9] Fielding praised *Clarissa* privately in a letter to Richardson in 1748: "Believe me . . . if your Clarissa had not engaged my Affections more than this Mrs. [Fame] all your Art and all your Nature had not been able to extract a single Tear"; the *Jacobite's Journal* also celebrated Richardson's achievement: "Such Simplicity, such deep Penetration into Nature; such Power to raise and alarm the Passions, few writers, either ancient or modern, have been possessed of."[10] Critics have noted Fielding's attempt to write a more mimetic, less allegorical style of fiction, but Richardson's influence is most pronounced, I believe, in the novel's representation of women. It is significant that Amelia's battered nose links her to Charlotte

Cradock, an allusion which Richardson caught in 1752: "Amelia, even to her noselessness, is again his [Fielding's] first wife."[11] Fielding's decision to model Amelia after his deceased wife, even to the point of highlighting a physical flaw, adds to the novel's mimetic impetus and the atmosphere of individualized affect Fielding establishes around his heroine.

As J. Paul Hunter has aptly observed, "Given the guarded portrayals of women in the earlier novels, *Amelia* is for Fielding something of a risk, a challenge to his own double standard of morality and his own personal frets and fears."[12] Indeed, various components of the novel undermine the Richardsonian faith in female virtue that Fielding satirizes in *Shamela,* but which he wants to claim for the heroine of *Amelia.* Two moments in the opening chapters establish the problematic nature of interpreting female character. The first scene takes place in the prison:

> A very pretty Girl then advanced towards them, whose Beauty Mr. *Booth* could not help admiring the Moment he saw her; declaring, at the same time, he thought she had great Innocence in her Countenance. *Robinson* said she was committed thither as an idle and disorderly Person, and a common Streetwalker.[13]

The immediate difficulty facing Booth and the reader is that the beautiful face bears no relation to virtue—that in fact it serves as a mask, covering the disease and corruption inherent in the prostitute's body. Booth's cheerful optimism marks him not as a man of Good Heart but as dangerously naïve.[14] The interpretive community which, in earlier novels, ensured an understanding between the narrator and the reader breaks down here, and we are forced to choose between Booth's innocent blindness and Robinson's cynical insight. The prison marks the absence of a moral context within which we might make an informed decision about the streetwalker, and it is unclear how we can discover for ourselves what Robinson already knows.

The potential for visual signs to act duplicitously re-emerges even more menacingly a few pages later, when the narrator recounts a personal anecdote reminiscent of the scene that has just taken place between Booth and Robinson:

> One of the Ladies, I remember, said to the other—"Did you ever see any thing look so modest and so innocent as that Girl over the way?" . . . Now this Lady was no bad Physiognomist; for it was impossible to conceive a greater Appearance of Modesty, Innocence and Simplicity, than what Nature had displayed in the Countenance of that Girl; and yet, all Appearances notwithstanding, I myself (remember, Critic, it was in my Youth) had a few Mornings before seen that very identical Picture of all those ingaging Qualities in Bed with a Rake at a Bagnio, smoking Tobacco, drinking Punch, talking Obscenity, and swearing and cursing with all the Impudence and Impiety of the lowest and most abandoned Trull of a Soldier. (p. 47)

This passage is meant to warn us against Miss Mathews (who is busy seducing Booth at the moment of this narrative intrusion) and, more generally, to act as a commentary on the opacity of women's nature: what you see is not necessarily what you get. In the above passage the narrator assumes the position which Robinson took up *vis-à-vis* Booth, confronting an idealistic belief in the correspondence between surface and depth with a profound suspicion of the posturing of innocence. Fielding offers the reader no advice but rather abandons the unwary to his gullibility; in fact, the only hope for knowledge seems to involve participation in the world's corruption—in this case, a visit to the bawdy-house.[15]

The crux of the matter rests upon the "identical Picture of all those ingaging Qualities." Unlike the first scene, where Booth *thought* he saw innocence in the prostitute's face (and so perhaps had misinterpreted her look), here we are confronted with the certain knowledge that the look interpreted by "no bad Physiognomist" *is* identical with the usual expression of the whore. The "ingaging Qualities" can have no intrinsically moral meaning if they are the same at the opera and in the bagnio, and so the question of what, exactly, is engaging the viewer becomes the critical issue for the reader. Within this sceptical paradigm, Booth's "admiration" for the young lady appears to be possibly tainted by lust. As Allan Wendt has argued, Fielding appreciates the fact that erotic desire can render moral ideals appealing, but when the object changes from Sophia Western to a prostitute, the happy marriage of desire and ethics is placed in jeopardy. The moral virtue which the viewer attributes to the prostitute is only a *trompe-l'œil*, a façade which renders the innocent gaze dubious if only by revealing its lack of discernment.[16]

Fielding's recognition that visual signs may trick the unwary spectator is apparent in all his novels. In *Amelia,* however, this distrust threatens to undermine the narrative's desire to conflate surface and depth in the representation of its heroine. Amelia's physical appearance is identical with her moral excellence, and her broken nose provides an important link in this chain of correspondence. Booth places the destruction of Amelia's nose at the centre of his courtship history: "The Injury done to her Beauty by the overturning of a Chaise, by which, as you may well remember, her lovely Nose was beat all to pieces, gave me an Assurance that the Woman who had been so much adored for the Charms of her Person, deserved a much higher Adoration to be paid to her Mind" (p. 66). Brian McCrea has argued that Amelia's broken nose advances Booth's suit by eliminating competitors of higher social rank: "the injured nose places her within [Booth's reach]."[17] However, Amelia is never presented as a woman who would marry out of self-interest, and it is crucial we believe that her love-match with Booth transcends material concerns.

The nose marks Amelia, not as socially humiliated, but as morally superior, with a "Mind" deserving "a much higher Adoration." The scene in which she unmasks herself after the accident suggests how the visual and the moral may work together:

> I begged her to indulge my Curiosity by shewing me her Face. She answered in a most obliging Manner, "Perhaps, Mr. *Booth,* you will as little know me when my Mask is off as when it is on;" and at the same instant unmasked.—The Surgeon's Skill was the least I considered. A thousand tender Ideas rushed all at once on my Mind. I was unable to contain myself, and eagerly kissing her Hand, I cried—"Upon my Soul, Madam, you never appeared to me so lovely as at this Instant." (p. 68).

Amelia's statement warns Booth against disappointment, but we never discover what the visual grounds for Booth's response might be. As Terry Castle points out, "We are left only with the paradoxical assertion that disfigured, Amelia is not only still beautiful, but somehow more beautiful than before."[18] This paradox defines Amelia's nature and separates her from all of the other women Fielding represents in the novel, women whose moral disfigurement coincides with a flawless physical appearance.[19]

Fielding is not simply stressing Booth's admiration of Amelia's mind in this scene, for the moment is narrated as an intensely visual revelation. On the one hand, the absence of description about Amelia's appearance effectively prevents us from imagining a conventional beauty who might arouse us. Fielding's silence at this crucial moment stands in sharp contrast to his intensely detailed and eroticized account of Sophia Western's beauty in *Tom Jones.*[20] This shift foregrounds Fielding's move towards a more Richardsonian aesthetic, one which had been formulated earlier in the century in almost exactly the same terms: "When Adam is introduc'd by Milton describing Eve in Paradise . . . he does not represent her like a Grecian Venus by her Shape or Features, but by the Lustre of her Mind which shone in them, and gave them their Power of charming."[21] Instead of allowing us an erotic response as a means of ensuring our sympathy for the heroine, Fielding directs our attention towards Amelia's modesty. It is this modesty that, given the dearth of physical detail, seems in itself to inspire Booth's enthusiastic response.

On the other hand, we can guess (and later it is confirmed) that Amelia bears a scar on her nose. The scar grants Amelia a particularity, and it is this particularity that becomes linked to a moral standard. Unlike the allusion to the Venus de Medici which establishes Sophia's universal appeal in *Tom Jones,* here the presence of a scar renders Amelia's beauty ideal. It does so because it identifies Amelia's beauty as unexchangeable; it cannot be compared to that of other women or be judged by traditional standards. In other words, Amelia's looks can be translated only in reference to Amelia's moral character. Thus the effect of not describing Amelia's beauty in conventional terms serves to single it out and to grant Amelia an "incorrigible specificity."[22]

Castle suggests that the moment of Amelia's unmasking produces a type of "dialectical confusion," but I would argue that it achieves the opposite effect. Amelia's beauty is unambiguous because her moral purity makes it so. Deformity resides in the blank faces of the whores, whose lack of specificity enables deception. Amelia's face cannot shock when unmasked because it is always identical with Amelia's self. For his ability to appreciate Amelia's new beauty, Booth is rewarded with a wife truly singular in her virtue.

Amelia's beauty finds its only visual expression in a miniature portrait which is stolen early in the narrative. Richard Wendorf has observed that in the eighteenth century the miniature portrait constructed "the cult of the private and carefully individuated subject, represented in a simple and direct manner that severed almost all ties with its iconic forebears."[23] Given Fielding's interest in visual aesthetics, this observation casts light on the significance of the miniature portrait in *Amelia*. In earlier novels, Fielding was more likely to allude to Hogarth's satiric prints, as in his description of Bridget Allworthy as the figure represented in Hogarth's *Morning*. The turn towards the non-satiric Hogarth—Hogarth the portrait painter—marks the difference between the understanding of female subjectivity informing his representation of Sophia Western and the new ideas revealed in his characterization of Amelia.

And yet the portrait raises questions about the particularity of Amelia's beauty and its connection to her moral virtues. The act of replicating the visual experience Amelia generates seems to qualify the ideal of non-duplication that the experience initially represented. The theft of the portrait places even more stress on the paradigm of Amelia's unexchangeability that the narrative has so laboriously established. When Booth describes his departure for Gibraltar, he laments: "What would I have then given for a little Picture of my dear Angel, which she had lost from her Chamber about a Month before? and which we had the highest Reason in the world to imagine her Sister had taken away" (p. 108). Amelia's beauty, in replica, has now changed hands. Booth identifies the worth of the painting as residing, not in the jewels that surround it, but in its exact representation of Amelia: "next to *Amelia* herself, there was nothing which I valued so much as this little Picture: for such a Resemblance did it bear of the Original, that *Hogarth* himself did never, I believe, draw a stronger Likeness" (pp. 108–9). The portrait bears a contiguous relation to Amelia, its likeness generating a response so powerful that only the original has more worth in the catalogue of Booth's possessions. This moment places Amelia and the visual representation of her face on a continuum of value, one which will take on a new significance in the context of London, where commerce and virtue meet and clash.

The London that the novel represents so darkly has become morally bankrupt as a result of its unwillingness to pursue any but financial goals. Fielding identifies the problem immediately in his characterization of Judge Thrasher:

"the Justice was never indifferent in a Cause, but when he could get nothing on either Side" (p. 21). Far from establishing bonds between men as members of a newly prosperous commercial society, money only serves to intensify the degradation of those without sufficient funds.[24] William Booth is imprisoned for the first of many times almost immediately after he and his wife arrive in London, simply because he lacks the money to secure his release from the constable who arrests him on the street.

For Amelia, commercial vice takes on a particularly gendered and menacing aspect. In London a woman's beauty is always understood to be for sale. Indeed, almost all social and commercial transactions lead back to some kind of prostitution. The Booths' plight seems to originate in their unwillingness to barter Amelia's virtue, and their naïve trust in the benevolence of the noble peer, "cousin" of their landlady, is placed in exact opposition to the rules of the city: "few Men, as I have observed, have such disinterested Generosity as to serve a Husband the better, because they are in Love with his Wife, unless she will condescend to pay a Price beyond the Reach of a virtuous Woman" (p. 193). Almost all of the characters the Booths meet and befriend—the Trents, Miss Mathews, the Jameses, Mrs Ellison, and even Mrs Atkinson—have found ways to advance themselves by exchanging women's sexual favours. More generally, Fielding is echoing Swift and other Augustans, who frequently represent the sins of modernity, and particularly of modern capital, in metaphors of the sexually diseased, and usually female, body, a body which manages to hide its disgusting interior behind a veneer of social respectability.[25] The disease of commercial culture seems embodied in corrupt sexual behaviour which circulates, like money, unseen and unnamed.[26] A striking instance of this analogy appears in Fielding's representation of the noble peer, who remains nameless throughout the text, though he is the most politically and financially powerful figure in the novel. Only the lord's death reveals his "true" nature, when his "amours" finally leave him "so rotten, that he stunk above Ground" (p. 532).

The difficulty of establishing an icon of virtue whose meaning cannot be misunderstood emerges in Fielding's attempt to render Amelia an active heroine in a place where no one will recognize her moral value. Amelia remains confined within the home, as restricted as Clarissa imprisoned in Lovelace's brothel; there is certainly, as Hunter points out, the same "claustrophobic, smothering sense of frustration, panic, and doom" as in Richardson's novel.[27] Amelia's broken nose, which guaranteed her singularity in the country, only adds to the sense of her vulnerability in London. Mrs Ellison is delighted by Amelia's appearance, and upon the occasion of the women's first meeting the narrator remarks, "I know not whether the little Scar on her Nose did not rather add to, than diminish her Beauty" (p. 184). Fielding added this remark to the second edition of the novel, in order to remind his readers that Amelia's broken nose *did* heal.[28] But the narrative intrusion only adds an ironic twist to the scene, in light of Mrs Ellison's plan to literalize the symbolic meaning of the scarred nose by selling Amelia to the noble peer. The frequency with which Amelia becomes an object of desire in London confuses the earlier narrative trajectory aimed at establishing an ethical, rather than an erotic, aura around the heroine. The intensity of the erotic responses Amelia elicits places the reader in a curious scopic position: her praises are sung again and again, but only in order to account for yet another illicit passion. It is unclear how Fielding's ideal reader, presumably male, is meant to separate himself from these adulterous admirers. Indeed, the narrator comes dangerously close to situating himself and the reader in the position occupied by the novel's libertines, a danger also encountered by Richardson in the writing of *Clarissa*.[29]

Unlike Richardson's heroine, Amelia seems entirely passive in her efforts to achieve moral good. Cynthia Griffin Wolff argues that "Amelia's virtue is private, and its influence can be felt only in personal interaction," but it seems that even privately Amelia can effect very little change. Her husband repeatedly acts in a manner so irresponsible as to be immoral, and the men who seek her favours seem undaunted by her repeated demonstrations of moral excellence.[30] Fielding's reluctance to transform Amelia into a more aggressive heroine, coupled with his hyperbolic and intrusive pronouncements on her innocence, mark the gap between his and Richardson's confidence in women's ability to effect the moral transformation of society.[31]

London's corruption destroys the potential for the private, domestic sphere to effect any kind of social change, and the Booths' London home functions in the novel only as a precarious kind of refuge. Outside this refuge Amelia is unable to prevent the attacks on her virtue that she wards off, in however bungling and naïve a fashion, in her own home. When Amelia is accosted at Vauxhall by two aristocratic young men, the presence of clergymen and her children does nothing to thwart the attack: " 'D—n me,' says he that spoke first, and whom they called Jack, 'I will have a Brush at her, if she belonged to the whole Convocation' " (p. 396). Amelia is saved only by the arrival of Captain Trent:

> "It is impossible," cries my Lord, "to know everyone.—I am sure, if I had known the Lady to be a Woman of Fashion, and an Acquaintance of Captain *Trent*, I should have said nothing disagreeable to her; but if I have, I ask her Pardon, and the Company's." (p. 398)

The problem of "knowing" everyone, or indeed anyone, in London is Fielding's central concern. The social codes which the aristocracy should guarantee disappear when noblemen choose to disregard them, as no one else has the power to enforce them. Even at the moment Amelia is rescued she is compromised yet again, for it is her husband's friendship with Captain Trent, a notorious pimp, that saves her. "A Woman of Fashion" means very little when coupled with "an acquaintance of Captain *Trent*." Amelia's meaning is necessarily altered when she enters the corrupt public domain, and neither her appearance nor her actions can rectify that slippage. Increasingly the novel implicates all of its characters in the realm of moral turpitude; as Fielding himself observed, "no Man, I believe, ever removed great Quantities of Dirt from any Place, without finding some of it sticking to his Skirts."[32]

In an attempt to restore his ethical standards to their original unity, Fielding reinvokes the visual code he established earlier in the narrative. The bridging of the chasm which has opened up in Amelia's character begins with the reunion of the long-lost portrait and its owner. In a scene far removed from the crowds of dissolutes who torment the Booths, the narrative re-establishes the sentimental value of Amelia's face. Amelia visits Sergeant Atkinson when he becomes ill, and he confesses his earlier theft of the portrait:

> "Here then, Madam," said he, "is your Picture, I stole it when I was eighteen Years of Age, and have kept it ever since. It is set in Gold, with three little Diamonds; and yet I can truly say, it was not the Gold nor the Diamonds which I stole—it was that Face which, if I had been the Emperor of the World——"
> (p. 482)

The sergeant's assumed moral integrity, closely tied to his lower-class origins, differentiates his passion from that of the novel's multiple adulterers. And yet the child-like innocence which characterizes sentimental heroes seems oddly compromised in Sergeant Atkinson, in so far as he has retained a secret which links him to other, less well intentioned, bearers of illicit knowledge. Most significantly, the language of the above passage, which aims to separate Atkinson's love for Amelia's particular beauty from the lust it has elicited in London society, does not entirely escape the commercial mores of the city. The "three little diamonds" are diminutive, almost endearing, like Amelia; "if I had been the Emperor of the World," Atkinson begins, before Amelia interrupts him. Atkinson wishes he had been in a position socially advantageous enough to woo Amelia, to buy, in effect, her beautiful face. Even within the confines of the sentimental, marriage and prostitution—explicitly linked in London society—form part of the same continuum.

The scene becomes even more complex when Amelia responds in an ambiguous manner to the sergeant's declaration of love:

> To say the Truth, without any injury to her Chastity, that Heart which had stood firm as a Rock to all the Attacks of Title and Equipage, of Finery and Flattery, and which all the Treasures of the Universe could not have purchased, was yet a little softened by the plain, honest, modest, involuntary, delicate, heroic Passion of this poor and humble Swain; for whom, in spite of herself, she felt a momentary Tenderness and Complacence, at which *Booth,* if he had known it, would perhaps have been displeased. (pp. 482–83)

Amelia's response to Atkinson seems in part motivated by the lack of any danger his love might pose, a lack guaranteed by his status as a "poor and humble Swain." The narrator can sympathize with Amelia's momentary lapse because he knows it will not lead to any real transgression. But the humility of Atkinson also has the effect of rendering Amelia's response more powerful, in so far as she authorizes it—she allows herself to indulge in feelings of "Tenderness and Complacence." This self-authorization fits in with the larger Richardsonian effect the novel has been striving, ineffectually, to create—Castle notes that the scene reveals traits of "a more exacting psychological realism"—and marks the moment when Amelia finally achieves some degree of autonomy as a heroine.[33]

The effect of the psychological realism which characterizes this scene is a certain amount of epistemological disruption. The moment is transgressive both in its origins—the theft of the portrait—and in its dénouement—the revelation of Amelia's potential for desire. While we are meant to view Atkinson's restraint as moral, his desire is nonetheless immoral when judged by the strict codes of the novel. Amelia's response, however sympathetically represented, could also be understood as her first move away from the path of righteousness. Thus the portrait, reintroduced after such a long hiatus, does not allow the visual and the moral to dovetail in quite the way that we might have expected. Most important, neither category seems able to escape the demands of an increasingly commercialized society.

What follows the scene between Atkinson and Amelia confirms this discovery. The sentimental tableau which is meant to secure meaning outside the workings of exchange becomes firmly lodged within its confines when Amelia takes the miniature, the catalyst for her exchange with Atkinson, and sells it:

> she was scarce able to walk in her present Condition; for the Case of poor *Atkinson* had much affected her tender Heart, and her Eyes had overflown with many Tears. It occurred likewise to her at present, that she had not a single Shilling in her Pocket, or at home, to provide Food for herself and her Family. In this situation she resolved to go immediately to the Pawnbroker whither she had gone before, and to deposit her Picture for what she could raise upon it. She then immediately took a Chair, and put her Design in Execution. (p. 487)

At this point the strain of protecting virtue from the taint of commercial transactions becomes pronounced. The unfortunate consequence of having the pawnshop scene follow the love scene so directly is that it appears as though Amelia is banking on the response that her looks have elicited in Atkinson when she takes her portrait to the pawnshop. The narrative reassures us that "the prettiest Face in the World . . . was deposited, as of no Value into the Bargain," but the value Atkinson places in Amelia's face and the value residing in the gold and diamonds in which the picture is set are confused by their common status as precious objects (p. 487). Recognizing, perhaps, the futility of an affective exchange as a means of social survival, Amelia redetermines her own value, in all senses of the term.[34]

The undecidibility between the portrait's value as a piece of jewellery, with a pretty face thrown into the bargain, and its value as a representation of ideal beauty and moral excellence is essential to the restoration of the Booths to their previous state of innocence. The portrait is the means by which Amelia becomes rich; it takes the place of selling her favours to the noble peer. Because this exchange accomplishes the same end as prostitution, it links sentimentalism to a materialist eroticism. Moreover, the pawnbroker's admiring response to the portrait—"*Upon my Word this is the handomest Face I ever saw in my Life*"—serves as the moral catalyst of the narrative (p. 516). Robinson's voyeuristic desire to view the object of the pawnbroker's admiration immediately becomes transformed into a sentimental feeling when he recognizes Amelia: "My Guilt immediately flew in my Face, and told me I had been Accessary to this Lady's Undoing" (pp. 516–17). The term "undoing" echoes the pawnbroker's description of Amelia as an "undone Wretch"; the face which was meant to represent all that differentiated Amelia from morally ruined women becomes identical with them for a brief but crucial narrative moment.

Ironically, the comic ending of Fielding's novel is premised on the fact that Amelia takes *herself* to the market. Unlike Clarissa, Fielding's heroine is able to compromise without destroying herself. In fact, because Amelia is able to divide herself, both by sending Mrs Atkinson to the masquerade in her stead, and by selling the portrait which Booth and Atkinson believe to be, in some contiguous fashion, Amelia herself, she can retrieve the wealth which will allow her to retreat from the violence of London society and so ensure her family's domestic tranquility. The potential for the visual iconography of Amelia's broken nose to work as a sign both of a type of agency claimed by prostitutes and of an ideal virtue finally becomes enabling, rather than crippling, for Fielding's narrative. Amelia's battered nose may have caused Fielding much grief after he published his last novel, but it also allowed his heroine to achieve some of the complexity that he admired in Clarissa.

Allan Wendt attributes Fielding's inability to sustain a vision of "pure" Eros in *Amelia* to the moral bankruptcy of London in the mid-eighteenth century:

> Intellectually, Fielding seems to have sympathized with the benevolists; practically, as magistrate and journalist, he seems to have met so many people who could be moved only by threats, who lacked the finer sensibilities which might be attracted by the "naked beauty of virtue" that he was sometimes forced to qualify his benevolism.[35]

While Fielding might have agreed with this assessment, it does not account for the artistic goals the novel sets itself. The "naked beauty of virtue," so happily embodied in the representation of Sophia Western, could not stand up to the social realities which Fielding wanted to discuss in *Amelia*. Fielding was not only responding to a lack of "finer sensibilities," but also constructing a viable alternative to the "Good Heart" ethical model. The qualification of Fielding's paternalistic benevolism in favour of a social realism coincides with the emergence of a heroine who escapes, at least in part, the status of an allegorical representation. Fielding's characterization of Amelia does not situate her "outside of time," as Spacks asserts, but rather places her within a complex social and economic dynamic, one which created tensions that the eighteenth-century novel both explicated and sought to resolve. The doubling of Amelia's self, which occurs as the portrait circulates and accumulates various meanings, points to the larger effect eighteenth-century fiction achieved. Rather than seeking out stability of character as a means of asserting a particular moral lesson, the eighteenth-century novel allowed narrative desire to generate interpretive challenges, both painful and pleasurable, for the new reading public.

*Notes*

1. A departure from the trend in twentieth-century criticism can be found in George E. Haggerty, "Amelia's Nose; or, Sensibility and Its Symptoms," *The Eighteenth Century: Theory and Interpretation* 32:2 (1995), 139–56. Haggerty's article appeared while this study was in press.

2. Frederick Blanchard, *Fielding, the Novelist: A Study in Historical Criticism* (New Haven: Yale University Press, 1926), p. 84.

3. Blanchard, p. 95. For Johnson's assessment of *Amelia* see *Henry Fielding: The Critical Heritage*, ed. Ronald Paulson and Thomas Lockwood (London: Routledge and Kegan Paul, 1969), p. 445.

4. A. R. Towers, "*Amelia* and the State of Matrimony," *Review of English Studies* n.s. 5 (1954), 157; George Sherburn, "Fielding's *Amelia*: An Interpretation," in *Fielding: A Collection of Critical Essays*, ed. Ronald Paulson (Englewood Cliffs, N.J.: Prentice Hall, 1962), p. 149; Allan Wendt, "The Naked Virtue of Amelia," *ELH* 27 (1960), 131.

5. Patricia Meyer Spacks, "Female Changelessness, Or, What Do Women Want?," *Studies in the Novel* 19 (1987), 273–83; see also April London, "Controlling the Text: Women in *Tom Jones*," *Studies in the Novel* 19 (1987), 284–95. An exception to the general feminist critique of Fielding's aesthetics is Angela J. Smallwood's *Fielding and the Woman Question: The Novels of Henry Fielding and the Feminist Debate 1700–1750* (New York: St Martin's Press, 1989). I am not convinced by Smallwood's assertion that Sophia and Amelia are "products of rationalist-feminist thinking" (p. 126).

6. Terry Castle's discussion of *Amelia* is the exception to this rule. Castle's discussion of Amelia's duplicity in the masquerade incident points to a moment of inconsistency in Fielding's characterization of his heroine; the masquerade, she argues, "insinuate[s], in the place of moral certainty, a tropology of ambiguity and complexity." *Masquerade and Civilization* (Stanford: Stanford University Press, 1986), p. 242. I would extend Castle's analysis to suggest that the moral complexity which colours the masquerade scene haunts Amelia throughout the text.

7. For an account of the Thorton advertisement, see Blanchard, p. 88.

8. Henry Fielding, *The Covent-Garden Journal* (28 January 1752), ed. Bertrand A. Goldgar (Middletown, Conn.: Wesleyan University Press, 1988), p. 66.

9. Peter Sabor makes a related claim in "*Amelia* and *Sir Charles Grandison:* The Convergence of Fielding and Richardson," *Wascana Review* 17 (Fall 1982), 3–18.

10. *The Correspondence of Henry and Sarah Fielding,* ed. Martin C. Battestin and Clive T. Probyn (London: Oxford University Press, 1993), pp. 70–74; *The Jacobite's Journal and Related Writing,* ed. W. B. Coley (Middletown, Conn.: Wesleyan University Press, 1975), p. 119; see also p. 188.

11. *Selected Letters of Samuel Richardson,* ed. John J. Carroll (Oxford: Clarendon Press, 1964), p. 197.

12. J. Paul Hunter, *Occasional Form: Henry Fielding and the Chains of Circumstance* (Baltimore: Johns Hopkins University Press, 1975), p. 196.

13. Henry Fielding, *Amelia,* ed. Martin Battestin (Middletown, Conn.: Wesleyan University Press, 1983), p. 33. References are to this edition.

14. Frank Kermode identifies the "Good Heart" as the basis of Fielding's moral criteria, which assume "a supposedly instinctive understanding of both reader and writer of Right and Wrong." See "Richardson and Fielding," *Cambridge Journal* 4 (1950), 109.

15. As J. Paul Hunter and others have pointed out, the moral tone of *Amelia* is far more severe and strict than in Fielding's other novels. This rigidity seems proportionate to the potential for moral relativism apparent in the novel, a relativism which, as in this scene, seems to force the reader to choose between the knowingness of evil and the blindness of innocence. At other points in the narrative, Fielding's judicial voice defines a third option, that of moral laws which stand above the quagmire of experience.

16. For an interesting account of Fielding's ambivalence towards prostitutes in general, see Bertrand A. Goldgar, "Fielding and the Whores of London," *Philological Quarterly* 64 (Spring 1985), 265–73.

17. Brian McCrea, "Politics and Narrative Technique in Fielding's *Amelia,*" *Journal of Narrative Technique* 13 (1983), 136.

18. Castle, p. 179.

19. "No Woman is capable of being Beautiful, who is not capable of being False," Mr. "R.B." had written to Richard Steele forty years earlier. *Spectator* 33 (7 April 1711), ed. Donald F. Bond (Oxford: Clarendon Press, 1965), p. 140.

20. Henry Fielding, *Tom Jones,* ed. Martin C. Battestin and Fredson Bowers (Middletown, Conn.: Wesleyan University Press, 1975), book 6, chap. 2, pp. 155–57. That Fielding's account of Sophia is both highly literary and even ironic does not, I believe, detract from its erotic potential. The accumulation of descriptive detail fixes the reader's gaze on Sophia's imaginary body, and exerts a powerful ekphrastic force, so that even if Sophia is only *like* the famous paintings and statues to which Fielding compares her, she is equally represented as an aesthetic object.

21. Mr "R.B." in his letter to Steele, quoted in the *Spectator* 33 (7 April 1711), p. 140.

22. Castle, p. 249.

23. Richard Wendorf, *The Elements of Life: Biography and Portrait-Painting in Stuart and Georgian England* (New York: Oxford University Press, 1990), p. 127.

24. "In Fielding's attack on the decadent aristocracy in *Amelia,* social obligation has become explicitly financial, transformed into a kind of social capital deployed to oppress the lower classes," James Thompson argues. "Property and Possession in Fielding," *Eighteenth-Century Fiction* 3 (1990), 40.

25. J. G. A. Pocock makes the link between misogyny and anti-commercial sentiment: "The Augustan political journalists—Defoe, Steele, Addison, Mandeville—display an uneasy concern with the increasingly visible public role of women, and it would appear that this is connected with their increasing perception of the growth of credit finance." *Virtue, Commerce, and History* (Cambridge: Cambridge University Press, 1985), p. 99.

26. As Thompson suggests, "Fielding's obsession with prostitution in *Amelia* is connected with capitalization, as in the central contrast between the good wife, Amelia, who protects her virtue at all costs, and Mrs. Trent" (p. 40n40).

27. Hunter, p. 195.

28. See Battestin, ed., *Amelia,* appendix 6, p. 569 [184.24–6].

29. My thanks to Carol Knoll for reminding me of Richardson's defence of the fire scene in *Clarissa,* a defence in which he goes as far as to praise Lovelace's voyeuristic description of Clarissa: "Are his descriptions, the Character and the Delicacy of the Lady considered, above the Life?" His praise has the effect of aligning his own gaze with that of his notorious character. See Richardson's document, edited by T. C. Duncan Eaves and Ben D. Kimpel, in *Philological Quarterly* 43 (1984), 403.

30. Cynthia Griffin Wolff, "Fielding's *Amelia:* Private Virtue and Public Good," *Texas Studies in Language and Literature* 10 (1968), 54.

31. This difference, however pronounced, should not lead us to set up an easy anti-feminist/feminist opposition between Fielding and Richardson. Smallwood makes this point convincingly in the introduction to *Fielding and the Woman Question,* pp. 5–6. Certainly the manner in which Richardson represents prostitutes in *Clarissa,* for example, suggests that his sympathy towards women had very clear limits, and to a large extent operated at the expense of women's sexuality. Fielding, on the other hand, could draw a Molly Seagrim without condemning her to a disease-ridden death.

32. *Covent-Garden Journal* (18 January 1752), p. 44.

33. Castle, p. 241. Castle also argues, and I agree, that "however stylized, [this scene] is probably the most sympathetic, least ironic representation of female desire in all of Fielding's fiction" (p. 241).

34. Frederick Ribble has observed that Amelia "seems to have two constitutions, or a constitution with very puzzling, contradictory properties, a constitution both delicate and resilient." "The Constitution of the Mind and the Concept of Emotion in Fielding's *Amelia,*" *Philological Quarterly* 56 (1977), 116.

35. Wendt, p. 147.

# The Failure of *Amelia:* Fielding's Novel of Sentiment and Social Reform

## Martin C. Battestin

Unlike Fielding's comic masterpieces, *Joseph Andrews* and *Tom Jones, Amelia* would be an altogether different sort of novel—at once the most personal work of fiction he ever wrote and the product of his heightened awareness of disorders in England's "Constitution."

By 29 October, when Walter Harte predicted that publication was imminent, *Amelia* was near enough to completion that Fielding projected a fresh literary enterprise—a smart new periodical calculated in part to promote the Universal Register Office and to keep the public apprised of his activities at Bow Street. Remembering his satire of Paul Whitehead in 1749, he called it the *Covent-Garden Journal.* Announcements of the paper were included in advertisements for the Universal Register Office as early as 31 October, promising publication on 23 November.[1] In the event, the *Covent-Garden Journal* would not appear until 4 January 1752, six weeks later than promised. The delay is chiefly owing to the fact that Fielding did not finish *Amelia* until 12 December, the date subscribed to the Dedication to Ralph Allen; and he tampered with the narrative even as it went through the press.[2] Millar began "puffing" the novel in mid-November, but it was not published (in four volumes duodecimo) until Thursday, 19 December. As that moment approached, he tried to ensure that demand for the work would be at fever pitch. He added to his advertisements the following somewhat disingenuous notice, to which a pointing finger directed the attention of prospective customers dull enough to doubt Fielding's new novel would be as popular as his last:

> *To satisfy the earnest Demand of the Publick, this Work is now printing at four Presses; but the Proprietor notwithstanding finds it impossible to get them bound in Time without spoiling the Beauty of the Impression, and therefore will sell them sew'd at Half a Guinea a Sett.*

Reprinted from Martin C. Battestin, with Ruthe R. Battestin, *Henry Fielding: A Life* (1989), by permission of Routledge.

No such devices had been necessary to drum up interest in *Tom Jones,* every copy of which was bought up before the day of publication. But this time Millar was worried. Citing as his source the publisher Thomas Cadell, who later this decade became Millar's associate in the business, Nathaniel Wraxall recounted the circumstances of Millar's agreement with Fielding and his subsequent apprehension that he had on his hands a work rather less saleable than Fielding's masterpiece. Having paid Fielding the munificent sum of £800 for the copyright—at £200 per volume a rate doubling what he gave for *Tom Jones*—Millar asked his friend Andrew Mitchell for his opinion of the manuscript. Mitchell recognized the quality of the novel, but he also saw that it was an odd performance, much inferior to *Tom Jones*. He advised Millar to get rid of it quickly. Millar, who had ordered a massive printing of 5,000 copies, kept his friend's advice to himself and by strategies whetted the appetite of the public for this work which he feared would prove a drug. In Wraxall's account, Millar announced to the trade at his first sale:

> "Gentlemen, I have several works to put up, for which I shall be glad if you will bid; but as to 'Amelia,' every copy is already bespoke." This manoeuvre had its effect. The booksellers were anxious to get their names put down for copies of it, and the edition, though very large, was immediately sold.[3]

It is not true that Millar, canny Scot though he was, managed to sell off this huge edition "immediately." On 23 December, just four days after publication, Fielding was aware of the Town's verdict. Sending a copy of *Amelia* to Harris (who had anticipated the favor by making Fielding a present of *Hermes* and a chine of bacon)[4] he wrote the last extant letter of their correspondence. From the cordial manner of this exchange, it is good to find the friendship holding fast despite the recent awkwardness about money; but Fielding's disappointment at the reception of his novel reveals how quickly its fate was sealed:

> My Dear Friend,
> I do sincerely assure you, you would have reed my damned book (for so it is) by this very Coach, even without your having mentioned it. If you read it, you will do it more Honour than hath been done it by many here. Indeed I think I have been more abused in a Week than any other Author hath been; but tho' *our* favourite Authors have not taught me to write so as to avoid Censure, they have at least taught me to bear it with Patience.

On 28 December, John Upton wrote Harris from town, giving a more specific account of the disaster—and verifying that, in the company of his friends at least, Fielding was bearing up very philosophically indeed:

> Our friend's Amelia does not answer people's expectations in reading, or the bookseller in selling. They say 'tis deficient in characters; and see not a Parson

Adams, a Square & Thwackum & Western, in it. In short, the word condemnation, tho not Damnation, is given out. Millar expected to get thousands, &
there chiefly the disappointment lies; for as to Fielding himself he laughs, &
jokes, & eats well, as usual; & will continue so whilst rogues live in Covent
Garden, & he signs warrants.

The first call for the novel must nevertheless have been encouraging: Dr.
Johnson assured Mrs. Piozzi that the work sold so briskly "a new edition was
called for before night."[5] Millar did project a substantial new edition of 3,000
copies; but this optimism, he quickly saw, was ill founded. Strahan's ledgers
for January 1752 show that work on a second edition had scarcely begun
before it was terminated.[6] A mere two months after *Amelia* had been so
breathlessly ushered into the world, Richardson gloated to Mrs. Donnellan
that "The piece . . . is as dead as if it had been published forty years ago, as to
sale."[7] That huge first printing was sufficient to satisfy public demand for
years to come. Not until 1762, when Millar published Fielding's *Works,* did
*Amelia* appear in a true second edition.

How was it, then, that Fielding's hopes for *Amelia,* his "favourite
Child,"[8] were so cruelly dashed? The answer is plain enough from the reactions of readers who either regretted the new direction he had taken in the
novel—the unexpected earnestness of its satire and the novelty of its narrative method—or simply read it with a lust to misapply. The former sort found
it dull and indelicate; the others, seizing on its faults in a spirit of spitefulness
and puerile glee, turned it to scorn. Though the Town had already condemned it, the first reviews were in fact quite favorable. Remarking that "The
author takes up his heroine at the very point at which all his predecessors
have dropped their capital personages"—that is, after her marriage—John
Cleland in the *Monthly Review* applauded *Amelia* as "the boldest stroke that
has yet been attempted in this species of writing," and he commended both
Fielding's virtuous purpose and his artful conduct of the narrative.[9] The
reviewer in the *London Magazine* also saw merit in the book: "upon the
whole," he concluded, "the story is amusing, the characters kept up, and
many reflections . . . are useful, if the reader will take notice of them."[10]

Yet despite these commendations, there are signs in both reviews of the
troubles that had already begun to plague the novel. Cleland worried that
Fielding's candor in treating scenes of low-life would "disgust" the fastidious.
And his counterpart in the *London Magazine* drew attention to an unlucky slip
which was all the wags needed to turn *Amelia* into a standing jest. Having
censured Fielding for a "notorious" anachronism in the narrative (wherein the
masquerades at Ranelagh take place several years before they in fact began),
he moved on to the silliest fault of all: Fielding, who modeled his heroine
after his beloved first wife, subjected Amelia to the same injury Charlotte had
suffered—"by the overturning of a Chaise . . . her lovely Nose was beat all to
pieces" (II.i)—but he neglected to state that the injury had been skillfully

repaired by the surgeon. Once exposed to view by the critic, the noselessness of Fielding's heroine diverted the Town for months to come—prompting Samuel Foote, for example, to prefix to the published version of his comedy, *Taste* (January 1752), a frontispiece depicting the bust of Praxiteles' Venus of Paphos without a nose.

The painful yet amusing tale of *Amelia*'s damning is familiar enough that we need not rehearse it in detail.[11] As the New Year turned, the mockery of the critics grew more clamorous, stimulated in part by the rowdy "Paper War" in which Fielding became embroiled as author of the *Covent-Garden Journal*. Bonnell Thornton, for instance—in the guise of "Madam Roxana Termagant," authoress of the *Drury-Lane Journal*—kept up a continual ridicule of the novel, delivering in his fifth number (13 February 1751/2) a gross burlesque of Fielding's style and characters, entitled "A New Chapter in *Amelia*." Smollett was even more impudent. Having recently roasted Fielding and Lyttelton in *Peregrine Pickle,* he resumed the sport in his pamphlet, *A Faithful Narrative of the base and inhuman Arts that were lately practised upon the Brain of Habbakuk Hilding* (15 January 1751/2), in which Fielding, lunatic and astride an ass, appears at the head of his Bow Street myrmidons:

> riding up to a draggle-tail Bunter, who had lost her Nose in the Exercise of her Occupation, he addressed himself to her by the Appelation of the adorable *Amelia,* swore by all the Gods she was the Pattern of all earthly Beauty and Perfection; and that he had exhausted his whole Fancy in celebrating her Name—To this Compliment she answered in a snuffling Tone, "Justice, you're a comical Bitch; I wish you would treat me with a Dram this cold Morning" (p. 18)

—upon which, to oblige his liquorish darling, Fielding gives his tobacco box to Booth to pawn at the next gin shop.

No one who scribbled for bread in these weeks after *Amelia* appeared could refrain from heaping abuse on the novel and its "doting" author. What might pass for rational criticism, instead of mere vituperation, centered on two principal objections: first, by discarding his old formula of comic romance to write in a sentimental vein, Fielding had mistaken his true talent; second, by exposing the most odious moral and social evils with uncompromising candor, he had offended against good taste. On the first count, the judgment of the Richardsonians was of course predictable, for Fielding had dared to poach in the master's preserve. "Poor Fielding, I believe, designed to be good," wrote Mrs. Donnellan, "but did not know how, and in the attempt lost his genius, low humour."[12] And Thomas Edwards advised Fielding not to overreach himself by attempting to describe "either the great or the tender sentiments of the mind," which he was too coarse to feel: "indeed," he declared to a clerical acquaintance, "I think, if Hogarth and he knew their own talents, they should keep to the Dutch manner of painting, and be contented to make people laugh, since what is really great seems to be above their powers."[13] The verdict was not quite unanimous. James Harris's cousin, the fourth Earl of Shaftesbury, was so moved by the "tender Scenes" between Booth and Amelia that he had to put the novel aside while he recovered his composure: "I find," he wrote Harris on 31 December 1751, "it is not a greatly admir'd Performance but I think there are many fine sentiments in it and it is a further confirmation to me of the Humanity and tender Disposition of the author." Lord Shaftesbury, however, saw a side to Fielding's character that few others would allow him. On the whole, the Town agreed that Fielding's experiment in the pathetic mode was a failure.

The other principal criticism of *Amelia* is more interesting, revealing, as it does, that the audience for fiction at mid-century was ill prepared either for the kind of realism Fielding here attempted, or for the disturbing moral and social purpose it was meant to serve. In trying to give his Gallic readers some notion of this quality of the book, Pierre Clément was reduced to sarcasm. He cautioned the squeamish that the author of *Amelia,* being a justice of the peace, "has surprised Nature in *flagrante delicto,* has closely copied her, and there is no execrable object with which he is not familiar." He hopes, therefore, they would be prepared to admire "the pictures of prison, tavern, and gibbet, of scoundrels deserving execution, gaolers deserving to hang, and magistrates to be pilloried, of which the work . . . is formed."[14] The sensibilities of Fielding's English readers were hardly less offended by the frankness of the novel. The author of *Poetical Impertinence* (4 March 1751/2) reproached Fielding for corrupting the public taste: "Would it not be thought the highest *Impertinence* to tell a certain worshipful Author, that the horrid imprecations, made use of in the *Gatehouse* or *Newgate,* are far from being an agreeable entertainment to virtuous ears?" (pp. 3–4).

By modern standards, of course, the "realism" of Fielding's descriptions of prison life, or of the insides of police courts and sponging houses, seems very tame indeed, and no one who has read Dickens could mistake its social purpose. But Fielding's first readers expected romance-writers to make them laugh or cry, not to prick their consciences or offend their ears with the speech of whores and turnkeys. Disallowing the very premise of his didacticism, they preferred to think he wrote the way he did in such passages because, being a coarse and dissolute fellow, he enjoyed paddling in the mire. Richardson, having perused the first volume of *Amelia,* felt compelled to lecture Sarah Fielding on the "lowness" of her brother, who wrote as if he had "been born in a stable, or been a runner at a spunging house."[15] But even those who wished Fielding well found it embarrassing that he could so flagrantly disregard the proprieties of polite literature. In Dresden, Hanbury Williams was eager to obtain a copy of his friend's new novel and to have news of its reception. On 17 January 1751/2 Henry Harris reported that "Fielding has not succeeded, in his last story book, up to the wish of our criticks"—an opinion in which Harris generally concurred, implying that Fielding's insistence on rehearsing

in his fiction the unseemly experiences of his youth had spoiled him for genteel readers: "For my own part, I allow in it great knowledge of human
nature, and many masterly strokes of humour: but the low and habitual
profligacy of his early life will ever hang round him; and when he talks of
brothels, and spunging houses, one is sure that everything is painted from his
own experience, and inhabitancy."[16]

To be sure, not every reader of *Amelia* condemned it. But those who
approved, who understood what Fielding had attempted and how well he had
succeeded, were indeed a "judicious few."[17] Matthew Maty came closer than
any other critic to grasping the true qualities of the novel. In the *Journal Britannique* he declared his admiration of "an author whose pen is no less chaste
than spiritual, and who equally unveils Nature and ennobles humanity."
(What, one wonders, would Richardson have made of this!) Maty praised the
"truth" of Fielding's descriptions, the "finesse" of his dialogue, the "variety"
of his characters; but he also sensed what few others had seen in the book—
that Fielding's purpose was, by exposing "the faults of his compatriots and
those of their laws," to reform them: "The citizen and the magistrate appear
no less in this work than the philosopher and the Christian."[18] At home, the
boldest commendation came from an anonymous adversary of John Hill (who
was by now regularly disparaging the novel in the *London Daily Advertiser*):
defying Hill and "the Town," the writer protested that *Amelia* was "a most
finished Performance," written to promote the cause of "Religion and Virtue"
and evincing "all the Regularity and Beauties of epick, and all the Life of dramatick Poetry."[19] The most extravagant praise, however, would come much
later and from the most surprising source: Dr. Johnson, who could not bring
himself to read *Joseph Andrews* and who pronounced the author of *Tom Jones* "a
blockhead" and "a barren rascal," read the novel through at a sitting and,
despite his admiration for Richardson, preferred Amelia to Clarissa. She was,
he declared to Mrs. Piozzi, "the most pleasing heroine of all the romances."[20]

Most readers, however, disparaged Fielding's last, ambitious experiment
as a novelist. Though he put on a face of carefree indifference for the benefit
of his friends Upton and James Harris, he was hurt by the novel's failure.
How deeply is evident from the response he made to his critics in the early
numbers of the *Covent-Garden Journal*. On 25 January, by which time the verdict was already in, he carried *Amelia* before the "Court of Censorial Enquiry,"
indicted by "Counsellor Town" upon "the Statute of Dulness." The ensuing
trial—in which it is not *Amelia,* but the obtuseness and rancor of her critics
which are judged—reveals what Fielding took to be the principal complaints
against the novel: it was too earnest in promoting the cause of religion and
virtue; its heroine lacked spirit, as well as a nose; Dr. Harrison was unnatural
and Colonel Bath a fool; the prison scenes were "low." And to these weighty
allegations were added the cavils of genteel ladies who damned the book
without troubling to read it. In short, in the words of "Counsellor Town's"
summation: "the whole Book is a Heap of *sad Stuff, Dulness, and Nonsense;* . . .

it contains no Wit, Humour, Knowledge of human Nature, or of the World; indeed . . . the Fable, moral Characters, Manners, Sentiments, and Diction, are all alike bad and contemptible."

In concluding the trial on 28 January, Fielding was reduced to the always ineffectual—and always a little embarrassing—expedient of pleading his own cause. But the scene, as he defends the book that had sunk his reputation and wearily disowns his Muse, is poignant enough:

> If you, Mr. Censor, are yourself a Parent, you will view me with Compassion when I declare I am the Father of this poor Girl the Prisoner at the Bar; nay, when I go farther, and avow, that of all my Offspring she is my favourite Child. I can truly say that I bestowed a more than ordinary Pains in her Education; in which I will venture to affirm, I followed the Rules of all those who are acknowledged to have writ best on the Subject; and if her Conduct be fairly examined, she will be found to deviate very little from the strictest Observation of all those Rules; neither Homer nor Virgil pursued them with greater Care than myself, and the candid and learned Reader will see that the latter was the noble model, which I made use of on this Occasion.
>
> I do not think my Child is entirely free from Faults. I know nothing human that is so; but surely she doth not deserve the Rancour with which she hath been treated by the Public. However, it is not my Intention, at present, to make any Defence; but shall submit to a Compromise, which hath been always allowed in this Court in all Prosecutions for Dulness. I do, therefore, solemnly declare to you, Mr. Censor, that I will trouble the World no more with any Children of mine by the same Muse.

*Amelia* was, as he promised, Fielding's last work of fiction. For what it reveals about his changing literary and social concerns, and most especially for the light it sheds on the most private corners of his personality, it is also perhaps his most interesting work.

In dedicating *Amelia* to Ralph Allen, Fielding declared that his design in the novel was "to promote the Cause of Virtue, and to expose some of the most glaring Evils, as well public as private, which at present infest the Country." The idea for the book took form soon after Fielding began at Bow Street. Its purpose is didactic and much of a piece with that of his other writings of this period: namely, to urge reforms in England's "Constitution" both in the laws themselves, which he found inadequate to preserve order, and also in the "Customs, Manners, and Habits of the People"—the essential character and temper of the body politic. In the summer of 1749 he had charged the Westminster Grand Jury to present those who pandered to that "Fury after licentious and luxurious Pleasures" which had become "the Characteristic of the present Age"—among them infidels and Jacobites, the keepers of brothels and gaming houses, and the perpetrators of masquerades. At the same time he submitted to the Lord Chancellor the draft of a "Bill" which proposed to strengthen and reorganize the watch. Later that year, after lawless mobs endangered the city, he had defended the hated Riot Act and the exemplary punishment of Penlez. More recently he had tried to diagnose the causes of a spreading plague of violence and crime whose source, however—the hedonism of the rich which had corrupted the "useful" orders of society—was beyond the reach of the laws. All these sobering public concerns find expression in *Amelia,* which may fairly be called the first novel of social protest and reform in English—a kind of book scarcely attempted again on such a scale until Dickens. What is more, since as a novelist he could more freely attack the source of the disease, his satire is directed against the Establishment at every level—the watchmen and bailiffs, the magistrates and prison-keepers, worldly priests, profligate lords, the rotten members even of the government which as "Court Justice" he served. Thus in his dialogue with the noble lord who represents venal and wholly pragmatic ministerial policies, Dr. Harrison, Fielding's spokesman, advocates a kind of political idealism which had long been the stock in trade of the Opposition—and which Fielding had recently been hearing at the table of his friend Dodington, "one of the greatest Men," Harrison declares, "this Country ever produced" (XI.ii).[21]

In keeping with this didactic purpose, Fielding experimented with new narrative strategies and techniques. His manner of exposition, depending more on dialogue than on the narrator's commentary, resembles that of the dramatist—a grander version, as it were, of his early "heroic comedies," *Rape upon Rape* and *The Modern Husband.* His materials, drawn more from his own experience and observation, resemble those of the historian and (in tantalizing ways) the autobiographer. His tone now, wavering between indignation and a maudlin sentimentality, is darker and more monitory, as such a subject required—no longer the follies of men, but their errors and cupidities and the doubtful efficacy of those institutions, the law and the Church, which were meant to preserve the social order. Reinforcing our sense of the novel as a social document to be distinguished from Fielding's previous comic "biographies" of Joseph Andrews and Tom Jones is the remarkable device of withholding the identity of his hero until the third chapter: Booth is introduced as merely another of the faceless victims of a corrupt system who are paraded before Justice Thrasher. The story of Booth and Amelia is in fact framed by scenes whose function it is through negative and positive examples, to stress the importance of just laws and their proper execution to the health of society. Thrasher, ignorant and venal, sounds this theme at the start of the novel, and in its closing pages he is replaced by another magistrate, resembling Fielding himself, who, as the mob surges through the streets threatening to burst the dikes of civilization, distributes justice and restores innocence to its rightful estate. Cooperating in this work of redemption, furthermore, is another agent of social order, the good priest Dr. Harrison. Booth, infidel and debtor, is at a stroke released from prison and from his subtler bondage to error.

Nearly as prominent as the didactic social intent of *Amelia* is its extraordinary, and often puzzling, autobiographical dimension.[22] Fielding opens the novel by declaring that his subject will be "The various Accidents which befel a very worthy Couple, after their uniting in the State of Matrimony." As those who knew him immediately saw, the story of that worthy couple, Billy and Amelia Booth, is also the story—however much disguised and sentimental-ized—of Harry Fielding and his beloved first wife Charlotte. To Richardson, indeed, this was only the latest and most egregious instance of an autobio-graphical element in all Fielding's fiction which proved the impotency of his "invention."[23] And Lady Mary assured her daughter, Lady Bute, that Field-ing in *Amelia* had "given a true picture of himselfe and his first Wife in the Characters of Mr. and Mrs. Booth (some Complement to his own figure excepted) and I am persuaded several of the Incidents he mentions are real matters of Fact"[24]—incidents no doubt related to Fielding's imprudence and his incurable improvidence with money: the mounting debts incurred, the flight from bailiffs to a shabby sanctuary in the Verge of the Court, the con-finement in sponging houses, the threat of imprisonment. Lady Bute knew Charlotte personally and spoke of her "amiable qualities" and "her beauty," which, however, "had suffered a little from the accident related in the novel."[25] In later years her daughter, Lady Stuart, recorded her mother's impressions of the marriage:

> He loved her passionately, and she returned his affection; yet led no happy life, for they were almost always miserably poor, and seldom in a state of quiet and safety. All the world knows what was his imprudence; if ever he possessed a score of pounds, nothing could keep him from lavishing it idly, or make him think of to-morrow. Sometimes they were living in decent lodgings with toler-able comfort; sometimes in a wretched garret without necessaries; not to speak of the spunging-houses and hiding-places where he was occasionally to be found. His elastic gaiety of spirit carried him through it all; but, meanwhile, care and anxiety were preying upon her more delicate mind, and undermining her constitution.

In too many ways, however, the story Fielding relates conceals more than it discloses about his essential character and most intimate relationships. It tantalizes more than it rewards the biographical reader. Consider, for exam-ple, the setting of the novel. Unlike Fielding's other works of fiction, in which the action is more or less contemporaneous with the period of composition, the action of *Amelia* occurs sixteen years, and more, in the past: time present in the novel is the period from 1 April to June 1733, while the reminiscences of the characters recreate scenes that took place six or eight years earlier still.[26] Why should Fielding choose for his setting this particular moment— a time in his own life when he was riding high as a playwright at Drury Lane, his marriage to Charlotte more than a year in the future? What fascination did these months hold for him?

More interesting still is the puzzle of Booth's identity. In many respects he is obviously his author's double: his fondness for snuff, for instance (I.v);

his way of indulging himself by driving coaches he cannot afford (III.xii); his length of nose (XI.i)—not to mention such general matters as the delight he takes in Lucian's works (VIII.v) and his admiration for the edifying writings of Isaac Barrow (XII.v), Fielding's "favourite" divine.[27] It is Barrow's sermons on the Apostles' Creed which convert Booth from the infidelity that paralyzes him as a moral agent, an error founded in a belief his author, himself a man of strong passions, may well have shared: "Indeed," Booth assures Dr. Harrison, "I never was a rash Disbeliever; my chief Doubt was founded on this, that as Men appeared to me to act entirely from their Passions, their Actions could have neither Merit nor Demerit."

In certain other respects, however, Booth more nearly resembles Fielding's father than he does Fielding himself. Like Booth, Edmund was a military officer who had behaved gallantly in battle. The circumstances of his courtship of Sarah Gould, Fielding's mother, and the articles of their marriage settlement, also find parallels in the story of Booth and Amelia: Sir Henry Gould and his wife resisted Edmund's marriage to their daughter and, when they were finally reconciled to the match, made legally certain, as Amelia's mother does (II.iv), that Sarah's dowry would be applied exclusively to maintain her and her children. Like Booth, when Edmund's regiment was disbanded and he was reduced to half-pay, he tried his hand at farming, all too unprofitably. Again like Booth (X.v), he once allowed himself to be cheated at cards by a disreputable fellow officer and his accomplices in a fashionable St. James's coffee-house, his losses seriously embarrassing him financially. And like Booth, Edmund had been no stranger to bailiffs and sponging-houses.

Booth is, then, curiously, a character in whom Fielding and his father coalesce. In Booth, despite their estrangement during Edmund's lifetime, Fielding and his father quite literally become one. Might there be in this fictional reconciliation a symbolic significance? Earlier we saw that the strange interpolated episode of the death of Booth's sister on the eve of his marriage invites a Freudian explanation, hinting not only at the possibility of incest in Fielding's own story, but also, and more agreeably, at the maturing of the erotic side of his nature. It may be that *Amelia* also represents a final, happier stage in Fielding's relationship with his father. One would like to believe that he came to understand Edmund better and to forgive him—that he came to recognize, indeed, that whatever Edmund's faults and follies, they were very like his own. I suspect that in *Amelia* Fielding tried to expiate his former bitterness toward Edmund, that in the character of Captain Booth—a soldier too weak to follow his own good intentions, who nearly ruins his family through his gaming and dissipation—Fielding sought not only to come to terms with his own all too fallible nature, but to reconcile himself to his father's memory.

*Notes*

1. Goldgar (ed.), *Covent-Garden Journal,* pp. xxvi–xxvii.
2. Strahan, who was assigned the printing of Vols. I and III, charged Millar for "Extraordinary Corrections" made while the work was in press. For a detailed account of the history of publication, see Battestin (ed.), *Amelia,* pp. xliv–lxi.
3. N. Wraxall, *Historical and Posthumous Memoirs, 1772–84.* ed. H. B. Wheatley (1884), I.38–9.
4. Harris's *Hermes: or, A Philosophical Inquiry concerning Language and Universal Grammar* was published 16 Dec. 1751 (*London Daily Advertiser,* 13 Dec.). From Salisbury on 21 Dec., Harris wrote Fielding:

> I hope you have received Hermes, for which in return I have the assurance to
> Desire that you would Send me Amelia. Should you ask with indignation,
> what four Books, for one—I might answere, if I would, that put them in the
> Scales, and See how much heavier grammatical Speculation is than Wit, and
> Humour.

Replying to this letter on 23 Dec., Fielding acknowledged Harris's "very valuable Present. (I mean that of yʳ. Book) I sincerely think it among the best Books in our Language."
5. Mrs. Piozzi, *Anecdotes of the late Samuel Johnson,* ed. S. C. Roberts (Cambridge: 1925), p. 143.
6. BL: Add. Mss. 48800 f. 83.
7. Letter of 22 Feb. 1752, in Carroll (ed.), *Selected Letters,* p. 196.
8. *Covent-Garden Journal* (28 Jan. 1752).
9. *Monthly Review,* 5 (Dec. 1751), 510–15.
10. *London Magazine,* 20 (Dec. 1751), 531–5, 592–6.
11. See F. T. Blanchard, *Fielding the Novelist: A Study in Historical Criticism* (New Haven, Conn.: 1926), Ch. 3; Battestin (ed.), *Amelia,* pp. l–lix.
12. Letter to Richardson, 11 Feb. 1751/2; in A. L. Barbauld (ed.) *Correspondence of Samuel Richardson* (Oxford: 1804), IV.56.
13. Letter to Rev. Mr. Lawry, 12 Feb. 1751/2 (Bodley Ms. 1011, pp. 331–2).
14. From Lettre XCI, 1 Jan. 1752, in *Cinq années littéraires* (The Hague: 1754), III.267–80.
15. Letter to Lady Bradshaigh, 23 Feb. 1751/2; in Carroll (ed.), *Selected Letters,* p. 198.
16. Hanbury Williams Mss., Vol. 54, p. 249; in W. S. Lewis Collection.
17. *Some Remarks on the Life and Writings of Dr. J{ohn} H{ill}* (1752), p. 60.
18. *Journal Britannique,* 7 (Feb. 1752), 123–46; translated in R. Paulson and T. Lockwood (eds.), *Henry Fielding: The Critical Heritage* (London: 1969), No. 119.
19. *Some Remarks,* pp. 59–61.
20. Mrs. Piozzi, *Anecdotes,* p. 143.
21. On this surprising political dimension of *Amelia,* see Battestin (ed.), pp. xxxvii–xxxix.
22. Ibid, pp. xvi–xxi.
23. Richardson to Mrs. Donnellan, 22 Feb. 1751/2; in Carroll (ed.), *Selected Letters,* p. 197.
24. Letter of 23 Jul. [1754]; in Halsband (ed.), *Complete Letters,* III.66.
25. Lady Louisa Stuart, "Introductory Anecdotes," I.105–6.
26. On the time scheme of *Amelia,* see Battestin (ed.), Appendix I.
27. *Covent-Garden Journal* (11 Apr. 1752).

# The Journal of a Voyage to Lisbon: Body, City, Jest

## Tom Keymer

### I

"Perhaps it was worth dying in your forties if two hundred years later you were the only non-contemporary novelist who could be read with unaffected and whole-hearted interest, the only one who never had to be apologized for or excused on the grounds of changing taste." So thinks Garnet Bowen, hero of Kingsley Amis's *I Like It Here,* as he stands by Fielding's grave at Lisbon with a pompous sub-Jamesian novelist named Wulfstan Strether. Bowen has been sent to Portugal to make sure that the author of a manuscript called *One Word More* really is the reclusive Strether, whose previous novel had seemed to announce his retirement in self-imposed exile. The truth becomes clear when, to Bowen's laughing disbelief, Strether intones a flatulent tribute to "the darling of the comic muse," and adds: "In the field of the novel he is indeed the colossus of the eighteenth century, but I cannot feel that posterity will place him beside . . . will care to place him beside the colossus of the twentieth." No impostor would overact on such a scale, Bowen is sure: "if he was a fake . . . he wouldn't have dared to put himself on show as the kind of prancing, posturing phoney who'd say he was better than Fielding."[1]

Amis's scene at Fielding's tomb—a scene of solemnity for one participant, farce for the other—is apt as well as absurd. Not only does it reflect the mingled gravity and comedy of Fielding's own last work, *The Journal of a Voyage to Lisbon.* Its two participants—Bowen the stalwart xenophobe, Strether the exiled genius—perfectly represent the contrasting roles in which Fielding played out his final days. His withdrawal, acutely disillusioned with the literary and political cultures left behind him, was very much that of the disregarded sage, aloof in exile. Stung by attacks on *Amelia,* he had announced his

Reprinted from *The Journal of a Voyage to Lisbon,* ed. Tom Keymer (Harmondsworth: Penguin Classics, 1996), by permission of the author and the publisher. © 1996 Tom Keymer.

retirement as novelist by publicly swearing "that I will trouble the World no more with any Children of mine by the same Muse." Drained by the legal work to which he then devoted his energies, and gravely ill, he left England in June 1754 in hopes of surviving the milder winter of Portugal. There he settled near the Lisbon court, planning a learned indictment of deism (partly achieved in his "Fragment of a Comment on Lord Bolingbroke's Essays") and requesting his publisher Andrew Millar "to send him over all the Books which relate to Portugal, for some other Work, which he has in view."[2]

Yet Fielding voyaged to Lisbon with little of Strether's precious reverence for the antique South, and much of Bowen's gut distaste for all things foreign. The city he reached in August was the nastiest in the world, the *Journal* declares, and one from which Fielding would write to his brother for the needs of a homesick exile: "a Hamper of large Parsnips . . . a vast large cheshire cheese and one of Stilton if to be had good and mild." Within days of arrival he was railing to Millar about the extortionate prices of Lisbon, "where the Expence of living is near thrice what it is in England." In the same letter he adds that he has "almost finish'd the History of his Voyage thither, which he offers to Millar as the best of his performances."[3] Two months later he was dead.

Millar published *The Journal of a Voyage to Lisbon* in 1755, and early readers were struck above all by the work's generic confusion, its discordant mingling of satire and jest with the solemnity of valediction. Some condemned the effect. "Fielding's Voyage is the arrantest catch-penny that ever was published," wrote the poet and scholar Thomas Edwards. "I am amazed that a man who felt himself dying by inches could be so idly employed." Repeating his strictures to Fielding's rival Samuel Richardson, Edwards was scandalized "that a man, who had led such a life as he had, should trifle in that manner when immediate death was before his eyes." Nor was this unsettling sense of a writer trifling with death, mixing the grave with the comic, confined to Fielding's enemies. In the words of his early biographer Arthur Murphy, the *Journal* seemed to perform its work of valediction with a resolute wrongness of tone: "In this his last sketch he puts us in mind of a person, under sentence of death, jesting on the scaffold."[4]

Yet it would misrepresent the *Journal* to say that Fielding turns to gallows humour as a way of evading, or failing to confront, the reality of impending death. He explains that "the most amusing pages . . . were possibly the production of the most disagreeable hours which ever haunted the author," and with these words he puts himself in a tradition of comedy which, far from hiding pain beneath jest, keeps both in constant dialogue. Laurence Sterne was shortly to write that *Tristram Shandy* "was every word of it wrote in affliction; & under a constant uneasiness of mind," adding that "Cervantes wrote his humorous Satyr in a Prison—& Scarron his, in pain & Anguish."[5] Fielding himself, not only diseased but imprisoned, "shut up within the circumference of a few yards," exactly combines the predicaments of these two forebears. Like Sterne, moreover, he writes a comedy which does not deny the fact of death but arises directly from it, coexisting with pain and anguish in provocative ways.

Far from deflecting attention from suffering, indeed, the *Journal* turns a quite unblinking gaze on the body's decay. Though glimpses of health are caught at times, Fielding's narrative is one, above all, of approaching death, a work of despair "which, if I should live to finish it, a matter of no great certainty, if indeed of any great hope to me, will be probably the last I shall ever undertake." Diseases gather as the *Journal* unfolds, as though in alliance or siege: "no fewer or less diseases than a jaundice, a dropsy, and an asthma, altogether uniting their forces in the destruction of a body so entirely emaciated, that it had lost all its muscular flesh." In our terms, Fielding probably suffered from cirrhosis of the liver or peritoneal cancer.[6] In the laconic language which he turns on his own demise, "I was now, in the opinion of all men, dying of a complication of disorders."

Sickness presides over the book as surely (though now on a horribly personal scale) as it dominates that earlier narrative of a whole city's decay, Defoe's *Journal of the Plague Year*. The care with which Fielding measures his periodic draining of excess fluid subjects his dropsy, indeed, to a statistical rigour chillingly reminiscent of the bills of mortality used by Defoe to punctuate and calibrate his reports. After the first tapping (of fourteen quarts), it is only with difficulty that he begins "to draw my feet out of the grave." In the following months he undergoes the operation a further four times. Beginning the *Journal* "almost fatigued to death" (the literalization of cliché is typical of Fielding's carefully weighted prose), he remains "dead luggage," "as dead a luggage as any . . . in my decayed condition." The *Journal* turns a cool scrutiny on the repulsiveness of this decay. Unable to climb aboard the *Queen of Portugal,* Fielding's bloated body is winched on to the ship with pulleys. There it presents "a spectacle of the highest horror. The total loss of limbs was apparent to all who saw me, and my face contained marks of a most diseased state, if not of death itself." The unflinching frankness of such lines is all the more remarkable in the light of a witness's report that later in the voyage Fielding cursed his landlord at Ryde for tactlessly wishing him health, and shrouded a mirror there "that he might not be struck with his own figure."[7] It is as though the act of writing, of subjecting pain to the control of a measured language, enables Fielding to confront his predicament with a directness impossible in daily life.

The predicament is not Fielding's alone, however, for the *Journal* presents its author's disease as merely part of some larger, and seemingly inescapable, pattern of decay and pain in a hostile world. The pattern is traced with obsessive care, all misfortune coming to seem an amplification of Fielding's own. The tone is one of civic solemnity as he finds himself "at the worst on that memorable day when the public lost Mr. Pelham." It shifts to a comedy of petty mishap and frustration when his need for a surgeon to tap him seems mockingly echoed by the case of his wife, "in the utmost torments of the tooth-ach." At Rotherhithe (Redriffe in the text) the ship weighs anchor before a first tooth-drawer arrives; at Gravesend a second declares the tooth immovable; a third is called at Deal where, "after having put my poor wife to inexpressible torment, he was obliged to leave her tooth *in statu quo;* and she had now the comfortable prospect of a long fit of pain, which might have lasted her whole voyage." Heavy seas compound the affliction, leaving Fielding's companions "more inclined to empty their stomachs than to fill them" and his own bowels "almost twisted out of my belly;" when able to eat, he succumbs in turn to his wife's condition, his teeth too rotten to chew a portion of scrawny duck. Like the "scurvy and disasterous world" in which Tristram Shandy must endure "as pitiful misadventures and cross accidents as ever small HERO sustained,"[8] this is a world where all that can goes awry. A mock "tragical incident," in which a cat is washed overboard seems happily resolved when the boatswain dives to its rescue. In a casual aside, Fielding later applauds the captain's fondness for animals, "an instance of which we saw this evening, when the cat, which had shewn it could not be drowned, was found suffocated under a feather-bed." Having "wantonly endeavoured to raise the tender passions" in the first scene, Fielding shifts to a tone of amused indifference to mention the second in passing, as though only by chance.

This sense of a hostile world, perversely needling its inhabitants at every point, is reinforced by further analogies. It is not simply that Fielding finds his own mortality reflected in the death of a minister or the loss of a tooth. The elements seem bent on plaguing all creation, so that even an unripe fruit or a wind-bound ship comes to seem reflective, or horribly parodic, of his own hapless condition. He links the very seasons with his own decline, oscillating in parallel sentences ("I saw . . . I saw . . . I saw") between twin struggles, without and within, which leave him a mere helpless observer:

> I saw the summer mouldering away, or rather, indeed, the year passing away without intending to bring on any summer at all. In the whole month of May the sun scarce appeared three times. So that the early fruits came to the fulness of their growth, and to some appearance of ripeness, without acquiring any real maturity; having wanted the heat of the sun to soften and meliorate their juices. I saw the dropsy gaining rather than losing ground; the distance growing still shorter between the tappings. I saw the asthma likewise beginning again to become more troublesome. I saw the Midsummer quarter drawing towards a close (p. 20).

In a further twist to this passage, the false ripeness of the early fruit seems cruelly matched within Fielding's own diseased belly, "again ripe for the trochar." The verbal patterning is typical, and the same obsessiveness is at work when Fielding later links Mary's "intolerable pain from her tooth," in adjacent sentences, with the halting progress of the ship itself, "the wind being now full in our teeth." Even a turn for the better brings with it a similar equation. "While the surgeon was drawing away my water, the sailors were drawing up the anchor," Fielding writes as body and ship momentarily escape their respective ailments of excess water and adverse wind.

It is this wind-bound ship that is Fielding's presiding symbol, in the *Journal,* for the sheer cussedness of life. Here circumstances place him on the brink of a Shandean joke about thwarted progress: just as Sterne's *Life and Opinions of Tristram Shandy* leaves its hero in early childhood, while *A Sentimental Journey through France and Italy* ends no further south than Piedmont, so *The Journal of a Voyage to Lisbon* is less a book about Portugal than about London, Ryde and Tor Bay. It took Richard Twiss five days to sail from Falmouth to Lisbon in 1772, Joseph Baretti seven days in 1760, William Beckford nine in 1787. Fielding boarded the *Queen of Portugal* at Rotherhithe on 26 June, and was not to disembark in Lisbon for a full six weeks. In a letter from Tor Bay, he complains to his brother of "the almost miraculous Dilatoriness of our Voyage."[9] The *Journal* itself presents the wind as tireless, and cleverly capricious, in its efforts to frustrate all progress. Again and again it tempts Captain Veale into unsustainable advances. Having struggled for hours off Kent, Veale "was obliged to give over, and lost, in a few minutes, all that he had been so long a-gaining;" off Ryde, "the wind got the better of him, so that about three he gave up the victory"; off Portland, "the wind . . . shewed him a dog's trick, and slily slipt back again to his summer-house in the south-west." It is as though some mischievous intelligence is at work, by turns offering and dashing hope in ways that echo, in the larger environment, the fluctuations of Fielding's own health. The adverse wind is persistent enough for Veale to think himself bewitched. For Fielding it is a chance for comedy, as when he depicts himself and Veale lashed in mid-storm to the cabin floor, attempting to drink bowls of soup. Real solemnity enters his tone, however, as he at last draws out from the plight of the ship a grimly explicit moral:

> I could not help reflecting how often the greatest abilities lie wind-bound as it were in life; or if they venture out, and attempt to beat the seas, they struggle in vain against wind and tide, and if they have not sufficient prudence to put back, are most probably cast away on the rocks and quicksands, which are every day ready to devour them (p. 97).

## II

And here, the hint is, we find Fielding's own condition—the condition of the man of ability lost in the struggle with invincible forces. For there is one further analogy at work in the *Journal,* with its intertwined tales of physical and political crisis. A double emphasis links Fielding's disease not only metaphorically with the sickness of the public realm but also literally—indeed causally—with his own professional struggles, as magistrate, to find and work the cure.

The idea of the state as body politic is a commonplace often invoked by Fielding as an image of civic ills. The avarice and corruption of a ruling élite are his long-standing targets. In *The Historical Register* he writes that "corruption hath the same influence on all societies, all bodies, which it hath on corporeal bodies, where we see it always produce an entire destruction." *Amelia's* Dr Harrison fears likewise that "*Roman* and *British* Liberty will have the same Fate; for Corruption in the Body Politic as naturally tends to Dissolution as in the Natural Body." In the *Covent-Garden Journal* Misargus rails against "that national Corruption, Luxury, and Immorality, which have polluted our Morals," and thinks money "the true Fountain of that Complication of political Diseases which infests this Nation."[10]

Such analogies between physical and political constitutions (the latter meaning not only founding laws but also "the Customs, Manners, and Habits of the People") are most intensively used in *An Enquiry into the Causes of the Late Increase of Robbers*. In this legal work Fielding prudently disowns any wish "to satirize the Great." Yet even here he is quick to trace the "stubborn political Disease" of robbery to the originating social evil of prodigality and luxury above. "Vices no more than Diseases will stop with [the Great]," he insists; "for bad Habits are as infectious by Example, as the Plague itself by contact." At such moments, Fielding clearly anticipates the *Journal's* dual concern with sickness in both body and state:

> The great Increase of Robberies within these few Years, is an Evil which . . . seems (tho' already become so flagrant) not yet to have arrived to that Height of which it is capable, and which it is likely to attain: For Diseases in the Political, as in the Natural Body, seldom fail going on to their Crisis, especially when nourished and encouraged by Faults in the Constitution.[11]

The *Journal* is directly continuous with these grim analyses of a society vitiated at every level by the trickle-down corruption of a greedy élite. The state Fielding leaves is debased from top to toe: a state in which "the common bands of humanity" give way to "the language and behaviour of savages"; a state in which "every man spunges and raps whatever he can get." The petty extortions of watermen and innkeepers find inspiration in a government that taxes light itself; the rich luxuriate in turtle-meat while "a few monopolizing fishmongers" rig a market that starves the poor. At every level community decays, weakened above by an élite which neglects the traditional obligations of patrician politics, and threatened below by a mob grown licentious and grasping in imitation of their masters. The state needs healing, in short, and the language of medicine is rarely far from Fielding's mind. When he talks of "the whole mischief which infects this part of our œconomy," his verb draws directly on the traditional imagery of the body politic. He uses the same terms to present the *Journal* as a book which works "to propose the remedies" of the sickness, to point out "the facility of curing it," and to denounce in ruling powers "the shameful neglect of the cure."

Fielding has been accused of trite or unthinking use of the body-politic image, yet in the *Journal* he reanimates what might otherwise seem mere cliché in a startling way. Recalling his efforts as magistrate to rid the city of violent crime, his Introduction pursues an interweaved double narrative— though with two quite different trajectories—of sickness in body and state. Political metaphor gains urgency from physical fact; and while the analogy between body and state remains quiet, working more by juxtaposition and implication than direct statement, it is none the less pressing for that. Charged to quell an epidemic of crime, Fielding also fights a personal sickness which at once reflects the city's disease and feeds off his efforts to cure it. In his own person, the three diseases "uniting their forces" become so firmly entrenched as to be beaten only "by the tedious operation of undermining; and not by a sudden attack and storm." Organized crime, meanwhile, takes violent hold of the polity itself, and he is asked "to demolish the then reigning gangs, and to put the civil policy into such order, that no such gangs should ever be able, for the future, to form themselves into bodies, or at least to remain any time formidable to the public." Fielding's point is not that there is complete equivalence between these two dangers, however, for his struggles against them are far from proceeding in harmony. His energy is spent on one fight to the detriment of the other, a point kept in play by paragraphs which alternate between steady cure in the public weal and steady decline in the private. "Tho' my health was now reduced to the last extremity," Fielding reports, "I continued to act with the utmost vigour against these villains." The result is predictable. The robbers and cut-throats are duly dispersed; the jaundice, dropsy and asthma continue to thrive. It is as though Fielding taps the poison away from the body of the state, even as he neglects his own; it is as though he acts, indeed, as some healing leech, who drains it into himself.

Fielding's struggles with the criminal gangs of 1753, and his attempts to establish a police force against their resurgence, are described in something closer to the conventional legal discourse of the day by his successor and half-brother, John:

> About the latter End of the Year 1753, a most notorious Gang of Street-Robbers, in Number about fourteen, who divided themselves in Parties, committed such daring Robberies, and at the same Time such Barbarities, by cutting and wounding those they robbed, in every Part of this Metropolis, as spread a general Alarm through the Town, and deterred his Majesty's Subjects from passing and repassing on their lawful Occasions after Night. These Outrages induced his Majesty to issue a Proclamation, and offer a hundred Pounds Reward for apprehending each of these Violaters of the public Peace. And though this was

humanely intended as a Remedy for this dreadful Evil, instead of answering the End proposed, it soon begat a greater, by introducing a Set of Villains to decoy unwary and ignorant Wretches to commit Robberies, and then to make a Sacrifice of them for the Sake of the Reward; while the real Offenders not only escaped Justice, but encreased their Barbarities even to Murder. Upon which his Grace the Duke of *Newcastle* sent to the late *Henry Fielding* to desire him to form some Plan in Order to bring these desperate Villains to Justice. A Plan was immediately formed, and approved of, and encouraged by his Grace, which being put in vigorous Execution, very soon brought this Gang to condign Punishment. But it did not deter others from following the same wicked Practices, and a fresh Gang, as desperate, tho' not as numerous as the former, soon made its Appearance.

About this Time the late *Henry Fielding*'s want of Health totally disqualified him from continuing the fatiguing Office of Acting Magistrate in this Metropolis; he therefore resigned the Office to his Brother *John Fielding,* who had been an assisting Magistrate to him for three or four Years.[12]

Fielding's resignation and departure, however, did not mark complete retirement so much as the return to a former vocation. No longer the executor of laws, he uses the *Journal* to resume his role, if not as legislator, then as the recommender of legislation to ministers, "who are alone capable of applying the remedy, tho' they are the last to whom the notice of those evils would occur, without some such monitor as myself." With this word "monitor" ("One who warns of faults, or informs of duty"), Fielding harks back to the posture of his earlier journalism. Following the tradition of Addison and Steele, the *Jacobite's Journal* and *Covent-Garden Journal* had claimed for their author the office of "Censor" ("An officer of Rome, who had the power of correcting manners").[13] This pose had then been used to satirize or castigate aspects of the national life. As "monitor" in the *Journal,* however, Fielding moves increasingly beyond satire and into the realm of specific legislative recommendation. Not content simply to mock the wealthy consumers of turtle, he urges new measures to break the cartel that keeps fish from the mouths of the poor. In this sense the *Journal* mediates between the functions of Fielding's satirical journalism and the debilitating struggles of his magistracy. As he gravely announces, linking his words as an author with his deeds as a justice. "I have scattered my several remarks through this voyage, sufficiently satisfied in having finished my life, as I have, probably, lost it, in the service of my country."

## III

Yet there is more to the *Journal* than some simple attempt on Fielding's part to legislate to the public or extol his professional conduct. Certainly he does take the chance to set his magistracy in a context of classical heroism (not least in hopes of winning his dependants a posthumous pension), and he repeatedly invokes the moralizing mode of the eighteenth-century law-giver, with his professions of "public utility." Even at these most solemn and ambitious moments, however, a rogue strain of irony is at work. It is as though Fielding finds himself unable to stage an argument which does not at the same time tip its claims into comic overstatement or self-parody. In a passage reminiscent of his *Proposal for Making an Effectual Provision for the Poor* (1753), he describes in sober detail the abundance and wholesomeness of fish. But then his argument that a rigged market deprives the poor of such food lurches suddenly towards mania:

> And, first, I humbly submit the absolute necessity of immediately hanging all the fishmongers within the bills of mortality; and however it might have been some time ago the opinion of mild and temporizing men, that the evil complained of might be removed by gentler methods, I suppose at this day there are none who do not see the impossibility of using such with any effect (p. 85–6).

Fielding's closeness here to the crazed advocacy of cannibalism in Swift's *Modest Proposal* does not of course sink his case. He calls fleetingly on Swift's way of proposing deranged remedies in order to highlight an evil while hinting at saner measures. He works this effect, however, in his own autobiographical voice, and in an oddly deadpan manner that does little to demarcate the ironic from the serious or otherwise settle a balance between jest and earnest. The lofty contempt for gluttons and profiteers voiced here on behalf of the starving is further ironized by the conspicuously inept return to narrative which then follows: "After having, however, gloriously regaled myself with this food, I was washing it down with some good claret . . ."

Elsewhere Fielding subjects his position to a yet stranger mode of irony, in which key proposals and claims are destabilized by self-defeating appeal to authorities of the leakiest kind. At one point he likens himself not to Cervantes, author of *Don Quixote,* but to Cid Hamet, the work's preposterous narrator, and the gesture is typical. His very claim to be writing a didactic work able to inspire change is undermined in just this way. The problem is not that Fielding chooses (as the Preface declares) "to convey such instruction or information with an air of joke or laughter"; it is that the laugh is aimed precisely at his own pretensions. Even as he stakes his claim to didactic seriousness, he undermines it by the mock pomposity with which he wishes to "fall at once to the direct and positive praises of the work itself; of which indeed I could say a thousand good things." He then justifies his aims with reference to Samuel Richardson's theories of instruction, only (and almost in the same breath) to ridicule this very authority as a self-promoting humbug whose works are mere waste-paper. Having kicked away his first crutch, he then rests on even flimsier support. Declaring an extravagant ambition "to bring about at once, like the revolution in *The Rehearsal,* a perfect reformation of the laws relating to our maritime affairs," he likens his project to a scene from the comedy of that name in which two foolish opportunists contrive a merely nominal revolution that achieves nothing and is reversed in a matter of minutes.

It is not for want of choice that Fielding turns to such precedents as these. Literature offered him countless examples of didactic theory, drama countless scenes of successful change. Yet he insists on resting his case with a novelist whose didactic claims he had earlier destroyed in a lengthy parody (*Shamela,* which ridicules Richardson's *Pamela*); he then compares himself with a pair of low-life characters whose unsuccessful revolution he had earlier described as "absurd and ridiculous," "calculated to inspire the Audience with Contempt."[14] It is as though he finds himself impelled, even as he stakes his largest claims, to undercut these claims with a countervailing strain of ironic self-mockery.

Perhaps the most unsettling case of the awkwardness with which Fielding adopts the role of monitor comes as he pleads the case for a posthumous pension. Public rewards and punishments are sensible acts of policy, he claims, and in his own case a pension would encourage future magistrates to emulate his efforts. He gives two supporting examples of punishment and reward:

> "For it is very hard, my lord," said a convicted felon at the bar to the late excellent Judge Burnet, "to hang a poor man for stealing a horse." "You are not to be hanged, Sir," answered my ever-honoured and beloved friend, "for stealing a horse, but you are to be hanged that horses may not be stolen." In like manner it might have been said to the late Duke of Marlborough, when the parliament was so deservedly liberal to him, after the battle of Blenheim, "You receive not these honours and bounties on account of a victory past, but that other victories may be obtained" (p. 16).

On the face of it this is a simple enough, if unendearing, passage. Fielding cites the enrichment of Marlborough (whose leadership he admired) as a laudable instance of reward, and the sentence of Burnet (his sometime friend) as a laudable instance of punishment. For ears attuned to Fielding's irony at its most quietly dangerous, however, a warning is sounded by the more than necessary slavishness with which praise is here trowelled on: "the late excellent Judge Burnet"; "my ever-honoured and beloved friend"; "so deservedly liberal." Such words are at least in tension with Burnet's insouciance as he informs a poor man that his neck is to be snapped, on behalf of the horse-owning classes, as an edifying piece of theatre. There is tension, too, between Burnet's callous glibness and the far more troubled attitude towards capital punishment voiced elsewhere by Fielding himself. Public executions should end and capital punishment be practised only in private, he urges elsewhere; such punishment constitutes a "Scandal to our Polity" when inflicted on "an industrious poor Creature . . . forced by mere Want into Dishonesty, and that in a Nation of such Trade and Opulence"; it is "a dreadful Consideration," requiring urgent remedial measures, "that many Cart-loads of our Fellow-creatures are once in six Weeks carried to Slaughter."[15]

The tension remains unresolved, but Fielding's juxtaposition of bland compliment with barbed quotation clearly gives his excellent and ever-honoured friend ample rope to hang himself as well as his victim. It is hard to miss Burnet's kinship with his colleagues in Pope's *Rape of the Lock,* for whom the noose is a casual, if not cynical, resource: "The hungry Judges soon the Sentence sign, / And Wretches hang that Jury-men may dine."[16]

Nor is Fielding's apparent ambivalence about his first supporting example resolved by his next. His pose of bland approval is sustained by seemingly unreserved praise for Parliament's action. Yet here again there is an unspoken yet obvious catch, for Fielding's words conspicuously fail to register what he and his early readers knew perfectly well—that the riches showered by Parliament on a general who was shortly to be arraigned for peculation had been among the greatest scandals of the age. Famously exposed in Swift's wry contrast between the cost of Blenheim Palace and that of a Roman victor's laurel wreath, the affair is recalled in Fielding's own ironic proposal elsewhere that the notoriously acquisitive family of Prime Minister Walpole be enriched along similar lines, "the Conduct of *one* having proved as wise, successful and glorious in the *Cabinet,* as the *other*'s did in the *Field.*"[17]

Instead of commenting further, it is at this point that Fielding abruptly describes himself as "dying of a complication of disorders." Having linked himself on one level with judge and general, he effectively links himself on another with the horse-thief who waits to be hanged. The gesture is characteristic, and speaks volumes about the uneasiness with which Fielding occupied (and needed at times to detach himself from) his roles as magistrate and monitor. The paradox returns when he later combines applause for the severity of "the last vagrant act" with an amused report that he is himself in breach of its terms, "and this too after having been very singularly officious in putting that law in execution." It is also to be found outside the *Journal,* as in the wry words with which Fielding is reported to have greeted a temporary return to health: "If I am not hanged this Sessions, I know I shall ye next."[18] The inner source of these perverse yet very pervasive habits of identification with vagrants and felons can only be guessed at. What is clear is that Fielding has at least misgivings about the formal role of magistrate and monitor which he adopts throughout the *Journal.* Even as he plays this role he is also driven to rebel quietly against it—to throw it off, ham it up, subvert it in manifold ways.

# IV

At other points Fielding seems to identify the *Journal* as a work not of uneasy irony but of outright satire—a parody of travel writing and its didactic pretensions in which the voyaging narrator himself is the foremost target. Such hints begin in the Preface, which mocks the tendency of travel writers to lapse into the fantastic or the mundane. The latter fault is illustrated with reference to an unnamed play by Aphra Behn or Susanna Centlivre, "where this vice in a voyage-writer is finely ridiculed." Fielding's vagueness about the play (which in fact he recalls very well) suggests that he has half an eye on *Mar-plot,* Centlivre's sequel to *The Busie-Body,* which sends her celebrated fool as a tourist to Lisbon ("And tho' our *Mar-plot* has been shown before, / The Fool may differ, on a different Shore"). But the primary reference here is to Behn's *The Feign'd Curtezans,* in which Timothy Tickletext, tutor to Sir Signal Buffoon, combines ignorance, philistinism and self-importance. Tickletext is a tourist for whom all of Rome is inferior to its English equivalent. "Your Buildings are very pretty Buildings," he declares, "but not comparable to our University Building; your Fountains, I confess, are pretty Springs,—and your Statues reasonably well carv'd—but, Sir, they are so antient they are of no value: then your Churches are the worst that ever I saw." He records such comments in a journal "into which I transcribe the most memorable and remarkable Transactions of the Day." A typical extract is read: "*April* the twentieth, arose a very great Storm of Wind, Thunder, Lightning and Rain,—which was a shreud sign of foul Weather. The 22d 9 of our 12 Chickens getting loose, flew over-board, the other three miraculously escaping by being eaten by me that Morning for breakfast." On returning, Tickletext intends to publish this journal "for the good of the Nation."[19]

Fielding declares himself keen (in a characteristic image) "to steer clear" of such faults as these, yet he falls into them suspiciously often. Like Tickletext, he describes a city which (until the ruinous earthquake of 1755) was one of the wonders of Europe, and like Tickletext he is blind to its splendour. Lisbon is "the nastiest city in the world," he declares, while the only virtue of its hinterland is to "make an Englishman proud of and pleased with his own country, which in verdure excels, I believe, every other country." Fielding again moves oddly close to Tickletext in his apparent assumption that readers will relish minute details of his creature comforts. On leaving Ryde, a "dreadful calamity" is suffered in the loss of a teachest; the hunt that ensues is a brilliantly pointless set-piece in which Fielding himself adopts exactly the role mocked in his Preface—the role of a writer obsessed by trifles which have "no other right of being remembered, than as they had the honour of having happened to the author, to whom nothing seems trivial that in any manner happens to himself." Even Tickletext's certainty that his book will serve "the good of the Nation" is uncomfortably echoed by Fielding's own insistence on the "public utility" of his remarks. It is as though the mention of Behn's play, overtly there to illustrate what the *Journal* is not, serves instead as an implicit indication of what in part the *Journal* is—a parody of inept travel writing, ironically written at the expense of, and sending up, its own narrating voice.

Here Fielding has two kinds of precedent before him. Among the moderns, he gently mocks the fussy accuracy of the most celebrated travel book of the day, Anson's *Voyage round the World* (1748), and he dismisses most of the rest as "a heap of dulness." Yet he clearly knows more than a little about this heap, the literary conventions of which he had earlier satirized in *Jonathan Wild*.[20] No doubt he looked in particular at existing voyages to Lisbon, among which Udal ap Rhys's *Account of the Most Remarkable Places and Curiosities in Spain and Portugal* (printed by Richardson in 1749) and William Bromley's *Several Years Travels through Portugal, Spain, etc.* (1702) stand out.

Bromley was a Tory of Jacobite leanings (and later Speaker of the House of Commons) who had refused to recognize William III in the Parliament of 1689. He spent most of the ensuing reign abroad, citing "a Love to Foreign Travel, other Circumstances concording." Little of this love was lavished, however, on the capital city of Whiggish England's favourite ally. Scandalized by the Lenten processions of idolatrous monks, Bromley was unimpressed by Lisbon's churches, and thought the cathedral "neither large nor beautiful." Further cause for disgust lay underfoot. "Lisbon is Scituated on several high Hills; which makes walking the Streets very unpleasant, as the Filth and noisome Smells render them very offensive," he complains. "The Houses are generally high and the Streets so narrow that the Sun comes little into them, to dry up the wet and filth."[21]

Nothing could be further from the raptures of Udal ap Rhys, for whom Lisbon was another seven-hilled Rome, its buildings "magnificent," its squares "handsome," its views "inexpressibly fine." The city "has all the Charms that can be produced by an infinite Variety of the most sumptuous Edifices, reflecting uncommon Beauties upon each other by the Happiness of their Situation." The surrounding landscape is likewise "delicious, fertile, and agreeable . . . for it is not only shaded, enriched, and adorned with the finest Fruit-trees, but Beds of the most odoriferous Flowers shoot up as spontaneously as if they were animated by the enlivening Touch of the inchanting Foot of a Poet's Mistress." To visit the country is to be transported to a golden age, Rhys suggests—and one distinguished in particular by the marvellous livestock on which he turns a connoisseurly eye. The country's "Productions" are of the highest quality, and "in that of beautiful Women (which is infinitely the finest that Man can conceive) it is thought to surpass all *Europe.*" Pursuing his enthusiasm for husbandry, Rhys describes a soil "so fertile, and the Air so pure and wholesome, that many of their Women will breed till they are Fifty . . . The Plains are covered with Sheep, and the Mutton is the sweetest in all *Spain.* Here also they have a perpetual Spring."[22]

More magical still is the ancient genre of travel book to which Fielding's attention also turns. Among the best-known characteristics of his fiction (or "comic Epic-Poem in Prose," as he calls the genre in *Joseph Andrews*)[23] is its witty reworking of epic forms, and the *Journal* sustains this interest. Noting that "Homer himself is by some considered as a voyage-writer," he pays particular attention to the *Odyssey* and to Virgil's *Aeneid*. Both poems concern hazardous voyages away from the ruins of Troy, and it is the hero's fate in each to contend with supernatural forces such as the *Odyssey*'s Circe (a sorceress who drugs Ulysses's crewmen and turns them to swine) or the *Aeneid*'s Juno (who persuades the wind-god Aeolus to buffet Aeneas with storms). Fielding's Preface wryly censures such fanciful strokes as tending "to pervert and confuse the records of antiquity." For all his own professions of fidelity to fact, however, he takes much the same course himself. The *Journal* too is not unshaped report but contrived art, he makes clear, embellished with surplus details "of stile or diction, or even of circumstance." The underlying hint here—that some of the *Journal*'s events are simply fiction—emerges more plainly when Fielding later likens his own poetic licence to that of a sailor who

faithfully related what had happened on board our ship; we say faithfully, tho' from what happened it may be suspected that Tom chose to add, perhaps, only five or six immaterial circumstances, as is always, I believe, the case, and may possibly have been done by me in relating this very story (p. 87).

Yet again we witness the pattern of contradiction typical of this teasing work: on one hand a denigration of fiction, a preference for history, and a solemn commitment (as the Introduction puts it) to "relate facts plainly and simply as they are"; on the other, a witty undermining of the factual status of a text avowedly decorated by the kind of "immaterial circumstances" (i.e. lies) told by Tom. What is clear is that here, as much as in a novel of Fielding's, style and pattern will carry the day in any contest with mere fact.

An amusing example of the *Journal*'s fictionality—or proof that its factual status is at least in question—is provided by a letter written to Samuel Richardson from Ryde in March 1755 (reprinted below, Appendix I). Here the unknown writer claims to expose as fiction Fielding's report of the malignity of his landlady, the poverty of his lodging, and several further details. Far from resembling the classical furies, as the *Journal* reports, the aged and sickly landlady raises "nothing but compassion" in the letter-writer, "and in her behaviour we saw yet less of the character of those infernal deities." Nor was this Fielding's only untruth:

We found the circumstances of their dining in a barn a fiction, there was no such barn with a pleasant view to the fields, nor dined they out of the house.

> The venison so miraculously receiv'd on their coming to a place, whither they
> were by accident driven; was not in fact so great a miracle as it appears in the
> story, for Mr. F.'s servant was dispatch'd to Southampton to buy it, and paid
> half a guinea for it . . . Fortune indeed must have been a very cunning goddess
> and attended very closely the steps of our author; to have found him at casting
> anchor with a present of a buck ready for his acceptance; the circumstances
> then relating to the venison we were convinced were wholly misrepresented
> (p. 109).

As an attempt to discredit Fielding, this letter is of little importance. Yet the
discrepancies it exposes do have the usefulness of showing his real priorities in
the *Journal*. No doubt the historical Mrs Francis was indeed more complex,
and perhaps more genuinely pitiable, than the fury described by Fielding.
The conclusion to draw, however, is not that Fielding sets out to deceive, but
that he sets out to fashion quotidian experience into a work of art that owes
its shape to more than contingency alone. As his talk of embellishment and
"immaterial circumstances" makes clear, the *Journal* must be seen not as a
work of neutral documentation but as one in which the raw materials of life
are imaginatively transformed. One need only remember the fiction of the
day to see that Mrs Francis in the *Journal* is above all a literary construct, a
caricature who has as much in common with Mrs Tow-wouse, the landlady in
*Joseph Andrews,* as with the actual keeper of a tavern at Ryde. Claude Rawson
has argued, indeed, that Fielding may well have modelled her portrait as
much on Mrs Jewkes in Richardson's *Pamela* as on a living subject:

> She is a broad, squat, pursy, fat thing, quite ugly, if any thing human can be so
> called. She has a huge hand, and an arm as thick—I never saw such a thick
> arm in my life. Her nose is flat and crooked, and her brows grow down over
> her eyes; a dead, spiteful, grey, goggling eye: and her face is flat and broad; and
> as to colour, looks as if it had been pickled a month in saltpetre. I dare say she
> drinks. She has a hoarse man-like voice . . .[24]

Many details differ with Mrs Francis, but the structure of her portrait is so
similar that Fielding might almost have had Richardson's page before him:

> She was a short, squat woman; her head was closely joined to her shoulders,
> where it was fixed somewhat awry; every feature of her countenance was sharp
> and pointed; her face was furrowed with the small-pox; and her complexion,
> which seemed to be able to turn milk to curds, not a little resembled in colour
> such milk as had already undergone that operation. She appeared indeed to
> have many symptoms of a deep jaundice in her look; but the strength and
> firmness of her voice over-balanced them all (p. 57).

By drawing so obviously on the resources of fiction, and by pushing his portrait of Mrs Francis into the realm of caricature, Fielding only confirms what

his Preface announces—that here is a work in which literary effect is as important as literal fact.

There is more to Fielding's resort to the fictional, however, than a chance to trump his greatest rival, or to display his own talent for the grotesque. By detaching himself from mere mundane report, he allows himself to model the material of the *Journal,* in cleverly parodic ways, on both the kinds of travel literature described above. Little need be said about the two traditions represented by Bromley and Rhys: Fielding takes obvious delight in exaggerating the surly xenophobia of the first and in contradicting the rapturous extravagance of the second. The more strictly nautical repertoire of such works as Anson's *Voyage* is also a source of fun. One anecdote (about catching a shark) is recommended by Fielding as "exactly conformable to the rules and practice of voyage-writing," while the "most tragical incident" of the cat washed overboard is perhaps a wry reworking of a famous moment in Anson, where the loss of a sailor prompts the leaden lament on which Cowper was to base his poem "The Castaway."[25] Again, the voyage-writer's standard claim to have written a contribution to knowledge "for the good of the Nation" (as Behn's Tickletext puts it) receives its most sustained parody in a Swiftian passage of bogus scholarship in which Fielding solemnly appeals for election to the Society of Antiquaries.

More interesting still is the ironic use to which the *Journal* puts its classical sources. For this, no less than *Joseph Andrews* or *Tom Jones,* is a work of mock epic, in which Fielding casts himself in the mildly ludicrous role of some latter-day Ulysses or Aeneas. A few years later Joseph Baretti was to regret the impossibility of writing an "*Olisipossey,* or an epic account of my voyage from Falmouth to Olisipo, or Lisbon": modern conditions inhibit the task, Baretti muses, "and now instead of Syrens and Tritons we meet in our voyages with nothing else but a Bonito and a Flying-fish." Fielding, however, has no such inhibitions. Playing on the traditional association of Troy with London, and on another tradition which attributes to Ulysses the foundation of Lisbon,[26] he turns the mismatch between heroic forms and post-heroic achievement to clever comic effect. Certain echoes are quite overt, notably those which jestingly link his departure from London to unknown shores with Aeneas' flight from Troy. Threatened at one point by "that very wind which Juno would have solicited of Æolus, had Æneas been in our latitude bound for Lisbon," he returns to the same analogy on the *Journal*'s final page.

Similar connections are also pursued in the way of a private joke. Here it is worth recalling the anonymous letter from Ryde, which shows clearly how little interest Fielding has at this point in mere veracity. Instead he pursues a submerged epic analogy that is comically at odds with the realities of tavern life. By likening Mrs Francis to a fury and a witch, and by comparing the island she inhabits with some far-flung isle "where the few savage inhabitants have little of human in them besides their form," Fielding playfully lends his provincial inn the magical aura of epic. The effect is enhanced by the very landscape, which in "its extraordinary verdure . . . vies with the power of art, and in its wanton exuberancy greatly exceeds it." It is only later that the myth of the island-dwelling sorceress who drugs her victims with doctored wine is explicitly mentioned. But implicitly Fielding here transforms the Isle of Wight into a kind of Circe's island, while Mrs Francis herself becomes a kind of cut-price Circe who strands her victims by witchcraft and plies them at extortionate cost with counterfeit wine. It now becomes clear why Fielding is so mysterious about the venison he procures from Southampton: by writing simply that "fortune, for I am convinced she had a hand in it, sent me a present of a buck," he wryly identifies himself with Ulysses on Circe's island. "Some pow'r divine who pities human woe / Sent a tall stag," as Ulysses tells his crew on returning from hunting there, a buck slung over his shoulder.[27]

Yet the underlying joke of these epic analogies is in the end of a melancholy kind, for by comparison with the feats of epic Fielding's own troubles are mundane things, his halting voyage almost absurdly inglorious. "Windbound in life," he cannot reach the heroic status of a Ulysses or an Aeneas, and such comparisons can only be at his own expense. Where the heroes of epic conquer and overcome, he himself journeys to an obscure death, calling on a strain of ironic valediction that identifies his post-heroic predicament as at once comic and intensely pathetic. He had published a work entitled *A Journey from this World to the Next* in 1743. In the *Journal of a Voyage to Lisbon* he returns to the theme in a gloomier strain, voyaging in sickness through adverse winds not to some Ithaca or New Troy but instead to a kind of earthly hell, "the nastiest city in the world."

## V

Fielding's surviving letters from Lisbon, by turns amused and enraged, describe the aftermath of the voyage. Even now the pattern of comic mishap related in the *Journal* strangely persists. His footman flees homeward, "being pulled down with a Flux occasioned by drinking too much Wine, and frightened with the Apprehensions of dying in a strange Country." He is taken there by Captain Veale, for whom Fielding no longer has any good word: "The Truth is these Captains are all y$^e$ greatest Scoundrels in the World, but Veale is the greatest of them all." The septuagenarian captain is more highly regarded by Mary Fielding's maid, however: "Bell follows Captain Veal to England where he hath promised to marry her." Meanwhile Mary herself "cries and sighs all Day to return to England," while Fielding's own cravings for tastes of home are strong enough for him to press his brother to send "a very good perfect Cook, by the first Ship, but not by Veale." Only Mary's companion Margaret Collier thrives in her new role as "a fine young lady of

Portugal, a Toast of Lisbon." She sets her cap at the English chaplain: "He is smitten, and she would succeed, if I did not prevent it."[28]

Fielding died on 8 October, and even then the hint of farce remains. Eight days later the *Public Advertiser* reported "that Henry Fielding, Esq., is surprisingly recovered . . . His Gout has entirely left him, and his Appetite returned." The newspaper ate its words at the end of the month, but for the rest of the century would-be pilgrims to the English cemetery in Lisbon were to search for the grave in vain. An ugly monument was at last erected "on a spot selected by *guess*," as Dora Quillinan complained in 1847: "The bones it covers may possibly have belonged to an idiot." Even the authenticity of Fielding's death-bed book was for some a matter of doubt. On settling at Ryde in 1755 (minus the English chaplain), Margaret Collier was vexed to hear reports

> of my being the author of Mr. Fielding's last work, 'The Voyage to Lisbon:' the reason which was given for supposing it mine, was to the last degree mortifying, viz. that it was so very bad a performance, and fell so far short of his other works, it must needs be the person *with him* who wrote it.[29]

Such reports were probably based on an expurgated version of the *Journal* known to have been circulating early in 1755. The authentic text (followed here) is far from falling short of Fielding's earlier works, and on some counts it gives genuine weight to Fielding's own view of it as "the best of his performances." Performance, at any rate, is certainly the word for a work which fashions from its author's decline and death a brilliant final display in contrasting modes. The wry and deadpan humour of the *Journal* competes with the gravity of valediction and public address; the rigorous scrutiny which Fielding turns on his diseased body and the corrupted polity left behind him clashes uneasily with whimsical flights of parody and mock epic; a uniquely noncommittal mode of irony unsettles the whole.

Perhaps Fielding tells us what to make of the *Journal* when referring in his Preface to a famous passage in Longinus about declining literary greatness. Contrasting the two Homeric epics, Longinus talks partly in terms of an ocean becalmed or "the ebbing tide of Homer's greatness," and partly in terms of a sunset: "So in the *Odyssey* one may liken Homer to the setting sun; the grandeur remains without the intensity." Arthur Murphy was later to see a final display of just this kind in Fielding's *Amelia,* writing that this last novel "holds the same proportion to *Tom Jones,* that the *Odyssey of Homer* bears, in the estimation of *Longinus,* to the *Iliad.*"[30] Yet Fielding's hint, by citing Longinus here, is that it is his last *work,* and not simply his last *novel,* in which he mounts the kind of spectacle described by the classical critic. Not only does he explicitly compare his practice in the *Journal* with the *Odyssey,* while also drawing mock-epic analogies with specific episodes; he also uses the tortuous progress of the *Queen of Portugal,* with its wind-bound sails, becalmed seas and ebbing tides, to give constant prominence to Longinus' imagery of genius on the brink of death. It is as though the events literally experienced by the author become a metaphor not only for the man "wind-bound in life" but also for the author, close to death, who stages his art's great sunset. That, certainly, is the implication of the *Journal*'s conclusive moment of epiphany when, shortly before reaching Lisbon, Fielding and his party emerge on deck to view

> the serenest evening that can be imagined. Not a single cloud presented itself to our view, and the sun himself was the only object which engrossed our whole attention. He did indeed set with a majesty which is incapable of description, with which while the horizon was yet blazing with glory, our eyes were called off to the opposite part to survey the moon, which was then at full, and which in rising presented us with the second object that this world hath offered to our vision. Compared to these the pageantry of theatres, or splendor of courts, are sights almost below the regard of children (p. 101).

Having opened with the rise of "the most melancholy sun I had ever beheld," the *Journal* now draws to its logical close. The symmetry alone implies a moment of symbolic force, as Fielding bids farewell to his world of literary production and affairs of state—theatres and courts—and watches the onset of night.

## Notes

*When indicators refer to more than one quotation in a given paragraph, sources are listed consecutively in the note.*

1. *I Like It Here* (Harmondsworth: Penguin, 1968), pp. 167–8, 180.
2. *The Covent-Garden Journal*, ed. B. A. Goldgar (Oxford: Clarendon Press, 1988), p. 66 (no. 8, 28 Jan. 1752); *The Correspondence of Henry and Sarah Fielding*, ed. M. C. Battestin and C. T. Probyn (Oxford: Clarendon Press, 1993), p. 115n.
3. *Correspondence*, pp. 113, 115n.
4. *Henry Fielding: The Critical Heritage*, ed. R. Paulson and T. Lockwood (London: Routledge, 1969), p. 393; "An Essay on the Life and Genius of Henry Fielding, Esq.," in *The Works of Henry Fielding, Esq.* (1762), I, p. 46.
5. A. H. Cash, *Laurence Sterne: The Later Years* (London: Methuen, 1986), p. 360.
6. M. C. Battestin, with R. R. Battestin, *Henry Fielding: A Life* (London: Routledge, 1989), p. 577; D. Thomas, *Henry Fielding* (London: Weidenfeld, 1990), p. 391.
7. See the anonymous letter from Ryde reprinted in Appendix I.
8. *Tristram Shandy*, ed. M. New et al. (Gainesville: University Presses of Florida, 1978–84), pp. 8–9 (I, v).
9. *Correspondence*, p. 107.
10. *The Historical Register*, ed. W. W. Appleton (London: Edward Arnold, 1968), p. 5; *Amelia*, ed. M. C. Battestin (Oxford: Clarendon Press, 1983), p. 460 (XI, ii); *The Covent-Garden Journal*, p. 211 (no. 35, 2 May 1752).

11. *An Enquiry into the Causes of the Late Increase of Robbers,* ed. M. R. Zirker (Oxford: Clarendon Press, 1988), pp. 65, 77, 75. On the body politic in the *Journal,* see also A. J. Rivero, "Figurations of the Dying: Reading Fielding's *The Journal of a Voyage to Lisbon," Journal of English and Germanic Philology,* 93 (1994), 520–33.

12. *An Account of the Origin and Effects of a Police Set on Foot by His Grace the Duke of Newcastle in the Year 1753, upon a Plan Presented to His Grace by the Late Henry Fielding,* Esq. (1758), pp. 15–17.

13. Samuel Johnson, *A Dictionary of the English Language* (1755), "Monitor"; Johnson, Dictionary, "Censor."

14. *The True Patriot,* ed. W. B. Coley (Oxford: Clarendon Press, 1987), p. 220 (no. 16, 11–18 Feb. 1746).

15. *An Enquiry into the Causes of the Late Increase of Robbers,* p. 172.

16. *The Rape of the Lock,* ed. G. Tillotson, 3rd edn (London: Methuen, 1962), III, ll. 21–2.

17. *New Essays by Henry Fielding: His Contributions to the Craftsman and Other Early Journalism,* ed. M. C. Battestin (Charlottesville: University Press of Virginia, 1989), p. 82 (*Craftsman,* no. 469, 28 June 1735); see also Jonathan Swift, *Examiner,* no. 17 (23 Nov. 1710).

18. Battestin, *Henry Fielding: A Life,* p. 586.

19. *Mar-plot; or, The Second Part of the Busie-Body* (1711), Prologue; *The Feign'd Curtezans* (1679), I.ii, III.i.

20. See in particular IV, x and I, vii.

21. *Several Years Travels through Portugal, Spain, etc.* (1702), pp. 1, 3, 2, 4.

22. *Account of the Most Remarkable Places and Curiosities in Spain and Portugal* (1749), pp. 232–3, 237, 243, 219.

23. *Joseph Andrews,* ed. M. C. Battestin (Oxford: Clarendon Press, 1967), p. 4.

24. *Pamela,* ed. P. Sabor, intr. M. A. Doody (Harmondsworth: Penguin, 1980), p. 152; see Rawson, *Henry Fielding and the Augustan Ideal under Stress* (London: Routledge, 1972), pp. 56–66.

25. George Anson, *A Voyage round the World* (1748), pp. 79–80.

26. Joseph Baretti, *A Journey from London to Genoa* (1770), pp. 56, 58; Charles Brockwell, *The Natural and Political History of Portugal* (1726), pp. 164–5.

27. Pope, *The Odyssey of Homer,* ed. M. Mack (London: Methuen, 1967), X, ll. 182–3.

28. *Correspondence,* pp. 109–13.

29. R. Macaulay, *They Went to Portugal* (London: Cape, 1948), pp. 92, 94–5; *The Correspondence of Samuel Richardson,* ed. A. L. Barbauld (1804), II, p. 77.

30. Longinus, *On the Sublime,* tr. W. H. Fyfe, Loeb Classical Library (London: Heinemann, 1965), p. 153 (sect. ix, par. 13); "An Essay on the Life and Genius of Henry Fielding, Esq." in *The Works of Henry Fielding, Esq.* (1762), I, p. 45.

# Index

# The Volume Editor

Albert J. Rivero teaches in the department of English at Marquette University, where he is director of undergraduate studies. He has published articles on Petrarch and eighteenth-century British literature as well as *The Plays of Henry Fielding: A Critical Study of his Dramatic Career* (University Press of Virginia, 1989). He has edited (and contributed to) *New Essays on Samuel Richardson* (St. Martin's Press, 1996) and *Augustan Subjects: Essays in Honor of Martin C. Battestin* (University of Delaware Press, 1997); he is also volume editor of Smollett's *Miscellaneous Writings* for the University of Georgia Press edition of *The Works of Tobias Smollett* (in progress). He is currently working on a book-length project tentatively titled *Duplicitous Representations: Fashioning Fiction from Behn to Burney* for Oxford University Press.

# *The General Editor*

Zack Bowen is professor of English at the University of Miami. He holds degrees from the University of Pennsylvania (B.A.), Temple University (M.A.), and the State University of New York at Buffalo (Ph.D.). In addition to being general editor of this G. K. Hall series, he is editor of the James Joyce series for the University of Florida Press and the *James Joyce Literary Supplement.* He is author of six books and editor of three others, all on modern British, Irish, and American literature. He has also published more than one hundred monographs, essays, scholarly reviews, and recordings related to literature. He is past president of the James Joyce Society (1977–86), former chair of the Modern Language Association Lowell Prize Committee, and current president of the International James Joyce Foundation.